CANADIAN CASES
IN THE
PHILOSOPHY OF LAW

CANADIAN CASES
IN THE
PHILOSOPHY OF LAW

FIFTH EDITION

EDITED BY J.E. BICKENBACH,
KEITH C. CULVER, AND MICHAEL GIUDICE

broadview press

BROADVIEW PRESS – www.broadviewpress.com
Peterborough, Ontario, Canada

Founded in 1985, Broadview Press remains a wholly independent publishing house. Broadview's focus is on academic publishing; our titles are accessible to university and college students as well as scholars and general readers. With over 600 titles in print, Broadview has become a leading international publisher in the humanities, with world-wide distribution. Broadview is committed to environmentally responsible publishing and fair business practices.

The interior of this book is printed on 100% recycled paper.

Library and Archives Canada Cataloguing in Publication

Canadian cases in the philosophy of law / edited by J.E. Bickenbach, Keith C. Culver, and Michael Giudice. — Fifth edition.

Includes bibliographical references.
ISBN 978-1-55481-271-4 (softcover)

1. Law—Canada—Philosophy. 2. Law—Canada—Cases. I. Bickenbach, Jerome Edmund, editor II. Culver, Keith Charles, 1969-, editor III. Giudice, Michael, 1978-editor

KE427 C35 2018   349.71   C2018-901183-1

Broadview Press handles its own distribution in North America:
PO Box 1243, Peterborough, Ontario K9J 7H5, Canada
555 Riverwalk Parkway, Tonawanda, NY 14150, USA
Tel: (705) 743-8990; Fax: (705) 743-8353
email: customerservice@broadviewpress.com

Distribution is handled by Eurospan Group in the UK, Europe, Central Asia, Middle East, Africa, India, Southeast Asia, Central America, South America, and the Caribbean. Distribution is handled by Footprint Books in Australia and New Zealand.

Broadview Press acknowledges the financial support of the Government of Canada through the Canada Book Fund for our publishing activities.

Copy-edited by Robert M. Martin

Book design by Chris Rowat Design

PRINTED IN CANADA

Contents

Preface to the Fifth Edition

As new editors of *Canadian Cases*, we are delighted to carry Professor Bickenbach's vision for this textbook into a fifth edition. Since its first appearance in 1991, *Canadian Cases* has become a Canadian standard: it is read and used by instructors and students from coast to coast. This new edition preserves the key features of previous editions, while responding to changes in law and legal theory by adding new cases selected in consultation with other instructors who have also relied on *Canadian Cases* in their classes. We have also created two new parts, one introducing a range of issues associated with First Nations as partners in Canada, and the second providing a view of international law and Canada's place in what many view as an emerging global legal order. The need for these two new parts is a reflection of the increasing complexity of Canada's legal system and its relation to a rapidly globalizing world. In recognition of this complexity, this edition includes two new tools to help students. We have added a general introduction explaining key concepts and terms associated with law, legal reasoning, and courts in Canada and elsewhere. A glossary defining legal terms and expressions has also been added.

The goal of this textbook remains the same as it was in its first edition: to display for students some of the distinctive features of Canadian legal culture, and to do so in a way which draws out theoretical questions benefiting from the attention of philosophers of law and other social theorists in many other disciplinary and interdisciplinary inquiries. The opportunity for readers also remains the same. Whether you are new to Canada or a citizen of long standing, the case excerpts provided here offer you new insights into a legal culture you may live within, seek to change, or perhaps use as a model for change elsewhere. We hope these insights accompany you far beyond your first readings of these cases, into life as a citizen who is both a subject and an author of our shared legal culture.

Keith Culver and Michael Giudice

Introduction

Courts are one of the most familiar yet fundamentally mysterious of our social institutions. We may pass them daily, see news of an important court decision, or even watch justice dispensed live by celebrity TV judges. Yet at the same time courts may seem beyond the understanding of the ordinary person, even while we all share the understanding that courts make decisions bearing directly on the course of our daily lives. Courts are often organized in complex hierarchies, and their judgements may be expressed in what appear to be unnecessarily complex terms—all while judges wear costumes signalling an attachment to ancient traditions distant from the modern world. Demystifying the nature and role of courts is probably beyond any one book, course, or even professional career. It is, however, possible to begin to understand the role of courts quite quickly, especially if we begin with the kinds of courts and kinds of decisions with the greatest force in our daily lives: courts of final appeal, deciding the meaning and application of the constitutional law establishing the fundamental structures of the state, and the relation of the state to the citizen.

This book is focused on the Supreme Court of Canada and its interpretation of Canada's constitutional law, with additional examination of what it means for Canada to be a state in a world of states interacting under international law. Our focus is on Canada in part because the editors are professors at Canadian universities, and in part because Canada's relatively recent adoption of a Charter of Rights in 1982 has created a new relation between Canadian courts, Canadian legislatures, and Canadian citizens. Canadian legislatures are constrained in their ability to organize social life by a set of fundamental rights and freedoms held by citizens, capable of being overridden only in special circumstances verified by courts. Courts are now said to have a much stronger power of "review" of legislation in Canada, giving courts a more prominent role in Canadian social life. This increased prominence of courts gives Canadian citizens and those interested in Canadian affairs good reason to inquire into just how Canadian courts, and especially the Supreme Court of Canada, express and develop some of the most fundamental commitments of the Canadian legal system. The organization of this book responds to those interests.

The general introduction to the book explains the nature and operations of courts, presuming that readers have some familiarity with courts through attention to news, use of law by friends and family, and popular media depictions of law in social life. The introduction is not, however, a compressed trip through law school. Rather, the introduction is intended to prepare citizens to read cases, likely guided by a professor's introductory remarks in class, and likely in conjunction with another book exploring in greater depth the range of ideas and issues arising in the theory of law—called philosophy of law, or jurisprudence. The cases chosen are familiar to judges and lawyers, but the excerpts we have included are not necessarily the portions of each case most important to judges and lawyers in their day-to-day operation of the legal system. Case excerpts have been chosen to illustrate philosophical or theoretical issues arising in judicial reasoning about fundamental commitments and aspects of Canada's legal system. From consideration of how constitutionally-permitted imposition of "reasonable limits" on fundamental rights and freedoms may affect your daily life, to exploration of how judges are developing the meaning of constitutional guarantees to equality, you will gain a deeper appreciation of the way courts and their reasoning shape and are shaped by the societies they serve.

1. COURTS AND CASES

We are so familiar with the film and television portrayals of courts and judges that it may not occur to us to ask whether those portrayals are reliable guides to what courts and judges actually do in Canada and elsewhere. It is worth reviewing some of the central features of the role courts and judges play in law. Above all, wherever courts are found, they provide an official venue for resolution of disputes, operated by a judge or a panel of judges delivering decisions which provide parties to the disputes with certainty as to what the law requires of them in the case of their dispute. Sometimes, depending upon the legal system, a court's decision in a particular dispute provides guidance to other disputants regarding the way their dispute may be resolved if brought before the court. In other systems, each dispute is taken in its own

right, and decided as if unique. Perhaps the practically most important feature of the operation of courts is the fact that their decisions
on a given matter are said to be binding. The parties to the decision
are bound to accept the court's decision as the final resolution of the
dispute—except if there is another court capable of overriding the
decision of the first court, a situation where an "appeal" to the second
court may result in a different decision. Most of the issues discussed
in decisions excerpted in this book arise from appeals, where there is
disagreement as to whether the law has been applied properly, often
motivated by disagreement as to what the law requires.

This picture of courts and their operations captures both Canadian
courts and courts of other countries. All courts resolve disputes with
respect to a variety of kinds of claims the law makes and allows to
be made—rights, obligations, permissions, prohibitions, and so on,
gathering accounts of the relevant facts in various ways and applying
the law of a given jurisdiction to those facts. Yet as the different types
of legal claims noted above begin to indicate by their diversity, not all
disputes are the same. The most obvious distinctions are among (1)
disputes involving individuals, and (2) disputes involving individuals
and a state, and (3) disputes involving just states. When one state has
a dispute with another, they may seek resolution from a court applying international law. When a state is involved in a dispute with an
individual, the matter may be either civil, where the interests involved
are limited to the parties of the dispute, or criminal, where the state
represents the interests of the country as a whole as they are claimed
to be harmed by an individual. Criminal matters are nearly always
prosecuted by states. When individuals seek to resolve disputes among
them, the matter is nearly always civil. (Beyond this general distinction,
it is important to remember that while we will refer in a general way to
"persons," "individuals," and "citizens" in this introduction, cases may
involve individuals, groups or various forms of organization capable
of bearing legal rights and duties, such as companies, co-operatives,
societies, and so on.) In Canada, some of the cases of each of the kinds
we have just discussed are "review" cases, in which courts must review
what appears to be applicable law to determine whether it is in fact valid
law according to the requirements of the Canadian Constitution. In the
next section of this introduction we will look at each type of case more
closely, explaining in the Canadian context matters which are familiar
to any judge or lawyer in the systems of law descended from English law. We will leave to one side the role of administrative tribunals,

specialized bodies handling disputes which legislators have chosen to assign to bodies operating for the most part outside the court system. We will also note but leave for your own investigation the additional complexity found in Quebec, where a civil law system descended from French law governs civil matters.

1.1 Disputes between individuals. We are all familiar with reality television programs in which a judge hears cases brought by one person against another, resulting in the judge finding in favour of one person and requiring actions such as repaying a debt. These disputes between individuals with competing interests are civil cases in which the state is not a party, and the possible outcomes do not include imprisonment. Usually the small, fast-moving print on screen at the end of the program indicates that the decisions are based on the law of some particular jurisdiction with respect to civil matters only, but often that fact is lost in the drama as the tough but sensible judge uses what seems to be mostly common sense to resolve the dispute. In real courts, civil disputes are more complex than those produced for our entertainment. The parties to the dispute may be individual persons, or they may be non-state organizations such as companies or clubs or non-profit organizations; and disputes may take months rather than minutes of court time before they are resolved. Complex disputes may range over matters of contract, property, inheritance, employment and so on, with some disputes going beyond parties' seeking certainty as to the requirements of the law, and on to seeking compensation for wrongs suffered.

1.2 Disputes between the state and individuals. We observed above that when the state is involved in a dispute with individuals, the matter may be criminal, or it may be civil. Examples of such civil matters include cases where individuals challenge decisions of the state for wrongful termination of benefits, or where the state seeks the return of overpayment of benefits. In civil cases such as these, the possible outcomes or decisions do not include imprisonment, in part because the interests addressed by civil law are largely individual interests where resolution often is monetary or orders to act or cease acting, rather than punishment in the form of restriction of liberty, which is difficult to imagine as applying in any meaningful way to a state.

The border between civil and criminal law cases may sometimes appear to be unclear. The kinds of actions understood as civil wrongs warranting compensation may seem to overlap with the criminal harms considered to be of such social importance that the outcomes of a trial may include not just financial penalties but imprisonment and naming to a permanent public record of persons convicted of crimes. The Canadian and many other legal systems attempt nonetheless to maintain the distinction, and many of the criminal cases you see here will display relatively clear instances of criminal conduct.

When looking to determine whether a particular dispute involving the state is a civil or a criminal matter, it is important to see how the courts have named the case which has come before them. Criminal cases can often be identified by their identifying one party by the abbreviation "R." meaning Rex (Latin for *King*) or Regina (Latin for *Queen*), or sometimes the full term "King" or "Queen," as may be seen in cases such as *R. v. Butler* and *Perka v. the Queen*. In all instances of "R" or "King" or "Queen" the intention is to represent the Government of Canada using a formal term reflecting our long history of constitutional monarchy, in which a King or Queen is an almost entirely ceremonial head of state, whose name is used to mark acts undertaken on behalf of all Canadians. Familiar examples of criminal matters include murder, arson, and drug trafficking. In cases of these matters brought to courts, the nature of the harm transcends its particular instance, and is considered to display a dangerous attitude or disposition towards society—a willful disregard for the very nature of a society and social living. This is what is meant by the expression that crimes are in fact "harms against the state." Unlike civil cases, possible outcomes or decisions in criminal cases do include imprisonment.

1.3 Disputes between states. When disputes between states are brought to courts for resolution, they are adjudicated by courts outside any single state, such as the International Court of Justice (ICJ) and the Court of Justice of the European Union. States often dispute matters associated with borders—about their precise location, or about compensation for activities in one state with negative effects in another state. States also dispute the correct applications of various agreements—international treaties, conventions, and protocols.

1.4 Review cases. In a review case, existing legislation is tested for its conformity with constitutional standards. Many of the cases included in this textbook are review cases, such as *R. v. Oakes* and *R. v. Keegstra*. In a typical review case, an existing law is challenged on the basis that it violates a constitutionally-recognized right or freedom. The court must then review the law, to determine whether there is a constitutional violation and whether the law must be declared invalid and struck down, or modified in some way saving part of the law that does not violate constitutional requirements, or given temporary validity until the appropriate legislature can amend it.

Review cases may also be of a different kind. In Canada, the *Supreme Court Act* empowers either the federal government or one or more provincial governments to "refer" for opinion to the Supreme Court of Canada "important questions of law or fact." This procedure is usually saved for difficult questions of constitutional law, in particular those concerning the division of legislative powers or other politically fraught issues. The procedure enables either level of government to test the constitutionality of legislation, or political or executive action, and to avoid the dangers associated with implementing legislation without knowledge of how it will be regarded by the courts. Unlike other kinds of cases, in which the legal issues addressed by the Supreme Court of Canada have already been addressed by lower courts, reference cases are brought directly to the Supreme Court of Canada. Two examples of reference cases included in Part I are *Reference Re Resolution to Amend the Constitution of Canada* and *Reference Re Secession of Quebec*. In Part VIII we have also included an example of the international equivalent of a reference case, *Accordance with International Law of the Unilateral Declaration of Independence in Respect of Kosovo*, in which several states asked the ICJ for an "advisory opinion" on the legality of Kosovo's unilateral declaration of independence from Serbia in 2008.

2. CHARACTERISTICS OF COURTS

Courts in the systems of law descended from the English legal system share a number of general characteristics. These characteristics help to explain both the role and status of particular courts within a legal system. Let us survey some of these characteristics, bearing in mind that we are identifying most prominent features of the most familiar courts, leaving aside for present purposes the details associated with special variations of courts such as military courts and family courts.

2.1 Open. It is often said that a hallmark of justice is that it can be seen to be done, applying laws and using procedures known to all in advance, in courts that are said to be "open." The formal processes of legal dispute resolution used in such courts are not kept hidden or secret, but are made transparent and displayed publicly. In particularly significant cases a record is kept of the activity of the courts and compiled in what are often called "reporters" showing how courts have decided particular kinds of questions.

In certain circumstances even legal systems committed to the ideal of openness find it important to operate closed proceedings. Where, for example, important privacy interests or the interests of young persons are at stake, proceedings may be closed, or publication of proceedings may be banned. In such cases, the ideal of openness is respected by publicly available statement of the exact circumstances in which a court proceeding may be closed, so closed proceedings are specific, known exceptions to the general practice of openness.

2.2 Adversarial. Courtroom television dramas gain much of their appeal from their depiction of the adversarial dimension of proceedings in courts. Sometimes a state prosecutor matches wits with a public defender in a criminal case, or a small-town lawyer representing the little guy battles valiantly against slick city lawyers in a civil matter. Often the judge or judges appear to take a very active role in the drama, giving the impression of a three-way discussion aimed at finding the truth of the matter, and enabling the judge to dispense justice accordingly. The actual operation of courts is often much less dramatic, and judges play a much less active role. In the part of a court case where lawyers attempt to convince the court of a particular picture of the facts and the way relevant law ought to be applied to the facts, the lawyers for each party to a dispute are in opposition to one another, adversaries in what is often called an adversarial trial system. Each works within established rules of procedure, argument and evidence to support a conclusion which the other must oppose, almost inevitably requiring what may be seen as attacks on the opponent. So a criminal prosecutor may seek to show that the accused is guilty beyond reasonable doubt, while a lawyer for the defence attempts to show that the prosecutor has failed to show this. And in a civil matter, the lawyer for the plaintiff attempts to show that it is more probable than not that the plaintiff has suffered a specified legal wrong at the hands of the defendant. It is important to realize that in this process, lawyers are not expected to recognize the merits of the opponent's argument. Rather, each lawyer attempts to build the strongest possible argument and the judge (or sometimes judges, or sometimes judge and jury) decides which argument prevails and to what extent. In the adversarial system the judge may ask lawyers to clarify what they have said, and the judge may use various rules of court procedure to ensure that evidence is appropriately heard, but the judge does not conduct an independent investigation into the facts—the judge hears what is brought before the court by the lawyers representing the two opposing parties.

2.3 Application of existing legal norms. One of the main features of the ideal of the rule of law is that laws are made known to those subject to them, so citizens have "protected expectations" regarding the kinds of action they can undertake without fear that what they believed was legally acceptable is suddenly unacceptable with various negative consequences suffered by citizens. So while courts can sometime be quite creative in applying existing law to new facts as a society evolves, and we may sometimes feel that judges are making entirely new laws rather than extending the meaning of existing laws, the ideal remains that courts apply existing law, and courts cannot simply make up entirely new laws for particular cases appearing before them.

2.4 Authoritative. One of the central features distinguishing courts from other means to resolution of disputes is found in the authority of courts. In modern systems of law serving modern societies, there are many kinds of social conflict which rarely reach the attention of courts. From referees applying the rules of sports to a game, to social clubs creating and applying membership rules allowing some in and keeping some out, we use many means to resolve many disputes. Disputes reaching courts do so for various reasons largely decided by legislators, who tend to try to reserve the time and energy of the court system for particularly serious matters in which a final judgement is needed for the sake of the disputants and in the interest of their surrounding society. For example, while rough play in a game of hockey is usually governed by the rules of hockey as applied by a referee, if rough play goes so far as to count as an assault as prohibited by criminal law, the courts may be required to rule on the question of whether a particular hockey player committed an assault deserving of criminal conviction. Such a judgement from a court sets the bounds on rough play in an authoritative way: while the rules of hockey might be varied in several ways, those rules cannot be varied to permit play so rough as to amount to criminal assault. Courts have the final say over sports associations, and have the power of the state to back their say in various ways, up to and including the use of force to compel disputants to abide by the court's ruling. Courts are said to be authoritative, as the final judges of various kinds of disputes, and in our system, their judgements in the cases they decide serve as authoritative "precedents" showing how future relevantly similar cases should be decided.

   The final, authoritative nature of court decisions can be easily over-looked within legal systems such as Canada's, which have a hierarchical system of courts, ranging, for example, from provincial trial courts to provincial courts of appeal to the Supreme Court of Canada. This hierarchy serves several purposes, including provision for particular matters to go directly to courts most suited to those matters, and provision for decisions by one court to be re-considered by another court where there is a basis for "appeal" if there is new evidence, a mistake in law, or a right to appeal. Generally speaking, in Canada a matter raising sufficiently serious legal issues to reach the Supreme Court of Canada will have begun as a case in what is sometimes called a "lower level" court in a province, followed by an appeal to a provincial appeals court, followed by an appeal to the Supreme Court of Canada. The names and layers vary across the provinces and territories, but the principles are very similar. As the case proceeds, a lower level court reasons on a basis which takes care to avoid departing from the reasoning of prior decisions by the appellate court above it, and the provincial appeals court similarly takes care to respect the reasoning of the Supreme Court of Canada while perhaps varying from the reasoning of lower level courts in its province. Once a matter reaches the Supreme Court of Canada, it is the court of final jurisdiction, beyond which there is no appeal. It is not bound by the decisions of the provincial appeals court from which an appeal arose, but its decisions bind the provincial supreme court and the lower level provincial courts.

   The layered, hierarchical nature of the court system may give the impression that cases are expected to bounce from one level of courts to the next with reversal following reversal. Most of the time, however, courts apply law in ways consistent with prior decisions on the same matters, deferring to higher courts as providing binding statements of what the law requires. Courts at the same level—and even the same court from one decision to another—try to follow each other's decisions. The doctrine that courts should "stand by decided matters" and lower courts should defer to higher courts is known by its Latin expression *stare decisis*. This promotes consistency of application of principles of law. Another familiar procedural constraint is the doctrine of "double jeopardy," which bars the repeat prosecution or trial of an accused for the same offence. So once a matter has been heard and decided by a court and no possibility of appeal exists, the decision is final. At the same time, the legal system permits flexibility when cases presenting new facts arrive. Sometimes courts decide they are not bound by *stare decisis* in a particular case, by "distinguishing" the present case from the facts or law of past similar cases, or distinguishing binding from persuasive decisions by higher courts and choosing to limit the degree to which their decision is influenced by a merely persuasive higher court decision. A further dimension of the way the court system balances authoritative finality with flexibility may be seen in the way courts composed of more than one judge tend to present their decisions. The decision of such a court is composed of opinions expressed by each judge, or sometimes one judge writes on behalf of a group of judges. A typical opinion states a finding of fact, a finding of law, and an application of law to fact resulting in a decision on the matter at hand. The reasons for the decision are called the "ratio," an abbreviation for the Latin expression "ratio decidendi," which means "reasons for decision." When a court is composed of several judges who do not all agree on the final resolution of a case, the ratio serves as the grounds for disagreement between majority and minority opinions. It is also possible for judges to agree with a final decision but for different reasons. These are known as "concurring opinions." Commentary and reasoning which does not fall within the ratio of a case but is still offered by a court on the occasion of a particular decision is known as "obiter dicta," which is Latin for "by the way" or "said in passing." The authoritative decision of the court is that of the majority, but the opinions expressed by the minority and obiter dicta offered by any judge can give important indications as to how slightly different cases might be decided, contributing to the flexibility of the system as it provides guidance even in reasoning that is not ultimately binding as a matter of precedent-setting case law.

Many legal disputes in Canada and similar legal systems are resolved without needing to be brought before a court, and those which are heard by a court are mostly given final resolution by that court. Appeals, as we have said, occur under certain conditions and are not an automatic matter. So while it is fun to see an actor in a gripping film shout "we'll take this all the way to the Supreme Court!" the reality of courts is often less dramatic. A lower court may decide a case in a way bringing an end to the dispute between the parties or the state's prosecution of someone accused of a crime, and if there is no basis for appeal, the decision is just as final as the decision of the Supreme Court of Canada in some other matter found eligible for appeal. Courts provide authoritative, final resolution of disputes, and that finality has an important value as it enables parties to move on with their lives, or enables legislators to recognize that a legally binding and final decision nonetheless falls short of our society's aspirations to greater justice which then requires legislators to revise the law they required the courts to apply.

3. HOW COURTS INTERPRET LAW

Over centuries of development, courts have devised, and legislators have required, an array of practices regarding the progress of a case from initial problem to final conclusion. The complexity of these rules provides endless fodder to writers of fiction exploring the ways in which blind rule-following can lead to injustice, or overzealous pursuit of justice can ignore rules which must be respected if real justice is to be delivered. Fictional portrayals of courts, and even reading of real cases, may give the sense that courts are all ancient procedure, gowns and wigs, a social situation where "technicalities" rule and real justice is illusory at both the level of the individual case and the legal system. This pessimistic assessment of courts is undeniably somewhat grounded in fact, as courts have been historically complicit in serious moral wrongdoing. At the same time, however, it is important to see beyond the procedures guiding day to day operation of courts. Evaluation of the doctrines and principles governing courts' interpretation and application of law soon builds understanding that the system of courts, taken as a whole, has built-in means to self-correction and to refinement. Courts can, over time, seek to deliver as much of the ideal of justice as can be hoped for from a human-run institution addressing human social affairs.

3.1 Construction rules. Laws and applications of laws in matters such as contracts and wills contain words and phrases whose meaning is crucial to how judges, lawyers, and citizens are to understand what the law requires. When judges read law and attempt to determine its meaning in order to apply it to facts before them, what are called "construction rules" constrain how judges may use or understand words and terms contained in the law. Some construction rules are quite simple. For example, judges are required to understand a word or phrase as having its "plain meaning" as understood by the ordinary person, unless that term is specifically required to be interpreted differently, as might be required by a statute or a portion of a contract. Another example may be found in the way judges are required to approach vague terms and standards which appear to be open to widely different interpretations. Courts are often required to interpret terms and standards according to the perspective of the reasonable person. So what is a "fair" contract or what amounts to "due care" is to be understood by asking what a reasonable person would count as fair or demonstrating due care. The reasonable person standard requires courts to develop understandings of reasonableness in the context of changing social norms, while using that standard consistently across the cases that require it, permitting gradual interpretive change corresponding to gradual social change.

3.2 Guidance in statutory interpretation. When thinking of where law comes from, perhaps the most obvious answer is enactments of legislatures, often in the form of statutes created as "acts" of a legislature. Statutes establish what law requires on some particular matter using a combination of general and specific language to set standards. Familiar examples in Canadian federal law include the *Canada Elections Act* specifying the requirements of a valid election, from naming roles of officials through specifying voting procedures. A fuller picture of law would add other elements such as custom, past court decisions, and the constitution as a special sort of statute (all discussed further below in section 5); but even that fuller account of law is still likely to give statutes a central role. Statutes as acts of legislatures generally displace judge-made law found in precedents set by decisions in particular cases, and similarly, statutes may displace and override customary law.

Since statutes are written in both general and specific terms intended to capture present and future facts in some given area of concern to legislators, questions of interpretation often arise with respect to facts unanticipated by legislators. Courts are guided in various ways as they interpret and apply statutes. Guidance ranges from stand-alone interpretation statutes, such as the *Interpretation Act* in Canada, which guide interpretation in general of statutes within a particular legal system, to definition sections within statutes, together with other statutes, the legislative history (including legislative debates) of a statute, and the context in which a statute's provisions are to be applied.

3.3 Presumptions. Finally, courts are required to observe various presumptions in their reasoning and procedures. For example, in criminal and taxation prosecution, accused persons are presumed innocent until proven otherwise. If a sufficient case is not made against an accused person, no opposing evidence or defense is required on their part. In Canada, the right to be presumed innocent until proven guilty in a criminal proceeding is enshrined in section 11(d) of the *Canadian Charter of Rights and Freedoms* (the *Charter* is reproduced in this text-book as an Appendix).

4. COURT PARTICIPANTS

Since this book is intended to help citizens and other inquirers to better understand some of the features of Canadian case law benefiting from philosophical or theoretical investigation, we will provide a broad and general overview of the roles of various persons seen in courts. As we have observed already, the daily processes of courts are highly complex, historically-informed matters, and while you would need a thorough understanding of these processes to act as a lawyer or a judge, a general understanding is sufficient. Within that general understanding of courts as social institutions composed of various persons acting in various roles, it is worth noting how some of these roles have changed and how new roles are emerging in Canada. Since we have already noted above that the parties to disputes can be individual persons, groups, and various forms of organization, we will focus here on other roles in courts.

4.1 Judges. Hollywood has done a very good job of situating judges as anchors of their courts, holding the proceedings down to earth while lawyers do their adversarial best—all with the sense that judges are in it for the long haul, grizzled veterans of human life who may look as though they were born as judges and will remain as judges until the end of time. This picture does a great deal to communicate the seriousness of the job of courts and the gravity judges often bring to their tasks, yet it glosses over some details that matter. Judges are central to many contemporary legal systems, but this is a choice rather than a necessity. In ancient Athens, for example, a court consisted of a special assembly of citizens, convened for the purpose of deciding a legal dispute. Even now, the choice of just who becomes a judge is a matter of varied practice. Judges are almost always former lawyers who enjoy the respect of their peers for their knowledge of law and commitment to justice. In Canada, judges are appointed by government after consultation with the legal profession and others. In the United States, the situation is often quite different: judges in some courts and jurisdictions are appointed, while others are elected. All share in common the judicial obligation to hear the claims of disputants, sometimes making a finding of fact, and to interpret and apply the relevant law to reach a decision which is final unless overturned by a higher court.

4.2 Juries. In some matters of law, legal systems require or make it optional for a case to be heard by both a judge, and a group of ordinary citizens constituting a jury. In some systems, juries are used to determine whether a matter ought to be heard by a court at all. The formation of juries is increasingly a question of concern to lawyers, since undetected bias toward one or the other party in a trial may result in exactly the sort of injustice the jury system is meant to avoid by bringing the collective sense and wisdom of a community to bear on a dispute before a court. Depending on the law to be applied, juries sometimes make findings of fact, and deliver verdicts based on judicial direction as to the meaning of law. Juries have a very long history, serving as a living reminder of the way justice in our system of law is very closely tied to the way contemporaries of the accused or plaintiff or defendant understand the meaning of our law in the context of our shared social life.

4.3 Lawyers. Much like judges, lawyers are often viewed as essential to court processes. In complex matters, lawyers nearly always represent disputants, but in less complex matters, it is common for disputants to represent themselves in court. Small claims court, for example, offers disputants an opportunity to resolve disputes worth relatively small sums of money in a way resulting in an authoritative, final judgement, but without the cost associated with hiring lawyers. Self-representation in court can be a challenge, but it is an available option, and an important demonstration that in at least parts of a legal system in need of constant improvement, access to justice can be inexpensive and available to all.

4.4 Witnesses. Witnesses are often called to provide testimony regarding relevant facts of some dispute, especially if they were present during some alleged offence or can offer reliable evidence regarding the context of some dispute. Sometimes witnesses are "expert witnesses," and provide expert testimony. Physicians and psychiatrists, for example, often provide expert testimony to courts on such matters as medical conditions of a physical and mental nature. In *R. v. Lavallee*, reproduced in Part VI, you will find an example of the Supreme Court of Canada relying on the testimony of a psychiatrist regarding the nature of "battered wife syndrome." The court's reliance on such testimony helped to re-define the notion of self-defence in Canadian criminal law.

4.5 Interveners. Since the 1982 proclamation of the *Canadian Charter of Rights and Freedoms* and the growth of courts' role in evaluating the constitutional validity of law, an old role and practice has gained new weight in Canadian law. An intervener (or intervenor) in a trial is neither a party to the dispute nor a judge. An intervener is an advocate for a perspective believed to be important to the court's reasoning, either permitted by the court to make a submission or in some cases entitled to do so. Interveners seek to ensure that the court is fully informed as to the context of the dispute, often emphasizing the consequences of particular interpretations of the law for particular groups. Decisions of the Supreme Court of Canada have far-reaching consequences, so interveners are highly motivated to intervene in cases reaching the Supreme Court. Examples of frequent interveners include professional associations, such as the Canadian Medical Association, and civil and human rights groups, such as Amnesty International, feminist groups such as LEAF (Women's Legal Education and Action Fund), and religious groups. Courts take care to note which interveners have been heard, to the extent that interveners are listed in reports of court proceedings and in the "header" indicating the parties to a legal dispute. While we have not reproduced the full headers of the cases included in this textbook, full headers list all of the intervening parties. For example, here is the full header for *Canada v. Khadr*:

Prime Minister of Canada, Minister of Foreign Affairs, Director of the Canadian Security Intelligence Service and Commissioner of the Royal Canadian Mounted Police (*Appellants*)

v.

Omar Ahmed Khadr (*Respondent*)

and

Amnesty International (Canadian Section, English Branch), Human Rights Watch, University of Toronto, Faculty of Law—International Human Rights Program, David Asper Centre for Constitutional Rights, Canadian Coalition for the Rights of Children, Justice for Children and Youth, British Columbia Civil Liberties Association, Criminal Lawyers' Association (Ontario), Canadian Bar Association, Lawyers Without Borders Canada, Barreau du Québec, Groupe d'étude en droits et libertés de la Faculté de droit de l'Université Laval, Canadian Civil Liberties Association and National Council for the Protection of Canadians Abroad (*Interveners*)

5. SOURCES OF LAW

The bulk of this general introduction has been occupied with how courts engage with law, all without saying a great deal about what counts as law, how judges are to distinguish law from non-law, and how judges are to weigh the relative importance of various sources of law. We have focused on the nature and operations of courts to enable readers to understand the context of the case excerpts following this introduction. It will be helpful, however, to bridge our explanation of courts to particular excerpts with further explanation of the sources of law judges use in their reasoning captured in each excerpt.

In Canada, (setting to one side the special case of Quebec), as in many common law countries there are several sources of law applied by judges. Among what might be called the formally enacted sources of law are the constitutional law at the foundation of our legal system, together with federal, provincial and territorial statutes enacted by legislatures, and precedent established by judges interpreting law in deciding particular cases. Constitutional law, statute, and precedent are hierarchically ranked in the Canadian legal system. Where they conflict, constitutional law has priority over statutes, and statutes have priority over precedent. Formal legislative enactments and their consequences are not the only sources of law on which citizens, lawyers and judges may rely. Customary law may be found in established practices regarded by participants as law. While much customary law in common law systems has been displaced by statute and judge-made law, the importance of customary law has been recognized once again, as First Nations customary law has become an element of legal disputes and decisions.

As the example of customary law tends to show, while it is convenient to presume that what is law and what ought to influence interpretation of law can all be known and fixed in place as a set of books on a shelf, legal practice is more complex. Citizens, lawyers, and judges seeking to understand the meaning of some generally stated word or phrase quite naturally look to similar other social situations for guidance. It is a matter of routine for Canadian lawyers to refer to American court decisions or the decisions of English, Australian, or New Zealand courts, when in our very similar legal systems a case has arisen and has been resolved in ways offering lessons to the others. Decisions in other legal systems are persuasive rather than binding in Canadian

courts, but their persuasive force can be very significant when bor-
rowed reasoning is applicable in a new context. Similar borrowing of
reasoning may be found in courts' recognition of the way ancient legal
systems, such as Roman law, treated facts still arising today. Courts
also sometimes refer to the writing of professors when choosing how to
understand and apply law, or draw on social science research, or on our
best available understandings of our moral obligations to one another,
when courts are asked to reach "fair" decisions. While these sources
of law generally have less force than what we have identified as formal
sources of law, it is important to realize that the distinction between
formal and informal sources of law is not a hard line—informal sources
may be very influential.

6. THE CANADIAN CHARTER OF RIGHTS AND FREEDOMS

Many of the cases in this book treat issues arising since the introduction of the *Canadian Charter of Rights and Freedoms* in 1982. The
introduction of the *Charter* is significant in several ways. Politically,
the arrival of the *Charter* and the patriation of the Canadian Constitution gave Canada the power to amend its own constitution without the
need to petition the Westminster Parliament in the United Kingdom.
The *Charter* specifies fundamental legal relationships between federal
and provincial governments, and private citizens, and protects those
arrangements with amendment formulas which make changes to those
relationships much more difficult than was previously the case. (The
Charter's protection of Canadians' fundamental rights and freedoms
was preceded by the Bill of Rights in 1960—a federal statute like any
other, capable of being varied or eliminated by the government of the
day whenever it wished.) The *Charter* also significantly expanded the
scope and power of judicial review of legislation for validity under the
requirements of the *Charter*. Since 1982 courts have found legislation
to be defective in various ways. Sometimes this has led to legislation's
being "struck down" as invalid; sometimes additional terms have
been "read into" legislation to enable its continued validity; sometimes courts have suspended invalidity while requiring governments
to alter laws to make them valid. Politicians and the public alike have
raised concerns regarding what some view as a new political role for

courts historically conceived to be politically neutral, while defenders of courts point to the fact that they are only exercising responsibilities created for them by legislatures. No matter how one views this debate, it is clear that courts have greater political power than ever, even without having asked for it.

The root of the new power of the courts lies in section 52 of the *Charter*, which makes the validity of all law in Canada conditional on consistency with the *Charter*. It reads very simply: "The Constitution of Canada is the supreme law of Canada, and any law that is inconsistent with the provisions of the Constitution is, to the extent of the inconsistency, of no force or effect." The job of assessing consistency of this sort is by default the responsibility of the courts, so the *Charter* gives judges the power to review and declare valid or invalid legislation enacted by elected representatives. Otherwise put, the law-creating power of government is limited by the *Charter*, and the extent of that limitation is determined by judges. Much of the concern expressed regarding the role of courts and judges in the post-*Charter* era is associated with the ways judges determine the limits to the law-creating power of government. For better or for worse, it is widely recognized that the *Charter* often requires judges to engage in moral reasoning regarding the content of *Charter* language specified in general, open terms. Equality rights asserted in the *Charter*, for example, require that judges explore just what equality is and what it might require in Canadian society as it grows and changes, enabling judges to assess whether an instance of legislation infringes equality guarantees so must be declared invalid, or meets the requirements of equality so may stand as valid. This is a significant change from the practice of interpreting the Canadian Bill of Rights, which typically took a very formal approach deferring to prior law and the intentions of Parliament.

It is appropriate that we end this introduction with a note on the *Charter*'s practical significance for ordinary citizens. In some ways, introduction of the *Charter* made Canadian law more American, as the *Charter* provides an American-style guarantee of fundamental freedoms against governmental intrusion. Yet it does so in an un-American way to the extent that it guarantees both individual and collective rights in a country now accustomed to recognizing itself as originating in the acts of three founding nations and cultures—First Nations, the United Kingdom, and France. In other words, both individual citizens and specified groups have a clear means by which to challenge laws with which governments are claimed to violate basic constitutional rights and freedoms.

Structurally, the *Charter* contains two kinds of rights. Positive rights protect claims *to* some particular condition, such as the right to education in a particular language. Negative rights protect claims to freedom *from* some particular condition, such as freedom from discrimination. It is important to note that the *Charter*'s very substantial protections apply mostly to civil and political rights, including rights to certain safeguards in the criminal process and rights to be free from various kinds of government interference, as well as rights to political participation in various forms. The *Charter* protects very few of what are called "socio-economic rights," such as the right to food, the right to shelter, or the right to healthcare or a minimum income.

There are also some important limitations to the fundamental rights and freedoms protected by the *Charter*, and those limitations are understandably the subject of great social concern. The very first major limitation is found in the first section of the *Charter*. Section 1 reads: "The Canadian Charter of Rights and Freedoms guarantees the rights and freedoms set out in it subject only to such reasonable limits prescribed by law as can be demonstrably justified in a free and democratic society." As majestic as this may sound, this guarantee arrives with several conditions requiring deeper consideration. Since the *Charter* is the result of legislators stating their intentions at the level of generality they think is appropriate to a foundational document, it is up to courts to determine the meaning of the standards stated by legislators. The courts must determine just what may be considered "reasonable limits" to fundamental rights and freedoms, and the courts must determine what standard must be reached for a limit to be "demonstrably justified," and what can be tolerated and what cannot be tolerated in a "free and democratic society." You will soon see exactly how the Supreme Court of Canada handled these questions in *R. v. Oakes*, one of the early *Charter* cases included in Part I. The second major limitation contained in the *Charter* is found in section 33, which is known as the "notwithstanding clause." This section allows governments the option of passing legislation which they know violates particular rights in the *Charter* so long as they do so explicitly and for a fixed period of time with the possibility of renewal. Invoking the notwithstanding clause can be a politically risky move for a government. Except in Quebec, it has rarely been used.

7. A QUICK OVERVIEW OF THE PARTS
OF THE BOOK

Our introduction to courts and the Canadian legal system is just that—an introduction to help you begin your own lifelong journey into informed citizenship in Canada or in another country. That journey can include at its beginning a set of glimpses into actual cases decided by judges in Canada, together with some examples of judicial reasoning regarding international law, and some key supporting documents. We have organized the parts of the book in an order which can be followed as if chapters in a story, or you or your instructor may wish to read parts in a different order better suited to the questions you are asking.

The first part of the book begins with constitutional law, the law which constitutes the foundations of the Canadian legal system. In the second part cases treat fundamental freedoms exercised largely by individuals, and the circumstances in which they can conflict with other social priorities and how such conflicts can be resolved by courts. The third part explores the *Charter*'s guarantee of the equality of individuals "before and under the law," and the special provision made in the *Charter* for affirmative action laws benefiting disadvantaged individuals or groups. The fourth part ranges over issues arising from individuals' choices which conflict with prevailing standards, and in the fifth part you will find cases examining how these and other conflicts raise questions as to how they are to be handled by courts in ways which are procedurally fair not just in paper rules but in actual effect. The sixth part introduces issues regarding responsibility in both criminal and civil contexts, exploring how we attribute acts to persons, and how we measure wrongdoing found in a particular act. In the last two parts of the book, new to this edition, we provide a lens on legal disputes and their resolution in two often overlooked contexts: the situation of First Nations peoples within Canada, and Canada's relation to other states under international law. Each of these sections is prefaced by a brief introduction, so you can move among sections in any order you wish.

With that, we'll leave you to your reading, with just one small request. We believe you ought to read critically and even sceptically as you learn how courts, especially appellate courts, have developed law in Canada. We also believe that it's worth at least a moment's pause to appreciate that our system of laws developed over centuries does a remarkable job of enabling us to live peacefully together—for the most part! As you consider whether one judge or court or another has made a mistake justifying someone's outrage, we suggest a policy of patient inquiry, considering the possibility that the judge or court made an honest error for reasons we ought to investigate and bear in mind as our generation does its best to perfect our legal system. We're all in this together, generation over generation, as citizens, lawyers, and judges trying to create a legal system capable of taking us toward justice for all.

SUGGESTED READINGS

Patrick Fitzgerald, Barry Wright, and Vincent Kazmierski, *Looking at Law: Canada's Legal System*, 6th edition (Toronto: LexisNexis, 2010).

Gerald L. Gall, *The Canadian Legal System*, 5th edition (Toronto: Carswell, 2004).

Patrick J. Monahan, Byron Shaw, and Padraic Ryan, *Constitutional Law*, 5th edition (Toronto: Irwin Law, 2017).

Robert J. Sharpe and Kent Roach, *The Charter of Rights and Freedoms*, 5th edition (Toronto: Irwin Law, 2013).

PART I

Constitutional Law

No matter how hard judges try to express their reasoning about constitutional matters in ways easily understood by all Canadians, thinking through constitutional issues can remain challenging. The greatest challenge may be a little surprising, especially to readers who have long heard plenty of talk about constitutional law from TV or movie characters saying things like "I'm not saying anything—I plead the fifth, I'm not going to incriminate myself" and "I'm exercising my right to free speech—I've got a constitutional right to have my say!" Both of these often-heard lines reflect American constitutional law, not Canadian constitutional law. The way Canadian constitutional law protects the rights of persons accused of committing a crime is similar to the American practice, but it isn't exactly the same, and there is no fifth amendment to the Canadian constitution. Similarly, Canadian constitutional protection of "freedom of expression" is similar to US constitutional protection of "freedom of speech," with the crucial difference that this and other fundamental rights and freedoms in Canada are "to such reasonable limits prescribed by law as can be demonstrably justified in a free and democratic society"—a condition nowhere present in American constitutional law. These differences are enough to show the greatest challenge to thinking about Canadian constitutional law: the long American experience of very similar constitutional commitments is so familiar in Canada that it can be very easy to underestimate the importance of the differences found in Canadian constitutional law. The Canadian constitution, especially its key elements the *Constitution Act, 1982* and the *Charter of Rights and Freedoms* it contains, is much newer than the US constitution. Yet at the same time the Canadian constitution has a long history—Canada's history as a country predates the current form of its constitution—so when Canadian judges come to interpret the Canadian constitution they do so with resources in both the similar American constitution and experience, and Canadian experience in advance of the post-1982 form of the Canadian constitution. In these differences we may find the grounds of the range of particularly Canadian constitutional issues exhibited by the case excerpts contained in this part.

Just like other countries, Canada's constitution sets out the elements of our legal system and their operation, specifying matters such as the powers of executive authorities who operate a legal system, the powers of legislatures who determine the content of the law of the system, and the powers of the judiciary who interpret and apply the laws of the system. Some countries and legal systems, but not all, assemble foundational elements of their legal systems in a specifically identified body of laws, often established in ways which make those foundational laws very difficult to change and very powerful in their overriding all conflicting laws. Such systems are often said to have a "unitary" constitution with "entrenched" provisions which can be varied only by use of amendment processes requiring much more agreement than the typical simple majority of votes required to pass or vary other kinds of law. Other countries, such as the United Kingdom, are entirely aware of the benefits of a unitary constitution protecting certain core parts of the legal system as foundational guarantees for all, yet prefer to retain the flexibility associated with permitting each succeeding body of legislators the power to change the legal system as much as seems necessary at a given moment.

Canada's entrenchment of specific constitutional provisions in the *Constitution Act, 1982* has raised a number of questions associated with the nature of constitutions and their force. Cases excerpted in this part offer readers an opportunity to investigate the idea of a constitution and the question of whether it is simply a set of specified documents, or whether it must be considered as those documents plus the way they are used—including, for example, the conventions guiding use of constitutional law, and the way respect for ideals such as the rule of law influence judges' interpretation of what constitutional law requires. The extent to which a constitution is a living practice, not just written commitments, is explored in excerpts determining what is meant at a particular time in a society's life by "reasonable limits" on protections of individual rights and freedoms, and group rights and freedoms. Other cases demonstrate the way a newly expressed constitution and new assembly and expression of fundamental rights and freedoms demands that judges look to history, consider the practices of similar legal systems, and engage in moral reasoning to give specific meaning to general terms chosen by legislators. A particularly Canadian interpretive task may be seen in judges' reasoning regarding group rights, especially minority rights, as Canadian political commitment to multiculturalism shapes Canadian thinking regarding the claims of linguistic and cultural minorities to a particular place in Canadian life. Some of the Canadian experience of a new constitution knitting together three founding nations can be seen to bear on constitutional reasoning in a case excerpt taking up a question often left unaddressed in unitary constitutions: how to dissolve a country that a constitution is largely devoted to assembling and sustaining. Throughout these case excerpts, readers will find constitutional law in Canada to be anything but dusty old stories of far off beginnings. Canada's constitution is better viewed by what legal scholars call the "living tree" doctrine, likening the constitution and its interpretation to an organic process of growth and development.

A: THE CONSTITUTION

Reference Re Resolution to Amend the Constitution of Canada
Supreme Court of Canada
[1981] 1 S.C.R. 753

At issue in this historic reference case was the procedure being followed to patriate the constitution: was it proper for the federal government to break the constitutional links between the United Kingdom and Canada and add the *Canadian Charter of Rights and Freedoms* to the constitution of Canada without the consent of all the provinces? Along the way to dealing with this complex question, the court paused to consider the nature of the Canadian constitution and the difference between law and convention.

Justice Martland (for the majority):

The Nature of Constitutional Conventions

A substantial part of the rules of the Canadian Constitution are written. They are contained not in a single document called a Constitution but in a great variety of statutes some of which have been enacted by the Parliament of Westminster, such as the *British North America Act 1867*, or by the Parliament of Canada, such as the *Alberta Act, 1905*, or by the provincial legislatures, such as the provincial electoral acts. They are also to be found in orders in council like the Imperial Order in Council of May 16, 1871, admitting British Columbia into the Union, and the Imperial Order in Council of June 26, 1873, admitting Prince Edward Island into the Union.

Another part of the Constitution of Canada consists of the rules of the common law. These are rules which the courts have developed over the centuries in the discharge of their judicial duties. An important portion of these rules concerns the prerogative of the Crown. Sections 9 and 15 of the *B.N.A. Act* provide:

> 9. The Executive Government and authority of and over Canada is hereby declared to continue and be vested in the Queen.

15. The Commander-in-Chief of the Land and Naval Militia, and all Naval and Military Forces, of and in Canada, is hereby declared to continue and be vested in the Queen.

But the Act does not otherwise say very much with respect to the elements of "Executive Government and authority" and one must look at the common law to find out what they are, apart from authority delegated to the Executive by statute.

The common law provides that the authority of the Crown includes for instance the prerogative of mercy or clemency, and the power to incorporate by charter so as to confer a general capacity analogous to that of a natural person. The royal prerogative puts the Crown in a preferred position as a creditor, or with respect to the inheritance of lands for defect of heirs, or in relation to the ownership of precious metals. It is also under the prerogative and the common law that the Crown appoints and receives ambassadors, declares war, concludes treaties and it is in the name of the Queen that passports are issued.

Those parts of the Constitution of Canada which are composed of statutory rules and common law rules are generically referred to as the law of the Constitution. In cases of doubt or dispute, it is the function of the courts to declare what the law is and since the law is sometimes breached, it is generally the function of the courts to ascertain whether it has in fact been breached in specific instances and, if so, to apply such sanctions as are contemplated by the law, whether they be punitive sanctions or civil sanctions such as a declaration of nullity. Thus, when a federal or provincial statute is found by the courts to be in excess of the legislative competence of the legislature which has enacted it, it is declared null and void and the courts refuse to give effect to it. In this sense it can be said that the law of the Constitution is administered or enforced by the courts.

But many Canadians would perhaps be surprised to learn that important parts of the Constitution of Canada, with which they are the most familiar because they are directly involved when they exercise their right to vote at federal and provincial elections, are nowhere to be found in the law of the Constitution. For instance it is a fundamental requirement of the Constitution that if the Opposition obtains the majority at the polls, the government must tender its resignation forthwith. But fundamental as it is, this requirement of the Constitution does not form part of the law of the Constitution.

It is also a constitutional requirement that the person who is appointed Prime Minister or Premier by the Crown and who is the effective head of the government should have the support of the elected branch of the legislature; in practice this means in most cases the leader of the political party which has won a majority of seats at a general election. Other ministers are appointed by the Crown on the advice of the Prime Minister or Premier when he forms or reshuffles his cabinet. Ministers must continuously have the confidence of the elected branch of the legislature, individually and collectively. Should they lose it, they must either resign or ask the Crown for a dissolution of the legislature and the holding of a general election. Most of the powers of the Crown under the prerogative are exercised only upon the advice of the Prime Minister or the Cabinet which means that they are effectively exercised by the latter, together with the innumerable statutory powers delegated to the Crown in council.

Yet none of these essential rules of the Constitution can be said to be a law of the Constitution. It was apparently [A.V.] Dicey who, in the first edition of his *Law of the Constitution*, in 1885, called them "the conventions of the constitution," (see W.S. Holdsworth, "The Conventions of the Eighteenth Century Constitution" [1932], 17 Iowa Law Rev. 161) an expression which quickly became current. What Dicey described under these terms are the principles and rules of responsible government, several of which are stated above and which regulate the relations between the Crown, the Prime Minister, the Cabinet, and the two Houses of Parliament. These rules developed in Great Britain by way of custom and precedent during the nineteenth century and were exported to such British colonies as were granted self-government.

Dicey first gave the impression that constitutional conventions are a peculiarly British and modern phenomenon. But he recognized in later editions that different conventions are found in other constitutions. As Sir William Holdsworth wrote (*supra*, at p. 162):

> In fact conventions must grow up at all times and in all places where the powers of government are vested in different persons or bodies—where in other words there is a mixed constitution. "The constituent parts of a state," said Burke, "are obliged to hold their public faith with each other, and with all those who derive any serious interest under their engagements, as much as the whole state is bound to keep its faith with separate communities." Necessarily conventional rules spring up to regulate the working of the various parts of the constitution, their relations to one another, and to the subject.

Within the British Empire, powers of government were vested in different bodies which provided a fertile ground for the growth of new constitutional conventions unknown to Dicey whereby self-governing colonies acquired equal and independent status within the Commonwealth. Many of these culminated in the *Statute of Westminster, 1931*.

A federal constitution provides for the distribution of powers between various legislatures and governments and may also constitute a fertile ground for the growth of constitutional conventions between those legislatures and governments. It is conceivable for instance that usage and practice might give birth to conventions in Canada relating to the holding of federal-provincial conferences, the appointment of Lieutenant-Governors, the reservation and disallowance of provincial legislation. [...]

The main purpose of constitutional conventions is to ensure that the legal framework of the Constitution will be operated in accordance with the prevailing constitutional values or principles of the period. For example, the constitutional value which is the pivot of the conventions stated above and relating to responsible government is the democratic principle: the powers of the state must be exercised in accordance with the wishes of the electorate; and the constitutional value or principle which anchors the conventions regulating the relationship between the members of the Commonwealth is the independence of the former British colonies.

Being based on custom and precedent, constitutional conventions are usually unwritten rules. Some of them however may be reduced to writing and expressed in the proceedings and documents of imperial conferences, or in the preamble of statutes such as the *Statute of Westminster, 1931*, or in the proceedings and documents of federal-provincial conferences. They are often referred to and recognized in statements made by members of governments.

The conventional rules of the Constitution present one striking peculiarity. In contradistinction to the laws of the Constitution, they are not enforced by the courts. One reason for this situation is that, unlike common law rules, conventions are not judge-made rules. They are not based on judicial precedents but on precedents established by the institutions of government themselves. Nor are they in the nature of statutory commands which it is the function and duty of the courts to obey and enforce. Furthermore, to enforce them would mean to administer some formal sanction when they are breached. But the legal system from which they are distinct does not contemplate formal sanctions for their breach.

Perhaps the main reason why conventional rules cannot be enforced by the courts is that they are generally in conflict with the legal rules which they postulate and the courts are bound to enforce the legal rules. The conflict is not of a type which would entail the commission of any illegality. It results from the fact that legal rules create wide powers, discretions and rights which conventions prescribe should be exercised only in a certain limited manner, if at all. Some examples will illustrate this point.

As a matter of law, the Queen, or the Governor General or the Lieutenant-Governor could refuse assent to every bill passed by both Houses of Parliament or by a Legislative Assembly as the case may be. But by convention they cannot of their own motion refuse to assent to any such bill on any ground, for instance because they disapprove of the policy of the bill. We have here a conflict between a legal rule which creates a complete discretion and a conventional rule which completely neutralizes it. But conventions, like laws, are sometimes violated. And if this particular convention were violated and assent were improperly withheld, the courts would be bound to enforce the law, not the convention. They would refuse to recognize the validity of a vetoed bill. This is what happened in *Gallant v. The King* (1949). The Lieutenant-Governor who had withheld assent in *Gallant* apparently did so towards the end of his term of office. Had it been otherwise, it is not inconceivable that his withholding of assent might have produced a political crisis leading to his removal from office which shows that if the remedy for a breach of a convention does not lie with the courts, still the breach is not necessarily without a remedy. The remedy lies with some other institutions of government; furthermore it is not a formal remedy and it may be administered with less certainty or regularity than it would be by a court.

Another example of the conflict between law and convention is provided by a fundamental convention already stated above: if after a general election where the Opposition obtained the majority at the polls the government refused to resign and clung to office, it would thereby commit a fundamental breach of convention, one so serious indeed that it could be regarded as tantamount to a *coup d'état*. The remedy in this case would lie with the Governor General or the Lieutenant-Governor as the case might be, who would be justified in dismissing the Ministry and in calling on the Opposition to form the government. But should the Crown be slow in taking this course, there is nothing the courts could do about it except at the risk of creating a state of legal discontinuity, that is a form of revolution. An order or a regulation passed by a Minister under statutory authority and otherwise valid could not be invalidated on the ground that, by convention, the Minister ought no longer to be a Minister. Required to say by what warrant they occupy their ministerial office, they would answer that they occupy it by the pleasure of the Crown under a commission issued by the Crown and this answer would be a complete one at law; for at law, the government is in office by the pleasure of the Crown although by convention it is there by the will of the people.

This conflict between convention and law which prevents the courts from enforcing conventions also prevents conventions from crystallizing into laws, unless it be by statutory adoption.

It is because the sanctions of conventions rest with institutions of government other than courts, such as the Governor General or the Lieutenant-Governor, or the Houses of Parliament, or with public opinion and, ultimately, with the electorate that it is generally said that they are political.

We respectfully adopt the definition of a convention given by the learned Chief Justice of Manitoba, Freedman C.J.M. in the *Manitoba Reference*, *supra*, at pp. 13–14:

> What is a constitutional convention? There is general agreement that a convention occupies a position somewhere in between a usage or custom on the one hand and a constitutional law on the other. There is general agreement that if one sought to fix that position with greater precision he would place convention nearer to law than to usage or custom. There is also general agreement that "a convention is a rule which is regarded as obligatory by the officials to whom it applies" [P. Hogg, *Constitutional Law of Canada* (1977)]. There is, if not general agreement, at least weighty authority, that the sanction for breach of a convention will be political rather than legal.

It should be borne in mind however that, while they are not laws, some conventions may be more important than some laws. Their importance depends on that of the value or principle which they are meant to safeguard. Also they form an integral part of the Constitution and of the constitutional system.

That is why it is perfectly appropriate to say that to violate a convention is to do something which is unconstitutional although it entails no direct legal consequence. But the words "constitutional" and "unconstitutional" may also be used in a strict legal sense, for instance with respect to a statute which is found *ultra vires* or unconstitutional. The foregoing may perhaps be summarized in an equation: constitutional conventions plus constitutional law equal the total Constitution of the country.

Edwards v. Attorney-General of Canada
Judicial Committee of the Privy Council
[1930] A.C. 124

This is the famous "persons" case in which five prominent Alberta women—Henrietta Muir Edwards, Emily F. Murphy, Nellie L. McClung, Louise C. McKinney, and Irene Parlby asked the Supreme Court of Canada whether the Governor General's power to appoint "qualified persons" to the Senate meant that women were eligible. The Supreme Court could not find in Canada's constitutional doctrine, *The British North America Act, 1867,* any reason for extending the phrase to include women and so unanimously dismissed the appeal. At the time, however, the final court of appeal for Canada was the Judicial Committee of the Privy Council, and this court reversed the judgment. The case is noteworthy for its discussion of early constitutional relationships between Canada and the United Kingdom, soon to be dramatically changed by the *Statute of Westminster, 1931,* but more importantly how the law, even constitutional law, can evolve.

Lord Chancellor Sankey:

By s. 24 of the B.N.A. Act, 1867, it is provided that "The Governor General shall from Time to Time, in the Queen's Name, by Instrument under the Great Seal of Canada, summon qualified Persons to the Senate; and, subject to the Provisions of this Act, every Person so summoned shall become and be a Member of the Senate and a Senator."

The question at issue in this appeal is whether the words "qualified Persons" in that section include a woman, and consequently whether women are eligible to be summoned to and become members of the Senate of Canada. [...]

No doubt in any code where women were expressly excluded from public office the problem would present no difficulty, but where instead of such exclusion those entitled to be summoned to or placed in public office are described under the word "person" different considerations arise.

The word is ambiguous and in its original meaning would undoubtedly embrace members of either sex. On the other hand, supposing in an Act of Parliament several centuries ago it had been enacted that any person should be entitled to be elected to a particular office it would have been understood that the word only referred to males, but the cause of this was not because the word "person" could not include females but because at Common Law a woman was incapable of serving a public office. The fact that no woman had served or had claimed to serve such an office is not of great weight when it is remembered that custom would have prevented the claim being made, or the point being contested.

Customs are apt to develop into traditions which are stronger than law and remain unchallenged long after the reason for them has disappeared. The appeal to history therefore in this particular matter is not conclusive. [...]

Over and above that, their Lordships do not think it right to apply rigidly to Canada of today the decisions and the reasons therefore which commended themselves, probably rightly, to those who had to apply the law in different circumstances, in different centuries to countries in different stages of development. Referring therefore to the judgment of the Chief Justice [of Canada] and those who agreed with him, their Lordships think that the appeal to Roman law and to early English decisions is not of itself a secure foundation on which to build the interpretation of the British North America Act of 1867. [...]

Before discussing the various sections [of the B.N.A. Act] they think it necessary to refer to the circumstances which led up to the passing of the Act.

The communities included within the Britannic system embrace countries and peoples in every stage of social, political and economic development and undergoing a continuous process of evolution.

His Majesty the King in Council is the final Court of Appeal from all these communities, and this Board must take great care therefore not to interpret legislation meant to apply to one community by a rigid adherence to the customs and traditions of another. Canada had its difficulties both at home and with the mother country, but soon discovered that union was strength. Delegates from the three maritime Provinces met in Charlottetown on September 1, 1864 to discuss proposals for a maritime union. A delegation from the coalition government of that day proceeded to Charlottetown and placed before the maritime delegates their schemes for a union embracing the Canadian Provinces. As a result the Quebec conference assembled on October 10, continued in session till October 28, and framed a number of resolutions. These resolutions as revised by the delegates from the different Provinces in London in 1866 were based upon a consideration of the rights of others and expressed in a compromise which will remain a lasting monument to the political genius of Canadian statesmen. Upon those resolutions the British North America Act of 1867 was framed and passed by the Imperial legislature. [...]

The British North America Act planted in Canada a living tree capable of growth and expansion within its natural limits. The object of the Act was to grant a Constitution to Canada. "Like all written constitutions it has been subject to development through usage and convention": *Canadian Constitutional Studies*, Sir Robert Borden (1922), p. 55.

Their Lordships do not conceive it to be the duty of this Board—it is certainly not their desire—to cut down the provisions of the Act by a narrow and technical construction, but rather to give it a large and liberal interpretation so that the Dominion to a great extent, but within certain fixed limits, may be mistress in her own house, as the provinces to a great extent, but within certain fixed limits, are mistresses in theirs. "The Privy council, indeed, has laid down that Courts of law must treat the provisions of the British North America Act by the same methods of construction and exposition which they apply to other statutes. But there are statutes and statutes; and the strict construction deemed proper in the case, for example, of a penal or taxing statute or one passed to regulate the affairs of an English parish, would be often subversive of Parliament's real intent if applied to an Act passed to ensure the peace, order and good government of a British Colony": see Clement's *Canadian Constitution*, 3rd ed., p. 347.

The learned author of that treatise quotes from the argument of Mr. Mowat and Mr. Edward Blake before the Privy Council in *St. Catherine's Milling and Lumber Co. v. The Queen* (1888): "The Act should be on all occasions interpreted in a large, liberal and comprehensive spirit, considering the magnitude of the subjects with which it purports to deal in very few words."

With that their Lordships agree, but as was said by the Lord Chancellor in *Brophy v. Attorney-General of Manitoba* (1895), the question is not what may be supposed to have been intended, but what has been said.

It must be remembered, too, that their Lordships are not here considering the question of the legislative competence either of the Dominion or its Provinces which arises under ss. 91 and 92 of the Act providing for the distribution of legislative powers and assigning to the dominion and its Provinces their respective spheres of Government.

Their Lordships are concerned with the interpretation of an Imperial Act, but an Imperial Act which creates a constitution for a new country. Nor are their Lordships deciding any questions as to the rights of women but only a question as to their eligibility for a particular position. No one either male or female has a right to be summoned to the Senate. The real point at issue is whether the Governor-General has a right to summon women to the Senate.

The Act consists of a number of separate heads.

The preamble states that the Provinces of Canada, Nova Scotia and New Brunswick have expressed their desire to be federally united into one Dominion under the Crown of the United Kingdom of Great Britain and Ireland with a constitution similar in principle to that of the United Kingdom.

Head No. 2 refers to the union. Head no. 3, ss. 9 to 16, to the executive power.

It is in s. 11 that the word "persons," which is used repeatedly in the Act, occurs for the first time.

It provides that the persons who are members of the Privy Council shall be from time to time chosen and summoned by the Governor General.

The word "person" as above mentioned may include members of both sexes, and to those who ask why the word should include females, the obvious answer is why should it not.

In these circumstances the burden is upon those who deny that the word includes women to make out their case. [...]

A heavy burden lies on an appellant who seeks to set aside a unanimous judgment of the Supreme Court, and this Board will only set aside such a decision after convincing argument and anxious consideration, but having regard:

> (1.) To the object of the Act—namely, to provide a constitution for Canada, a responsible and developing State; (2.) That the word "person" is ambiguous and may include members of either sex; (3.) That there are sections in the Act above referred to which show that in some cases the word "person" must include females; (4.) That in some sections the words "male persons" is expressly used when it is desired to confine the matter in issue to males; and (5.) to the provisions of the *Interpretation Act*; [...]

[T]heir Lordships have come to the conclusion that the word "persons" in s. 24 includes members both of the male and female sex and that, therefore, the question propounded by the Governor-General must be answered in the affirmative and that women are eligible to be summoned to and become members of the Senate of Canada, and they will humbly advise His Majesty accordingly.

Reference Re Manitoba Language Rights
Supreme Court of Canada
[1985] 1 S.C.R. 721

By section 23 of the *Manitoba Act, 1870*, all Acts of the Manitoba Legislature were to be enacted, printed and published in both English and French. This had not been done, and the government of Manitoba used the device of the reference to bring the issue before the Supreme Court of Canada. Since the law was clear on the point, the Supreme Court had to conclude that all of the unilingual Acts passed since 1870 were invalid and of no force or effect. This meant that everything that had been done, or not done, in the province in accordance with these laws was also invalid. It was a relatively simple matter to translate the legislation into French, but that would take time. In the meantime, what was to be done with the legal vacuum? The court came to the philosophically interesting conclusion that when all specific laws are found to be invalid, there still remains a kind of legal residue that fills the vacuum. What fills the vacuum is the rule of law itself.

The Court:

This Reference combines legal and constitutional questions of the utmost subtlety and complexity with political questions of great sensitivity. [...]

In the present case the unilingual enactments of the Manitoba Legislature are inconsistent with s. 23 of the *Manitoba Act, 1870* since the constitutionally required manner and form for their enactment has not been followed. Thus they are invalid and of no force or effect.

The Rule of Law

1. The Principle

The difficulty with the fact that the unilingual Acts of the Legislature of Manitoba must be declared invalid and of no force or effect is that, without going further, a legal vacuum will be created with consequent legal chaos in the Province of Manitoba. The Manitoba Legislature has, since 1890, enacted nearly all of its laws in English only. Thus, to find that the unilingual laws of Manitoba are invalid and of no force or effect would mean that only laws enacted in both French and English before 1890 would continue to be valid, and would still be in force even if the law had purportedly been repealed or amended by a post-1890 unilingual statute; matters that were not regulated by laws enacted before 1890 would now be unregulated by law, unless a pre-confederation law or the common law provided a rule.

The situation of the various institutions of provincial government would be as follows: the courts, administrative tribunals, public officials, municipal corporations, school boards, professional governing bodies, and all other bodies created by law, to the extent that they derive their existence from or purport to exercise powers conferred by Manitoba laws enacted since 1890 in English only, would be acting without legal authority.

Questions as to the validity of the present composition of the Manitoba Legislature might also be raised. [...]

Finally, all legal rights, obligations and other effects which have purportedly arisen under all Acts of the Manitoba Legislature since 1890 would be open to challenge to the extent that their validity and enforceability depends upon a regime of unconstitutional unilingual laws.

In the present case, declaring the Acts of the Legislature of Manitoba invalid and of no force or effect would, without more, undermine the principle of the rule of law. The rule of law, a fundamental principle of our Constitution, must mean at least two things. First, that the law is supreme over officials of the government as well as private individuals, and thereby preclusive of the influence of arbitrary power. Indeed, it is because of the supremacy of law over the government, as established in s. 23 of the *Manitoba Act, 1870* and s. 52 of the *Constitution Act, 1982*, that this Court must find the unconstitutional laws of Manitoba to be invalid and of no force and effect.

Second, the rule of law requires the creation and maintenance of an actual order of positive laws which preserves and embodies the more general principle of normative order. Law and order are indispensable elements of civilized life. "The rule of law in this sense implies...simply the existence of public order" (W.I. Jennings, *The Law and the Constitution* [5th ed. 1959] at p. 43). As John Locke once said, "A government without laws is, I suppose, a mystery in politics, inconceivable to human capacity and inconsistent with human society." (quoted by Lord Wilberforce in *Carl-Zeiss-Stiftung v. Rayner and Keeler Ltd.* [No. 2], [1966] 2 All E.R. 536 [H.L.] at p. 577) According to Wade and Phillips, *Constitutional and Administrative Law* (9th ed. 1977), at p. 89: "...the rule of law expresses a preference for law and order within a community rather than anarchy, warfare and constant strife. In this sense, the rule of law is a philosophical view of society which in the Western tradition is linked with basic democratic notions."

It is this second aspect of the rule of law that is of concern in the present situation. The conclusion that the Acts of the Legislature of Manitoba are invalid and of no force or effect means that the positive legal order which has purportedly regulated the affairs of the citizens of Manitoba since 1890 will be destroyed and the rights, obligations and other effects arising under these laws will be invalid and unenforceable. As for the future, since it is reasonable to assume that it will be impossible for the Legislature of Manitoba to rectify *instantaneously* the constitutional defect, the Acts of the Manitoba Legislature will be invalid and of no force or effect until they are translated, re-enacted, printed and published in both languages.

Such results would certainly offend the rule of law. As we stated in the *Patriation Reference*, supra, at pp. 805–06:

> The "rule of law" is a highly textured expression...conveying, for example, a sense of orderliness, of subjection to known legal rules and of executive accountability to legal authority.

Dr. [Joseph] Raz has said: "'The rule of law' means literally what it says: the rule of the law. It has two aspects: (1) that people should be ruled by the law and obey it, and (2) that the law should be such that people will be able to be guided by it" (*The Authority of Law* [1979], at pp. 212–13). The rule of law simply cannot be fulfilled in a province that has no positive law.

The constitutional status of the rule of law is beyond question. The preamble to the *Constitution Act, 1982* states:

> Whereas Canada is founded upon principles that recognize the supremacy of God and *the rule of law*. [Emphasis added]

This is explicit recognition that "the rule of law [is] a fundamental postulate of our constitutional structure" (Rand J., *Roncarelli v. Duplessis* [1959]). The rule of law has always been understood as the very basis of the English Constitution characterising the political institutions of England from the time of the Norman Conquest. (A.V. Dicey, *The Law of the Constitution* [10th ed. 1959], at p. 183) It becomes a postulate of our own constitutional order by way of the preamble to the *Constitution Act, 1982*, and its implicit inclusion in the preamble of the *Constitution Act, 1867* by virtue of the words "with a Constitution similar in principle to that of the United Kingdom."

Additional to the inclusion of the rule of law in the preambles of the *Constitution Acts* of 1867 and 1982, the principle is clearly implicit in the very nature of a constitution. The Constitution, as the supreme law, must be understood as a purposive ordering of social relations providing a basis upon which an actual order of positive laws can be brought into existence. The founders of this nation must have intended, as one of the basic principles of nation building, that Canada be a society of legal order and normative structure: one governed by rule of law. While this is not set out in a specific provision, the principle of the rule of law is clearly a principle of our Constitution.

This Court cannot take a narrow and literal approach to constitutional interpretation. The jurisprudence of the court evidences a willingness to supplement textual analysis with historical, contextual and purposive interpretation in order to ascertain the intent of the makers of our Constitution. [...]

2. Application of the Principle of the Rule of Law

It is clear from the above that: (i) the law as stated in s. 23 of the *Manitoba Act, 1870* and s. 52 of the *Constitution Act, 1982* requires that the unilingual Acts of the Manitoba Legislature be declared to be invalid and of no force or effect, and (ii) without more, such a result would violate the rule of law. The task the Court faces is to recognize the unconstitutionality of Manitoba's unilingual laws and the Legislature's duty to comply with the "supreme law" of this country, while avoiding a legal vacuum in Manitoba and ensuring the continuity of the rule of law.

A number of the parties and interveners have suggested that the Court declare the unilingual Acts of the Manitoba Legislature to be invalid and of no force or effect and leave it at that, relying on the legislatures to work out a constitutional amendment. This approach, because it would rely on a future and uncertain event, would be inappropriate. A declaration that the laws of Manitoba are invalid and of no legal force or effect would deprive Manitoba of its legal order and cause a transgression of the rule of law. For the Court to allow such a situation to arise and fail to resolve it would be an abdication of its responsibility as protector and preserver of the Constitution. [...]

The only appropriate solution for preserving the rights, obligations and other effects which have arisen under invalid Acts of the Legislature of Manitoba and which are not saved by the *de facto* or other doctrines is to declare that, in order to uphold the rule of law, these rights, obligations and other effects have, and will continue to have, the same force and effect they would have had if they had arisen under valid enactments, for that period of time during which it would be impossible for Manitoba to comply with its constitutional duty under s. 23 of the *Manitoba Act, 1870*. The Province of Manitoba would be faced with chaos and anarchy if the legal rights, obligations and other effects which have been relied upon by the people of Manitoba since 1890 were suddenly open to challenge. The constitutional guarantee of rule of law will not tolerate such chaos and anarchy.

Nor will the constitutional guarantee of rule of law tolerate the Province of Manitoba being without a valid and effectual legal system for the present and future. Thus, it will be necessary to deem temporarily valid and effective the unilingual Acts of the Legislature of Manitoba which would be currently in force, were it not for their constitutional defect, for the period of time during which it would be impossible for the Manitoba Legislature to fulfill its constitutional duty. Since this temporary validation will include the legislation under which the Manitoba Legislature is presently constituted, it will be legally able to re-enact, print and publish its laws in conformity with the dictates of the Constitution once they have been translated. [...]

As concerns the future, the Constitution requires that, from the date of this judgment, all new Acts of the Manitoba Legislature be enacted, printed and published in both French and English. Any Acts of the Legislature that do not meet this requirement will be invalid and of no force or effect.

Reference Re Secession of Quebec
Supreme Court of Canada
[1998] 2 S.C.R. 217

This is a reference case in which the Supreme Court of Canada was asked to "hear and consider important questions of law and fact" concerning Canada's constitution, in particular an issue of enormous importance to the country, and the source of endless political and social controversy: under the Constitution of Canada, can Quebec secede from Canada unilaterally? The answer was no. (The Court was also asked whether Quebec has the right to secede under international law, and came to the same conclusion: no.) Of course, a negotiated secession is possible, if agreement of the rest of Canada can be secured; even an illegal secession (or *coup d'état*) is possible, although its success would depend on the reaction of the international community. But here the question is one of law, one that can only be answered by first exposing the most fundamental principles of Canada's constitution, the "vital unstated assumptions" underpinning Canada's Constitution.

––––––––––

The Court:

Pursuant to s. 53 of the *Supreme Court Act*, the Governor in Council referred the following question to this Court:

> 1. Under the Constitution of Canada, can the National Assembly, legislature or government of Quebec effect the secession of Quebec from Canada unilaterally? [...]

[1] This Reference requires us to consider momentous questions that go to the heart of our system of constitutional government. The observation we made more than a decade ago in *Reference re Manitoba Language Rights*, [1985] 1 S.C.R. 721 (*Manitoba Language Rights Reference*), at p. 728, applies with equal force here: as in that case, the present one "combines legal and constitutional questions of the utmost subtlety and complexity with political questions of great sensitivity." In our view, it is not possible to answer the questions that have been put to us without a consideration of a number of underlying principles. An exploration of the meaning and nature of these underlying principles is not merely of academic interest. On the contrary, such an exploration is of immense practical utility. Only once those underlying principles have been examined and delineated may a considered response to the questions we are required to answer emerge. [...]

[49] What are those underlying principles? Our Constitution is primarily a written one, the product of 131 years of evolution. Behind the written word is an historical lineage stretching back through the ages, which aids in the consideration of the underlying constitutional principles. These principles inform and sustain the constitutional text: they are the vital unstated assumptions upon which the text is based. The following discussion addresses the four foundational constitutional principles that are most germane for resolution of this Reference: federalism, democracy, constitutionalism and the rule of law, and respect for minority rights. These defining principles function in symbiosis. No single principle can be defined in isolation from the others, nor does any one principle trump or exclude the operation of any other. [...]

Federalism

[55] It is undisputed that Canada is a federal state. [...]

[56] In a federal system of government such as ours, political power is shared by two orders of government: the federal government on the one hand, and the provinces on the other. Each is assigned respective spheres of jurisdiction by the *Constitution Act, 1867*. In interpreting our Constitution, the courts have always been concerned with the federalism principle, inherent in the structure of our constitutional arrangements, which has from the beginning been the lodestar by which the courts have been guided. [...]

[58] The principle of federalism recognizes the diversity of the component parts of Confederation, and the autonomy of provincial governments to develop their societies within their respective spheres of jurisdiction. The federal structure of our country also facilitates democratic participation by distributing power to the government thought to be most suited to achieving the particular societal objective having regard to this diversity. [...]

Democracy

[61] Democracy is a fundamental value in our constitutional law and political culture. While it has both an institutional and an individual aspect, the democratic principle was also argued before us in the sense of the supremacy of the sovereign will of a people, in this case potentially to be expressed by Quebecers in support of unilateral secession. It is useful to explore in a summary way these different aspects of the democratic principle. [...]

[64] Democracy is not simply concerned with the process of government. On the contrary... democracy is fundamentally connected to substantive goals, most importantly, the promotion of self-government. Democracy accommodates cultural and group identities. [...] Put another way, a sovereign people exercises its right to self-government through the democratic process. In considering the scope and purpose of the *Charter*, the Court in *R. v. Oakes* articulated some of the values inherent in the notion of democracy (at p. 136):

> The Court must be guided by the values and principles essential to a free and democratic society which I believe to embody, to name but a few, respect for the inherent dignity of the human person, commitment to social justice and equality, accommodation of a wide variety of beliefs, respect for cultural and group identity, and faith in social and political institutions which enhance the participation of individuals and groups in society.

In institutional terms, democracy means that each of the provincial legislatures and the federal Parliament is elected by popular franchise. These legislatures, we have said, are "at the core of the system of representative government." [...]

[66] It is, of course, true that democracy expresses the sovereign will of the people. Yet this expression, too, must be taken in the context of the other institutional values we have identified as pertinent to this Reference. The relationship between democracy and federalism means, for example, that in Canada there may be different and equally legitimate majorities in different provinces and territories and at the federal level. No one majority is more or less "legitimate" than the others as an expression of democratic opinion, although, of course, the consequences will vary with the subject matter. A federal system of government enables different provinces to pursue policies responsive to the particular concerns and interests of people in that province. At the same time, Canada as a whole is also a democratic community in which citizens construct and achieve goals on a national scale through federal government acting within the limits of its jurisdiction. The function of federalism is to enable citizens to participate concurrently in different collectivities and to pursue goals at both a provincial and a federal level.

[67] The consent of the governed is a value that is basic to our understanding of a free and democratic society. Yet democracy in any real sense of the word cannot exist without the rule of law. It is the law that creates the framework within which the "sovereign will" is to be ascertained and implemented. To be accorded legitimacy, democratic institutions must rest, ultimately, on a legal foundation. That is, they must allow for the participation of, and accountability to, the people, through public institutions created under the Constitution. Equally, however, a system of government cannot survive through adherence to the law alone. A political system must also possess legitimacy, and in our political culture, that requires an interaction between the rule of law and the democratic principle. The system must be capable of reflecting the aspirations of the people. But there is more. Our law's claim to legitimacy also rests on an appeal to moral values, many of which are imbedded in our constitutional structure. It would be a grave mistake to equate legitimacy with the "sovereign will" or majority rule alone, to the exclusion of other constitutional values.

[68] Finally, we highlight that a functioning democracy requires a continuous process of discussion. The Constitution mandates government by democratic legislatures, and an executive accountable to them, "resting ultimately on public opinion reached by discussion and the interplay of ideas" (*Saumur v. City*

of Quebec, supra, at p. 330). At both the federal and provincial level, by its very nature, the need to build majorities necessitates compromise, negotiation, and deliberation. No one has a monopoly on truth, and our system is predicated on the faith that in the marketplace of ideas, the best solutions to public problems will rise to the top. Inevitably, there will be dissenting voices. A democratic system of government is committed to considering those dissenting voices, and seeking to acknowledge and address those voices in the laws by which all in the community must live. [...]

Constitutionalism and the Rule of Law

[70] The principles of constitutionalism and the rule of law lie at the root of our system of government. [...] At its most basic level, the rule of law vouchsafes to the citizens and residents of the country a stable, predictable and ordered society in which to conduct their affairs. It provides a shield for individuals from arbitrary state action.

[71] In the *Manitoba Language Rights Reference, supra*, at pp. 747–52, this Court outlined the elements of the rule of law. We emphasized, first, that the rule of law provides that the law is supreme over the acts of both government and private persons. There is, in short, one law for all. Second, we explained, at p. 749, that "the rule of law requires the creation and maintenance of an actual order of positive laws which preserves and embodies the more general principle of normative order." [...] A third aspect of the rule of law is, as recently confirmed in the *Provincial Judges Reference, supra*, at para 10, that "the exercise of all public power must find its ultimate source in a legal rule." Put another way, the relationship between the state and the individual must be regulated by law. Taken together, these three considerations make up a principle of profound constitutional and political significance.

[72] The constitutionalism principle bears considerable similarity to the rule of law, although they are not identical. The essence of constitutionalism in Canada is embodied in s. 52(1) of the *Constitution Act, 1982*, which provides that "[t]he Constitution of Canada is the supreme law of Canada, and any law that is inconsistent with the provisions of the Constitution is, to the extent of the inconsistency, of no force or effect." Simply put, the constitutionalism principle requires that all government action comply with the Constitution. The rule of law principle requires that all government action must comply with the law, including the Constitution. [...]

[73] An understanding of the scope and importance of the principles of the rule of law and constitutionalism is aided by acknowledging explicitly why a constitution is entrenched beyond the reach of simple majority rule. There are three overlapping reasons.

[74] First, a constitution may provide an added safeguard for fundamental human rights and individual freedoms which might otherwise be susceptible to government interference. Although democratic government is generally solicitous of those rights, there are occasions when the majority will be tempted to

ignore fundamental rights in order to accomplish collective goals more easily or effectively. Constitutional entrenchment ensures that those rights will be given due regard and protection. Second, a constitution may seek to ensure that vulnerable minority groups are endowed with the institutions and rights necessary to maintain and promote their identities against the assimilative pressures of the majority. And third, a constitution may provide for a division of political power that allocates political power amongst different levels of government. That purpose would be defeated if one of those democratically elected levels of government could usurp the powers of the other simply by exercising its legislative power to allocate additional political power to itself unilaterally. [...]

[76] Canadians have never accepted that ours is a system of simple majority rule. Our principle of democracy, taken in conjunction with the other constitutional principles discussed here, is richer. Constitutional government is necessarily predicated on the idea that the political representatives of the people of a province have the capacity and the power to commit the province to be bound into the future by the constitutional rules being adopted. These rules are "binding" not in the sense of frustrating the will of a majority of a province, but as defining the majority which must be consulted in order to alter the fundamental balances of political power (including the spheres of autonomy guaranteed by the principle of federalism), individual rights, and minority rights in our society. Of course, those constitutional rules are themselves amenable to amendment, but only through a process of negotiation which ensures that there is an opportunity for the constitutionally defined rights of all the parties to be respected and reconciled.

[77] In this way, our belief in democracy may be harmonized with our belief in constitutionalism. Constitutional amendment often requires some form of substantial consensus precisely because the content of the underlying principles of our Constitution demand it. By requiring broad support in the form of an "enhanced majority" to achieve constitutional change, the Constitution ensures that minority interests must be addressed before proposed changes which would affect them may be enacted. [...]

Protection of Minorities

[79] The fourth underlying constitutional principle we address here concerns the protection of minorities. There are a number of specific constitutional provisions protecting minority language, religion and education rights. Some of those provisions are, as we have recognized on a number of occasions, the product of historical compromises. As this Court observed, the protection of minority religious education rights was a central consideration in the negotiations leading to Confederation. In the absence of such protection, it was felt that the minorities in what was then Canada East and Canada West would be submerged and assimilated. [...]

[80] However, we highlight that even though those provisions were the product of negotiation and political compromise, that does not render them

unprincipled. Rather, such a concern reflects a broader principle related to the protection of minority rights. Undoubtedly, the three other constitutional principles inform the scope and operation of the specific provisions that protect the rights of minorities. We emphasize that the protection of minority rights is itself an independent principle underlying our constitutional order. [...]

[81] The concern of our courts and governments to protect minorities has been prominent in recent years, particularly following the enactment of the *Charter*. Undoubtedly, one of the key considerations motivating the enactment of the *Charter*, and the process of constitutional judicial review that it entails, is the protection of minorities. However, it should not be forgotten that the protection of minority rights had a long history before the enactment of the *Charter*. Indeed, the protection of minority rights was clearly an essential consideration in the design of our constitutional structure even at the time of Confederation. Although Canada's record of upholding the rights of minorities is not a spotless one, that goal is one towards which Canadians have been striving since Confederation, and the process has not been without successes. The principle of protecting minority rights continues to exercise influence in the operation and interpretation of our Constitution. [...]

Conclusions

[149] The Reference requires us to consider whether Quebec has a right to *unilateral* secession. Those who support the existence of such a right found their case primarily on the principle of democracy. Democracy, however, means more than simple majority rule. As reflected in our constitutional jurisprudence, democracy exists in the larger context of other constitutional values such as those already mentioned. In the 131 years since Confederation, the people of the provinces and territories have created close ties of interdependence (economically, socially, politically and culturally) based on shared values that include federalism, democracy, constitutionalism and the rule of law, and respect for minorities. A democratic decision of Quebecers in favour of secession would put those relationships at risk. The Constitution vouchsafes order and stability, and accordingly secession of a province "under the Constitution" could not be achieved unilaterally, that is, without principled negotiation with other participants in Confederation within the existing constitutional framework.

[150] The Constitution is not a straitjacket. Even a brief review of our constitutional history demonstrates periods of momentous and dramatic change. Our democratic institutions necessarily accommodate a continuous process of discussion and evolution, which is reflected in the constitutional right of each participant in the federation to initiate constitutional change. This right implies a reciprocal duty on the other participants to engage in discussions to address any legitimate initiative to change the constitutional order. While it is true that some attempts at constitutional amendment in recent years have faltered, a clear majority vote in Quebec on a clear question in favour of secession would

confer democratic legitimacy on the secession initiative which all of the other participants in Confederation would have to recognize.

[151] Quebec could not, despite a clear referendum result, purport to invoke a right of self-determination to dictate the terms of a proposed secession to the other parties to the federation. The democratic vote, by however strong a majority, would have no legal effect on its own and could not push aside the principles of federalism and the rule of law, the rights of individuals and minorities, or the operation of democracy in the other provinces or in Canada as a whole. Democratic rights under the Constitution cannot be divorced from constitutional obligations. Nor, however, can the reverse proposition be accepted. The continued existence and operation of the Canadian constitutional order could not be indifferent to a clear expression of a clear majority of Quebecers that they no longer wish to remain in Canada. The other provinces and the federal government would have no basis to deny the right of the government of Quebec to pursue secession, should a clear majority of the people of Quebec choose that goal, so long as in doing so, Quebec respects the rights of others. The negotiations that followed such a vote would address the potential act of secession as well as its possible terms should in fact secession proceed. There would be no conclusions predetermined by law on any issue. Negotiations would need to address the interests of the other provinces, the federal government, Quebec and indeed the rights of all Canadians both within and outside Quebec, and specifically the rights of minorities. No one suggests that it would be an easy set of negotiations.

[152] The negotiation process would require the reconciliation of various rights and obligations by negotiation between two legitimate majorities, namely, the majority of the population of Quebec, and that of Canada as a whole. A political majority at either level that does not act in accordance with the underlying constitutional principles we have mentioned puts at risk the legitimacy of its exercise of its rights, and the ultimate acceptance of the result by the international community.

[153] The task of the Court has been to clarify the legal framework within which political decisions are to be taken "under the Constitution," not to usurp the prerogatives of the political forces that operate within that framework. The obligations we have identified are binding obligations under the Constitution of Canada. However, it will be for the political actors to determine what constitutes "a clear majority on a clear question" in the circumstances under which a future referendum vote may be taken. Equally, in the event of demonstrated majority support for Quebec secession, the content and process of the negotiations will be for the political actors to settle. The reconciliation of the various legitimate constitutional interests is necessarily committed to the political rather than the judicial realm precisely because that reconciliation can only be achieved through the give and take of political negotiations. To the extent issues addressed in the course of negotiation are political, the courts, appreciating their proper role in the constitutional scheme, would have no supervisory role. [...]

[155] Although there is no right, under the Constitution or at international law, to unilateral secession, that is secession without negotiation on the basis just discussed, this does not rule out the possibility of an unconstitutional declaration of secession leading to a *de facto* secession. The ultimate success of such a secession would be dependent on recognition by the international community, which is likely to consider the legality and legitimacy of secession having regard to, amongst other facts, the conduct of Quebec and Canada, in determining whether to grant or withhold recognition. Such recognition, even if granted, would not, however, provide any retroactive justification for the act of secession, either under the Constitution of Canada or at international law.

B: THE SCOPE AND OPERATION OF THE *CHARTER*

Retail, Wholesale and Department Store Union, Local 580 v. Dolphin Delivery Ltd.
Supreme Court of Canada
[1986] 2 S.C.R. 573

What is the scope of judicial review under the *Charter*? Is there a tension between the sweeping words of section 52(1) ("supreme law of Canada") and the more restrained language of section 32(1)? The concern here is not the purely technical one it might seem on first glance. At stake is the traditional liberal view that there is a fundamental distinction between the "public" and the "private" spheres, and that constitutional guarantees are only required to constrain government action within the public sphere. Does this mean, for example, that powerful private organizations such as corporations can violate our freedoms of speech and association with impunity?

In the *Dolphin Delivery* case precisely this question is at issue. During a labour dispute involving Purolator Courier, the union representing the employees believed that Dolphin Delivery, by continuing to do business with Purolator during the lockout, was conspiring to defeat the union. The union proposed to engage in "secondary picketing" of Dolphin Delivery. Before they could do so, Dolphin Delivery asked for and was granted an injunction on the grounds that secondary picketing comprises a common law tort of inducing breach of contract. The union appealed arguing that the injunction, and the "private" common law on which it was based, violated their right to freedom of expression and association. The majority based its rejection of the union's appeal on the issue of whether the *Charter* applies to the law concerning "private" matters.

Mr. Justice McIntyre (for the majority):

Does the Charter Apply to the Common Law?

[25] In my view, there can be no doubt that it does apply. [...] The English text [of s. 52] provides that "any law that is inconsistent with the provisions of the Constitution is, to the extent of the inconsistency, of no force or effect." If this language is not broad enough to include the common law, it should be observed as well that the French text adds strong support to this conclusion in its employment of the words "elle rend inopérantes les dispositions incompatibles *de toute autre règle de droit.*" [Emphasis added] To adopt a construction of s. 52(1) which would exclude from *Charter* application the whole body of the common law which in great part governs the rights and obligations of the individuals in society, would be wholly unrealistic and contrary to the clear language employed in s. 52(1) of the Act.

Does the Charter Apply to Private Litigation?

[26] This question involves consideration of whether or not an individual may found a cause of action or defence against another individual on the basis of a breach of a *Charter* right. In other words, does the *Charter* apply to private litigation divorced completely from any connection with Government? This is a subject of controversy in legal circles and the question has not been dealt with in this Court. One view of the matter rests on the proposition that the *Charter*, like most written constitutions, was set up to regulate the relationship between the individual and the Government. It was intended to restrain government action and to protect the individual. It was not intended in the absence of some governmental action to be applied in private litigation. [...]

[33] I am in agreement with the view that the *Charter* does not apply to private litigation. It is evident from the authorities that that approach has been adopted by most judges and commentators who have dealt with this question. In my view, s. 32 of the *Charter*, especially dealing with the question of *Charter* application, is conclusive on this issue. [...] Section 32(1) refers to the Parliament and Government of Canada and to the legislatures and governments of the Provinces in respect of all matters within their respective authorities. In this, it may be seen that Parliament and the legislatures are treated as separate or specific branches of government, distinct from the executive branch of government, and therefore where the word "government" is used in s. 32 it refers not to government in its generic sense meaning the whole of the governmental apparatus of the state—but to a branch of government. The word "government," following as it does the words "Parliament" and "Legislature," must then, it would seem, refer to the executive or administrative branch of government. This is the sense in which one generally speaks of the Government of Canada or of a province. I am of the opinion that the word "government" is used in s. 32 of the *Charter* in the sense of the executive government of Canada and the Provinces. [...]

[34] It is my view that s. 32 of the *Charter* specifies the actors to whom the *Charter* will apply. They are the legislative, executive and administrative branches of government. It will apply to those branches of government whether or not their action is invoked in public or private litigation. It would seem that legislation is the only way in which a legislature may infringe a guaranteed right or freedom. Action by the executive or administrative branches of government will generally depend upon legislation, that is, statutory authority. Such action may also depend, however, on the common law, as in the case of the prerogative. To the extent that it relies on statutory authority which constitutes or results in an infringement of a guaranteed right or freedom, the *Charter* will apply and it will be unconstitutional. The action will also be unconstitutional to the extent that it relies for authority or justification on a rule of the common law which constitutes or creates an infringement of a *Charter* right or freedom. In this way the *Charter* will apply to the common law, whether in public or private litigation. It will apply to the common law, however, only in so far as the common law is the basis of some governmental action which, it is alleged, infringes a guaranteed right or freedom.

[35] The element of governmental intervention necessary to make the *Charter* applicable in an otherwise private action is difficult to define. We have concluded that the *Charter* applies to the common law but not between private parties. The problem here is that this is an action between private parties in which the appellant resists the common law claim of the respondent on the basis of a *Charter* infringement. The argument is made that the common law, which is itself subject to the *Charter*, creates the tort of civil conspiracy and that of inducing a breach of contract. The respondent has sued and has procured the injunction which has enjoined the picketing on the basis of the commission of these torts. The appellants say the injunction infringes their *Charter* right of freedom of expression under s. 2 (b). Professor [Peter] Hogg meets this problem when he suggests, at p. 677 of his text, after concluding that the *Charter* does not apply to private litigation, that:

> Private action is, however, a residual category from which it is necessary to subtract those kinds of action to which s. 32 does make the *Charter* applicable. The *Charter* will apply to any rule of the common law that specifically authorizes or directs an abridgement of a guaranteed right.
>
> The fact that a court order is governmental action means that the *Charter* will apply to a purely private arrangement, such as a contract or proprietary interest, but only to the extent that the *Charter* will preclude judicial enforcement of any arrangement in derogation of a guaranteed right. [p. 678]

Professor Hogg rationalized his position in these words:

> In a sense, the common law authorizes any private action that is not prohibited by a positive rule of law. If the *Charter* applied to the com-

mon law in that attenuated sense, it would apply to all private activity. But it seems more reasonable to say that the common law offends the *Charter* only when it crystallizes into a rule that can be enforced by the courts. Then, if an enforcement order would infringe a *Charter* right, the *Charter* will apply to preclude the order, and, by necessary implication, to modify the common law rule. [p. 678]

[36] I find the position thus adopted troublesome and, in my view, it should not be accepted as an approach to this problem. While in political science terms it is probably acceptable to treat the courts as one of the three fundamental branches of government, that is, legislative, executive, and judicial, I cannot equate for the purposes of *Charter* application the order of a court with an element of governmental action. This is not to say that the courts are not bound by the *Charter*. The courts are, of course, bound by the *Charter* as they are bound by all law. It is their duty to apply the law, but in doing so they act as neutral arbiters, not as contending parties involved in a dispute. To regard a court order as an element of governmental intervention necessary to invoke the *Charter* would, it seems to me, widen the scope of *Charter* application to virtually all private litigation. All cases must end, if carried to completion, with an enforcement order and if the *Charter* precludes the making of the order, where a *Charter* right would be infringed, it would seem that all private litigation would be subject to the *Charter*. In my view, this approach will not provide the answer to the question. A more direct and a more precisely-defined connection between the element of government action and the claim advanced must be present before the *Charter* applies.

[37] An example of such a direct and close connection is to be found in *Re Blainey and Ontario Hockey Ass'n et al.* (1986). In that case, proceedings were brought against the hockey association in the Supreme Court of Ontario on behalf of a 12-year-old girl who had been refused permission to play hockey as a member of a boys' team competing under the auspices of the association. A complaint against the exclusion of the girl on the basis of her sex alone had been made under the provisions of the *Human Rights Code, 1981* to the Ontario Human Rights Commission. It was argued that the hockey association provided a service ordinarily available to members of the public without discrimination because of sex, and therefore that the discrimination against the girl contravened this legislation. The commission considered that it could not act in the matter because of the provisions of s. 19(2) of the *Code*, which are set out hereunder:

19(2) The right under section 1 to equal treatment with respect to services and facilities is not infringed where membership in an athletic organization or participation in an athletic activity is restricted to persons of the same sex.

In the Supreme Court of Ontario it was claimed that s. 19(2) of the *Code* was contrary to s. 15(1) of the *Charter* and that it was accordingly void. The application was dismissed. In the Court of Appeal, the appeal was allowed. Dubin J.A. writing for the majority, stated the issue in these terms:

> Indeed, it was on the premise that the ruling of the Ontario Human Rights Commission was correct that these proceedings were launched and which afforded the status to the applicant to complain now that, by reason of s. 19(2) of the *Code*, she is being denied the equal protection and equal benefit of the *Code* by reason of her sex, contrary to the provision of s. 15(1) of the *Charter*.

He concluded that the provisions of s. 19(2) were in contradiction of the *Charter* and hence of no force or effect. In the *Blainey* case, a lawsuit between private parties, the *Charter* was applied because one of the parties acted on the authority of a statute, i.e., s. 19(2) of the Ontario *Human Rights Code*, which infringed the *Charter* rights of another. *Blainey* then affords an illustration of the manner in which *Charter* rights of private individuals may be enforced and protected by the courts, that is, by measuring legislation—government action against the *Charter*.

[38] As has been noted above, it is difficult and probably dangerous to attempt to define with narrow precision that element of governmental intervention which will suffice to permit reliance on the *Charter* by private litigants in private litigation. Professor Hogg has dealt with this question, at p. 677, *supra*, where he said:

> [T]he *Charter* would apply to a private person exercising the power of arrest that is granted to "anyone" by the Criminal Code, and to a private railway company exercising the power to make by-laws (and impose penalties for their breach) that is granted to a "railway company" by the Railway Act; all action taken in exercise of a statutory power is covered by the *Charter* by virtue of the references to "Parliament" and "legislature" in s. 32. The *Charter* would also apply to the action of a commercial corporation that was an agent of the Crown, by virtue of the reference to "government" in s. 32.

[39] It would also seem that the *Charter* would apply to many forms of delegated legislation, regulations, orders in council, possibly municipal by-laws, and by-laws and regulations of other creatures of Parliament and the Legislatures. It is not suggested that this list is exhaustive. Where such exercise of, or reliance upon, governmental action is present and where one private party invokes or relies upon it to produce an infringement of the *Charter* rights of another, the *Charter* will be applicable. Where, however, private party "A" sues private party "B" relying on the common law and where no act of government is relied upon to support the action, the *Charter* will not apply. I should make it clear, however, that this is a distinct issue from the question whether the judiciary ought to apply and develop the principles of the common law in a manner consistent with the fundamental values enshrined in the Constitution. The answer to

this question must be in the affirmative. In this sense, then, the *Charter* is far from irrelevant to private litigants whose disputes fail to be decided at common law. But this is different from the proposition that one private party owes a constitutional duty to another, which proposition underlies the purported assertion of *Charter* causes of action or *Charter* defences between individuals.

[40] Can it be said in the case at bar that the required element of government intervention or intrusion may be found? In *Blainey*, s. 19(2) of the Ontario *Human Rights Code*, an Act of a legislature, was the factor which removed the case from the private sphere. If in our case one could point to a statutory provision specifically outlawing secondary picketing of the nature contemplated by the appellants, the case—assuming for the moment an infringement of the *Charter*—would be on all fours with *Blainey* and, subject to s. 1 of the *Charter*, the statutory provision could be struck down. In neither case, would it be, as Professor Hogg would have it, the order of a court which would remove the case from the private sphere. It would be the result of one party's reliance on a statutory provision violative of the *Charter*.

[41] In the case at bar, however, we have no offending statute. We have a rule of the common law which renders secondary picketing tortious and subject to injunctive restraint, on the basis that it induces a breach of contract. While, as we have found, the *Charter* applies to the common law, we do not have in this litigation between purely private parties any exercise of or reliance upon governmental action which would invoke the *Charter*. It follows then that the appeal must fail.

R. v. Oakes
Supreme Court of Canada
[1986] 1 S.C.R. 103

A unique feature of Canada's constitutional framework for the protection of rights and freedoms is section 1 of the *Charter*. This section reads: "*The Canadian Charter of Rights and Freedoms* guarantees the rights and freedoms set out in it subject only to such reasonable limits prescribed by law as can be demonstrably justified in a free and democratic society." In effect, section 1 asserts that sometimes a law or state action that violates rights or freedoms may nonetheless be constitutionally acceptable. When are limits on our rights and freedoms "reasonable" and when can they be "demonstrably justified"? Should our rights and freedoms only be reasonably limited to preserve or enhance other, more important rights and freedoms, or should any state interest—from security to cost-savings or administrative convenience—do the job?

In the *Oakes* case Chief Justice Dickson attempted to answer these questions by offering a sophisticated test for the application of section 1. David Oakes had been charged with unlawful possession of a narcotic for the purpose of trafficking. In the course of his trial, he challenged the constitutionality of the "reverse onus" provision of section 8 of the *Narcotic Control Act*. That section provided that once the court found that Oakes was in possession of the narcotic, he was presumed to be in possession for the purposes of trafficking (a much more serious offence), and that it was up to him to prove otherwise. The Supreme Court of Canada quickly found that this provision violated Oakes's *Charter* section 11(d) right to be presumed innocent until proven guilty. But the question remained whether, given that drug trafficking is a serious social problem, this infringement of Oakes's rights could be justified in a "free and democratic society." Chief Justice Dickson's analysis of the application of section 1 has had a profound effect on all subsequent *Charter* jurisprudence. As many of the *Charter* cases found in this book attest, a substantial part of our constitutional jurisprudence now involves section 1 and the *Oakes* test.

Chief Justice Dickson (for the majority):

[62] The Crown submits that even if s. 8 of the *Narcotic Control Act* violates s. 11(d) of the *Charter*, it can still be upheld as a reasonable limit under s. 1 which provides:

> 1. The *Canadian Charter of Rights and Freedoms* guarantees the rights and freedoms set out in it subject only to such reasonable limits pre-scribed by law as can be demonstrably justified in a free and democratic society. [...]

[63] It is important to observe at the outset that s. 1 has two functions: first, it constitutionally guarantees the rights and freedoms set out in the provisions which follow; and, second, it states explicitly the exclusive justificatory criteria (outside of s. 33 of the *Constitution Act, 1982*) against which limitations on those rights and freedoms must be measured. Accordingly, any s. 1 inquiry must be premised on an understanding that the impugned limit violates constitutional rights and freedoms—rights and freedoms which are part of the supreme law of Canada. As Wilson J. stated in *Singh v. Minister of Employment and Immigration* (1985), at p. 218: "...it is important to remember that the courts are conducting this inquiry in light of a commitment to uphold the rights and freedoms set out in the other sections of the *Charter*."

[64] A second contextual element of interpretation of s. 1 is provided by the words "free and democratic society." Inclusion of these words as the final standard of justification for limits on rights and freedoms refers the Court to the very purpose for which the *Charter* was originally entrenched in the Con-stitution: Canadian society is to be free and democratic. The Court must be guided by the values and principles essential to a free and democratic society which I believe embody, to name but a few, respect for the inherent dignity of the human person, commitment to social justice and equality, accommodation of a wide variety of beliefs, respect for cultural and group identity, and faith in social and political institutions which enhance the participation of individu-als and groups in society. The underlying values and principles of a free and democratic society are the genesis of the rights and freedoms guaranteed by the *Charter* and the ultimate standard against which a limit on a right or freedom must be shown, despite its effect, to be reasonable and demonstrably justified.

[65] The rights and freedoms guaranteed by the *Charter* are not, however, absolute. It may become necessary to limit rights and freedoms in circum-stances where their exercise would be inimical to the realization of collective goals of fundamental importance. For this reason, s. 1 provides criteria of justification for limits on the rights and freedoms guaranteed by the *Charter*. These criteria impose a stringent standard of justification, especially when understood in terms of the two contextual considerations discussed above, namely, the violation of a constitutionally guaranteed right or freedom and the fundamental principles of a free and democratic society.

[66] The onus of proving that a limit on a right and freedom guaranteed by the *Charter* is reasonable and demonstrably justified in a free and democratic society rests upon the party seeking to uphold the limitation. It is clear from the text of s. 1 that limits on the rights and freedoms enumerated in the *Charter* are exceptions to their general guarantee. The presumption is that the rights and freedoms are guaranteed unless the party invoking s. 1 can bring itself within the exceptional criteria which justify their being limited. This is further substantiated by the use of the word "demonstrably" which clearly indicates that the onus of justification is on the party seeking to limit. [...]

[67] The standard of proof under s. 1 is the civil standard, namely, proof by a preponderance of probability. The alternative criminal standard, proof beyond a reasonable doubt, would, in my view, be unduly onerous on the party seeking to limit. Concepts such as "reasonableness," "justifiability" and "free and democratic society" are simply not amenable to such a standard. Nevertheless, the preponderance of probability test must be applied rigorously. Indeed, the phrase "demonstrably justified" in s. 1 of the *Charter* supports this conclusion. [...]

[68] Having regard to the fact that s. 1 is being invoked for the purpose of justifying a violation of the constitutional rights and freedoms the *Charter* was designed to protect, a very high degree of probability will be, in the words of Lord Denning, "commensurate with the occasion." Where evidence is required in order to prove the constituent elements of an s. 1 inquiry, and this will generally be the case, it should be cogent and persuasive and make clear to the Court the consequences of imposing or not imposing the limit. [...] A court will also need to know what alternative measures for implementing the objective were available to the legislators when they made their decisions. I should add, however, that there may be cases where certain elements of the s. 1 analysis are obvious or self-evident.

[69] To establish that a limit is reasonable and demonstrably justified in a free and democratic society, two central criteria must be satisfied. First, the objective, which the measures responsible for a limit on a *Charter* right and freedom are designed to serve, must be "of sufficient importance to warrant overriding a constitutionally protected right or freedom": *R. v. Big M Drug Mart Ltd.* (1985), *supra*, at p. 352. The standard must be high in order to ensure that objectives which are trivial or discordant with the principles integral to a free and democratic society do not gain s. 1 protection. It is necessary, at a minimum, that an objective relate to concerns which are pressing and substantial in a free and democratic society before it can be characterized as sufficiently important.

[70] Second, once a sufficiently significant objective is recognized, then the party invoking s. 1 must show that the means chosen are reasonable and demonstrably justified. This involves "a form of proportionality test": *R. v. Big M Drug Mart Ltd.* (1985), *supra*, at p. 352. Although the nature of the proportionality test will vary depending on the circumstances, in each case courts will

be required to balance the interests of society with those of individuals and groups. There are, in my view, three important components of a proportionality test. First, the measures adopted must be carefully designed to achieve the objective in question. They must not be arbitrary, unfair or based on irrational considerations. In short, they must be rationally connected to the objective. Second, the means, even if rationally connected to the objective in this first sense, should impair "as little as possible" the right or freedom in question: *R. v. Big M Drug Mart Ltd.* (1985), *supra*, at p. 352. Third, there must be a proportionality between the *effects* of the measures which are responsible for limiting the *Charter* right or freedom, and the objective which has been identified as of "sufficient importance."

[71] With respect to the third component, it is clear that the general effect of any measure impugned under s. 1 will be the infringement of a right or freedom guaranteed by the *Charter*, this is the reason why resort to s. 1 is necessary. The inquiry into effects must, however, go further. A wide range of rights and freedoms are guaranteed by the *Charter*, and an almost infinite number of factual situations may arise in respect of these. Some limits on rights and freedoms protected by the *Charter* will be more serious than others in terms of the nature of the right or freedom violated, the extent of the violation, and the degree to which the measures which impose the limit trench upon the integral principles of a free and democratic society. Even if an objective is of sufficient importance, and the first two elements of the proportionality test are satisfied, it is still possible that, because of the severity of the deleterious effects of a measure on individuals or groups, the measure will not be justified by the purposes it is intended to serve. The more severe the deleterious effects of a measure, the more important the objective must be if the measure is to be reasonable and demonstrably justified in a free and democratic society.

[72] Having outlined the general principles of an s. 1 inquiry, we must apply them to s. 8 of the *Narcotic Control Act*. Is the reverse onus provision in s. 8 a reasonable limit on the right to be presumed innocent until proven guilty beyond a reasonable doubt as can be demonstrably justified in a free and democratic society?

[73] The starting point for formulating a response to this question is, as stated above, the nature of Parliament's interest or objective which accounts for the passage of s. 8 of the *Narcotic Control Act*. According to the Crown, s. 8 is aimed at curbing drug trafficking by facilitating the conviction of drug traffickers. In my opinion, Parliament's concern that drug trafficking be decreased can be characterized as substantial and pressing. The problem of drug trafficking has been increasing since the 1950's at which time there was already considerable concern. [...] Throughout this period, numerous measures were adopted by free and democratic societies, at both the international and national levels. [...]

[76] The objective of protecting our society from the grave ills associated with drug trafficking, is, in my view, one of sufficient importance to warrant

overriding a constitutionally protected right or freedom in certain cases. More-over, the degree of seriousness of drug trafficking makes its acknowledgement as a sufficiently important objective for the purposes of s. 1, to a large extent, self-evident. The first criterion of an s. 1 inquiry, therefore, has been satisfied by the Crown.

[77] The next stage of inquiry is a consideration of the means chosen by Parliament to achieve its objective. The means must be reasonable and demon-strably justified in a free and democratic society. As outlined above, this pro-portionality test should begin with a consideration of the rationality of the provision: is the reverse onus clause in s. 8 rationally related to the objective of curbing drug trafficking? At a minimum, this requires that s. 8 be internally rational; there must be a rational connection between the basic fact of possession and the presumed fact of possession for the purpose of trafficking. Otherwise, the reverse onus clause could give rise to unjustified and erroneous convictions for drug trafficking of persons guilty only of possession of narcotics.

[78] In my view, s. 8 does not survive this rational connection test. As Martin J.A. of the Ontario Court of Appeal concluded, possession of a small or neg-ligible quantity of narcotics does not support the inference of trafficking. In other words, it would be irrational to infer that a person had an intent to traffic on the basis of his or her possession of a very small quantity of narcotics. The presumption required under s. 8 of the *Narcotic Control Act* is over-inclusive and could lead to results in certain cases which would defy both rationality and fairness. In light of the seriousness of the offence in question, which carries with it the possibility of imprisonment for life, I am further convinced that the first component of the proportionality test has not been satisfied by the Crown.

[79] Having concluded that s. 8 does not satisfy this first component of proportionality, it is unnecessary to consider the other two components.

[Therefore, s. 8 of the *Narcotic Control Act* is inconsistent with s. 11 (d) of the *Charter* and thus is of no force and effect.]

Canada (Justice) v. Khadr
Supreme Court of Canada
[2008] 2 S.C.R. 125

Omar Khadr is a Canadian who was detained by the US military at Guantanamo Bay, Cuba in 2002 for alleged war crimes. In 2003 and 2004 he was interrogated by two of Canada's intelligence agencies, the Canadian Security Intelligence Service (CSIS) and the Foreign Intelligence Division of the Department of Foreign Affairs and International Trade (DFAIT). Some of these interrogations took place with knowledge that Khadr had been subjected to sleep deprivation techniques by US authorities to make him less resistant to interrogation. At issue for the court was whether Khadr was entitled, upon request, to disclosure of the records of those interrogations, and whether the *Canadian Charter of Rights and Freedoms* applies extra-territorially or whether principles of comity preclude such application.

The excerpt reproduced below focuses on the question of extra-territorial application of Canadian law, and in particular on how the principle of comity can be limited where international human rights law is relevant.

The court found that Khadr was entitled to disclosure of the interrogation records, and that the *Canadian Charter of Rights and Freedoms* does apply extra-territorially when Canada's international human rights obligations are at stake.

The Court:

[1] This appeal raises the issue of the relationship between Canada's domestic and international human rights commitments. Omar Khadr currently faces prosecution on murder and other charges before a US Military Commission in Guantanamo Bay, Cuba. Mr. Khadr asks for an order under s. 7 of the *Canadian Charter of Rights and Freedoms* that the appellants be required to disclose to him all documents relevant to these charges in the possession of the Canadian Crown, including interviews conducted by Canadian officials with him in 2003 at Guantanamo Bay. The Minister of Justice opposes the request, arguing that the *Charter* does not apply outside Canada and hence did not govern the actions of Canadian officials at Guantanamo Bay. [...]

(i) Does the Charter Apply?

[15] As discussed, CSIS, a Canadian government organization, interviewed Mr. Khadr at his prison in Guantanamo Bay and shared the contents of these interviews with US authorities. Mr. Khadr seeks an order that the appellants be required to disclose to him all documents in the possession of the Canadian Crown relevant to the charges he is facing, for the purpose of his defence.

[16] Had the interviews and process been in Canada, Mr. Khadr would have been entitled to full disclosure under the principles in *Stinchcombe*, which held that persons whose liberty is at risk as a result of being charged with a criminal offence are entitled to disclosure of the information in the hands of the Crown under s. 7 of the *Charter*. The Federal Court of Appeal applied *Stinchcombe* to Mr. Khadr's situation and ordered disclosure.

[17] The government argues that this constituted an error, because the *Charter* does not apply to the conduct of Canadian agents operating outside Canada. It relies on *R. v. Hape*, [2007] 2 S.C.R. 292, 2007 SCC 26, where a majority of this Court held that Canadian agents participating in an investigation into money laundering in the Caribbean were not bound by *Charter* constraints in the manner in which the investigation was conducted. This conclusion was based on international law principles against extraterritorial enforcement of domestic laws and the principle of comity which implies acceptance of foreign laws and procedures when Canadian officials are operating abroad.

[18] In *Hape*, however, the Court stated an important exception to the principle of comity. While not unanimous on all the principles governing extraterritorial application of the *Charter*, the Court was united on the principle that comity cannot be used to justify Canadian participation in activities of a foreign state or its agents that are contrary to Canada's international obligations. It was held that the deference required by the principle of comity "ends where clear violations of international law and fundamental human rights begin" (*Hape*, at para. 52, *per* LeBel J.; see also paras. 51 and 101). The Court further held that in interpreting the scope and application of the *Charter*, the courts should seek to ensure compliance with Canada's binding obligations under international law (para. 56, *per* LeBel J.).

[19] If the Guantanamo Bay process under which Mr. Khadr was being held was in conformity with Canada's international obligations, the *Charter* has no application and Mr. Khadr's application for disclosure cannot succeed: *Hape*. However, if Canada was participating in a process that was violative of Canada's binding obligations under international law, the *Charter* applies to the extent of that participation.

[20] At this point, the question becomes whether the process at Guantanamo Bay at the time that CSIS handed the products of its interviews over to US officials was a process that violated Canada's binding obligations under international law.

[21] Issues may arise about whether it is appropriate for a Canadian court to pronounce on the legality of the process at Guantanamo Bay under which Mr.

Khadr was held at the time that Canadian officials participated in that process. We need not resolve those issues in this case. The United States Supreme Court has considered the legality of the conditions under which the Guantanamo detainees were detained and liable to prosecution during the time Canadian officials interviewed Mr. Khadr and gave the information to US authorities, between 2002 and 2004. With the benefit of a full factual record, the United States Supreme Court held that the detainees had illegally been denied access to *habeas corpus* and that the procedures under which they were to be prosecuted violated the *Geneva Conventions*. Those holdings are based on principles consistent with the *Charter* and Canada's international law obligations. In the present appeal, this is sufficient to establish violations of these international law obligations, to which Canada subscribes.

[22] In *Rasul v. Bush*, 542 U.S. 466 (2004), the United States Supreme Court held that detainees at Guantanamo Bay who, like Mr. Khadr, were not US citizens, could challenge the legality of their detention by way of the statutory right of *habeas corpus* provided for in 28 U.S.C. § 2241. This holding necessarily implies that the order under which the detainees had previously been denied the right to challenge their detention was illegal. In his concurring reasons, Kennedy J. noted that "the detainees at Guantanamo Bay are being held indefinitely, and without benefit of any legal proceeding to determine their status" (pp. 487–88). Mr. Khadr was detained at Guantanamo Bay during the time covered by the *Rasul* decision, and Canadian officials interviewed him and passed on information to US authorities during that time.

[23] At the time he was interviewed by CSIS officials, Mr. Khadr also faced the possibility of trial by military commission pursuant to Military Commission Order No. 1. In *Hamdan v. Rumsfeld*, 126 S. Ct. 2749 (2006), the United States Supreme Court considered the legality of this Order. The court held that by significantly departing from established military justice procedure without a showing of military exigency, the procedural rules for military commissions violated both the Uniform Code of Military Justice (10 U.S.C. § 836) and Common Article 3 of the *Geneva Conventions*. Different members of the majority of the United States Supreme Court focused on different deviations from the *Geneva Conventions* and the Uniform Code of Military Justice. But the majority was unanimous in holding that, in the circumstances, the deviations were sufficiently significant to deprive the military commissions of the status of "a regularly constituted court, affording all the judicial guarantees which are recognized as indispensable by civilized peoples," as required by Common Article 3 of the *Geneva Conventions*.

[24] The violations of human rights identified by the United States Supreme Court are sufficient to permit us to conclude that the regime providing for the detention and trial of Mr. Khadr at the time of the CSIS interviews constituted a clear violation of fundamental human rights protected by international law.

[25] Canada is a signatory of the four *Geneva Conventions* of 1949, which it ratified in 1965 (Can. T.S. 1965 No. 20) and has incorporated into Canadian

law with the *Geneva Conventions Act*, R.S.C. 1985, c. G-3. The right to challenge the legality of detention by *habeas corpus* is a fundamental right protected both by the *Charter* and by international treaties. It follows that participation in the Guantanamo Bay process which violates these international instruments would be contrary to Canada's binding international obligations.

[26] We conclude that the principles of international law and comity that might otherwise preclude application of the *Charter* to Canadian officials acting abroad do not apply to the assistance they gave to US authorities at Guantanamo Bay. Given the holdings of the United States Supreme Court, the *Hape* comity concerns that would ordinarily justify deference to foreign law have no application here. The effect of the United States Supreme Court's holdings is that the conditions under which Mr. Khadr was held and was liable for prosecution were illegal under both US and international law at the time Canadian officials interviewed Mr. Khadr and gave the information to US authorities. Hence no question of deference to foreign law arises. The *Charter* bound Canada to the extent that the conduct of Canadian officials involved it in a process that violated Canada's international obligations.

RELATED CASES

Minister of Justice of Canada v. Borowski [1981] 2 S.C.R. 575
(This case addresses the issue of standing, namely who has standing to challenge the constitutional validity of legislation.)

The Queen in Right of Canada v. Beauregard [1986] 2 S.C.R. 56
(This case discusses in general terms the nature of judicial independence in Canada.)

Schachter v. Canada [1992] 2 S.C.R. 679
(This case surveys a variety of remedial approaches under sections 24 and 52 of the *Charter* for addressing unjustified violations of *Charter* rights.)

Bertrand v. Attorney-General of Quebec [1995] R.J.Q. 2500
(This case examines whether a referendum in Quebec on the question of secession is unconstitutional since it could have the effect of disqualifying Quebec residents from the guarantees of the *Charter* if secession were chosen.)

PART II

Fundamental Freedoms

The reliance upon law for the protection of rights and freedoms within a social structure is a fundamental feature of our legal tradition, as basic as the rule of law itself. Part I, Schedule B of the *Constitution Act, 1982*—better known as the *Charter of Rights and Freedoms*—sets out the traditional and familiar rights and freedoms of a liberal constitutional order. Since 1982 our courts have cautiously crafted a jurisprudence of these rights and freedoms. Despite the immense gravitational force from the United States, which has a two-hundred-year jurisprudence to draw upon, distinctive features of the Canadian jurisprudence have emerged.

Section 2 of the *Charter* enumerates four basic liberal freedoms: freedom of conscience and religion; freedom of thought and expression; freedom of peaceful assembly; and freedom of association. The first two of these classic freedoms have been the most heavily litigated. Much of that litigation has focused on the meaning and scope of freedoms protected by these provisions. In several decisions the Supreme Court has implemented what is called a "purposive" approach to interpretation, expressed in *Big M Drug Mart* (excerpted here) as an approach to understanding each freedom "in the light of the interests it was meant to protect" [para. 116]. As readers will see in *Big M Drug Mart*, a purposive approach to interpretation goes hand in hand with consideration of the effects of a given law, and a law may be declared invalid in light of its purpose or its effects.

The purposive approach often requires judges to consider the meaning of a particular freedom in light of s. 1 considerations regarding justifiable limits to freedom in a free and democratic society. Ever since the decision in *R. v. Oakes*, excerpted in Part I, judges have applied the

"*Oakes* test" to determine whether a law found to be constitutionally invalid can be "saved" by being demonstrably justifiable in a free and democratic society. Judicial reasoning regarding justifiable limits on freedom of expression is demonstrated in several cases excerpted here, as judges attempt to identify standards and evidence for regarding some expression as so harmful, even if only expression and not physical action, that it is justifiably limited. Along the way, in *Little Sisters*, the Supreme Court makes clear just how restrictions on freedom of expression are to operate: the burden lies with legislators to justify a restraint, so it is not up to citizens to demonstrate that their expression is not justifiably limited—expression is presumed to be protected unless and until it can be shown to be justifiably limited. These cases take up highly controversial, complex matters including pornography depicting particular sexual practices, and "hate propaganda" advocating hatred of an identifiable group. Judicial reasoning regarding justifiable limits to the right to life, liberty, and security of the person is also presented here, in a case regarding the power of the provincial government of Quebec to prohibit citizens from choosing health care options outside the public health care system provided by Quebec.

R. v. Big M Drug Mart Ltd.
Supreme Court of Canada
[1985] 1 S.C.R. 295

Federal and provincial legislation declaring Sundays to be the official "day of rest" for business purposes has frequently come before Canadian courts, but this time the Supreme Court of Canada had the opportunity to test the legislation against standards of section 2 of the *Charter*. As in pre-*Charter* cases, the government insists that its "Lord's Day" legislation is not intended to put into law the dictates of any particular religion; the purpose is rather to ensure that workers have at least one day off to enjoy social and leisure activities with family and friends. From the other side, it is argued that, even if the legislation's *purpose* is not of compelling sabbatical observance, its *effect* is to attach an economic penalty to those who close on Saturdays for religious reasons since those businesses are required to be closed two days in a week rather than one.

Before tackling these arguments, Chief Justice Dickson had to address a legal issue that is highly significant in its own right. This is the issue of "standing." The plaintiff who is complaining about a violation of rights is a corporation, not an individual human being. Does it make sense for a corporation, or some other artificial, legal person, to complain that its freedom of religion is being infringed? Do corporations have constitutional rights? Is that what the *Charter* is about?

Chief Justice Dickson (for the majority):

Standing and Jurisdiction

[33] As a preliminary issue the Attorney-General for Alberta challenges the standing of Big M to raise the question of a possible infringement of the guarantee of freedom of conscience and religion and the jurisdiction of the provincial court to declare the *Lord's Day Act* inoperative.

[34] As best I understand the first submission, the assertion is that Big M is not entitled to any relief pursuant to s. 24(1) of the *Charter*. It is urged that freedom of religion is a personal freedom and that a corporation, being a statutory creation, cannot be said to have a conscience or hold a religious belief. It cannot, therefore, be protected by s. 2(a) of the *Charter*, nor can its rights and freedoms have been infringed or denied under s. 24(1); Big M's application under that section must consequently fail. [...]

[39] Any accused, whether corporate or individual, may defend a criminal charge by arguing that the law under which the charge is brought is constitutionally invalid. Big M is urging that the law under which it has been charged is inconsistent with s. 2(a) of the *Charter* and by reason of s. 52 of the *Constitution Act, 1982*, it is of no force or effect.

[40] Whether a corporation can enjoy or exercise freedom of religion is therefore irrelevant. The respondent is arguing that the legislation is constitutionally invalid because it impairs freedom of religion—if the law impairs freedom of religion it does not matter whether the company can possess religious belief. An accused atheist would be equally entitled to resist a charge under the Act. The only way this question might be relevant would be if s. 2(a) were interpreted as limited to protecting only those persons who could prove a genuinely held religious belief. I can see no basis to so limit the breadth of s. 2(a) in this case.

[41] The argument that the respondent, by reason of being a corporation, is incapable of holding religious belief and therefore incapable of claiming rights under s. 2 (a) of the *Charter*, confuses the nature of this appeal. A law which itself infringes religious freedom is, by that reason alone, inconsistent with s. 2(a) of the *Charter* and it matters not whether the accused is a Christian, Jew, Muslim, Hindu, Buddhist, atheist, agnostic or whether an individual or a corporation. It is the nature of the law, not the status of the accused, that is in issue. [...]

The Characterization of the Lord's Day Act

[48] There are obviously two possible ways to characterize the purpose of Lord's Day legislation, the one religious, namely, securing public observance of the Christian institution of the Sabbath and the other secular, namely, providing a uniform day of rest from labour. It is undoubtedly true that both elements may be present in any given enactment, indeed it is almost inevitable that they will be, considering that such laws combine a prohibition of ordinary employment for one day out of seven with a specification that this day of rest shall be the Christian Sabbath—Sunday. [...]

Purpose and Effect of Legislation

[78] A finding that the *Lord's Day Act* has [only] a secular purpose is, on the authorities, simply not possible. Its religious purpose, in compelling sabbatical observance, has been long-established and consistently maintained by the courts of this country.

[79] The Attorney-General for Alberta concedes that the Act is characterized by this religious purpose. He contends, however, that it is not the purpose but the effects of the Act which are relevant. In his submission, *Robertson and Rosetanni v. The Queen* (1963) is support for the proposition that it is effects alone which must be assessed in determining whether legislation violates a constitutional guarantee of freedom of religion.

[80] I cannot agree. In my view, both purpose and effect are relevant in determining constitutionality; either an unconstitutional purpose or an unconstitutional effect can invalidate legislation. All legislation is animated by an object the legislature intends to achieve. This object is realized through the impact produced by the operation and application of the legislation. Purpose and effect respectively, in the sense of the legislation's object and its ultimate impact, are clearly linked, if not indivisible. Intended and actual effects have often been looked to for guidance in assessing the legislation's object and thus, its validity.

[81] Moreover, consideration of the object of legislation is vital if rights are to be fully protected. The assessment by the courts of legislative purpose focuses scrutiny upon the aims and objectives of the legislature and ensures they are consonant with the guarantees enshrined in the *Charter*. The declaration that certain objects lie outside the legislature's power checks governmental action at the first stage of unconstitutional conduct. Further, it will provide more ready and more vigorous protection of constitutional rights by obviating the individual litigant's need to prove effects violative of *Charter* rights. It will also allow courts to dispose of cases where the object is clearly improper, without inquiring into the legislation's actual impact. [...]

[85] If the acknowledged purpose of the *Lord's Day Act*, namely, the compulsion of sabbatical observance, offends freedom of religion, it is then unnecessary to consider the actual impact of Sunday closing upon religious freedom. Even if such effects were found inoffensive, as the Attorney-General of Alberta urges, this could not save legislation whose purpose has been found to violate the *Charter's* guarantees. In any event, I would find it difficult to conceive of legislation with an unconstitutional purpose, where the effects would not also be unconstitutional. [...]

[93] While the effect of such legislation as the *Lord's Day Act* may be more secular today than it was in 1677 or in 1906, such a finding cannot justify a conclusion that its purpose has similarly changed. In result, therefore, the *Lord's Day Act* must be characterized as it has always been, a law the primary purpose of which is the compulsion of sabbatical observance.

Freedom of Religion

[94] A truly free society is one which can accommodate a wide variety of beliefs, diversity of tastes and pursuits, customs and codes of conduct. A free society is one which aims at equality with respect to the enjoyment of fundamental freedoms and I say this without any reliance upon s. 15 of the *Charter*. Freedom must surely be founded in respect for the inherent dignity and the inviolable rights of the human person. The essence of the concept of freedom of religion is the right to entertain such religious beliefs as a person chooses, the right to declare religious beliefs openly and without fear of hindrance or reprisal, and the right to manifest belief by worship and practice or by teaching and dissemination. But the concept means more than that.

[95] Freedom can primarily be characterized by the absence of coercion or constraint. If a person is compelled by the State or the will of another to a course of action or inaction which he would not otherwise have chosen, he is not acting of his own volition and he cannot be said to be truly free. One of the major purposes of the *Charter* is to protect, within reason, from compulsion or restraint. Coercion includes not only such blatant forms of compulsion as direct commands to act or refrain from acting on pain of sanction, coercion includes indirect forms of control which determine or limit alternative courses of conduct available to others. Freedom in a broad sense embraces both the absence of coercion and constraint, and the right to manifest beliefs and practices. Freedom means that, subject to such limitations as are necessary to protect public safety, order, health, or morals or the fundamental rights and freedoms of others, no one is to be forced to act in a way contrary to his beliefs or his conscience.

[96] What may appear good and true to a majoritarian religious group, or to the state acting at their behest, may not, for religious reasons, be imposed upon citizens who take a contrary view. The *Charter* safeguards religious minorities from the threat of "the tyranny of the majority."

[97] To the extent that it binds all to a sectarian Christian ideal, the *Lord's Day Act* works a form of coercion inimical to the spirit of the *Charter* and the dignity of all non-Christians. In proclaiming the standards of the Christian faith, the Act creates a climate hostile to, and gives the appearance of discrimination against, non-Christian Canadians. It takes religious values rooted in Christian morality and, using the force of the state, translates them into a positive law binding on believers and non-believers alike. The theological content of the legislation remains as a subtle and constant reminder to religious minorities within the country of their differences with, and alienation from, the dominant religious culture.

[98] Non-Christians are prohibited for religious reasons from carrying out activities which are otherwise lawful, moral and normal. The arm of the state requires all to remember the Lord's day of the Christians and to keep it holy. The protection of one religion and the concomitant non-protection of others imports disparate impact destructive of the religious freedom of the collectivity.

[99] I agree with the submission of the respondent that to accept that Parliament retains the right to compel universal observance of the day of rest preferred by one religion is not consistent with the preservation and enhancement of the multicultural heritage of Canadians. To do so is contrary to the expressed provisions of s. 27. […]

[100] If I am a Jew or a Sabbatarian or a Muslim, the practice of my religion at least implies my right to work on a Sunday if I wish. It seems to me that any law purely religious in purpose, which denies me that right, must surely infringe my religious freedom. […]

The Purpose of Protecting Freedom of Conscience and Religion

[121] What unites enunciated freedoms in the American First Amendment, s. 2(a) of the *Charter* and in the provisions of other human rights documents in which they are associated is the notion of the centrality of individual conscience and the inappropriateness of governmental intervention to compel or to constrain its manifestation. In *Hunter v. Southam Inc.* (1984), the purpose of the *Charter* was identified as "the unremitting protection of individual rights and liberties." It is easy to see the relationship between respect for individual conscience and the valuation of human dignity that motivates such unremitting protection.

[122] It should also be noted, however, that an emphasis on individual judgment also lies at the heart of our democratic political tradition. The ability of each citizen to make free and informed decisions is the absolute prerequisite for the legitimacy, acceptability, and efficacy of our system of self government. It is because of the centrality of the rights associated with freedom of individual conscience both to basic beliefs about human worth and dignity and to a free and democratic political system that American jurisprudence has emphasized the primacy or "firstness" of the First Amendment. It is this same centrality that in my view underlies their designation in the *Canadian Charter of Rights and Freedoms* as "fundamental." They are the *sine qua non* of the political tradition underlying the *Charter.*

[123] Viewed in this context, the purpose of freedom of conscience and religion becomes clear. The values that underlie our political and philosophic traditions demand that every individual be free to hold and to manifest whatever beliefs and opinions his or her conscience dictates, provided, *inter alia*, only that such manifestations do not injure his or her neighbours or their parallel rights to hold and manifest beliefs and opinions of their own. Religious belief and practice are historically prototypical and, in many ways, paradigmatic of conscientiously held beliefs and manifestations and are therefore protected by the *Charter.* Equally protected, and for the same reasons, are expressions and manifestations of religious non-belief and refusals to participate in religious practice. It may perhaps be that freedom of conscience and religion extends beyond these principles to prohibit other sorts of governmental involvement in matters having to do with religion. For the present case it is sufficient in my opinion to say that whatever else freedom of conscience and religion may mean, it must at the very least mean this: government may not coerce individuals to affirm a specific religious belief or to manifest a specific religious practice for a sectarian purpose. I leave to another case the degree, if any, to which the government may, to achieve a vital interest or objective, engage in coercive action which s. 2(a) might otherwise prohibit.

R. v. Keegstra
Supreme Court of Canada
[1990] 3 S.C.R. 697

Section 319 of the *Criminal Code* prohibits the willful promotion of hatred, other than in private conversation, towards any section of the public distinguished by colour, race, religion, or ethnic origin. Keegstra was charged under this section because of his activities, in the role of high school teacher, of communicating anti-semitic sentiment to his students. This section of the *Code* is one of the few explicit, statutory limitations of freedom of speech in Canada, and the Supreme Court had no difficulty finding it to infringe section 2(b) of the *Charter.* The real question, though, was whether this kind of infringement is justifiable as a reasonable limit in a free and democratic society under section 1 of the *Charter.* In deciding that it was, Chief Justice Dickson found it necessary to explore the meaning and rationale of freedom of expression.

Chief Justice Dickson (for the majority):

Objective of Section 319(2)

I now turn to the specific requirements of the *Oakes* approach in deciding whether the infringement of s. 2(b) occasioned by s. 319(2) is justifiable in a free and democratic society. According to *Oakes,* the first aspect of the s. 1 analysis is to examine the objective of the impugned legislation. Only if the objective relates to concerns which are pressing and substantial in a free and democratic society can the legislative limit on a right or freedom hope to be permissible under the *Charter.* In examining the objective of s. 319(2), I will begin by discussing the harm caused by hate propaganda as identified by the Cohen Committee and subsequent study groups, and then review in turn the impact upon this objective of international human rights instruments and ss. 15 and 27 of the *Charter.*

Harm Caused by Expression Promoting the Hatred of Identifiable Groups

Looking to the legislation challenged in this appeal, one must ask whether the amount of hate propaganda in Canada causes sufficient harm to justify legislative intervention of some type. The Cohen Committee, speaking in 1965, found that the incidence of hate propaganda in Canada was not insignificant (at p. 24):

> ... there exists in Canada a small number of persons and a somewhat larger number of organizations, extremist in outlook and dedicated

to the preaching and spreading of hatred and contempt against certain identifiable minority groups in Canada. It is easy to conclude that because the number of persons and organizations is not very large, they should not be taken too seriously. The Committee is of the opinion that this line of analysis is no longer tenable after what is known to have been the result of hate propaganda in other countries, particularly in the 1930s when such material and ideas played a significant role in the creation of a climate of malice, destructive to the central values of Judaic-Christian society, the values of our civilization. The Committee believes, therefore, that the actual and potential danger caused by present hate activities in Canada cannot be measured by statistics alone.

Even the statistics, however, are not unimpressive, because while activities have centered heavily in Ontario, they nevertheless have extended from Nova Scotia to British Columbia and minority groups in at least eight Provinces have been subjected to these vicious attacks.

In 1984, the House of Commons Special Committee on Participation of Visible Minorities in Canadian Society in its report, entitled *Equality Now!*, observed that increased immigration and periods of economic difficulty "have produced an atmosphere that may be ripe for racially motivated incidents" (p. 69). With regard to the dissemination of hate propaganda, the Special Committee found that the prevalence and scope of such material had risen since the Cohen Committee made its report, stating (at p. 69):

> There has been a recent upsurge in hate propaganda. It has been found in virtually every part of Canada. Not only is it anti-semitic and anti-black, as in the 1960s, but it is also now anti-Roman Catholic, anti-East Indian, anti-aboriginal people and anti-French. Some of this material is imported from the United States but much of it is produced in Canada. Most worrisome of all is that in recent years Canada has become a major source of supply of hate propaganda that finds its way to Europe, and especially to West Germany.

As the quotations above indicate, the presence of hate propaganda in Canada is sufficiently substantial to warrant concern. Disquiet caused by the existence of such material is not simply the product of its offensiveness, however, but stems from the very real harm which it causes. Essentially, there are two sorts of injury caused by hate propaganda. First, there is harm done to members of the target group. It is indisputable that the emotional damage caused by words may be of grave psychological and social consequence. In the context of sexual harassment, for example, this Court has found that words can in themselves constitute harassment (*Janzen v. Platy Enterprises Ltd.*, [1989] 1 S.C.R. 1252). In a similar manner, words and writings that wilfully promote hatred can constitute a serious attack on persons belonging to a racial or religious group, and in this regard the Cohen Committee noted that these persons are humiliated and degraded (p. 214).

In my opinion, a response of humiliation and degradation from an individual targeted by hate propaganda is to be expected. A person's sense of human dignity and belonging to the community at large is closely linked to the concern and respect accorded the groups to which he or she belongs (see I. Berlin, "Two Concepts of Liberty," in *Four Essays on Liberty* [1969], 118, at p. 155). The derision, hostility and abuse encouraged by hate propaganda therefore have a severely negative impact on the individual's sense of self-worth and acceptance. This impact may cause target group members to take drastic measures in reaction, perhaps avoiding activities which bring them into contact with non-group members or adopting attitudes and postures directed towards blending in with the majority. Such consequences bear heavily in a nation that prides itself on tolerance and the fostering of human dignity through, among other things, respect for the many racial, religious and cultural groups in our society.

A second harmful effect of hate propaganda which is of pressing and substantial concern is its influence upon society at large. The Cohen Committee noted that individuals can be persuaded to believe "almost anything" (p. 30) if information or ideas are communicated using the right technique and in the proper circumstances (at p. 8):

> ... we are less confident in the 20th century that the critical faculties of individuals will be brought to bear on the speech and writing which is directed at them. In the 18th and 19th centuries, there was a widespread belief that man was a rational creature, and that if his mind was trained and liberated from superstition by education, he would always distinguish truth from falsehood, good from evil. So Milton, who said "let truth and falsehood grapple: who ever knew truth put to the worse in a free and open encounter."
>
> We cannot share this faith today in such a simple form. While holding that over the long run, the human mind is repelled by blatant falsehood and seeks the good, it is too often true, in the short run, that emotion displaces reason and individuals perversely reject the demonstrations of truth put before them and forsake the good they know. The successes of modern advertising, the triumphs of impudent propaganda such as Hitler's, have qualified sharply our belief in the rationality of man. We know that under strain and pressure in times of irritation and frustration, the individual is swayed and even swept away by hysterical, emotional appeals. We act irresponsibly if we ignore the way in which emotion can drive reason from the field.

It is thus not inconceivable that the active dissemination of hate propaganda can attract individuals to its cause, and in the process create serious discord between various cultural groups in society. Moreover, the alteration of views held by the recipients of hate propaganda may occur subtly, and is not always attendant upon conscious acceptance of the communicated ideas. Even if the message of hate propaganda is outwardly rejected, there is evidence that its premise of racial or religious inferiority may persist in a recipient's mind as an idea that holds some truth, an incipient effect not to be entirely discounted (see Matsuda, op. cit., at pp. 2339–40).

The threat to the self-dignity of target group members is thus matched by the possibility that prejudiced messages will gain some credence, with the attendant result of discrimination, and perhaps even violence, against minority groups in Canadian society. With these dangers in mind, the Cohen Committee made clear in its conclusions that the presence of hate propaganda existed as a baleful and pernicious element, and hence a serious problem, in Canada (at p. 59):

> The amount of hate propaganda presently being disseminated and its measurable effects probably are not sufficient to justify a description of the problem as one of crisis or near crisis proportions. Nevertheless the problem is a serious one. We believe that, given a certain set of socio-economic circumstances, such as a deepening of the emotional tensions or the setting in of a severe business recession, public susceptibility might well increase significantly. Moreover, the potential psychological and social damage of hate propaganda, both to a desensitized majority and to sensitive minority target groups, is incalculable. As Mr. Justice Jackson of the United States Supreme Court wrote in *Beauharnais v. Illinois*, such "sinister abuses of our freedom of expression…can tear apart a society, brutalize its dominant elements, and persecute even to extermination, its minorities."

As noted previously, in articulating concern about hate propaganda and its contribution to racial and religious tension in Canada, the Cohen Committee recommended that Parliament use the *Criminal Code* in order to prohibit wilful, hate-promoting expression and underline Canada's commitment to end prejudice and intolerance. [...]

Conclusion Respecting Objective of Section 319(2)

In my opinion, it would be impossible to deny that Parliament's objective in enacting s. 319(2) is of the utmost importance. Parliament has recognized the substantial harm that can flow from hate propaganda, and in trying to prevent the pain suffered by target group members and to reduce racial, ethnic and religious tension in Canada has decided to suppress the willful promotion of hatred against identifiable groups. The nature of Parliament's objective is supported not only by the work of numerous study groups, but also by our collective historical knowledge of the potentially catastrophic effects of the promotion of hatred. Additionally, the international commitment to eradicate hate propaganda and the stress placed upon equality and multiculturalism in the *Charter* strongly buttress the importance of this objective. I consequently find that the first part of the test under s. 1 of the *Charter* is easily satisfied and that a powerfully convincing legislative objective exists such as to justify some limit on freedom of expression.

Proportionality

The second branch of the *Oakes* test—proportionality—poses the most challenging questions with respect to the validity of s. 319(2) as a reasonable limit on freedom of expression in a free and democratic society. It is therefore not surprising to find most commentators, as well as the litigants in the case at bar, agreeing that the objective of the provision is of great importance, but to observe considerable disagreement when it comes to deciding whether the means chosen to further the objective are proportional to the ends. [...]

Relation of the Expression at Stake to Free Expression Values

From the outset, I wish to make clear that in my opinion the expression prohibited by s. 319(2) is not closely linked to the rationale underlying s. 2(b). [...]

At the core of freedom of expression lies the need to ensure that truth and the common good are attained, whether in scientific and artistic endeavors or in the process of determining the best course to take in our political affairs. Since truth and the ideal form of political and social organization can rarely, if at all, be identified with absolute certainty, it is difficult to prohibit expression without impeding the free exchange of potentially valuable information. Nevertheless, the argument from truth does not provide convincing support for the protection of hate propaganda. Taken to its extreme, this argument would require us to permit the communication of all expression, it being impossible to know with absolute certainty which factual statements are true, or which ideas obtain the greatest good. The problem with this extreme position, however, is that the greater the degree of certainty that a statement is erroneous or mendacious, the less its value in the quest for truth. Indeed, expression can be used to the detriment of our search for truth; the state should not be the sole arbiter of truth, but neither should we overplay the view that rationality will overcome all falsehoods in the unregulated marketplace of ideas. There is very little chance that statements intended to promote hatred against an identifiable group are true, or that their vision of society will lead to a better world. To portray such statements as crucial to truth and the betterment of the political and social milieu is therefore misguided.

Another component central to the rationale underlying s. 2(b) concerns the vital role of free expression as a means of ensuring individuals the ability to gain self-fulfillment by developing and articulating thoughts and ideas as they see fit. It is true that s. 319(2) inhibits this process among those individuals whose expression it limits, and hence arguably works against freedom of expression values. On the other hand, such self-autonomy stems in large part from one's ability to articulate and nurture an identity derived from membership in a cultural or religious group. The message put forth by individuals who fall within the ambit of s. 319(2) represents a most extreme opposition to the idea that members of identifiable groups should enjoy this aspect of the s. 2(b) benefit. The extent to which the unhindered promotion of this message furthers free expression values must therefore be tempered insofar as it advocates with inordinate vitriol an intolerance and prejudice which views as execrable the process of individual self development and human flourishing among all members of society.

Moving on to a third strain of thought said to justify the protection of free expression, one's attention is brought specially to the political realm. The connection between freedom of expression and the political process is perhaps the linchpin of the s. 2(b) guarantee, and the nature of this connection is largely derived from the Canadian commitment to democracy. Freedom of expression is a crucial aspect of the democratic commitment, not merely because it permits the best policies to be chosen from among a wide array of proffered options, but additionally because it helps to ensure that participation in the political process is open to all persons. Such open participation must involve to a substantial degree the notion that all persons are equally deserving of respect and dignity. The state therefore cannot act to hinder or condemn a political view without to some extent harming the openness of Canadian democracy and its associated tenet of equality for all.

The suppression of hate propaganda undeniably muzzles the participation of a few individuals in the democratic process, and hence detracts somewhat from free expression values, but the degree of this limitation is not substantial. I am aware that the use of strong language in political and social debate— indeed, perhaps even language intended to promote hatred—is an unavoidable part of the democratic process. Moreover, I recognize that hate propaganda is expression of a type which would generally be categorized as "political," thus putatively placing it at the very heart of the principle extolling freedom of expression as vital to the democratic process. Nonetheless, expression can work to undermine our commitment to democracy where employed to propagate ideas anathemic to democratic values. Hate propaganda works in just such a way, arguing as it does for a society in which the democratic process is subverted and individuals are denied respect and dignity simply because of racial or religious characteristics. This brand of expressive activity is thus wholly inimical to the democratic aspirations of the free expression guarantee.

Indeed, one may quite plausibly contend that it is through rejecting hate propaganda that the state can best encourage the protection of values central to freedom of expression, while simultaneously demonstrating dislike for the vision forwarded by hate-mongers. In this regard, the reaction to various types of expression by a democratic government may be perceived as meaningful expression on behalf of the vast majority of citizens. I do not wish to be construed as saying that an infringement of s. 2(b) can be justified under s. 1 merely because it is the product of a democratic process; the *Charter* will not permit even the democratically elected legislature to restrict the rights and freedoms crucial to a free and democratic society. What I do wish to emphasize, however, is that one must be careful not to accept blindly that the suppression of expression must always and unremittingly detract from values central to freedom of expression. (L.C. Bollinger, *The Tolerant Society: Freedom of Speech and Extremist Speech in America* [1986], at pp. 87–93).

I am very reluctant to attach anything but the highest importance to expression relevant to political matters. But given the unparalleled vigour with which hate propaganda repudiates and undermines democratic values, and in particular its condemnation of the view that all citizens need be treated with equal respect and dignity so as to make participation in the political process meaningful, I am unable to see the protection of such expression as integral to the democratic ideal so central to the s. 2(b) rationale. Together with my comments as to the tenuous link between communications covered by s. 319(2) and other values at the core of the free expression guarantee, this conclusion leads me to disagree with the opinion of McLachlin J. [in dissent] that the expression at stake in this appeal mandates the most solicitous degree of constitutional protection. In my view, hate propaganda should not be accorded the greatest of weight in the s. 1 analysis.

As a caveat, it must be emphasized that the protection of extreme statements, even where they attack those principles underlying the freedom of expression, is not completely divorced from the aims of s. 2 (b) of the *Charter*. As noted already, suppressing the expression covered by s. 319(2) does to some extent weaken these principles. It can also be argued that it is partly through a clash with extreme and erroneous views that truth and the democratic vision remain vigorous and alive. In this regard, judicial pronouncements strongly advocating the importance of free expression values might be seen as helping to expose prejudiced statements as valueless even while striking down legislative restrictions that proscribe such expression. Additionally, condoning a democracy's collective decision to protect itself from certain types of expression may lead to a slippery slope on which encroachments on expression central to s. 2(b) values are permitted. To guard against such a result, the protection of communications virulently unsupportive of free expression values may be necessary in order to ensure that expression more compatible with these values is never unjustifiably limited.

None of these arguments is devoid of merit, and each must be taken into account in determining whether an infringement of s. 2(b) can be justified under s. 1. It need not be, however, that they apply equally or with the greatest of strength in every instance. As I have said already, I am of the opinion that hate propaganda contributes little to the aspirations of Canadians or Canada in either the quest for truth, the promotion of individual self-development or the protection and fostering of a vibrant democracy where the participation of all individuals is accepted and encouraged. While I cannot conclude that hate propaganda deserves only marginal protection under the s. 1 analysis, I can take cognizance of the fact that limitations upon hate propaganda are directed at a special category of expression which strays some distance from the spirit of s. 2(b), and hence conclude that restrictions on expression of this kind might be easier to justify than other infringements of s. 2(b).

Having made some preliminary comments as to the nature of the expression at stake in this appeal, it is now possible to ask whether s. 319(2) is an acceptably proportional response to Parliament's valid objective. As stated above, the proportionality aspect of the *Oakes* test requires the Court to decide whether the impugned state action: i) is rationally connected to the objective; ii) minimally impairs the *Charter* right or freedom at issue; and iii) does not produce effects of such severity so as to make the impairment unjustifiable. [...]

Rational Connection

Section 319(2) makes the willful promotion of hatred against identifiable groups an indictable offence, indicating Parliament's serious concern about the effects of such activity. Those who would uphold the provision argue that the criminal prohibition of hate propaganda obviously bears a rational connection to the legitimate Parliamentary objective of protecting target group members and fostering harmonious social relations in a community dedicated to equality and multiculturalism. I agree, for in my opinion it would be difficult to deny that the suppression of hate propaganda reduces the harm such expression does to individuals who belong to identifiable groups and to relations between various cultural and religious groups in Canadian society.

Doubts have been raised, however, as to whether the actual effect of s. 319(2) is to undermine any rational connection between it and Parliament's objective. As stated in the reasons of McLachlin J., there are three primary ways in which the effect of the impugned legislation might be seen as an irrational means of carrying out the Parliamentary purpose. First, it is argued that the provision may actually promote the cause of hate-mongers by earning them extensive media attention. In this vein, it is also suggested that persons accused of intentionally promoting hatred often see themselves as martyrs, and may actually generate sympathy from the community in the role of underdogs engaged in battle against the immense powers of the state. Second, the public may view the suppression of expression by the government with suspicion, making it possible that such expression—even if it is hate propaganda—is perceived as containing an element of truth. Finally, it is often noted, citing the writings of A. Neier, *Defending my Enemy: American Nazis, the Skokie Case, and the Risks of Freedom* (1979), that Germany of the 1920s and 1930s possessed and used hate propaganda laws similar to those existing in Canada, and yet these laws did nothing to stop the triumph of a racist philosophy under the Nazis.

If s. 319(2) can be said to have no impact in the quest to achieve Parliament's admirable objectives, or in fact works in opposition to these objectives, then I agree that the provision could be described as "arbitrary, unfair or based on irrational considerations." In my view, however, the position that there is no strong and evident connection between the criminalization of hate propaganda and its suppression is unconvincing. I come to this conclusion for a number of reasons, and will elucidate these by answering in turn the three arguments just mentioned.

It is undeniable that media attention has been extensive on those occasions when s. 319(2) has been used. Yet from my perspective, s. 319(2) serves to illustrate to the public the severe reprobation with which society holds messages of hate directed towards racial and religious groups. The existence of a particular criminal law, and the process of holding a trial when that law is used, is thus itself a form of expression, and the message sent out is that hate propaganda is harmful to target group members and threatening to a harmonious society. [...]

In this context, it can also be said that government suppression of hate propaganda will not make the expression attractive and hence increase acceptance of its content. Similarly, it is very doubtful that Canadians will have sympathy for either propagators of hatred or their ideas. Governmental disapproval of hate propaganda does not invariably result in dignifying the suppressed ideology. Pornography is not dignified by its suppression, nor are defamatory statements against individuals seen as meritorious because the common law lends its support to their prohibition. [...]

As for the use of hate propaganda laws in pre-World War Two Germany, I am skeptical as to the relevance of the observation that legislation similar to s. 319(2) proved ineffective in curbing the racism of the Nazis. No one is contending that hate propaganda laws can in themselves prevent the tragedy of a Holocaust; conditions particular to Germany made the rise of Nazi ideology possible despite the existence and use of these laws. Rather, hate propaganda laws are one part of a free and democratic society's bid to prevent the spread of racism, and their rational connection to this objective must be seen in such a context. [...]

Conclusion as to Minimal Impairment

To summarize the above discussion, in light of the great importance of Parliament's objective and the discounted value of the expression at issue I find that the terms of s. 319(2) create a narrowly confined offence which suffers from neither overbreadth nor vagueness. This interpretation stems largely from my view that the provision possesses a stringent *mens rea* requirement, necessitating either an intent to promote hatred or knowledge of the substantial certainty of such, and is also strongly supported by the conclusion that the meaning of the word "hatred" is restricted to the most severe and deeply-felt form of opprobrium. Additionally, however, the conclusion that s. 319(2) represents a minimal impairment of the freedom of expression gains credence through the exclusion of private conversation from its scope, the need for the promotion of hatred to focus upon an identifiable group and the presence of the s. 319(2) defences [these are: (a) truth; (b) good faith opinion on a religious matter; (c) public interest; (d) good faith attempt to point out, so as to remove, matters producing feelings of hatred toward an identifiable group]. As for the argument that other modes of combating hate propaganda eclipse the need for a criminal provision, it is eminently reasonable to utilize more than one type of legislative tool in working to prevent the spread of racist expression and its resultant harm. [...]

Effects of the Limitation

The third branch of the proportionality test entails a weighing of the importance of the state objective against the effect of limits imposed upon a *Charter* right or guarantee. Even if the purpose of the limiting measure is substantial and the first two components of the proportionality test are satisfied, the deleterious effects of a limit may be too great to permit the infringement of the right or guarantee in issue.

I have examined closely the significance of the freedom of expression values threatened by s. 319(2) and the importance of the objective which lies behind the criminal prohibition. It will by now be quite clear that I do not view the infringement of s. 2(b) by s. 319(2) as a restriction of the most serious kind. The expressive activity at which this provision aims is of a special category, a category only tenuously connected with the values underlying the guarantee of freedom of speech. Moreover, the narrowly drawn terms of s. 319(2) and its defences prevent the prohibition of expression lying outside of this narrow category. Consequently, the suppression of hate propaganda affected by s. 319(2) represents an impairment of the individual's freedom of expression which is not of a most serious nature.

It is also apposite to stress yet again the enormous importance of the objective fueling s. 319(2), an objective of such magnitude as to support even the severe response of criminal prohibition. Few concerns can be as central to the concept of a free and democratic society as the dissipation of racism, and the especially strong value which Canadian society attaches to this goal must never be forgotten in assessing the effects of an impugned legislative measure. When the purpose of s. 319(2) is thus recognized, I have little trouble in finding that its effects, involving as they do the restriction of expression largely removed from the heart of free expression values, are not of such a deleterious nature as to outweigh any advantage gleaned from the limitation of s. 2(b).

R. v. Butler
Supreme Court of Canada
[1992] 1 S.C.R. 452

Section 163 of the Criminal Code makes it an offence to make, publish, or sell obscene material, defined as "any publication a dominant characteristic of which is the undue exploitation of sex, or of sex and... crime, horror, cruelty and violence." Manitoba sex shop owner Donald Butler had no trouble convincing the Supreme Court of Canada that section 163 violates his *Charter* section 2(b) right of freedom of expression. But, in this ground-breaking decision, the court unanimously agreed that section 163 constitutes a reasonable limit on this freedom. In coming to this conclusion, the court argued that the objective of Canada's anti-obscenity provision is not to express moral disapprobation about sexual behaviour, but to avoid the harm to society's basic values that is involved in portraying women as a class as objects for sexual exploitation and abuse.

Mr. Justice Sopinka (for the majority):

Is Section 163 Justified under Section 1 of the Charter?

(1) Objective

The respondent [the Crown] argues that there are several pressing and sub-stantial objectives which justify overriding the freedom to distribute obscene materials. Essentially, these objectives are the avoidance of harm resulting from antisocial attitudinal changes that exposure to obscene material causes and the public interest in maintaining a "decent society." On the other hand, the appellant [Butler] argues that the objective of s. 163 is to have the state act as "moral custodian" in sexual matters and to impose subjective standards of morality.

The obscenity legislation and jurisprudence prior to the enactment of s. 163 were evidently concerned with prohibiting the "immoral influences" of obscene publications and safeguarding the morals of individuals into whose hands such works could fall. The *Hicklin* (1868) philosophy posits that explicit sexual depic-tions, particularly outside the sanctioned contexts of marriage and procreation, threatened the morals or the fabric of society. [...] In this sense, its exclusive purpose was to advance a particular conception of morality. Any deviation from such morality was considered to be inherently undesirable, independently of any harm to society. As Judson J. described the test in *Brodie* (1962):

[The work under attack] has none of the characteristics that are often described in judgments dealing with obscenity—dirt for dirt's sake, the leer of the sensualist, depravity in the mind of an author with an obsession for dirt, pornography, an appeal to a prurient interest, etc.

I agree with Twaddle J.A. of the [Manitoba] Court of Appeal that this particular objective is no longer defensible in view of the *Charter*. To impose a certain standard of public and sexual morality, solely because it reflects the conventions of a given community, is inimical to the exercise and enjoyment of individual freedoms, which form the basis of our social contract. David Dyzenhaus, "Obscenity and the Charter: Autonomy and Equality" (1991), 1 C.R. (4th) 367, at p. 370, refers to this as "legal moralism," of a majority deciding what values should inform individual lives and then coercively imposing those values on minorities. The prevention of "dirt for dirt's sake" is not a legitimate objective which would justify the violation of one of the most fundamental freedoms enshrined in the *Charter*.

On the other hand, I cannot agree with the suggestion of the appellant that Parliament does not have the right to legislate on the basis of some fundamental conception of morality for the purposes of safeguarding the values which are integral to a free and democratic society. As Dyzenhaus, *supra*, at p. 376, writes: "Moral disapprobation is recognized as an appropriate response when it has its basis in *Charter* values."

As the respondent and many of the interveners have pointed out, much of the criminal law is based on moral conceptions of right and wrong and the mere fact that a law is grounded in morality does not automatically render it illegitimate. In this regard, criminalizing the proliferation of materials which undermine another basic *Charter* right may indeed be a legitimate objective.

In my view, however, the overriding objective is not moral disapprobation but the avoidance of harm to society. In *Towne Cinema Theatres Ltd.* (1985), Dickson C.J.C. stated: "It is harm to society from undue exploitation that is aimed at by the section, not simply lapses in propriety or good taste."

The harm was described in the following way in the *Report on Pornography* by the Standing Committee on Justice and Legal Affairs (MacGuigan Report) (1978):

The clear and unquestionable danger of this type of material is that it reinforces some unhealthy tendencies in Canadian society. The effect of this type of material is to reinforce male-female stereotypes to the detriment of both sexes. It attempts to make degradation, humiliation, victimization, and violence in human relationships appear normal and acceptable. A society which holds that egalitarianism, non-violence, consensualism, and mutuality are basic to any human interaction, whether sexual or other, is clearly justified in controlling and prohibiting any medium of depiction, description or advocacy which violates these principles. [...]

This being the objective, is it pressing and substantial? Does the prevention of the harm associated with the dissemination of certain obscene materials constitute a sufficiently pressing and substantial concern to warrant a restriction on the freedom of expression? In this regard, it should be recalled that in *Keegstra* (1990), this court unanimously accepted that the prevention of the influence of hate propaganda on society at large was a legitimate objective. [...]

This Court has thus recognized that the harm caused by the proliferation of materials which seriously offend the values fundamental to our society is a substantial concern which justifies restricting the otherwise full exercise of the freedom of expression. In my view, the harm sought to be avoided in the case of the dissemination of obscene materials is similar. In the words of Nemetz C.J.B.C. in *Red Hot Video Ltd.* (1985), there is a growing concern that the exploitation of women and children, depicted in publications and films can, in certain circumstances, lead to "abject and servile victimization." As Anderson J.A. also noted in that same case, if true equality between male and female persons is to be achieved, we cannot ignore the threat to equality resulting from exposure to audiences of certain types of violent and degrading material. Materials portraying women as a class as objects for sexual exploitation and abuse have a negative impact on "the individual's sense of self-worth and acceptance." [...]

Finally, it should be noted that the burgeoning pornography industry renders the concern even more pressing and substantial than when the impugned provisions were first enacted. I would therefore conclude that the objective of avoiding the harm associated with the dissemination of pornography in this case is sufficiently pressing and substantial to warrant some restriction on full exercise of the right to freedom of expression. The analysis of whether the measure is proportional to the objective must, in my view, be undertaken in light of the conclusion that the objective of the impugned section is valid only insofar as it relates to the harm to society associated with obscene materials. Indeed, the section as interpreted in previous decisions and in these reasons is fully consistent with that objective. The objective of maintaining conventional standards of propriety, independently of any harm to society, is no longer justified in light of the values of individual liberty which underlie the *Charter*. This, then, being the objective of s. 163, which I have found to be pressing and substantial, I must now determine whether the section is rationally connected and proportional to this objective. As outlined above, s. 163(8) criminalizes the exploitation of sex and sex and violence, when, on the basis of the community test, it is undue. The determination of when such exploitation is undue is directly related to the immediacy of a risk of harm to society which is reasonably perceived as arising from its dissemination. [...]

(2) Proportionality

(i) General

The values which underlie the protection of freedom of expression relate to the search for truth, participation in the political process, and individual self-fulfillment. The Attorney-General for Ontario argues that of these, only "individual self-fulfillment," and only in its most base aspect, that of physical arousal, is engaged by pornography. On the other hand, the civil liberties groups argue that pornography forces us to question conventional notions of sexuality and thereby launches us into an inherently political discourse. In their factum, the British Columbia Civil Liberties Association adopts a passage from R. West, "The Feminist-Conservative Anti-Pornography Alliance and the 1986 Attorney General's Commission on Pornography Report" (1987), 4 *Am. Bar Found. Res. Jo.* 681, at p. 696:

> Good pornography has value because it validates women's will to pleasure. It celebrates female nature. It validates a range of female sexuality that is wider and truer than that legitimated by the nonpornographic culture. Pornography when it is good celebrates both female pleasure and male rationality.

A proper application of the test should not suppress what West refers to as "good pornography." The objective of the impugned provision is not to inhibit the celebration of human sexuality. However, it cannot be ignored that the realities of the pornography industry are far from the picture which the British Columbia Civil Liberties Association would have us paint. Shannon J., in *Wagner* (1985), described the materials more accurately when he observed at p. 331:

> Women, particularly, are deprived of unique human character or identity and are depicted as sexual playthings, hysterically and instantly responsive to male sexual demands. They worship male genitals and their own value depends upon the quality of their genitals and breasts.

In my view, the kind of expression which is sought to be advanced does not stand on equal footing with other kinds of expression which directly engage the "core" of the freedom of expression values.

This conclusion is further buttressed by the fact that the targeted material is expression which is motivated, in the overwhelming majority of cases, by economic profit. This court held in *Rocket v. Royal College of Dental Surgeons of Ontario* (1990), that an economic motive for expression means that restrictions on the expression might "be easier to justify than other infringements."

I will now turn to an examination of the three basic aspects of the proportionality test.

(ii) Rational Connection

The message of obscenity which degrades and dehumanizes is analogous to that of hate propaganda. As the Attorney-General of Ontario has argued in its factum, obscenity wields the power to wreak social damage in that a significant portion of the population is humiliated by its gross misrepresentations.

Accordingly, the rational link between s. 163 and the objective of Parliament relates to the actual causal relationship between obscenity and the risk of harm to society at large. On this point, it is clear that the literature of the social sciences remains subject to controversy. [...]

The recent conclusions of the Fraser Report [*Pornography and Prostitution in Canada: Report of the Special Committee on Pornography and Prostitution*] (1985), could not postulate any causal relationship between pornography and the commission of violent crimes, the sexual abuse of children, or the disintegration of communities and society. This is in contrast to the findings of the MacGuigan Report (1978).

While a direct link between obscenity and harm to society may be difficult, if not impossible, to establish, it is reasonable to presume that exposure to images bears a causal relationship to changes in attitudes and beliefs. [...]

In the face of inconclusive social science evidence, the approach adopted by our court in *Irwin Toy Ltd.* (1989) is instructive. In that case, the basis for the legislation was that television advertising directed at young children is *per se* manipulative. The Court made it clear that in choosing its mode of intervention, it is sufficient that Parliament had a *reasonable basis*. [...]

Similarly, in *R v. Keegstra* (1990), the absence of proof of a causative link between hate propaganda and hatred of an identifiable group was discounted as a determinative factor in assessing the constitutionality of the hate literature provisions of the *Criminal Code*. [...]

I am in agreement with Twaddle J.A. who expressed the view that Parliament was entitled to have a "reasoned apprehension of harm" resulting from the desensitization of individuals exposed to materials which depict violence, cruelty, and dehumanization in sexual relations.

Accordingly, I am of the view that there is a sufficiently rational link between the criminal sanction, which demonstrates our community's disapproval of the dissemination of materials which potentially victimize women and which restricts the negative influence which such materials have on changes in attitudes and behaviour, and the objective.

Finally, I wish to distinguish this case from *Keegstra*, in which the minority adopted the view that there was no rational connection between the criminalization of hate propaganda and its suppression. As McLachlin J. noted, prosecutions under the *Criminal Code* for racist expression have attracted extensive media coverage. The criminal process confers on the accused publicity for his or her causes and succeeds even in generating sympathy. The same cannot be said of the kinds of expression sought to be suppressed in the present case. The general availability of the subject materials and the rampant pornography industry are such that, in the words of Dickson C.J.C. in *Keegstra*, "pornography is not dignified by its suppression." In contrast to the hatemonger who may succeed, by the sudden media attention, in gaining an audience, the prohibition of obscene materials does nothing to promote the pornographer's cause. [...]

(iii) Minimal Impairment

There are several factors which contribute to the finding that the provision minimally impairs the freedom which is infringed.

First, the impugned provision does not proscribe sexually explicit erotica without violence that is not degrading or dehumanizing. It is designed to catch material that creates a risk of harm to society. It might be suggested that proof of actual harm should be required. It is apparent from what I have said above that it is sufficient in this regard for Parliament to have a reasonable basis for concluding that harm will result and this requirement does not demand actual proof of harm.

Second, materials which have scientific, artistic or literary merit are not captured by the provision. As discussed above, the court must be generous in its application of the "artistic defence." For example, in certain cases, materials such as photographs, prints, books and films which may undoubtedly be produced with some motive for economic profit, may nonetheless claim the protection of the *Charter* insofar as their defining characteristic is that of aesthetic expression, and thus represent the artist's attempt at individual fulfillment. The existence of an accompanying economic motive does not, of itself, deprive a work of significance as an example of individual artistic or self-fulfillment.

Third, in considering whether the provision minimally impairs the freedom in question, it is legitimate for the court to take into account Parliament's past abortive attempts to replace the definition with one that is more explicit. The attempt to provide exhaustive instances of obscenity has been shown to be destined to fail. It seems that the only practicable alternative is to strive towards a more abstract definition of obscenity which is contextually sensitive and responsive to progress in the knowledge and understanding of the phenomenon to which the legislation is directed. In my view, the standard of "undue exploitation" is therefore appropriate. The intractable nature of the problem and the impossibility of precisely defining a notion which is inherently elusive makes the possibility of a more explicit provision remote. In this light, it is appropriate to question whether, and at what cost, greater legislative precision can be demanded. [...]

Finally, I wish to address the arguments of the interveners, Canadian Civil Liberties Association and Manitoba Association for Rights and Liberties, that the objectives of this kind of legislation may be met by alternative, less intrusive measures. First, it is submitted that reasonable time, manner and place restrictions would be preferable to outright prohibition. I am of the view that this argument should be rejected. Once it has been established that the objective is the avoidance of harm caused by the degradation which many women feel as "victims" of the message of obscenity, and of the negative impact exposure to such material has on perceptions and attitudes towards women, it is untenable to argue that these harms could be avoided by placing restrictions on access to such material. Making the materials more difficult to obtain by increasing their cost and reducing their availability does not achieve the same objective. Once Parliament has reasonably concluded that certain acts are harmful to certain groups in society and to society in general, it would be inconsistent, if not hypocritical, to argue that such acts could be committed in more restrictive conditions. The harm sought to be avoided would remain the same in either case.

It is also submitted that there are more effective techniques to promote the objectives of Parliament. For example, if pornography is seen as encouraging violence against women, there are certain activities which discourage it—counseling rape victims to charge their assailants, provision of shelter and assistance for battered women, campaigns for laws against discrimination on the grounds of sex, education to increase the sensitivity of law enforcement agencies and other governmental authorities. In addition, it is submitted that education is an under-used response.

It is noteworthy that many of the above suggested alternatives are in the form of *response* to the harm engendered by negative attitudes against women. The role of the impugned provision is to control the dissemination of the very images that contribute to such attitudes. Moreover, it is true that there are additional measures which could alleviate the problem of violence against women. However, given the gravity of the harm, and the threat to the values at stake, I do not believe that the measure chosen by Parliament is equaled by the alternatives which have been suggested. Education, too, may offer a means of combating negative attitudes to women, just as it is currently used as a means of addressing other problems dealt with in the *Criminal Code*. However, there is no reason to rely on education alone. It should be emphasized that this is in no way intended to deny the value of other educational and counseling measures to deal with the roots and effects of negative attitudes. Rather, it is only to stress the arbitrariness and unacceptability of the claim that such measures represent the sole legitimate means of addressing the phenomenon. Serious social problems such as violence against women require multi-pronged approaches by government. Education and legislation are not alternatives but complements in addressing such problems. There is nothing in the *Charter* which requires Parliament to choose between such complementary measures.

(iv) Balance between Effects of Limiting Measures and Legislative Objective

The final question to be answered in the proportionality test is whether the effects of the law so severely trench on a protected right that the legislative objective is outweighed by the infringement. The infringement on freedom of expression is confined to a measure designed to prohibit the distribution of sexually explicit material accompanied by violence, and those without violence that are degrading or dehumanizing. As I have already concluded, this kind of expression lies far from the core of the guarantee of freedom of expression. It appeals only to the most base aspect of individual fulfillment, and it is primarily economically motivated.

The objective of the legislation, on the other hand, is of fundamental importance in a free and democratic society. It is aimed at avoiding harm, which

Parliament has reasonably concluded will be caused directly or indirectly, to individuals, groups such as women and children, and consequently to society as a whole, by the distribution of these materials. It thus seeks to enhance respect for all members of society, and non-violence and equality in their relations with each other.

I therefore conclude that the restriction on freedom of expression does not outweigh the importance of the legislative objective. [...] I conclude that while s. 163(8) infringes s. 2(b) of the *Charter* freedom of expression—it constitutes a reasonable limit and is saved by virtue of the provisions of s. 1.

Little Sisters Book and Art Emporium v. Canada (Minister of Justice)
Supreme Court of Canada
[2000] 2 S.C.R. 1120

When assessing whether legislation is constitutionally valid, courts must interpret legislation in light of its purpose, and must assess its effects, sometimes in contexts where it may appear that conflicts between legislation and constitutional requirements might be avoided by greater attention to proper implementation of legislators' intentions. Courts faced with such situations must decide just how much they ought to intervene in declaring law to be invalid, preserving the intentions of legislators so far as possible. In *Little Sisters* the Supreme Court finds that Parliament is justified in its attempts to regulate obscene expression, while rejecting a "reverse onus" provision of the *Customs Act* requiring a person accused of importing obscene materials to show that the materials are not obscene.

Justice Binnie (for the majority):

[71] The appellants say a regulatory structure that is open to the level of malad-ministration described in the trial judgment is unconstitutionally underprotec-tive of their constitutional rights and should be struck down in its entirety. In effect they argue that Parliament was required to proceed by way of legislation rather than the creation of a delegated power of regulation in s. 164(1)(*j*), which authorizes the Governor in Council to "make regulations... generally, to carry out the purposes and provisions of this Act," or by ministerial directive. My colleague Iacobucci J. accepts the propositions that "[t]his Court's precedents demand suf-ficient safeguards in the legislative scheme itself to ensure that government action will not infringe constitutional rights" (para. 204) and because "the legislation makes no reasonable effort to ensure that it will be applied constitutionally to expressive materials" (para. 211), Code 9956 should be struck from the *Customs Tariff.* I do not think there is any constitutional rule that requires Parliament to deal with Customs' treatment of constitutionally protected expressive mate-rial by legislation (as the appellants contend) rather than by way of regulation (as Parliament contemplated in s. 164(1)(*j*)) or even by ministerial directive or departmental practice. Parliament is entitled to proceed on the basis that its enactments "will be applied constitutionally" by the public service.

[72] The authorities relied on by my colleague all deal with legislation that itself contained problematic provisions. In this case, the complaint is about the *absence* of affirmative provisions, *per* Iacobucci J., at para. 166: "The Customs legislation lacks the most basic procedures necessary for a fair and accurate

determination of whether something is obscene." To put it another way, the appellants' complaint is about what Parliament did *not* enact rather than what it *did* enact. The imposition on Parliament of a constitutional obligation to deal itself with *Charter*-sensitive matters rather than by permitting Parliament the option of enacting a delegated regulation-making power has serious ramifications for the machinery of government. I do not agree that Parliament's options are so limited. [...]

[97] The constitutional question challenges the validity of s. 71 of the *Customs Act*, on which the redetermination and court proceedings are based. In part, the challenge relies on the "reverse onus" provision applied in such proceedings by virtue of s. 152(3) of the *Customs Act*, as explained in oral argument by counsel for the appellants:

> We challenge the entire scheme, not just the power of the Customs officer at the front line to do that detention and prohibition, but the scheme *insofar as it puts the onus on the importer*, whether the importer is a bookstore or a regular individual to seek a redetermination, or review, or appeal, would have you through a byzantine bureaucratic process and ultimately to the Courts in order to prove that the material is *not* obscene. [Emphasis added.]

[98] Section 152(3) is not specific to obscenity or even to prohibited goods generally, but applies to "any proceeding under this Act," including the appeals process authorized by s. 71. Section 152(3) directs the decision-maker to assume that Customs officials are right unless and until the importer proves them to be wrong. It provides:

> 152. ...
>
> (3) Subject to subsection (4), in any proceeding under this Act, the burden of proof in any question relating to
>
> ...
>
> (*d*) the compliance with any of the provisions of this Act or the regulations in respect of any goods lies on the person, other than Her Majesty, who is a party to the proceeding or the person who is accused of an offence, and not on Her Majesty.

[99] The appellants did not directly impugn the constitutionality of the reverse onus provision in their application to state the constitutional questions, presumably because they intended to rely on its continued validity as a lever to overturn the rest of the Customs legislation in relation to expressive materials. In my view, however, the appellants' attack on s. 71 and the procedures it authorizes is inextricably bound up with the reverse onus provision, and the Court is not bound to accept the application of the latter as valid when considering the constitutionality of the former. The constitutional question in relation to s. 71 encompasses both aspects of the appellants' argument. [...]

[101] An importer has a *Charter* right to receive expressive material unless the state can justify its denial. It is not open to the state to put the onus on an individual to show why he or she should be allowed to exercise a *Charter* right. It is for the state to establish that a limitation on the *Charter* right is justified: *R. v. Oakes*, [1986] 1 S.C.R. 103, *per* Dickson C.J., at pp. 136–37: "The onus of proving that a limit on a right or freedom guaranteed by the *Charter* is reasonable and demonstrably justified in a free and democratic society rests upon the party seeking to uphold the limitation."

[102] As to the obscenity determination at the departmental level, I do not think s. 152(3) applies at all. The Crown does not contend that all expressive material entering Canada is presumptively obscene until shown to be otherwise. The earliest the reverse onus *could* apply with any logic is in the re-determination, but at that stage the importer is given neither sufficient notice nor a sufficient opportunity to be heard to discharge the onus. The reality is that once the front-line officer has made the initial determination that he or she considers the publication to be obscene, the question for the Deputy Minister or designate on the re-determination is whether the Department is ready, willing and able, if required, to establish in court that the detained material is obscene.

[103] The Crown received notice in *Glad Day Bookshop Inc. v. Canada (Deputy Minister of National Revenue, Customs and Excise)*, [1992] O.J. No. 1466 (QL) (Gen. Div.) ("*Glad Day (No. 2)*") that s. 152(3) could not reverse the onus of proof on the obscenity issue onto the importer, and in this Court the Crown tried neither to defend the application of s. 152(3) to obscenity nor to advance any s. 1 justification. These concessions were, I believe, quite correct.

[104] In *Glad Day (No. 2)*, Hayes J. went on to rule that not only did the Crown carry the burden of proof but it must establish obscenity to the criminal standard. This goes too far. Although the *Customs Tariff* incorporates by reference the *Criminal Code* definition of obscenity, it does so into a civil proceeding which generally requires proof only on a balance of probabilities. The incorporation was made in response to *Luscher v. Deputy Minister, Revenue Canada, Customs and Excise, supra*, which held that the prohibition of "immoral" and "indecent" materials in earlier Customs legislation was so vague as to be an unreasonable limit on s. 2 (*b*) and to that extent was of no force or effect. We are dealing with the imposition in civil proceedings of a limitation on freedom of expression, and the imposition on the Crown of a civil standard of proof is consistent with the usual *Charter* requirement that the Crown need only justify an infringement to the civil standard.

[105] As mentioned, s. 152(3) is not restricted to obscenity but has a broad application across the whole Customs process. It may be appropriate when dealing with imports of materials that ordinarily would not have much constitutional sensitivity (such as Minister Nowlan's "cabbages and cucumbers") to put the onus on the importer at the court level to show that the Customs official has made an erroneous tariff classification. What may work as a general rule in circumstances where Customs procedures are not limited by constitu-

tional rights does not, however, work in relation to constitutionally protected expressive materials. In these circumstances, however, the proper order should be limited to the matters pertinent to the disposition of this appeal. I would therefore declare that s. 152(3) is not to be construed and applied so as to place on an importer the onus to establish that goods are *not* obscene within the meaning of s. 163(8) of the *Criminal Code*. The burden of proving obscenity rests on the Crown or other person who alleges it. [...]

[123] There was ample evidence to support the trial judge's conclusion that the adverse treatment meted out by Canada Customs to the appellants and through them to Vancouver's gay and lesbian community violated the appellants' legitimate sense of self-worth and human dignity. The Customs treatment was high-handed and dismissive of the appellants' right to receive lawful expressive material which they had every right to import. When Customs officials prohibit and thereby censor lawful gay and lesbian erotica, they are making a statement about gay and lesbian culture, and the statement was reasonably interpreted by the appellants as demeaning gay and lesbian values. The message was that their concerns were less worthy of attention and respect than those of their heterosexual counterparts.

[124] While here it is the interests of the gay and lesbian community that were targeted, other vulnerable groups may similarly be at risk from overzealous censorship. Little Sisters was targeted because it was considered "different." On a more general level, it seems to me fundamentally unacceptable that expression which is free within the country can become stigmatized and harassed by government officials simply because it crosses an international boundary, and is thereby brought within the bailiwick of the Customs department. The appellants' constitutional right to receive perfectly *lawful* gay and lesbian erotica should not be diminished by the fact their suppliers are, for the most part, located in the United States. Their freedom of expression does not stop at the border.

[125] That having been said, there is nothing on the face of the Customs legislation, or in its necessary effects, which contemplates or encourages differential treatment based on sexual orientation. The definition of obscenity, as already discussed, operates without distinction between homosexual and heterosexual erotica. The differentiation was made here at the administrative level in the implementation of the Customs legislation. [...]

[152] In my view Parliament has struck an appropriate balance between the limiting effects of the Customs legislation and the legislative objective of prohibiting the entry of socially harmful material. As held in *Butler*, at p. 509, the benefits sought by the criminalization of obscenity are the avoidance of harm and the enhancement of respect for all members of society, and the promotion of non-violence and equality in their relations with each other. If I am correct that the source of the appellants' problem lies at the administrative level rather than the legislative level, the restriction imposed by Parliament to catch expressive materials that violate s. 163 of the *Criminal Code* at the international border does not outweigh the importance of the legislative objective.

Deleterious Effects versus Salutary Benefits

[153] The deleterious effects on the appellants found by the trial judge went way beyond any salutary benefits for Canadian society in this case, but that is not the test. The test is whether the deleterious effects of the Customs legislation, properly administered, exceed the salutary effect of the Customs legislation. The Customs legislation, properly administered, is designed to prevent entry into Canada of material that in all probability is obscene, i.e., likely to cause harm in excess of the community's standard of tolerance. That is a salutary benefit, although there is little evidence in the record on this point, apart from identification of some adult heterosexual pornographic magazines which are regularly and apparently effectively monitored. Against this, the deleterious effect on importers of lawful material is expected by Parliament to be no more than temporary detention and the various costs in time and money reasonably occasioned by the processing of the goods. If the Customs legislation operated as intended, as it apparently does across a broad range of commercial and other goods, the deleterious effects would be outweighed by its salutary benefit. The problem, to repeat, is in the implementation and it is to the remedy for the deficient administration of the Customs legislation that I now turn. [...]

[159] The appeal is therefore allowed in part, and a declaration will issue under s. 52 of the *Constitution Act, 1982* that s. 152(3) of the *Customs Act* is not to be construed and applied so as to place on an importer the onus to establish that goods are *not* obscene within the meaning of s. 163(8) of the *Criminal Code*. The burden of proving obscenity rests on the Crown or other person who alleges it.

R. v. Sharpe
Supreme Court of Canada
[2001] 1 S.C.R. 45

None deny the importance of legislation to protect the most vulnerable in our society. Criminal law prohibiting possession of child pornography is an instance of such law. Yet even when a social objective is universally acknowledged as important, the means of achieving the objective may be inadequate in various ways. In the case excerpted below, the Supreme Court examines the justifiability of a law which might criminalize an author's thoughts expressed in writing or in images intended for the author's sole use, and further explores the consequences of prohibition of child pornography for teenagers who while not yet adults possess images of their legally permitted sexual activity with each other.

Chief Justice McLachlin (for the majority):

[75] [...] The interpretation of the legislation suggested above reveals that the law may catch some material that particularly engages the value of self-fulfilment and poses little or no risk of harm to children. This material may be grouped in two classes. The first class consists of self-created, privately held expressive materials. Private journals, diaries, writings, drawings and other works of the imagination, created by oneself exclusively for oneself, may all trigger the s. 163.1(4) offence. The law, in its prohibition on the possession of such materials, reaches into a realm of exceedingly private expression, where s. 2 (*b*) values may be particularly implicated and state intervention may be markedly more intrusive. Further, the risk of harm arising from the private creation and possession of such materials, while not eliminated altogether, is low.

[76] The second class of material concerns privately created visual recordings of lawful sexual activity made by or depicting the person in possession and intended only for private use. Sexually explicit photographs taken by a teenager of him- or herself, and kept entirely in private, would fall within this class of materials. Another example would be a teenaged couple's private photographs of themselves engaged in lawful sexual activity. Possession of such materials may implicate the values of self-fulfilment and self-actualization, and therefore, like the material in the first category, reside near the heart of the s. 2 (*b*) guarantee. And like the material in the first category, this material poses little risk of harm to children. It is privately created and intended only for personal use. It depicts only lawful sexual activity. Indeed, because the law

reaches depictions of persons who are or appear to be under 18, the person or persons depicted may not even appear to be children.

[77] These examples suggest that s. 163.1(4), at the margins of its application, prohibits deeply private forms of expression, in pursuit of materials that may pose no more than a nominal risk of harm to children. It is these potential applications that present the most significant concerns at the stage of justification.

[...]

Proportionality: The Final Balance

[102] This brings us to the third and final branch of the proportionality inquiry: whether the benefits the law may achieve in preventing harm to children outweigh the detrimental effects of the law on the right of free expression. The final proportionality assessment takes all the elements identified and measured under the heads of Parliament's objective, rational connection and minimal impairment, and balances them to determine whether the state has proven on a balance of probabilities that its restriction on a fundamental *Charter* right is demonstrably justifiable in a free and democratic society.

[103] In the vast majority of the law's applications, the costs it imposes on freedom of expression are outweighed by the risk of harm to children. The Crown has met the burden of demonstrating that the possession of child pornography poses a reasoned apprehension of harm to children and that the goal of preventing such harm is pressing and substantial. Explicit sexual photographs and videotapes of children may promote cognitive distortions, fuel fantasies that incite offenders, enable grooming of victims, and may be produced using real children. Written material that advocates or counsels sexual offences with children can pose many of the same risks. Although we recently held in *Little Sisters Book and Art Emporium v. Canada (Minister of Justice)*, [2000] 2 S.C.R. 1120, 2000 SCC 69, that it may be difficult to make the case of obscenity against written texts, materials that advocate or counsel sexual offences with children may qualify. The Crown has also met the burden of showing that the law will benefit society by reducing the possibility of cognitive distortions, the use of pornography in grooming victims, and the abuse of children in the manufacture and continuing existence of this material. Explicit sexual photographs of children, videotapes of pre-pubescent children, and written works advocating sexual offences with children—all these and more pose a reasoned risk of harm to children. Thus we may conclude that in its main impact, s. 163.1(4) is proportionate and constitutional.

[104] I say this having given full consideration to the law's chilling effect. It is argued that fear of prosecution under s. 163.1(4), and the attendant social stigma, will deter people from keeping legal material and thus chill legitimate expression. However, the interpretation of the law offered in this decision may go some distance to reducing the uncertainty that feeds the chilling effect. Families need not fear prosecution for taking pictures of bare-bottomed toddlers

at the beach or children playing in the backyard, given the requirement that the dominant purpose be sexual. As case law develops, greater certainty may be expected, further reducing the law's chilling effect. On the record before us, the chilling effect, while not insignificant, does not appear to represent a major cost as it relates to the vast majority of material captured under s. 163.1(4).

[105] However, the prohibition also captures in its sweep materials that arguably pose little or no risk to children, and that deeply implicate the freedoms guaranteed under s. 2 (*b*). The ban, for example, extends to a teenager's sexually explicit recordings of him- or herself alone, or engaged in lawful sexual activity, held solely for personal use. It also reaches private materials, created by an individual exclusively for him- or herself, such as personal journals, writings, and drawings. It is in relation to these categories of materials that the costs of the prohibition are most pronounced. At the same time, it is here that the link between the proscribed materials and any risk of harm to children is most tenuous, for the reasons discussed earlier: children are not exploited or abused in their production; they are unlikely to induce attitudinal effects in their possessor; adolescents recording themselves alone or engaged in lawful sexual activity will generally not look like children; and the fact that this material is held privately renders the potential for its harmful use by others minimal. Consequently, the law's application to these materials, while peripheral to its objective, poses the most significant problems at this final stage of the proportionality analysis.

[106] As noted in discussing the values at stake in this appeal, privacy interests going to the liberty of the subject are also engaged by the legislation in question. However, these interests largely overlap with the s. 2 (*b*) values and are properly considered in the final balancing stage under s. 1.

[107] I turn first to consider the law's application to self-created works of the imagination, written or visual, intended solely for private use by the creator. The intensely private, expressive nature of these materials deeply implicates s. 2 (*b*) freedoms, engaging the values of self-fulfilment and self-actualization and engaging the inherent dignity of the individual: *Ford, supra*, at p. 765; see also my comments in *Keegstra, supra*, at p. 804. Personal journals and writings, drawings and other forms of visual expression may well be of importance to self-fulfilment. Indeed, for young people grappling with issues of sexual identity and self-awareness, private expression of a sexual nature may be crucial to personal growth and sexual maturation. The fact that many might not favour such forms of expression does not lessen the need to insist on strict justification for their prohibition. As stated in *Irwin Toy, supra*, at p. 976, "the diversity in forms of individual self-fulfilment and human flourishing ought to be cultivated in an essentially tolerant, indeed welcoming, environment."

[108] The restriction imposed by s. 163.1(4) regulates expression where it borders on thought. Indeed, it is a fine line that separates a state attempt to control the private possession of self-created expressive materials from a state attempt to control thought or opinion. The distinction between thought and

expression can be unclear. We talk of "thinking aloud" because that is often what we do: in many cases, our thoughts become choate only through their expression. To ban the possession of our own private musings thus falls perilously close to criminalizing the mere articulation of thought.

[109] The same concerns arise in relation to auto-depictions; that is, visual recordings made by a person of him- or herself alone, held privately and intended only for personal use. Again, such materials may be of significance to adolescent self-fulfilment, self-actualization and sexual exploration and identity. Similar considerations apply where the creator of the recordings is not the sole subject; that is, where lawful sexual acts are documented in a visual recording, such as photographs or a videotape, and held privately by the participants exclusively for their own private use. Such materials could conceivably reinforce healthy sexual relationships and self-actualization. For example, two adolescents might arguably deepen a loving and respectful relationship through erotic pictures of themselves engaged in sexual activity. The cost of including such materials to the right of free expression outweighs any tenuous benefit it might confer in preventing harm to children.

[110] I conclude that in broad impact and general application, the limits s. 163.1(4) imposes on free expression are justified by the protection the law affords children from exploitation and abuse. I cannot, however, arrive at the same conclusion in regard to the two problematic categories of materials described above. The legislation prohibits a person from articulating thoughts in writing or visual images, even if the result is intended only for his or her own eyes. It further prohibits a teenager from possessing, again exclusively for personal use, sexually explicit photographs or videotapes of him- or herself alone or engaged with a partner in lawful sexual activity. The inclusion of these peripheral materials in the law's prohibition trenches heavily on freedom of expression while adding little to the protection the law provides children. To this extent, the law cannot be considered proportionate in its effects, and the infringement of s. 2 (b) contemplated by the legislation is not demonstrably justifiable under s. 1. [...]

L'Heureux-Dubé, Gonthier and Bastarache JJ. (concurring):

[237] The impugned legislation is said to have a deleterious effect on both the right to free expression as guaranteed by s. 2 (b) and on the value of privacy. We turn first to the effect of the provision on the freedom of expression. As we discussed above, the law does not trench significantly on speech possessing social value; there is a very tenuous connection between the possession of child pornography and the right to free expression. At most, the law has a detrimental cost to those who find base fulfilment in the possession of child pornography.

[238] As we have stated, we do not find objections to the restriction of auto-depictions of adolescent sexuality compelling. In our view, the provision is consistent with the protection of children and does not serve as an unjusti-

fied impediment to the self-fulfilment of adolescents. As the Fraser Committee noted, restrictions on children's liberties are sometimes necessary because of their vulnerability. The cases involving depictions of teenagers engaged in explicit sexual activity demonstrate that pornography depicting teenagers is sometimes produced under conditions of exploitation, rather than mutuality and consent. Any deleterious effect on the self-fulfilment of teenagers who produce permanent records of their own sexual activity in an environment of mutual consent is, therefore, far outweighed by the salutary effects on all children resulting from the prohibition of the possession of child pornography.

[239] In most cases, the prohibition's restriction on expression will affect adults who seek fulfilment through the possession of child pornography. These adults seek to fulfill themselves by deriving sexual pleasure from images and writings which objectify and degrade children. It is important to emphasize that the self-fulfilment denied by the law is closely connected to the harm to children. The benefits of the prohibition of the possession of child pornography far outweigh any deleterious effect on the right to free expression.

[240] The legislation affects privacy interests because it extends its reach into the home. However, we must be careful not to exaggerate the severity of this deleterious effect. The privacy of those who possess child pornography is also protected by the right against unreasonable search and seizure as guaranteed by s. 8 of the *Charter*. Before any police investigation could take place within the home, a judicial officer would first have to make a determination that the law enforcement interests of the state were, in the particular situation, demonstrably superior to the affected individual's interest in being left alone. The law intrudes into the private sphere because doing so is necessary to achieve its salutary objectives. Child pornography is produced in private, and child pornography is used privately to entice children into sexual activity. Thus, the privacy interest restricted by the law is closely related to the specific harmful effects of child pornography.

[241] In examining the law's effect on privacy interests, it is important not to lose sight of the beneficial effects of the provision in protecting the privacy interests of children. When children are depicted in pornographic representations, the camera captures their abuse and creates a permanent record of it. This constitutes an extreme violation of their privacy interests. By criminalizing the possession of such materials, Parliament has created an incentive to destroy those pornographic representations which already exist. In our view, this beneficial effect on the privacy interests of children is proportional to the detrimental effects on the privacy of those who possess child pornography.

[242] When the effects of the provision are examined in their overall context, the benefits of the legislation far outweigh any harms to freedom of expression and the interests of privacy. The legislation hinders the self-fulfilment of a few, but this form of self-fulfilment is at a base and prurient level. Those who possess child pornography are self-fulfilled to the detriment of the rights of all children.

The prohibition of the possession of such materials is thus consistent with our *Charter* values. It fosters and supports the dignity of children and sends the message that they are to be accorded equal respect with other members of the community. In our view, Parliament has enacted a law which is reasonable, and which is justified in a free and democratic society.

Chaoulli v. Quebec (Attorney General)
Supreme Court of Canada
[2005] 1 S.C.R. 791

In Quebec, the *Health Insurance Act* and the *Hospital Insurance Act* prohibited private health insurance for services and treatment provided by the public health system. The appellants challenged the validity of the prohibition, claiming that the prohibition's combination with certain medical conditions (and associated stress and anxiety) and unreasonable waiting times in the public health system violated the right to life, liberty, and security of the person, which is protected in similar ways by both the *Quebec Charter of Rights and Freedoms* and the *Canadian Charter of Rights and Freedoms*.

The case raises the controversial issue of single-tiered versus two-tiered health systems, and how far the right to life, liberty, and security of the person limits legislative objectives on social and policy issues.

By a majority of 4–3, the Supreme Court decided that the prohibition was unconstitutional, under both the *Canadian Charter* as well as the quasi-constitutional *Quebec Charter*.

———————

McLachlin C.J. and Major J. (for the majority):

[103] The appellants do not seek an order that the government spend more money on health care, nor do they seek an order that waiting times for treatment under the public health care scheme be reduced. They only seek a ruling that because delays in the public system place their health and security at risk, they should be allowed to take out insurance to permit them to access private services.

[104] The *Charter* does not confer a freestanding constitutional right to health care. However, where the government puts in place a scheme to provide health care, that scheme must comply with the *Charter*. [...]

[105] The primary objective of the *Canada Health Act*, R.S.C. 1985, c. C-6, is "to protect, promote and restore the physical and mental wellbeing of residents of Canada and *to facilitate reasonable access* to health services without financial or other barriers" (s. 3). By imposing exclusivity and then failing to provide public health care of a reasonable standard within a reasonable time, the government creates circumstances that trigger the application of s. 7 of the *Charter*.

[106] The *Canada Health Act*, the *Health Insurance Act*, and the *Hospital Insurance Act* do not expressly prohibit private health services. However, they

limit access to private health services by removing the ability to contract for private health care insurance to cover the same services covered by public insurance. The result is a virtual monopoly for the public health scheme. The state has effectively limited access to private health care except for the very rich, who can afford private care without need of insurance. This virtual monopoly, on the evidence, results in delays in treatment that adversely affect the citizen's security of the person. Where a law adversely affects life, liberty or security of the person, it must conform to the principles of fundamental justice. This law, in our view, fails to do so.

[107] While the decision about the type of health care system Quebec should adopt falls to the Legislature of that province, the resulting legislation, like all laws, is subject to constitutional limits, including those imposed by s. 7 of the *Charter*. The fact that the matter is complex, contentious or laden with social values does not mean that the courts can abdicate the responsibility vested in them by our Constitution to review legislation for *Charter* compliance when citizens challenge it. [...]

[108] The government defends the prohibition on medical insurance on the ground that the existing system is the only approach to adequate universal health care for all Canadians. The question in this case, however, is not whether single-tier health care is preferable to two-tier health care. Even if one accepts the government's goal, the legal question raised by the appellants must be addressed: is it a violation of s. 7 of the *Charter* to prohibit private insurance for health care, when the result is to subject Canadians to long delays with resultant risk of physical and psychological harm? The mere fact that this question may have policy ramifications does not permit us to avoid answering it.

Section 7 of the Charter

[109] Section 7 of the *Charter* guarantees that "[e]veryone has the right to life, liberty and security of the person and the right not to be deprived thereof except in accordance with the principles of fundamental justice." The disposition of this appeal therefore requires us to consider (1) whether the impugned provisions deprive individuals of their life, liberty or security of the person; and (2) if so, whether this deprivation is in accordance with the principles of fundamental justice: see, e.g., *R. v. Malmo-Levine*, [2003] 3 S.C.R. 571, 2003 SCC 74, at para. 83.

Deprivation of Life, Liberty or Security of the Person

[110] The issue at this stage is whether the prohibition on insurance for private medical care deprives individuals of their life, liberty or security of the person protected by s. 7 of the *Charter*.

[111] The appellants have established that many Quebec residents face delays in treatment that adversely affect their security of the person and that they would not sustain but for the prohibition on medical insurance. It is common

ground that the effect of the prohibition on insurance is to allow only the very rich, who do not need insurance, to secure private health care in order to avoid the delays in the public system. Given the ban on insurance, most Quebeckers have no choice but to accept delays in the medical system and their adverse physical and psychological consequences. [...]

[123] Not every difficulty rises to the level of adverse impact on security of the person under s. 7. The impact, whether psychological or physical, must be serious. However, because patients may be denied timely health care for a condition that is clinically significant to their current and future health, s. 7 protection of security of the person is engaged. Access to a waiting list is not access to health care. As we noted above, there is unchallenged evidence that in some serious cases, patients die as a result of waiting lists for public health care. Where lack of timely health care can result in death, s. 7 protection of life itself is engaged. The evidence here demonstrates that the prohibition on health insurance results in physical and psychological suffering that meets this threshold requirement of seriousness.

[124] We conclude, based on the evidence, that prohibiting health insurance that would permit ordinary Canadians to access health care, in circumstances where the government is failing to deliver health care in a reasonable manner, thereby increasing the risk of complications and death, interferes with life and security of the person as protected by s. 7 of the *Charter*. [...]

[134] As discussed above, interference with life, liberty and security of the person is impermissibly arbitrary if the interference lacks a real connection on the facts to the purpose the interference is said to serve.

[135] The government argues that the interference with security of the person caused by denying people the right to purchase private health insurance is necessary to providing effective health care under the public health system. It argues that if people can purchase private health insurance, they will seek treatment from private doctors and hospitals, which are not banned under the Act. According to the government's argument, this will divert resources from the public health system into private health facilities, ultimately reducing the quality of public care.

[136] In support of this contention, the government called experts in health administration and policy. Their conclusions were based on the "common sense" proposition that the improvement of health services depends on exclusivity (R.R., at p. 591). They did not profess expertise in waiting times for treatment. Nor did they present economic studies or rely on the experience of other countries. They simply assumed, as a matter of apparent logic, that insurance would make private health services more accessible and that this in turn would undermine the quality of services provided by the public health care system.

[137] The appellants, relying on other health experts, disagreed and offered their own conflicting "common sense" argument for the proposition that prohibiting private health insurance is neither necessary nor related to maintaining high quality in the public health care system. Quality public care, they argue,

depends not on a monopoly, but on money and management. They testified that permitting people to buy private insurance would make alternative medical care more accessible and reduce the burden on the public system. The result, they assert, would be better care for all. The appellants reinforce this argument by pointing out that disallowing private insurance precludes the vast majority of Canadians (middle-income and low-income earners) from accessing additional care, while permitting it for the wealthy who can afford to travel abroad or pay for private care in Canada.

[138] To this point, we are confronted with competing but unproven "common sense" arguments, amounting to little more than assertions of belief. We are in the realm of theory. But as discussed above, a theoretically defensible limitation may be arbitrary if in fact the limit lacks a connection to the goal.

[139] This brings us to the evidence called by the appellants at trial on the experience of other developed countries with public health care systems which permit access to private health care. The experience of these countries suggests that there is no real connection in fact between prohibition of health insurance and the goal of a quality public health system.

[140] The evidence adduced at trial establishes that many western democracies that do not impose a monopoly on the delivery of health care have successfully delivered to their citizens medical services that are superior to and more affordable than the services that are presently available in Canada. This demonstrates that a monopoly is not necessary or even related to the provision of quality public health care. [...]

[152] When we look to the evidence rather than to assumptions, the connection between prohibiting private insurance and maintaining quality public health care vanishes. The evidence before us establishes that where the public system fails to deliver adequate care, the denial of private insurance subjects people to long waiting lists and negatively affects their health and security of the person. The government contends that this is necessary in order to preserve the public health system. The evidence, however, belies that contention.

[153] We conclude that on the evidence adduced in this case, the appellants have established that in the face of delays in treatment that cause psychological and physical suffering, the prohibition on private insurance jeopardizes the right to life, liberty and security of the person of Canadians in an arbitrary manner, and is therefore not in accordance with the principles of fundamental justice.

[154] Having concluded that the prohibition on private health insurance constitutes a breach of s. 7, we must now consider whether that breach can be justified under s. 1 of the *Charter* as a reasonable limit demonstrably justified in a free and democratic society. The evidence called in this case falls short of demonstrating such justification.

[155] The government undeniably has an interest in protecting the public health regime. However, given the absence of evidence that the prohibition on the purchase and sale of private health insurance protects the health care system, the rational connection between the prohibition and the objective is

not made out. Indeed, we question whether an arbitrary provision, which by reason of its arbitrariness cannot further its stated objective, will ever meet the rational connection test under *R. v. Oakes*, [1986] 1 S.C.R. 103.

[156] In addition, the resulting denial of access to timely and effective medical care to those who need it is not proportionate to the beneficial effects of the prohibition on private insurance to the health system as a whole. On the evidence here and for the reasons discussed above, the prohibition goes further than necessary to protect the public system: it is not minimally impairing.

[157] Finally, the benefits of the prohibition do not outweigh the deleterious effects. Prohibiting citizens from obtaining private health care insurance may, as discussed, leave people no choice but to accept excessive delays in the public health system. The physical and psychological suffering and risk of death that may result outweigh whatever benefit (and none has been demonstrated to us here) there may be to the system as a whole.

[158] In sum, the prohibition on obtaining private health insurance, while it might be constitutional in circumstances where health care services are reasonable as to both quality and timeliness, is not constitutional where the public system fails to deliver reasonable services. Life, liberty and security of the person must prevail. To paraphrase Dickson C.J. in *Morgentaler*, at p. 73, if the government chooses to act, it must do so properly. [...]

Binnie and Lebel, JJ. (for the minority):

[161] The question in this appeal is whether the province of Quebec not only has the constitutional authority to establish a comprehensive single-tier health plan, but to discourage a second (private) tier health sector by prohibiting the purchase and sale of private health insurance. The appellants argue that timely access to needed medical service is not being provided in the publicly funded system and that the province cannot therefore deny to those Quebeckers (who can qualify) the right to purchase private insurance to pay for medical services whenever and wherever such services can be obtained for a fee, i.e., in the private sector. This issue has been the subject of protracted debate across Canada through several provincial and federal elections. We are unable to agree with our four colleagues who would allow the appeal that such a debate can or should be resolved as a matter of law by judges. We find that, on the *legal* issues raised, the appeal should be dismissed.

[162] Our colleagues the Chief Justice and Major J. state at para. 105:

> By imposing exclusivity and then failing to provide *public health care of a reasonable standard within a reasonable time*, the government creates circumstances that trigger the application of s. 7 of the [*Canadian*] *Charter*. [Emphasis added.]

[163] The Court recently held in *Auton (Guardian ad litem of) v. British Columbia (Attorney General)*, [2004] 3 S.C.R. 657, 2004 SCC 78, that the government was not required to fund the treatment of autistic children. It did not on that

occasion address in constitutional terms the scope and nature of "reasonable" health services. Courts will now have to make that determination. What, then, are constitutionally required "reasonable health services"? What is treatment "within a reasonable time"? What are the benchmarks? How short a waiting list is short enough? How many MRIs does the Constitution require? The majority does not tell us. The majority lays down no manageable constitutional standard. The public cannot know, nor can judges or governments know, how much health care is "reasonable" enough to satisfy s. 7 of the *Canadian Charter of Rights and Freedoms* ("*Canadian Charter*") and s. 1 of the *Charter of Human Rights and Freedoms*, R.S.Q. c. C-12 ("*Quebec Charter*"). It is to be hoped that we will know it when we see it.

[164] The policy of the *Canada Health Act*, R.S.C. 1985, c. C-6, and its provincial counterparts is to provide health care based on need rather than on wealth or status. The evidence certainly established that the public health care system put in place to implement this policy has serious and persistent problems. This does not mean that the courts are well placed to perform the required surgery. The resolution of such a complex fact-laden policy debate does not fit easily within the institutional competence or procedures of courts of law. The courts can use s. 7 of the *Canadian Charter* to pre-empt the ongoing public debate only if the current health plan violates an established "principle of fundamental justice." Our colleagues McLachlin C.J. and Major J. argue that Quebec's enforcement of a single-tier health plan meets this legal test because it is "arbitrary." In our view, with respect, the prohibition against private health insurance is a rational consequence of Quebec's commitment to the goals and objectives of the *Canada Health Act*.

[165] Our colleague Deschamps J. states at para. 4:

> In essence, the question is whether Quebeckers *who are prepared to spend money* to get access to health care that is, in practice, not accessible in the public sector because of waiting lists may be validly prevented from doing so by the state. [Emphasis added.]

This is so, but of course it must be recognized that the liberty and security of Quebeckers who do *not* have the money to afford private health insurance, who cannot qualify for it, or who are not employed by establishments that provide it, are not put at risk by the absence of "upper tier" health care. It is Quebeckers who have the money to afford private medical insurance and can qualify for it who will be the beneficiaries of the appellants' constitutional challenge.

[166] The Quebec government views the prohibition against private insurance as essential to preventing the current single-tier health system from disintegrating into a *de facto* two-tier system. The trial judge found, and the evidence demonstrated, that there is good reason for this fear. The trial judge concluded that a private health sector fuelled by private insurance would frustrate achievement of the objectives of the *Canada Health Act*. She thus found no *legal* basis to intervene, and declined to do so. This raises the issue of *who* it is that *should*

resolve these important and contentious issues. Commissioner Roy Romanow makes the following observation in his Report:

> Some have described it as a perversion of Canadian values that they cannot use their money to purchase faster treatment from a private provider for their loved ones. I believe it is a far greater perversion of Canadian values to accept a system where money, rather than need, determines who gets access to care.

(*Building on Values: The Future of Health Care in Canada: Final Report* [2002] ["Romanow Report"], at p. xx).

Whether or not one endorses this assessment, his premise is that the debate is about *social* values. It is not about constitutional law. We agree.

[167] We believe our colleagues the Chief Justice and Major J. have extended too far the strands of interpretation under the *Canadian Charter* laid down in some of the earlier cases, in particular the ruling on abortion in *R. v. Morgentaler*, [1988] 1 S.C.R. 30 (which involved criminal liability, not public health policy). We cannot find in the constitutional law of Canada a "principle of fundamental justice" dispositive of the problems of waiting lists in the Quebec health system. In our view, the appellants' case does not rest on constitutional law but on their disagreement with the Quebec government on aspects of its social policy. The proper forum to determine the social policy of Quebec in this matter is the National Assembly.

RELATED CASES

Regina v. Jack and Charlie [1982] 5 W.W.R. 193
(In this case the British Columbia Court of Appeal had to decide whether deer shot and killed out of season for use in a religious ceremony by an Indigenous group was permissible under freedom of religion.)

Attorney-General of Quebec v. Irwin Toy Inc. [1989] 1 S.C.R. 927
(This case examines whether the prohibition of commercial speech aimed at children unjustifiably infringes freedom of expression.)

Native Women's Association of Canada v. Canada [1994] 3 S.C.R. 627
(In this case the Supreme Court of Canada explored whether there might be a positive dimension to freedom of expression, which would require governments to facilitate expression, rather than merely protect it from interference.)

Ross v. The Board of School Trustees, District No. 15 [1996] 1 S.C.R. 825
(This case examines the extent to which educational environments can constitute a justifiable limitation on school teachers' freedom to express discriminatory statements in public contexts outside the classroom.)

RJR-Macdonald Inc. v. Attorney-General of Canada [1995] 3 S.C.R. 199
(In this case the Supreme Court of Canada had to determine whether a tobacco company's right to advertise was protected under the *Charter* right of freedom of expression.)

PART III

Equality Rights

Equality is as fundamental a political value as any mentioned in the *Charter*, yet it is also notoriously open to competing interpretations, both legal and philosophical. Section 15 identifies four kinds of equality, ("equality *before* and *under* the law and... *equal protection* and *equal benefit* of the law") although it remains unclear how they differ. Federal and provincial human rights codes also contain provisions that attempt to secure equality, but with respect to the more concrete concerns of employment, housing, and other everyday, private matters. Both Section 15 and human rights code sections express equality in terms of "non-discrimination," raising the question whether legal equality is mostly, or entirely, a matter of protecting people against the unequal actions, rules, or policies of others. Does "guaranteeing equality" come to the same thing as "remedying discrimination" or does it mean that and more?

Legal and philosophical debates over the scope of equality have spawned several competing accounts of what a political commitment to equality entails. These range from formal guarantees of the equal application of the law, to prohibitions against discrimination and guarantees of equality of opportunity to, finally, affirmative commitments to equality of condition with substantial redistributive consequences. The cases in this Part set out some of these background debates.

Andrews v. Law Society of British Columbia
Supreme Court of Canada
[1989] 1 S.C.R. 143

Although the discrimination at issue in this case may not be a major social problem (Andrews successfully challenged the rule that he be a Canadian citizen before becoming a member of the BC bar), it gave the Supreme Court the opportunity to examine section 15 of the *Charter* more thoroughly than it had done before. The case has had a profound effect on the legal conception of equality in this country; this judgment is truly the starting point for equality jurisprudence in this country. Among the issues addressed here are: the so-called "similarly situated" or "formal" analysis of equality; the nature of, and test for, discriminatory laws; the relationship between the *Charter* and Human Rights Codes (which exist in every province, territory, and the federal government); and the relation between the equality provisions in section 15 and the "reasonable limitation" provision in section 1 of the *Charter*. (Although the judgment given below was in dissent, Justice McIntyre wrote the judgment for a unanimous court on the crucial issue of the interpretation of section 15.)

Justice McIntyre, dissenting:

The Concept of Equality

Section 15(1) of the *Charter* provides for every individual a guarantee of equality before and under the law, as well as the equal protection and equal benefit of the law without discrimination. This is not a general guarantee of equality; it does not provide for equality between individuals or groups within society in a general or abstract sense, nor does it impose on individuals or groups an obligation to accord equal treatment to others. It is concerned with the application of the law. No problem regarding the scope of the word "law," as employed in s. 15(1), can arise in this case because it is an Act of the Legislature which is under attack. Whether other governmental or *quasi*-governmental regulations, rules or requirements may be termed laws under s. 15(1) should be left for cases in which the issue arises.

The concept of equality has long been a feature of Western thought. As embodied in s. 15(1) of the *Charter*, it is an elusive concept and, more than any of the other rights and freedoms guaranteed in the *Charter*, it lacks precise definition. [...]

It is a comparative concept, the condition of which may only be attained or discerned by comparison with the conditions of others in the social and political setting in which the question arises.

It must be recognized at once, however, that every difference in treatment between individuals under the law will not necessarily result in inequality and, as well, that identical treatment may frequently produce serious inequality. This proposition has found frequent expression in the literature on the subject but, as I have noted on a previous occasion, nowhere more aptly than in the well-known words of Frankfurter J. in *Dennis v. United States*, 339 U.S. 162 (1950), at p. 184:

> It is a wise man who said that there is no greater inequality than the equal treatment of unequals.

The same thought has been expressed in this court in the context of s. 2(b) of the *Charter* in *R. v. Big M Drug Mart Ltd.* (1985) where Dickson C.J.C. said at p. 347:

> The equality necessary to support religious freedom does not require identical treatment of all religions. In fact, the interests of true equality may well require differentiation in treatment.

In simple terms, then, it may be said that a law which treats all identically and which provides equality of treatment between "A" and "B" might well cause inequality for "C," depending on differences in personal characteristics and situations. To approach the ideal of full equality before and under the law—and in human affairs an approach is all that can be expected—the main consideration must be the impact of the law on the individual or the group concerned. Recognizing that there will always be an infinite variety of personal characteristics, capacities, entitlements and merits among those subject to a law, there must be accorded, as nearly as may be possible, an equality of benefit and protection and no more of the restrictions, penalties or burdens imposed upon one than another. In other words, the admittedly unattainable ideal should be that a law expressed to bind all should not because of irrelevant personal differences have a more burdensome or less beneficial impact on one than another.

McLachlin J.A. in the Court of Appeal expressed the view, at p. 605, that:

> ...the essential meaning of the constitutional requirement of equal protection and equal benefit is that persons who are "similarly situated be similarly treated" and conversely, that persons who are "differently situated be differently treated."

In this, she was adopting and applying as a test a proposition which seems to have been widely accepted with some modifications in both trial and appeal court decisions throughout the country on s. 15(1) of the *Charter*. [...] The reliance on this concept appears to have derived, at least in recent times, from J.T. Tussman and J. tenBroek, "The Equal Protection of Laws" (1949), 37 *Calif. L. Rev.* 341.

The similarly situated test is a restatement of the Aristotelian principle of formal equality—that "things that are alike should be treated alike, while things that are unalike should be treated unalike in proportion to their unalikeness." (*Ethica Nichomacea*, trans. W. Ross, Book V3, at p. 1131a-6 [1925])

The test as stated, however, is seriously deficient in that it excludes any consideration of the nature of the law. If it were to be applied literally, it could be used to justify the Nuremberg laws of Adolf Hitler. Similar treatment was contemplated for all Jews. The similarly situated test would have justified the formalistic separate but equal doctrine of *Plessy v. Ferguson* (1896). [...]

[M]ere equality of application to similarly situated groups or individuals does not afford a realistic test for violation of equality rights. For, as has been said, a bad law will not be saved merely because it operates equally upon those to whom it has application. Nor will a law necessarily be bad because it makes distinctions.

A similarly situated test focusing on the equal application of the law to those to whom it has application could lead to results akin to those in *Bliss v. A.-G. Can.* (1978). In *Bliss*, a pregnant woman was denied unemployment benefits to which she would have been entitled had she not been pregnant. She claimed that the *Unemployment Insurance Act* violated the equality guarantees of the *Canadian Bill of Rights* because it discriminated against her on the basis of her sex. Her claim was dismissed by this court on the grounds that there was no discrimination on the basis of sex, since the class into which she fell under the Act was that of pregnant persons, and within that class, all persons were treated equally. This case, of course, was decided before the advent of the *Charter*.

I would also agree with the following criticism of the similarly situated test made by Kerans J.A. in *Mahe v. Alta.* (1987), at p. 244:

> ...the test accepts an idea of equality which is almost mechanical, with no scope for considering the reason for the distinction. In consequence, subtleties are found to justify a finding of dissimilarity which reduce the test to a categorization game. Moreover, the test is not helpful. After all, most laws are enacted for the specific purpose of offering a benefit or imposing a burden on some persons and not on others. The test catches every conceivable difference in legal treatment.

For the reasons outlined above, the test cannot be accepted as a fixed rule or formula for the resolution of equality questions arising under the *Charter*. Consideration must be given to the content of the law, to its purpose, and its impact upon those to whom it applies, and also upon those whom it excludes from its application. The issues which will arise from case to case are such that it would be wrong to attempt to confine these considerations within such a fixed and limited formula.

It is not every distinction or differentiation in treatment at law which will transgress the equality guarantees of s. 15 of the *Charter*. It is, of course, obvious that legislatures may—and to govern effectively must—treat different individuals and groups in different ways. Indeed, such distinctions are one of the main preoccupations of legislatures. The classifying of individuals and groups, the making of different provisions respecting such groups, the application of different rules, regulations, requirements and qualifications to different persons is necessary for the governance of modern society. As noted above, for the accommodation of differences, which is the essence of true equality, it will frequently be necessary to make distinctions. [...]

The principle of equality before the law has long been recognized as a feature of our constitutional tradition and it found statutory recognition in the *Canadian Bill of Rights*. However, unlike the *Canadian Bill of Rights*, which spoke only of equality before the law, s. 15(1) of the *Charter* provides a much broader protection. Section 15 spells out four basic rights: (1) the right to equality before the law; (2) the right to equality under the law; (3) the right to equal protection of the law; and (4) the right to equal benefit of the law. The inclusion of these last three additional rights in s. 15 of the *Charter* was an attempt to remedy some of the shortcomings of the right to equality in the *Canadian Bill of Rights*. It also reflected the expanded concept of discrimination being developed under the various Human Rights Codes since the enactment of the *Canadian Bill of Rights*. The shortcomings of the *Canadian Bill of Rights* as far as the right to equality is concerned are well known. [...] It is readily apparent that the language of s. 15 was deliberately chosen in order to remedy some of the perceived defects under the *Canadian Bill of Rights*. The antecedent statute is part of the "linguistic, philosophic and historical context" of s. 15 of the *Charter*.

It is clear that the purpose of s. 15 is to ensure equality in the formulation and application of the law. The promotion of equality entails the promotion of a society in which all are secure in the knowledge that they are recognized at law as human beings equally deserving of concern, respect and consideration. It has a large remedial component.

It must be recognized, however, as well that the promotion of equality under s. 15 has a much more specific goal than the mere elimination of distinctions. If the *Charter* was intended to eliminate all distinctions, then there would be no place for sections such as s. 27 (multicultural heritage); s. 2(a) (freedom of conscience and religion); s. 25 (aboriginal rights and freedoms); and other such provisions designed to safeguard certain distinctions. Moreover, the fact that identical treatment may frequently produce serious inequality is recognized in s. 15(2), which states that the equality rights in s. 15(1) do "not preclude any law, program or activity that has as its object the amelioration of conditions of disadvantaged individuals or groups."

Discrimination

The right to equality before and under the law, and the rights to the equal protection and benefit of the law contained in s. 15, are granted with the direction contained in s. 15 itself that they be without discrimination. Discrimination is unacceptable in a democratic society because it epitomizes the worst effects of the denial of equality, and discrimination reinforced by law is particularly repugnant. The worst oppression will result from discriminatory measures having the force of law. It is against this evil that s. 15 provides a guarantee.

Discrimination as referred to in s. 15 of the *Charter* must be understood in the context of *pre-Charter* history. Prior to the enactment of s. 15(1), the legislatures of the various provinces and the federal Parliament had passed during the previous fifty years what may be generally referred to as Human Rights Acts. With the steady increase in population from the earliest days of European emigration into Canada and with the consequential growth of industry, agriculture and commerce and the vast increase in national wealth which followed, many social problems developed. The contact of the European immigrant with the indigenous population, the steady increase in immigration bringing those of neither French nor British background, and in more recent years the greatly expanded role of women in all forms of industrial, commercial and professional activity led to much inequality and many forms of discrimination. In great part these developments, in the absence of any significant legislative protection for the victims of discrimination, called into being the Human Rights Acts. In 1944, the *Racial Discrimination Act, 1944* was passed, to be followed in 1947 by the *Saskatchewan Bill of Rights Act, 1947* and in 1960 by the *Canadian Bill of Rights*. Since then every jurisdiction in Canada has enacted broad-ranging Human Rights Acts which have attacked most of the more common forms of discrimination found in society. [...]

What does discrimination mean? The question has arisen most commonly in a consideration of the Human Rights Acts and the general concept of discrimination under those enactments has been fairly well settled. There is little difficulty, drawing upon the cases in this court, in isolating an acceptable definition. [...]

I would say then that discrimination may be described as a distinction, whether intentional or not but based on grounds relating to personal characteristics of the individual or group, which has the effect of imposing burdens, obligations, or disadvantages on such individual or group not imposed upon others, or which withholds or limits access to opportunities, benefits, and advantages available to other members of society. Distinctions based on personal characteristics attributed to an individual solely on the basis of association with a group will rarely escape the charge of discrimination, while those based on an individual's merits and capacities will rarely be so classed.

The Court in the case at bar must address the issue of discrimination as the term is used in s. 15(1) of the *Charter*. In general, it may be said that the principles which have been applied under the Human Rights Acts are equally applicable in considering questions of discrimination under s. 15(1). Certain differences arising from the difference between the *Charter* and the Human Rights Acts must, however, be considered. To begin with, discrimination in s. 15(1) is limited to discrimination caused by the application or operation of law, whereas the Human Rights Acts apply also to private activities. Furthermore, and this is a distinction of more importance, all the Human Rights Acts passed in Canada specifically designate a certain limited number of grounds upon which discrimination is forbidden. Section 15(1) of the *Charter* is not so limited. The enumerated grounds in s. 15(1) are not exclusive and the limits, if any, on grounds for discrimination which may be established in future cases await definition. The enumerated grounds do, however, reflect the most common and probably the most socially destructive and historically practised bases of discrimination and must, in the words of s. 15(1), receive particular attention. Both the enumerated grounds themselves and other possible grounds in discrimination recognized under s. 15(1) must be interpreted in a broad and generous manner, reflecting the fact that they are constitutional provisions not easily repealed or amended but intended to provide a "continuing framework for the legitimate exercise of governmental power" and, at the same time, for "the unremitting protection" of equality rights. [...]

It should be noted as well that when the Human Rights Acts create exemptions or defences, such as a *bona fide* occupational requirement, an exemption for religious and political organizations, or definitional limits on age discrimination, these generally have the effect of completely removing the conduct complained of from the reach of the Act. [...] Where discrimination is forbidden in the Human Rights Acts, it is done in absolute terms, and where a defence or exception is allowed, it, too, speaks in absolute terms and the discrimination is excused. There is, in this sense, no middle ground. In the *Charter*, however, while s. 15(1), subject always to subs. (2), expresses its prohibition of discrimination in absolute terms, s. 1 makes allowance for a reasonable limit upon the operation of s. 15(1). A different approach under s. 15(1) is therefore required. While discrimination under s. 15(1) will be of the same nature and in descriptive terms will fit the concept of discrimination developed under the Human Rights Acts, a further step will be required in order to decide whether discriminatory laws can be justified under s. 1. The onus will be on the state to establish this. This is a distinct step called for under the *Charter* which is not found in most Human Rights Acts, because in those Acts justification for or defence to discrimination is generally found in specific exceptions to the substantive rights.

Relationship Between s. 15(1) and s. 1 of the Charter

In determining the extent of the guarantee of equality in s. 15(1) of the *Charter*, special consideration must be given to the relationship between subs. 15(1) and s. 1. It is indeed the presence of s. 1 in the *Charter* and the interaction between these sections which has led to the differing approaches to a definition of the s. 15(1) right, and which has made necessary a judicial approach differing from that employed under the *Canadian Bill of Rights*. Under the *Canadian Bill of Rights*, a test was developed to distinguish between justified and unjustified legislative distinctions within the concept of equality before the law itself in the absence of anything equivalent to the s. 1 limit. [...]

It may be noted as well that the 14th Amendment to the American Constitution, which provides that no state shall deny to any person within its jurisdiction the "equal protection of the laws," contains no limiting provisions similar to s. 1 of the *Charter*. As a result, judicial consideration has led to the development of varying standards of scrutiny of alleged violations of the equal protection provision which restrict or limit the equality guarantee within the concept of equal protection itself. Again, article 14 of the *European Convention of Human Rights*, which secures the rights guaranteed therein without discrimination, lacks a s. 1 or its equivalent and has also developed a limit within the concept itself. [...]

The distinguishing feature of the *Charter*, unlike the other enactments, is that consideration of such limiting factors is made under s. 1. This court has described the analytical approach to the *Charter* in *R. v. Oakes* (1986) the essential feature of which is that the right guaranteeing sections be kept analytically separate from s. 1. In other words, when confronted with a problem under the *Charter*, the first question which must be answered will be whether or not an infringement of a guaranteed right has occurred. Any justification of an infringement which is found to have occurred must be made, if at all, under the broad provisions of s. 1. It must be admitted at once that the relationship between these two sections may well be difficult to determine on a wholly satisfactory basis. It is, however, important to keep them analytically distinct if for no other reason than the different attribution of the burden of proof. It is for the citizen to establish that his or her *Charter* right has been infringed and for the state to justify the infringement.

Approaches to s. 15(1)

Three main approaches have been adopted in determining the role of s. 15(1), the meaning of discrimination set out in that section, and the relationship between s. 15(1) and s. 1. The first one, which was advanced by Professor Peter Hogg in *Constitutional Law of Canada* (1985), would treat every distinction drawn by law as discrimination under s. 15(1). There would then follow a consideration of the distinction under the provisions of s. 1 of the *Charter*. [...]

[Hogg] reached this conclusion on the basis that, where the *Charter* right is expressed in unqualified terms, s. 1 supplies the standard of justification for any abridgment of the right. He argued that the word "discrimination" in s. 15(1) could be read as introducing a qualification in the section itself, but he preferred to read the word in a neutral sense because this reading would immediately send the matter to s. 1, which was included in the *Charter* for this purpose.

The second approach put forward by McLachlin J.A. in the Court of Appeal involved a consideration of the reasonableness and fairness of the impugned legislation under s. 15(1). She stated, at p. 610:

The ultimate question is whether a fair-minded person, weighing the purposes of legislation against its effects on the individuals adversely affected, and giving due weight to the right of the Legislature to pass laws for the good of all, would conclude that the legislative means adopted are reasonable or unfair.

She assigned a very minor role to s. 1 which would, it appears, be limited to allowing in times of emergency, war, or other crises the passage of discriminatory legislation which would normally be impermissible.

A third approach, sometimes described as an "enumerated or analogous grounds" approach, adopts the concept that discrimination is generally expressed by the enumerated grounds. Section 15(1) is designed to prevent discrimination based on these and analogous grounds. The approach is similar to that found in human rights and civil rights statutes which have been enacted throughout Canada in recent times. The following excerpts from the judgment of Hugessen J. in *Smith, Kline & French Laboratories Ltd. v. A.-G. Can.* (1986), at pp. 367–69, illustrate this approach:

> [...] The answer, in my view, is that the text of the section itself contains its own limitations. It only proscribes discrimination amongst the members of categories which are themselves similar. Thus the issue, for each case, will be to know which categories are permissible in determining similarity of situation and which are not. It is only in those cases where the categories themselves are not permissible, where equals are not treated equally, that there will be a breach of equality rights.
>
> As far as the text of s. 15 itself is concerned, one may look to whether or not there is "discrimination," in the pejorative sense of that word, and as to whether the categories are based upon the grounds enumerated or grounds analogous to them. The inquiry, in effect, concentrates upon the personal characteristics of those who claim to have been unequally treated. Questions of stereotyping, of historical disadvantagement, in a word, of prejudice, are the focus and there may even be a recognition that for some people equality has a different meaning than for others.

The analysis of discrimination in this approach must take place within the context of the enumerated grounds and those analogous to them. The words "without discrimination" require more than a mere finding of distinction between the treatment of groups or individuals. Those words are a form of qualifier built into s. 15 itself and limit those distinctions which are forbidden by the section to those which involve prejudice or disadvantage.

I would accept the criticisms of the first approach made by McLachlin J.A. in the Court of Appeal. She noted that the labelling of every legislative distinction as an infringement of s. 15(1) trivializes the fundamental rights guaranteed by the *Charter* and, secondly, that to interpret "without discrimination" as "without distinction" deprives the notion of discrimination of content. [...]

In rejecting the Hogg approach, I would say that it draws a straight line from the finding of a distinction to a determination of its validity under s. 1, but my objection would be that it virtually denies any role for s. 15(1).

I would reject, as well, the approach adopted by McLachlin J.A. She seeks to define discrimination under s. 15(1) as an unjustifiable or unreasonable distinction. In so doing she avoids the mere distinction test but also makes a radical departure from the analytical approach to the *Charter* which has been approved by this Court. In the result, the determination would be made under s. 15(1) and virtually no role would be left for s. 1.

The third or "enumerated and analogous grounds" approach most closely accords with the purposes of s. 15 and the definition of discrimination outlined above and leaves questions of justification to s. 1. However, in assessing whether a complainant's rights have been infringed under s. 15(1), it is not enough to focus only on the alleged ground of discrimination and decide whether or not it is an enumerated or analogous ground. The effect of the impugned distinction or classification on the complainant must be considered. Once it is accepted that not all distinctions and differentiations created by law are discriminatory, then a role must be assigned to s. 15(1) which goes beyond the mere recognition of a legal distinction. A complainant under s. 15(1) must show not only that he or she is not receiving equal treatment before and under the law or that the law has a differential impact on him or her in the protection or benefit accorded by law but, in addition, must show that the legislative impact of the law is discriminatory.

Where discrimination is found, a breach of s. 15(1) has occurred and—where s. 15(2) is not applicable—any justification, any consideration of the reasonableness of the enactment, indeed, any consideration of factors which could justify the discrimination and support the constitutionality of the impugned enactment would take place under s. 1. This approach would conform with the directions of this court in earlier decisions concerning the application of s. 1 and at the same time would allow for the screening out of the obviously trivial and vexatious claim. In this, it would provide a workable approach to the problem.

Eaton v. Brant County Board of Education
Supreme Court of Canada
[1997] 1 S.C.R. 241

What does equality demand? In this case a 12-year-old child with cerebral palsy who is unable to speak or use sign language was moved out of the regular classroom, where she had been for three years, and into a special education class. Her parents refused to consent to this arguing that placement in a special class, even if motivated by a desire to meet her needs, amounts to "exclusion, segregation, and isolation from the mainstream," which is a denial of equal benefit of the law. The Identification, Placement and Review Committee argued that the placement was in Emily Eaton's best interests and indeed, given Emily's communication difficulties, leaving her in the regular class would only have the counter-productive effect of isolating and segregating her from her peers. In terms of section 15, the question before the court was this: was Emily Eaton denied an advantage or benefit other children received, or subjected to a disadvantage or burden other children were spared? Does s. 15 not only address discrimination, but also require the state to actively advance equality? When does "special treatment" result in inequality?

Sopinka, J (for the majority):

[5] The issue in this case is whether a decision of the Ontario Special Education Tribunal (the "tribunal") confirming the placement of a disabled child in a special education class contrary to the wishes of her parents contravenes the equality provisions of s. 15(1) of the *Canadian Charter of Rights and Freedoms*. [...]

Does the Decision of the Tribunal Contravene s. 15 of the Charter?

[57] The placement of children in special education programs and services is carried out pursuant to the provisions of the *Education Act*. Prior to 1980, there was no mandatory requirement that school boards provide such programs and a disabled person could be denied status as a resident pupil at elementary school if that person was "unable by reason of mental or physical handicap to profit by instruction in an elementary school." (*The Education Act, 1974*, S.O. 1974, c. 109, s. 34(1)).

[58] A change in attitude with respect to disabled persons was initiated by [The Williston report commissioned by Ontario's Department of Health

in 1971]. With it came the recognition of the desirability of integration and deinstitutionalization. The change in attitude was reflected in changes in the *Education Act*.

[59] The current legal framework for the education of exceptional pupils was adopted [in the 1980 *Education Amendment Act*]. The *Act* and regulations made it mandatory for all school boards to provide special education programs and services for exceptional pupils. The policy of the Ministry of Education is that "[e]very exceptional child has the right to be part of the mainstream of education to the extent to which it is profitable." (*Special Education Information Handbook* [1984]). [...]

[62] While there has not been unanimity in the judgments of the court with respect to all the principles relating to the application of s. 15 of the *Charter*, I believe that the issue in this case can be resolved on the basis of principles in respect of which there is no disagreement. There is general agreement that before a violation of s. 15 can be found, the claimant must establish that the impugned provision creates a distinction on a prohibited or analogous ground which withholds an advantage or benefit from, or imposes a disadvantage or burden on, the claimant. [...]

[66] The principles that not every distinction on a prohibited ground will constitute discrimination and that, in general, distinctions based on presumed rather than actual characteristics are the hallmarks of discrimination have particular significance when applied to physical and mental disability. Avoidance of discrimination on this ground will frequently require distinctions to be made taking into account the actual personal characteristics of disabled persons. In *Andrews v. Law Society of British Columbia*, [1989] 1 S.C.R. 143, at p. 169, McIntrye J. stated that the "accommodation of differences is the true essence of equality." This emphasizes that the purpose of s. 15(1) of the *Charter* is not only to prevent discrimination by the attribution of stereotypical characteristics to individuals, but also to ameliorate the position of groups within Canadian society who have suffered disadvantage by exclusion from mainstream society as has been the case with disabled persons.

[67] The principal object of certain of the prohibited grounds is the elimination of discrimination by the attribution of untrue characteristics based on stereotypical attitudes relating to immutable conditions such as race or sex. In the case of disability, this is one of the objectives. The other equally important objective seeks to take into account the true characteristics of this group which act as headwinds to the enjoyment of society's benefits and to accommodate them. Exclusion from the mainstream of society results from the construction of a society based solely on "mainstream" attributes to which disabled persons will never be able to gain access. Whether it is the impossibility of success at a written test for a blind person, or the need for ramp access to a library, the discrimination does not lie in the attribution of untrue characteristics to the disabled individual. The blind person cannot see and the person in a wheelchair needs a ramp. Rather, it is the failure to make reasonable accommodation, to

fine-tune society so that its structures and assumptions do not result in the relegation and banishment of disabled persons from participation, which results in discrimination against them. The discrimination inquiry which uses "the attribution of stereotypical characteristics" reasoning as commonly understood is simply inappropriate here. It may be seen rather as a case of reverse stereotyping which, by not allowing for the condition of a disabled individual, ignores his or her disability and forces the individual to sink or swim within the mainstream environment. It is recognition of the actual characteristics and reasonable accommodation of these characteristics which is the central purpose of s. 15(1) in relation to disability.

[68] The interplay of these objectives relating to disability is illustrated by the evolution of special education in Ontario. The earlier policy of exclusion to which I referred was influenced in large part by a stereotypical attitude to disabled persons that they could not function in a system designed for the general population. No account was taken of the true characteristics of individual members of the disabled population, nor was any attempt made to accommodate these characteristics. With the change in attitude influenced by the Williston report and other developments, the policy shifted to one which assessed the true characteristics of disabled persons with a view to accommodating them. Integration was the preferred accommodation but if the pupil could not benefit from integration a special program was designed to enable disabled pupils to receive the benefits of education which were available to others.

[69] It follows that disability, as a prohibited ground, differs from other enumerated grounds such as race or sex because there is no individual variation with respect to these grounds. However, with respect to disability, this ground means vastly different things depending upon the individual and the context. This produces, among other things, the "difference dilemma" referred to by the interveners whereby segregation can be both protective of equality and violative of equality depending upon the person and the state of disability. In some cases, special education is a necessary adaptation of the mainstream world which enables some disabled pupils access to the learning environment they need in order to have an equal opportunity in education. While integration should be recognized as the norm of general application because of the benefits it generally provides, a presumption in favour of integrated schooling would work to the disadvantage of pupils who require special education in order to achieve equality. Schools focused on the needs of the blind or deaf, and special education for students with learning disabilities indicate the positive aspects of segregated education placement. Integration can be either a benefit or a burden depending on whether the individual can profit from the advantages that integration provides.

[70] These are the basic principles in respect of which the tribunal's decision should be tested in order to determine whether that decision complies with s. 15(1). [...]

The Tribunal's Decision

A Distinction

[71] It is quite clear that a distinction is being made under the Act between "exceptional" children and others. Other children are placed in the integrated classes. Exceptional children, in some cases, face an inquiry into their placement in the integrated or special classes. It is clear that the distinction between "exceptional" and other children is based on the disability of the individual child.

Burden

[72] In its thorough and careful consideration of this matter, the tribunal sought to determine the placement that would be in the best interests of Emily from the standpoint of receiving the benefits that an education provides. In arriving at the conclusion, the tribunal considered Emily's special needs and strove to fashion a placement that would accommodate those special needs and enable her to benefit from the services that an educational program offers. The tribunal took into account the great psychological benefit that integration offers but found, based on the three years' experience in a regular class, that integration had had "the counter-productive effect of isolating her, of segregating her in the theoretically integrated setting." [...]

[76] The tribunal, therefore, balanced the various educational interests of Emily Eaton, taking into account her special needs, and concluded that the best possible placement was in the special class. [...] Finally, the tribunal stated:

> ...our decision in favour of a special class placement does not relieve the school board and the parents of the obligation to collaborate creatively in a continuing effort to meet her present and future needs. Emily's is so unusual a case that unusual responses may well be necessary for her. Such achievements can only be realized through cooperation, and most important, compromise.

It seems incongruous that a decision reached after such an approach could be considered a burden or a disadvantage imposed on a child. [...]

[78] The Court of Appeal was of the view that the tribunal's reasoning infringed s. 15(1) because the *Charter* mandates a presumption in favour of integration. This presumption is displaced if the parents consent to a segregated placement. This is reflected in the remedy that the Court of Appeal found to be appropriate. Section 8 of the [*Education Amendment Act*, 1980] was to be read to include a direction that, unless the parents of a disabled child consent to the placement of the child in a segregated environment, the presumption applies.

[79] In my view, the application of a test designed to secure what is in the best interests of the child will best achieve that objective if the test is unencumbered by a presumption. The operation of a presumption tends to render proceedings more technical and adversarial. Moreover, there is a risk that in some circumstances, the decision may be made by default rather than on the merits as to

what is in the best interests of the child. I would also question the view that a presumption as to the best interests of a child is a constitutional imperative when the presumption can be automatically displaced by the decision of the child's parents. Such a result runs counter to decisions of this court that the parents' view of their child's best interests is not dispositive of the question. [...]

[80] I conclude that the placement of Emily which was confirmed by the tribunal did not constitute the imposition of a burden or disadvantage nor did it constitute the withholding of a benefit or advantage from the child. Neither the tribunal's order nor its reasoning can be construed as a violation of s. 15(1). [...]

[81] In the result, the appeal is allowed.

Vriend v. Alberta
Supreme Court of Canada
[1998] 1 S.C.R. 493

Delwin Vriend was a college teacher in Alberta whose contract of employment was terminated once he had disclosed to the college that he was homosexual. Under the *Individual's Rights Protection Act (IRPA)*,[1] Alberta's provincial human rights legislation, sexual orientation was not included among the prohibited grounds of discrimination. The question before the Supreme Court was whether the *IRPA* was unconstitutional on the ground that it violated the *Charter* right to equality (s. 15).

At issue before the Court was not only the constitutionality of the exclusion of sexual orientation among the prohibited grounds of discrimination under the *IRPA*, but also the question of the appropriate remedy if the exclusion was found to be unconstitutional. Among the possible options available to the Court regarding the appropriate remedy were to strike down the *IRPA* in its entirety, to declare the unconstitutionality of the offending provisions of the *IRPA* but leave sufficient time for the government of Alberta to remedy the defects, or, more controversially, since it may appear as a quasi-legislative role assumed by the Court, to "read in" sexual orientation among the prohibited grounds already included in the *IRPA*.

The Court was unanimous in its decision that the *IRPA* unjustifiably violated the *Charter* right to equality, and with only one dissenting justice decided to read in sexual orientation among the prohibited grounds of discrimination covered by the *IRPA*.

———————

Cory, J. (for the majority):

[67] The rights enshrined in s. 15(1) of the *Charter* are fundamental to Canada. They reflect the fondest dreams, the highest hopes and finest aspirations of Canadian society. When universal suffrage was granted it recognized to some extent the importance of the individual. Canada by the broad scope and fundamental fairness of the provisions of s. 15(1) has taken a further step in the recognition of the fundamental importance and the innate dignity of

———————

1   Editors' note: The *Individual's Rights Protection Act* has since been renamed as the *Human Rights, Citizenship and Multiculturalism Act*.

the individual. That it has done so is not only praiseworthy but essential to achieving the magnificent goal of equal dignity for all. It is the means of giving Canadians a sense of pride. In order to achieve equality the intrinsic worthiness and importance of every individual must be recognized regardless of the age, sex, colour, origins, or other characteristics of the person. This in turn should lead to a sense of dignity and worthiness for every Canadian and the greatest possible pride and appreciation in being a part of a great nation.

[68] The concept and principle of equality is almost intuitively understood and cherished by all. It is easy to praise these concepts as providing the foundation for a just society which permits every individual to live in dignity and in harmony with all. The difficulty lies in giving real effect to equality. Difficult as the goal of equality may be it is worth the arduous struggle to attain. It is only when equality is a reality that fraternity and harmony will be achieved. It is then that all individuals will truly live in dignity.

[69] It is easy to say that everyone who is just like "us" is entitled to equality. Everyone finds it more difficult to say that those who are "different" from us in some way should have the same equality rights that we enjoy. Yet so soon as we say any enumerated or analogous group is less deserving and unworthy of equal protection and benefit of the law all minorities and all of Canadian society are demeaned. It is so deceptively simple and so devastatingly injurious to say that those who are handicapped or of a different race, or religion, or colour or sexual orientation are less worthy. Yet, if any enumerated or analogous group is denied the equality provided by s. 15 then the equality of every other minority group is threatened. That equality is guaranteed by our constitution. If equality rights for minorities had been recognized, the all too frequent tragedies of history might have been avoided. It can never be forgotten that discrimination is the antithesis of equality and that it is the recognition of equality which will foster the dignity of every individual.

[...]

[99] Apart from the immediate effect of the denial of recourse in cases of discrimination, there are other effects which, while perhaps less obvious, are at least as harmful. In *Haig*, the Ontario Court of Appeal based its finding of discrimination on both the "failure to provide an avenue for redress for prejudicial treatment of homosexual members of society" and "the possible inference from the omission that such treatment is acceptable" (p. 503). It can be reasonably inferred that the absence of any legal recourse for discrimination on the ground of sexual orientation perpetuates and even encourages that kind of discrimination. The respondents contend that it cannot be assumed that the "silence" of the *IRPA* reinforces or perpetuates discrimination, since governments "cannot legislate attitudes." However, this argument seems disingenuous in light of the stated purpose of the *IRPA*, to prevent discrimination. It cannot be claimed that human rights legislation will help to protect individuals from discrimination, and at the same time contend that an exclusion from the legislation will have no effect.

[100] However, let us assume, contrary to all reasonable inferences, that exclusion from the *IRPA's* protection does not actually contribute to a greater incidence of discrimination on the excluded ground. Nonetheless that exclusion, deliberately chosen in the face of clear findings that discrimination on the ground of sexual orientation does exist in society, sends a strong and sinister message. The very fact that sexual orientation is excluded from the *IRPA*, which is the Government's primary statement of policy against discrimination, certainly suggests that discrimination on the ground of sexual orientation is not as serious or as deserving of condemnation as other forms of discrimination. It could well be said that it is tantamount to condoning or even encouraging discrimination against lesbians and gay men. Thus this exclusion clearly gives rise to an effect which constitutes discrimination.

[101] The exclusion sends a message to all Albertans that it is permissible, and perhaps even acceptable, to discriminate against individuals on the basis of their sexual orientation. The effect of that message on gays and lesbians is one whose significance cannot be underestimated. As a practical matter, it tells them that they have no protection from discrimination on the basis of their sexual orientation. Deprived of any legal redress they must accept and live in constant fear of discrimination. These are burdens which are not imposed on heterosexuals.

[102] Perhaps most important is the psychological harm which may ensue from this state of affairs. Fear of discrimination will logically lead to concealment of true identity and this must be harmful to personal confidence and self-esteem. Compounding that effect is the implicit message conveyed by the exclusion, that gays and lesbians, unlike other individuals, are not worthy of protection. This is clearly an example of a distinction which demeans the individual and strengthens and perpetuates the view that gays and lesbians are less worthy of protection as individuals in Canada's society. The potential harm to the dignity and perceived worth of gay and lesbian individuals constitutes a particularly cruel form of discrimination.

[103] Even if the discrimination is experienced at the hands of private individuals, it is the state that denies protection from that discrimination. Thus the adverse effects are particularly invidious. This was recognized in the following statement from *Egan* (at para. 161):

> The law confers a significant benefit by providing state recognition of the legitimacy of a particular status. The denial of that recognition may have a serious detrimental effect upon the sense of self-worth and dignity of members of a group because it stigmatizes them.... Such legislation would clearly infringe s. 15(1) because its provisions would indicate that the excluded groups were inferior and less deserving of benefits.

This reasoning applies *a fortiori* in a case such as this where the denial of recognition involves something as fundamental as the right to be free from discrimination.

[104] In excluding sexual orientation from the *IRPA*'s protection, the Government has, in effect, stated that "all persons are equal in dignity and rights," except gay men and lesbians. Such a message, even if it is only implicit, must offend s. 15(1), the "section of the *Charter*, more than any other, which recognizes and cherishes the innate human dignity of every individual" (*Egan*, at para. 128). This effect, together with the denial to individuals of any effective legal recourse in the event they are discriminated against on the ground of sexual orientation, amount to a sufficient basis on which to conclude that the distinction created by the exclusion from the *IRPA* constitutes discrimination. [...]

[107] In summary, this Court has no choice but to conclude that the *IRPA*, by reason of the omission of sexual orientation as a protected ground, clearly violates s. 15 of the *Charter*. The *IRPA* in its underinclusive state creates a distinction which results in the denial of the equal benefit and protection of the law on the basis of sexual orientation, a personal characteristic which has been found to be analogous to the grounds enumerated in s. 15. This, in itself, would be sufficient to conclude that discrimination is present and therefore there is a violation of s. 15. The serious discriminatory effects of the exclusion of sexual orientation from the Act reinforce this conclusion. As a result, it is clear that the *IRPA*, as it stands, violates the equality rights of the appellant Vriend and of other gays and lesbians. [...]

Iacobucci, J. (concurring):

Remedy

Introduction: The Relationship between the Legislatures and the Courts under the Charter

[129] Having found the exclusion of sexual orientation from the *IRPA* to be an unjustifiable violation of the appellants' equality rights, I now turn to the question of remedy under s. 52 of the *Constitution Act, 1982*. Before discussing the jurisprudence on remedies, I believe it might be helpful to pause to reflect more broadly on the general issue of the relationship between legislatures and the courts in the age of the *Charter*.

[130] Much was made in argument before us about the inadvisability of the Court interfering with or otherwise meddling in what is regarded as the proper role of the legislature, which in this case was to decide whether or not sexual orientation would be added to Alberta's human rights legislation. Indeed, it seems that hardly a day goes by without some comment or criticism to the effect that under the *Charter* courts are wrongfully usurping the role of the legislatures. I believe this allegation misunderstands what took place and what was intended when our country adopted the *Charter* in 1981–82.

[131] When the *Charter* was introduced, Canada went, in the words of former Chief Justice Brian Dickson, from a system of Parliamentary supremacy

to constitutional supremacy ("Keynote Address," in *The Cambridge Lectures 1985* [1985], at pp. 3–4). Simply put, each Canadian was given individual rights and freedoms which no government or legislature could take away. However, as rights and freedoms are not absolute, governments and legislatures could justify the qualification or infringement of these constitutional rights under s. 1 as I previously discussed. Inevitably disputes over the meaning of the rights and their justification would have to be settled and here the role of the judiciary enters to resolve these disputes. Many countries have assigned the important role of judicial review to their supreme or constitutional courts. [...]

[132] We should recall that it was the deliberate choice of our provincial and federal legislatures in adopting the *Charter* to assign an interpretive role to the courts and to command them under s. 52 to declare unconstitutional legislation invalid.

[133] However, giving courts the power and commandment to invalidate legislation where necessary has not eliminated the debate over the "legitimacy" of courts taking such action. As eloquently put by A.M. Bickel in his outstanding work *The Least Dangerous Branch: The Supreme Court at the Bar of Politics* (2nd ed. 1986), "it thwarts the will of representatives of the...people" (p. 17). So judicial review, it is alleged, is illegitimate because it is antidemocratic in that unelected officials (judges) are overruling elected representatives (legislators). [...]

[134] To respond, it should be emphasized again that our *Charter*'s introduction and the consequential remedial role of the courts were choices of the Canadian people through their elected representatives as part of a redefinition of our democracy. Our constitutional design was refashioned to state that henceforth the legislatures and executive must perform their roles in conformity with the newly conferred constitutional rights and freedoms. That the courts were the trustees of these rights insofar as disputes arose concerning their interpretation was a necessary part of this new design.

[135] So courts in their trustee or arbiter role must perforce scrutinize the work of the legislature and executive not in the name of the courts, but in the interests of the new social contract that was democratically chosen. All of this is implied in the power given to the courts under s. 24 of the *Charter* and s. 52 of the *Constitution Act, 1982*.

[136] Because the courts are independent from the executive and legislature, litigants and citizens generally can rely on the courts to make reasoned and principled decisions according to the dictates of the constitution even though specific decisions may not be universally acclaimed. In carrying out their duties, courts are not to second-guess legislatures and the executives; they are not to make value judgments on what they regard as the proper policy choice; this is for the other branches. Rather, the courts are to uphold the Constitution and have been expressly invited to perform that role by the Constitution itself. But respect by the courts for the legislature and executive role is as important as ensuring that the other branches respect each others' role and the role of the courts. [...]

[138] As I view the matter, the Charter has given rise to a more dynamic interaction among the branches of governance. This interaction has been aptly described as a "dialogue" by some (see e.g., Hogg and Bushell, *supra*). In reviewing legislative enactments and executive decisions to ensure constitutional validity, the courts speak to the legislative and executive branches. As has been pointed out, most of the legislation held not to pass constitutional muster has been followed by new legislation designed to accomplish similar objectives (see Hogg and Bushell, *supra*, at p. 82). By doing this, the legislature responds to the courts; hence the dialogue among the branches.

[139] To my mind, a great value of judicial review and this dialogue among the branches is that each of the branches is made somewhat accountable to the other. The work of the legislature is reviewed by the courts and the work of the court in its decisions can be reacted to by the legislature in the passing of new legislation (or even overarching laws under s. 33 of the *Charter*). This dialogue between and accountability of each of the branches have the effect of enhancing the democratic process, not denying it.

[140] There is also another aspect of judicial review that promotes democratic values. Although a court's invalidation of legislation usually involves negating the will of the majority, we must remember that the concept of democracy is broader than the notion of majority rule, fundamental as that may be. In this respect, we would do well to heed the words of Dickson C.J. in *Oakes*, *supra*, at p. 136:

> The Court must be guided by the values and principles essential to a free and democratic society which I believe to embody, to name but a few, respect for the inherent dignity of the human person, commitment to social justice and equality, accommodation of a wide variety of beliefs, respect for cultural and group identity, and faith in social and political institutions which enhance the participation of individuals and groups in society.

[141] So, for example, when a court interprets legislation alleged to be a reasonable limitation in a free and democratic society as stated in s. 1 of the *Charter*, the court must inevitably delineate some of the attributes of a democratic society. Although it is not necessary to articulate the complete list of democratic attributes in these remarks, Dickson C.J.'s comments remain instructive. [...]

[142] Democratic values and principles under the *Charter* demand that legislators and the executive take these into account; and if they fail to do so, courts should stand ready to intervene to protect these democratic values as appropriate. As others have so forcefully stated, judges are not acting undemocratically by intervening when there are indications that a legislative or executive decision was not reached in accordance with the democratic principles mandated by the *Charter*. [...]

[143] With this background in mind, I now turn to discuss the jurisprudence on the specific question of the choice of the appropriate remedy that should apply in this appeal.

Remedial Principles

[144] The leading case on constitutional remedies is *Schachter, supra*. Writing on behalf of the majority in *Schachter*, Lamer C.J. stated that the first step in selecting a remedial course under s. 52 is to define the extent of the *Charter* inconsistency which must be struck down. In the present case, that inconsistency is the exclusion of sexual orientation from the protected grounds of the *IRPA*. As I have concluded above, this exclusion is an unjustifiable infringement upon the equality rights guaranteed in s. 15 of the *Charter*.

[145] Once the Charter inconsistency has been identified, the next step is to determine which remedy is appropriate. In *Schachter*, this Court noted that, depending upon the circumstances, there are several remedial options available to a court in dealing with a *Charter* violation that was not saved by s. 1. These include striking down the legislation, severance of the offending sections, striking down or severance with a temporary suspension of the declaration of invalidity, reading down, and reading provisions into the legislation.

[146] Because the *Charter* violation in the instant case stems from an omission, the remedy of reading down is simply not available. Further, I note that given the considerable number of sections at issue in this case and the important roles they play in the scheme of the *IRPA* as a whole, severance of these sections from the remainder of the Act would be akin to striking down the entire Act.

[147] The appellants suggest that the circumstances of this case warrant the reading in of sexual orientation into the offending sections of the *IRPA*. However, in the Alberta Court of Appeal, O'Leary J.A. and Hunt J.A. agreed that the appropriate remedy would be to declare the relevant provisions of the *IRPA* unconstitutional and to suspend that declaration for a period of time to allow the Legislature to address the matter. McClung J.A. would have gone further and declared the *IRPA* invalid in its entirety. With respect, for the reasons that follow, I cannot agree with either remedy chosen by the Court of Appeal.

[148] In *Schachter*, Lamer C.J. noted that when determining whether the remedy of reading in is appropriate, courts must have regard to the "twin guiding principles," namely, respect for the role of the legislature and respect for the purposes of the *Charter*, which I have discussed generally above. Turning first to the role of the legislature, Lamer C.J. stated at p. 700 that reading in is an important tool in "avoiding undue intrusion into the legislative sphere.... [T]he purpose of reading in is to be as faithful as possible within the requirements of the Constitution to the scheme enacted by the Legislature." [...]

[150] As I discussed above, the purpose of the *IRPA* is the recognition and protection of the inherent dignity and inalienable rights of Albertans through the elimination of discriminatory practices. It seems to me that the remedy of reading in would minimize interference with this clearly legitimate legislative purpose and thereby avoid excessive intrusion into the legislative sphere whereas striking down the *IRPA* would deprive all Albertans of human rights protection and thereby unduly interfere with the scheme enacted by the Legislature.

Law v. Canada (Minister of Employment and Immigration)
Supreme Court of Canada
[1999] 1 S.C.R. 497

This case involves survivor's benefits under the Canada Pension Plan. The appellant was only 30 years old when she was widowed, but under the Plan, her benefits (since she was neither disabled nor had dependent children) were substantially less than had she been widowed later in her life. The Pension Appeals Board concluded that the Plan's age distinctions did not violate her equality rights, and the Supreme Court agreed. Justice Iacobucci, writing for a unanimous Court, took the opportunity to summarize and comment upon the Post-*Andrews* jurisprudence on s. 15 equality rights and anti-discrimination law, in order "to provide a set of guidelines for courts that are called upon to analyze a discrimination claim under the *Charter*."

The appellant, a 30-year-old woman without dependent children or disability, was denied survivor's benefits under the Canada Pension Plan (CPP). The CPP gradually reduces the survivor's pension for able-bodied surviving spouses without dependent children who are between the ages of 35 and 45 by 1/120th of the full rate for each month that the claimant's age is less than 45 years at the time of the contributor's death so that the threshold age to receive benefits is age 35. The appellant unsuccessfully appealed first to the Minister of National Health and Welfare and then to the Pension Plan Review Tribunal, arguing that these age distinctions discriminated against her on the basis of age contrary to s. 15(1) of the *Canadian Charter of Rights and Freedoms*. A further appeal was made to the Pension Appeals Board, which, in a trial *de novo*, concluded that the impugned age distinctions did not violate the appellant's equality rights. The majority of the Board also found that, even if the distinctions did infringe s. 15(1) of the *Charter*, they could be justified under s. 1. A subsequent appeal to the Federal Court of Appeal was dismissed largely for the reasons of the Pension Appeals Board. The constitutional questions here queried whether ss. 44(1)(*d*) and 58 of the *Canada Pension Plan* infringe s. 15(1) of the *Charter* on the ground that they discriminate on the basis of age against widows and widowers under the age of 45, and if so, whether this infringement is demonstrably justified in a free and democratic society under s. 1.

Held: The appeal should be dismissed. The first constitutional question should be answered in the negative; the second constitutional question did not need to be answered.

Justice Iacobucci (for the majority):

[2] Section 15 of the *Charter* guarantees to every individual the right to equal treatment by the state without discrimination. It is perhaps the *Charter*'s most conceptually difficult provision. In this Court's first s. 15 case, *Andrews*, McIntyre J. noted that, as embodied in s. 15(1) of the *Charter*, the concept of equality is "an elusive concept," and that "more than any of the other rights and freedoms guaranteed in the *Charter*, it lacks precise definition." Part of the difficulty in defining the concept of equality stems from its exalted status. The quest for equality expresses some of humanity's highest ideals and aspirations, which are by their nature abstract and subject to differing articulations. The challenge for the judiciary in interpreting and applying s. 15(1) of the *Charter* is to transform these ideals and aspirations into practice in a manner which is meaningful to Canadians and which accords with the purpose of the provision. [...]

[42] What is the purpose of the s. 15(1) equality guarantee? There is great continuity in the jurisprudence of this Court on this issue. [...]

[51]...[T]he purpose of s. 15(1) is to prevent the violation of essential human dignity and freedom through the imposition of disadvantage, stereotyping, or political or social prejudice, and to promote a society in which all persons enjoy equal recognition at law as human beings or as members of Canadian society, equally capable and equally deserving of concern, respect and consideration. Legislation which effects differential treatment between individuals or groups will violate this fundamental purpose where those who are subject to differential treatment fall within one or more enumerated or analogous grounds, and where the differential treatment reflects the stereotypical application of presumed group or personal characteristics, or otherwise has the effect of perpetuating or promoting the view that the individual is less capable, or less worthy of recognition or value as a human being or as a member of Canadian society. Alternatively, differential treatment will not likely constitute discrimination within the purpose of s. 15(1) where it does not violate the human dignity or freedom of a person or group in this way, and in particular where the differential treatment also assists in ameliorating the position of the disadvantaged within Canadian society. [...]

[53] What is human dignity? There can be different conceptions of what human dignity means. For the purpose of analysis under s. 15(1) of the *Charter*, however, the jurisprudence of this Court reflects a specific, albeit non-exhaustive, definition. As noted by Lamer C.J. in *Rodriguez*, the equality guarantee in s. 15(1) is concerned with the realization of personal autonomy and self-determination. Human dignity means that an individual or group feels self-respect and self-worth. It is concerned with physical and psychological integrity and empowerment. Human dignity is harmed by unfair treatment premised upon personal traits or circumstances which do not relate to individual needs, capacities, or merits. It is enhanced by laws which are sensitive to the needs, capacities, and merits of different individuals, taking into account the context

underlying their differences. Human dignity is harmed when individuals and groups are marginalized, ignored, or devalued, and is enhanced when laws recognize the full place of all individuals and groups within Canadian society. Human dignity within the meaning of the equality guarantee does not relate to the status or position of an individual in society *per se*, but rather concerns the manner in which a person legitimately feels when confronted with a particular law. Does the law treat him or her unfairly, taking into account all of the circumstances regarding the individuals affected and excluded by the law?

[54] The equality guarantee in s. 15(1) of the *Charter* must be understood and applied in light of the above understanding of its purpose. The overriding concern with protecting and promoting human dignity in the sense just described infuses all elements of the discrimination analysis. [...]

[88] [...] I believe it would be useful to summarize some of the main guidelines for analysis under s. 15(1) to be derived from the jurisprudence of this Court, as reviewed in these reasons. As I stated above, these guidelines should not be seen as a strict test, but rather should be understood as points of reference for a court that is called upon to decide whether a claimant's right to equality without discrimination under the *Charter* has been infringed. Inevitably, the guidelines summarized here will need to be supplemented in practice by the explanation of these guidelines in these reasons and those of previous cases, and by a full appreciation of the context surrounding the specific s. 15(1) claim at issue. It goes without saying that as our s. 15 jurisprudence evolves it may well be that further elaborations and modifications will emerge.

General Approach

(1) It is inappropriate to attempt to confine analysis under s. 15(1) of the *Charter* to a fixed and limited formula. A purposive and contextual approach to discrimination analysis is to be preferred, in order to permit the realization of the strong remedial purpose of the equality guarantee, and to avoid the pitfalls of a formalistic or mechanical approach.

(2) The approach adopted and regularly applied by this Court to the interpretation of s. 15(1) focuses upon three central issues:

(A) whether a law imposes differential treatment between the claimant and others, in purpose or effect;

(B) whether one or more enumerated or analogous grounds of discrimination are the basis for the differential treatment; and

(C) whether the law in question has a purpose or effect that is discriminatory within the meaning of the equality guarantee.

The first issue is concerned with the question of whether the law causes differential treatment. The second and third issues are concerned with whether the differential treatment constitutes discrimination in the substantive sense intended by s. 15(1).

(3) Accordingly, a court that is called upon to determine a discrimination claim under s. 15(1) should make the following three broad inquiries:

(A) Does the impugned law (a) draw a formal distinction between the claimant and others on the basis of one or more personal characteristics, or (b) fail to take into account the claimant's already disadvantaged position within Canadian society resulting in substantively differential treatment between the claimant and others on the basis of one or more personal characteristics?

(B) Is the claimant subject to differential treatment based on one or more enumerated and analogous grounds?

and

(C) Does the differential treatment discriminate, by imposing a burden upon or withholding a benefit from the claimant in a manner which reflects the stereotypical application of presumed group or personal characteristics, or which otherwise has the effect of perpetuating or promoting the view that the individual is less capable or worthy of recognition or value as a human being or as a member of Canadian society, equally deserving of concern, respect, and consideration?

Purpose

(4) In general terms, the purpose of s. 15(1) is to prevent the violation of essential human dignity and freedom through the imposition of disadvantage, stereotyping, or political or social prejudice, and to promote a society in which all persons enjoy equal recognition at law as human beings or as members of Canadian society, equally capable and equally deserving of concern, respect and consideration.

(5) The existence of a conflict between the purpose or effect of an impugned law and the purpose of s. 15(1) is essential in order to found a discrimination claim. The determination of whether such a conflict exists is to be made through an analysis of the full context surrounding the claim and the claimant.

Comparative Approach

(6) The equality guarantee is a comparative concept, which ultimately requires a court to establish one or more relevant comparators. The claimant generally chooses the person, group, or groups with whom he or she wishes to be compared for the purpose of the discrimination inquiry. However, where the claimant's characterization of the comparison is insufficient, a court may, within the scope of the ground or grounds pleaded, refine the comparison presented by the claimant where warranted. Locating the relevant comparison group requires an examination of the subject-matter of the legislation and its effects, as well as a full appreciation of context.

Context

(7) The contextual factors which determine whether legislation has the effect of demeaning a claimant's dignity must be construed and examined from the perspective of the claimant. The focus of the inquiry is both subjective and objective. The relevant point of view is that of the reasonable person, in circumstances similar to those of the claimant, who takes into account the contextual factors relevant to the claim.

(8) There is a variety of factors which may be referred to by a s. 15(1) claimant in order to demonstrate that legislation demeans his or her dignity. The list of factors is not closed. Guidance as to these factors may be found in the jurisprudence of this Court, and by analogy to recognized factors.

(9) Some important contextual factors influencing the determination of whether s. 15(1) has been infringed are, among others:

(A) Pre-existing disadvantage, stereotyping, prejudice, or vulnerability experienced by the individual or group at issue. The effects of a law as they relate to the important purpose of s. 15(1) in protecting individuals or groups who are vulnerable, disadvantaged, or members of "discrete and insular minorities" should always be a central consideration. Although the claimant's association with a historically more advantaged or disadvantaged group or groups is not *per se* determinative of an infringement, the existence of these pre-existing factors will favour a finding that s. 15(1) has been infringed.

(B) The correspondence, or lack thereof, between the ground or grounds on which the claim is based and the actual need, capacity, or circumstances of the claimant or others. Although the mere fact that the impugned legislation takes into account the claimant's traits or circumstances will not necessarily be sufficient to defeat a s. 15(1) claim, it will generally be more difficult to establish discrimination to the extent that the law takes into account the claimant's actual situation in a manner that respects his or her value as a human being or member of Canadian society, and less difficult to do so where the law fails to take into account the claimant's actual situation.

(C) The ameliorative purpose or effects of the impugned law upon a more disadvantaged person or group in society. An ameliorative purpose or effect which accords with the purpose of s. 15(1) of the *Charter* will likely not violate the human dignity of more advantaged individuals where the exclusion of these more advantaged individuals largely corresponds to the greater need or the different circumstances experienced by the disadvantaged group being targeted by the legislation. This factor is more relevant where the s. 15(1) claim is brought by a more advantaged member of society.

and

(D) The nature and scope of the interest affected by the impugned law. The more severe and localized the consequences of the legislation for the affected group, the more likely that the differential treatment responsible for these consequences is discriminatory within the meaning of s. 15(1).

(10) Although the s. 15(1) claimant bears the onus of establishing an infringement of his or her equality rights in a purposive sense through reference to one or more contextual factors, it is not necessarily the case that the claimant must adduce evidence in order to show a violation of human dignity or freedom. Frequently, where differential treatment is based on one or more enumerated or analogous grounds, this will be sufficient to found an infringement of s. 15(1) in the sense that it will be evident on the basis of judicial notice and logical reasoning that the distinction is discriminatory within the meaning of the provision.

Reference Re ss. 193 and 195.1(1)(c) of the Criminal Code (Man.)
Supreme Court of Canada
[1990] 1 S.C.R. 1123

In this case the Supreme Court considers the boundaries of the protection of freedom of expression, answering questions sent to it as a reference matter by the province of Manitoba. At issue is the question of whether the scope of protection of freedom of expression extends to offers of sexual services and to operation of a brothel—matters prohibited in various ways by criminal law. The majority find that the *Criminal Code* provisions brought to the Court are justified as reasonable limits according to the s. 1 *Oakes* test. Justice Wilson and Justice L'Heureux-Dubé, dissenting, provide another view. They agree that the operation of a brothel does not amount to expression protected by the *Charter*, yet find that criminal prohibition of the expression seen in offering of sexual services is protected by the *Charter* and is not reasonably limited by the section of the *Criminal Code* at issue. In the difference between majority and minority opinions, the Court shows how judges may reasonably disagree in their assessment of the social context in which the goals of legislation run up against constitutional guarantees regarding the intrusion of the state into the lives of citizens. It is worth reading this case in conjunction with *Canada (Attorney General) v. Bedford*, also excerpted in this Part, to see how over time the same activity—offering sexual services—has come to be quite differently regarded by the Court. In the more than twenty years between the two decisions, social views have changed, enabling development of broader ways of understanding the lives of sex workers as persons whose expression of offers of sexual services occurs in the context of additional interests subject to legal protection, such as the right to security of the person. Seen in this light, cases treating freedom of expression and security of the person may together be viewed as engaging the question of equality as a fundamental social and legal value.

Dickson C.J. (for the majority):

I have had the advantage of reading the reasons of my colleagues, Justice Lamer and Justice Wilson. I agree, for the reasons given by Wilson J., that s. 195.1(1)(c) of the *Criminal Code*, R.S.C. 1970, c. C34, represents a *prima facie* infringement of s. 2 (*b*) of the *Canadian Charter of Rights and Freedoms*, while s. 193 does not. In my view, the scope of freedom of expression does extend to the activity of communication for the purpose of engaging in prostitution. With respect, however, I disagree with the conclusion reached by Wilson J. that this *prima facie* infringement is not justified as a reasonable limit under s. 1 of the *Charter*. On this issue, I reach the same conclusion as Lamer J., but prefer to rest my conclusion on an analysis which differs from that of my colleague.

[...]

Justice Lamer (concurring):

In my view then, the section at issue does impair freedom of expression as little as reasonably possible in order to achieve the legislative objective. Parliament was faced with a myriad of views and options from which to choose in respect of dealing with the problem of street solicitation for the purpose of prostitution. The role of this Court is not to second-guess the wisdom of policy choices made by our legislators. Prostitution, and specifically, the solicitation for the purpose thereof, is an especially contentious and at times morally laden issue, requiring the weighing of competing political pressures. The issue for this Court to determine is not whether Parliament has weighed those pressures and interests wisely, but rather whether the limit they have imposed on a *Charter* right or freedom is reasonable and justified. Parliament chose to enact s. 195.1 to deal with what was clearly viewed as a pressing and substantial social problem. It has done so in a way that is rationally connected to the legislative objective, and furthermore in a way that has specific regard for the place and purpose of the communication, thereby demonstrating a concern for limiting the impairment of expression to that which is minimally necessary to achieve the objective. Therefore, I conclude that s. 195.1(1)(*c*) satisfies the first two components of the proportionality test under s. 1 of the *Charter*. [...]

[...] [I]n weighing the serious social harms caused by public solicitation for the purpose of prostitution against the restriction on expression, I find that the challenged section is not disproportionate with its effects. In addition, it should be noted that concerns about the wisdom or effectiveness of the section have been taken into account by Parliament. The Act that amended the *Criminal Code* to enact the current s. 195.1 includes within it s. 2 which mandates that a comprehensive review of the provisions is to be undertaken by a committee of the House of Commons three years from the date of enactment, with a report on the review to be tabled in the House of Commons including a statement of any changes the committee recommends: see S.C. 1985, c. 50, s. 2. In summary then, when one weighs the nature of the legislative objective against the extent of the restriction on the freedom in question, there is no disproportionality.

[...]

Justice Wilson (dissenting):

Ms. Bennett submits that ss. 193 and 195.1(1)(*c*), both singly and together, violate s. 7 because they are too vague. While legislative provisions that are so vague as to be unintelligible to the citizen may well fail to accord with the principle of fundamental justice that requires persons to be given clear notice of that which is prohibited, in my view neither s. 193 nor s. 195.1(1)(*c*), read on their own or together, are so vague as to violate the requirement that the criminal law be clear. It is true that this Court has been called upon to interpret some of the terms used in these sections: see, for example, this Court's discussion of the term "common bawdyhouse" in *R. v. Cohen*, [1939] S.C.R. 212, and in *Patterson v. The Queen*, [1968] S.C.R. 157. This does not mean, however, that the legislation is so vague as to fail to accord with fundamental justice. The courts are regularly called upon to resolve ambiguities in legislation but this does not necessarily make such legislation vulnerable to constitutional attack.

In my view, the language of s. 195.1(1)(*c*) prohibits communication for the purposes of engaging in prostitution or of obtaining the sexual services of a prostitute. While I have previously noted that the wording of the provision may lead police officers to detain people on the mistaken assumption that they were communicating for the prohibited purposes, this does not mean that the section does not send a clear message to the citizen that communicating for those purposes is prohibited. Similarly, the fact that s. 193 does not itemize every situation that falls within the ambit of the prohibition against keeping a common bawdyhouse does not mean that citizens reading the provision will not know that they risk criminal sanctions if they are operating or found on premises used for the purpose of exchanging sex for money. Finally, while the combination of s. 193 and s. 195.1(1)(*c*) may seriously constrain the prostitute in the way in which he or she is able to carry on business, and may even make it difficult for the prostitute to know what avenues are left open to him or her, this does not necessarily mean that the provisions themselves, either individually or together, are not clear.

It is my view, however, that an infringement of a person's right to liberty cannot be said to accord with the principles of fundamental justice where the conduct alleged to constitute the infringement violates another *Charter* guarantee. My colleague Lamer J. observed in *Re B.C. Motor Vehicle Act*, *supra*, at p. 503:

> In other words, the principles of fundamental justice are to be found in the basic tenets of our legal system. They do not lie in the realm of general public policy but in the inherent domain of the judiciary as guardian of the justice system.

While the *Charter* reflects a number of principles which have traditionally been part of our legal system, it also gives specific constitutional protection to other principles which are now an integral part of our legal system. These are just as much, if not more so, "basic tenets of our legal system" and required to be protected by the judiciary. This Court emphasized in *Hunter v. Southam Inc.*, [1984] 2 S.C.R. 145, at p. 155, that "[t]he judiciary is the guardian of the constitution" and in *Oakes, supra*, at p. 135, Dickson C.J. expressed agreement with the proposition stated in *Singh v. Minister of Employment and Immigration*, [1985] 1 S.C.R. 177, at p. 218, that:

> . . . it is important to remember that the courts are conducting this inquiry [under s. 1] in light of a commitment to uphold the rights and freedoms set out in the other sections of the *Charter*.

The rights guaranteed in the *Charter* "do not," to quote Lamer J., "lie in the realm of general public policy." They are the laws of the land. Indeed, this Court pointed out in its very first *Charter* case, *Law Society of Upper Canada v. Skapinker*, [1984] 1 S.C.R. 357, at p. 366, that the *Charter* "is part of the fabric of Canadian law. Indeed, it 'is the supreme law of Canada.'"

In my view, it follows from these propositions that a law that infringes the right to liberty under s. 7 in a way that also infringes another constitutionally entrenched right (which infringement is not saved by s. 1) cannot be said to accord with the principles of fundamental justice. It must therefore be justified as a reasonable limit under s. 1 of the *Charter*.

I have already concluded that s. 195.1(1)(*c*) violates s. 2 (*b*) of the *Charter* because it violates the *Charter*'s guarantee of the right to freedom of expression and that it is not saved by s. 1. But s. 195.1(1)(*c*) also infringes a person's right to liberty by providing that those who communicate for the prohibited purposes may be sent to prison. In my view, a person cannot be sent to prison for exercising his or her constitutionally protected right to freedom of expression. This is clearly not in accordance with the principles of fundamental justice.

I noted in discussing s. 2 (*b*) that s. 193, either on its own or in combination with s. 195.1(1)(*c*), does not violate a person's right to freedom of expression. While s. 193 infringes a person's right to liberty through the threat of imprisonment, absent the infringement of some other *Charter* guarantee, this particular deprivation of liberty does not, in my view, violate a principle of fundamental justice. Nor are s. 193 and s. 195.1(1)(*c*) so intimately linked as to be part of a single legislative scheme enabling one to say that because part of the scheme violates a principle of fundamental justice the whole scheme violates that principle. I conclude therefore that no principle of fundamental justice is violated by s. 193 or the combination of ss. 193 and 195.1(1)(*c*).

Section 1 of the Charter

Where a legislative provision violates more than one section of the *Charter*, as I have found to be the case with s. 195.1(1)(*c*) of the *Criminal Code*, it may not be possible to provide a single answer to the question whether the legislation constitutes a reasonable limit justifiable under s. 1 of the *Charter*. This is because the nature of the justification will depend at least in part on the right which is being limited. Thus, in some instances legislation may limit one *Charter* right in a way that can be justified under s. 1 and at the same time limit another *Charter* right in a way that cannot be justified under s. 1. I make this point simply to emphasize that one cannot assume that the basis of justification under s. 1 will be the same in both instances. It is not enough, in other words, for the government to justify a breach of one *Charter* guarantee under s. 1. It must justify the breach of the other *Charter* guarantee as well.

In this case the respondent and each of the Attorneys General made the same submissions in support of s. 195.1(1)(*c*) as a reasonable limit on s. 7 as they made in its support as a reasonable limit on s. 2 (*b*).

I agree that their submissions as to the existence of a pressing and substantial concern and as to the rational connection between that concern and the impugned legislation are equally valid in relation to the infringement of the s. 7 right. The test of proportionality may, however, be different.

The question in relation to the s. 2 (*b*) infringement was whether it was reasonable and justifiable to limit freedom of expression in the broad terms of s. 195.1(1)(*c*) in order to deal with the nuisance caused by street solicitation. I concluded that it was not. The section was too broad. The question in relation to the s. 7 infringement, it seems to me, is whether it is reasonable and justifiable to deprive citizens of their liberty through imprisonment in order to deal with the nuisance caused by street solicitation. Again I conclude that it is not. It seems to me that where communication is a lawful (and, indeed, a constitutionally protected) activity and prostitution is also a lawful activity, the legislative response of imprisonment is far too drastic. I indicated elsewhere my view that an infringement of liberty which violates the principles of fundamental justice must be very difficult, if not impossible, to justify as a reasonable limit under s. 1. My colleague Lamer J. suggests in *Re B.C. Motor Vehicle Act, supra*, at p. 518, that it may be possible "in cases arising out of exceptional conditions, such as natural disasters, the outbreak of war, epidemics, and the like."

Be that as it may, it seems to me that to imprison people for exercising their constitutionally protected freedom of expression, even if they are exercising it for purposes of prostitution (which is not itself prohibited), is not a proportionate way of dealing with the public or social nuisance at which the legislation is aimed. I conclude, therefore, that s. 195.1(1)(*c*) violates s. 7 of the *Charter* and is not saved by s. 1.

Canada (Attorney General) v. Bedford
Supreme Court of Canada
[2013] 3 S.C.R 1101

This case is usefully read together with the excerpt from *Reference re ss. 193 and 195.1(1)(c) of the Criminal Code (Man.)*, a 1990 reference case also provided in this Part. In 1990, the Supreme Court was asked to determine whether a *Criminal Code* prohibition of communication regarding sale of sexual services and operation of a brothel amounted to reasonable limits on the right to freedom of expression. In the intervening years, social understanding of what is now known as "sex work" and "sex workers" has changed. New arguments have reached the Court, asking it to declare invalid several laws criminalizing activities associated with the legally permitted sale of sexual services. The effect of those laws, it is argued, is to deprive sex workers of the right to security of the person, so those laws must be invalidated as unconstitutional. The Court's decision is striking: it makes a "suspended declaration of invalidity" leaving the laws temporarily valid while Parliament finds another way to regulate sex work in a constitutionally valid manner. In reasoning regarding the nature of the right to security of the person, the Court examines the meaning of the idea of fundamental justice as a "qualifier" to the right to security of the person, with particular attention to the requirement that law not be arbitrary, overbroad, or disproportionate in its effects relative to its goals.

Chief Justice McLachlin (for the majority):

[1] It is not a crime in Canada to sell sex for money. However, it is a crime to keep a bawdy-house, to live on the avails of prostitution or to communicate in public with respect to a proposed act of prostitution. It is argued that these restrictions on prostitution put the safety and lives of prostitutes at risk, and are therefore unconstitutional.

[2] These appeals and the cross-appeal are not about whether prostitution should be legal or not. They are about whether the laws Parliament has enacted on how prostitution may be carried out pass constitutional muster. I conclude that they do not. I would therefore make a suspended declaration of invalidity, returning the question of how to deal with prostitution to Parliament.

[...]

Principles of Fundamental Justice

The Applicable Norms

[93] I have concluded that the impugned laws deprive prostitutes of security of the person, engaging s. 7. The remaining step in the s. 7 analysis is to determine whether this deprivation is in accordance with the principles of fundamental justice. If so, s. 7 is not breached.

[94] The principles of fundamental justice set out the minimum requirements that a law that negatively impacts on a person's life, liberty, or security of the person must meet. As Lamer J. put it, "[t]he term 'principles of fundamental justice' is not a right, but a qualifier of the right not to be deprived of life, liberty and security of the person; its function is to set the parameters of that right" (*Re B.C. Motor Vehicle Act*, [1985] 2 S.C.R. 486 ["*Motor Vehicle Reference*"], at p. 512).

[95] The principles of fundamental justice have significantly evolved since the birth of the *Charter*. Initially, the principles of fundamental justice were thought to refer narrowly to principles of natural justice that define procedural fairness. In the *Motor Vehicle Reference*, this Court held otherwise:

> ... it would be wrong to interpret the term "fundamental justice" as being synonymous with natural justice.... To do so would strip the protected interests of much, if not most, of their content and leave the "right" to life, liberty and security of the person in a sorely emaciated state. Such a result would be inconsistent with the broad, affirmative language in which those rights are expressed and equally inconsistent with the approach adopted by this Court toward the interpretation of *Charter* rights in *Law Society of Upper Canada v. Skapinker*, [1984] 1 S.C.R. 357, *per* Estey J., and *Hunter v. Southam Inc., supra*. [pp. 501–02]

[96] The *Motor Vehicle Reference* recognized that the principles of fundamental justice are about the basic values underpinning our constitutional order. The s. 7 analysis is concerned with capturing inherently bad laws: that is, laws that take away life, liberty, or security of the person in a way that runs afoul of our basic values. The principles of fundamental justice are an attempt to capture those values. Over the years, the jurisprudence has given shape to the content of these basic values. In this case, we are concerned with the basic values against arbitrariness, overbreadth, and gross disproportionality.

[97] The concepts of arbitrariness, overbreadth, and gross disproportionality evolved organically as courts were faced with novel *Charter* claims.

[98] Arbitrariness was used to describe the situation where there is no connection between the effect and the object of the law. In *Morgentaler*, the accused challenged provisions of the *Criminal Code* that required abortions to be approved by a therapeutic abortion committee of an accredited or approved hospital. The purpose of the law was to protect women's health. The majority found that the requirement that all therapeutic abortions take place in accredited hospitals

did not contribute to the objective of protecting women's health and, in fact, caused delays that were detrimental to women's health. Thus, the law violated basic values because the effect of the law actually contravened the objective of the law. Beetz J. called this "manifest unfairness" (*Morgentaler*, at p. 120), but later cases interpreted this as an "arbitrariness" analysis (see *Chaoulli v. Quebec (Attorney General)*, 2005 SCC 35, [2005] 1 S.C.R. 791, at para. 133, *per* McLachlin C.J. and Major J.).

[99] In *Chaoulli*, the applicant challenged a Quebec law that prohibited private health insurance for services that were available in the public sector. The purpose of the provision was to protect the public health care system and prevent the diversion of resources from the public system. The majority found, on the basis of international evidence, that private health insurance and a public health system could co-exist. Three of the four-judge majority found that the prohibition was "arbitrary" because there was no real connection on the facts between the effect and the objective of the law.

[100] Most recently, in *PHS*, this Court found that the Minister's decision not to extend a safe injection site's exemption from drug possession laws was arbitrary. The purpose of drug possession laws was the protection of health and public safety, and the services provided by the safe injection site actually contributed to these objectives. Thus, the effect of not extending the exemption—that is, prohibiting the safe injection site from operating—was contrary to the objectives of the drug possession laws.

[101] Another way in which laws may violate our basic values is through what the cases have called "overbreadth": the law goes too far and interferes with some conduct that bears no connection to its objective. In *R. v. Heywood*, [1994] 3 S.C.R. 761, the accused challenged a vagrancy law that prohibited offenders convicted of listed offences from "loitering" in public parks. The majority of the Court found that the law, which aimed to protect children from sexual predators, was overbroad; insofar as the law applied to offenders who did not constitute a danger to children, and insofar as it applied to parks where children were unlikely to be present, it was unrelated to its objective.

[102] In *R. v. Demers*, 2004 SCC 46, [2004] 2 S.C.R. 489, the challenged provisions of the *Criminal Code* prevented an accused who was found unfit to stand trial from receiving an absolute discharge, and subjected the accused to indefinite appearances before a review board. The purpose of the provisions was "to allow for the ongoing treatment or assessment of the accused in order for him or her to become fit for an eventual trial" (para. 41). The Court found that insofar as the law applied to permanently unfit accused, who would never become fit to stand trial, the objective did "not apply" and therefore the law was overbroad (paras. 42–43).

[103] Laws are also in violation of our basic values when the effect of the law is grossly disproportionate to the state's objective. In *Malmo-Levine*, the accused challenged the prohibition on the possession of marijuana on the basis that its effects were grossly disproportionate to its objective. Although the Court

agreed that a law with grossly disproportionate effects would violate our basic norms, the Court found that this was not such a case: "...the effects on accused persons of the present law, including the potential of imprisonment, fall within the broad latitude within which the Constitution permits legislative action" (para. 175).

[104] In *PHS*, this Court found that the Minister's refusal to exempt the safe injection site from drug possession laws was not in accordance with the principles of fundamental justice because the effect of denying health services and increasing the risk of death and disease of injection drug users was grossly disproportionate to the objectives of the drug possession laws, namely public health and safety.

[105] The overarching lesson that emerges from the case law is that laws run afoul of our basic values when the means by which the state seeks to attain its objective is fundamentally flawed, in the sense of being arbitrary, overbroad, or having effects that are grossly disproportionate to the legislative goal. To deprive citizens of life, liberty, or security of the person by laws that violate these norms is not in accordance with the principles of fundamental justice.

[106] As these principles have developed in the jurisprudence, they have not always been applied consistently. The Court of Appeal below pointed to the confusion that has been caused by the "commingling" of arbitrariness, overbreadth, and gross disproportionality (paras. 143–51). This Court itself recently noted the conflation of the principles of overbreadth and gross disproportionality (*R. v. Khawaja*, 2012 SCC 69, [2012] 3 S.C.R. 555, at paras. 38–40; see also *R. v. S.S.C.*, 2008 BCCA 262, 257 B.C.A.C. 57, at para. 72). In short, courts have explored different ways in which laws run afoul of our basic values, using the same words—arbitrariness, overbreadth, and gross disproportionality—in slightly different ways.

[107] Although there is significant overlap between these three principles, and one law may properly be characterized by more than one of them, arbitrariness, overbreadth, and gross disproportionality remain three distinct principles that stem from what Hamish Stewart calls "failures of instrumental rationality"—the situation where the law is "inadequately connected to its objective or in some sense goes too far in seeking to attain it" (*Fundamental Justice: Section 7 of the Canadian Charter of Rights and Freedoms* [2012], at p. 151). As Peter Hogg has explained:

> The doctrines of overbreadth, disproportionality and arbitrariness are all at bottom intended to address what Hamish Stewart calls "failures of instrumental rationality," by which he means that the Court accepts the legislative objective, but scrutinizes the policy instrument enacted as the means to achieve the objective. If the policy instrument is not a rational means to achieve the objective, then the law is dysfunctional in terms of its own objective. ("The Brilliant Career of Section 7 of the Charter" [2012], 58 *S.C.L.R.* [2d] 195, at p. 209 [citation omitted])

[108] The case law on arbitrariness, overbreadth and gross disproportionality is directed against two different evils. The first evil is the absence of a connection between the infringement of rights and what the law seeks to achieve—the situation where the law's deprivation of an individual's life, liberty, or security of the person is not connected to the purpose of the law. The first evil is addressed by the norms against arbitrariness and overbreadth, which target the absence of connection between the law's purpose and the s. 7 deprivation.

[109] The second evil lies in depriving a person of life, liberty or security of the person in a manner that is grossly disproportionate to the law's objective. The law's impact on the s. 7 interest is connected to the purpose, but the impact is so severe that it violates our fundamental norms.

Reference Re Same-Sex Marriage
Supreme Court of Canada
[2004] 3 S.C.R. 698

In this reference case the Governor in Council of Canada requested an opinion regarding the constitutionality of a proposed act of Parliament which would extend the capacity to marry to persons of the same sex. In the excerpt reproduced below the Supreme Court addressed the philosophical question of the nature of marriage, as well as the protection of the *Charter* rights to equality and freedom of religion.

The Court was unanimous in finding that same-sex marriage is not only consistent with *Charter* values, but flows from them.

The Court:

The Meaning of Marriage Is Not Constitutionally Fixed

[21] Several interveners say that the *Constitution Act, 1867* effectively entrenches the common law definition of "marriage" as it stood in 1867. That definition was most notably articulated in *Hyde v. Hyde* (1866), L.R. 1 P. & D. 130, at p. 133:

> What, then, is the nature of this institution as understood in Christendom? Its incidents may vary in different countries, but what are its essential elements and invariable features? If it be of common acceptance and existence, it must needs (however varied in different countries in its minor incidents) have some pervading identity and universal basis. I conceive that marriage, as understood in Christendom, may for this purpose be defined as the voluntary union for life of one man and one woman, to the exclusion of all others.

[22] The reference to "Christendom" is telling. *Hyde* spoke to a society of shared social values where marriage and religion were thought to be inseparable. This is no longer the case. Canada is a pluralistic society. Marriage, from the perspective of the state, is a civil institution. The "frozen concepts" reasoning runs contrary to one of the most fundamental principles of Canadian constitutional interpretation: that our Constitution is a living tree which, by way of progressive interpretation, accommodates and addresses the realities of modern life. In the 1920s, for example, a controversy arose as to whether women as well as men were capable of being considered "qualified persons" eligible for appointment to the Senate of Canada. Legal precedent stretching back to Roman Law was cited for the proposition that women had always been considered "unqualified" for public office, and it was argued that this common

understanding in 1867 was incorporated in s. 24 of the *Constitution Act, 1867* and should continue to govern Canadians in succeeding ages. Speaking for the Privy Council in *Edwards v. Attorney-General for Canada*, [1930] A.C. 124 (P.C.) (the *"Persons"* case), Lord Sankey L.C. said at p. 136:

> Their Lordships do not conceive it to be the duty of this Board—it is certainly not their desire—to cut down the provisions of the [B.N.A.] Act by a narrow and technical construction, but rather to give it a *large and liberal interpretation* so that the Dominion to a great extent, but within certain fixed limits, may be mistress in her own house, as the Provinces to a great extent, but within certain fixed limits, are mistresses in theirs. [Emphasis added.]

This approach applies to the construction of the powers enumerated in ss. 91 and 92 of the *Constitution Act, 1867.*

[23] A large and liberal, or progressive, interpretation ensures the continued relevance and, indeed, legitimacy of Canada's constituting document. By way of progressive interpretation our Constitution succeeds in its ambitious enterprise, that of structuring the exercise of power by the organs of the state in times vastly different from those in which it was crafted. For instance, Parliament's legislative competence in respect of telephones was recognized on the basis of its authority over interprovincial "undertakings" in s. 92(10)(*a*) even though the telephone had yet to be invented in 1867: *Toronto Corporation v. Bell Telephone Co. of Canada*, [1905] A.C. 52 (P.C.). Likewise, Parliament is not limited to the range of criminal offences recognized by the law of England in 1867 in the exercise of its criminal law power in s. 91(27): *Proprietary Articles Trade Association v. Attorney-General for Canada*, [1931] A.C. 310 (P.C.), at p. 324. Lord Sankey L.C. noted in the *Persons* case, at p. 135, that early English decisions are not a "secure foundation on which to build the interpretation" of our Constitution. We agree.

[24] The arguments presented to this Court in favour of a departure from the "living tree" principle fall into three broad categories: (1) marriage is a prelegal institution and thus cannot be fundamentally modified by law; (2) even a progressive interpretation of s. 91(26) cannot accommodate same-sex marriage since it falls outside the "natural limits" of that head of power, a corollary to this point being the objection that s. 15 of the *Charter* is being used to "amend" s. 91(26); and (3) in this instance, the intention of the framers of our Constitution should be determinative. As we shall see, none of these arguments persuade.

[25] First, it is argued, the institution of marriage escapes legislative redefinition. Existing in its present basic form since time immemorial, it is not a legal construct, but rather a supra-legal construct subject to legal incidents. In the *Persons* case, Lord Sankey L.C., writing for the Privy Council, dealt with this very type of argument, though in a different context. In addressing whether the fact that women never had occupied public office was relevant to whether they

could be considered "persons" for the purposes of being eligible for appointment to the Senate, he said at p. 134:

> The fact that no woman had served or has claimed to serve such an office is not of great weight when it is remembered that custom would have prevented the claim being made or the point being contested.
>
> Customs are apt to develop into traditions which are stronger than law and remain unchallenged long after the reason for them has disappeared.
>
> The appeal to history therefore in this particular matter is not conclusive.

Lord Sankey L.C. acknowledged, at p. 134, that "several centuries ago" it would have been understood that "persons" should refer only to men. Several centuries ago it would have been understood that marriage should be available only to opposite-sex couples. The recognition of same-sex marriage in several Canadian jurisdictions as well as two European countries belies the assertion that the same is true today.

[26] Second, some interveners emphasize that while Lord Sankey L.C. envisioned our Constitution as a "living tree" in the *Persons* case, he specified that it was "capable of growth and expansion within its natural limits" (p. 136). These natural limits, they submit, preclude same-sex marriage. As a corollary, some suggest that s. 1 of the *Proposed Act* would effectively amount to an amendment to the *Constitution Act, 1867* by interpretation based on the values underlying s. 15(1) of the *Charter*.

[27] The natural limits argument can succeed only if its proponents can identify an objective core of meaning which defines what is "natural" in relation to marriage. Absent this, the argument is merely tautological. The only objective core which the interveners before us agree is "natural" to marriage is that it is the voluntary union of two people to the exclusion of all others. Beyond this, views diverge. We are faced with competing opinions on what the natural limits of marriage may be.

[28] Lord Sankey L.C.'s reference to "natural limits" did not impose an obligation to determine, in the abstract and absolutely, the core meaning of constitutional terms. Consequently, it is not for the Court to determine, in the abstract, what the natural limits of marriage must be. Rather, the Court's role is to determine whether marriage as defined in the *Proposed Act* falls within the subject matter of s. 91(26).

[29] In determining whether legislation falls within a particular head of power, a progressive interpretation of the head of power must be adopted. The competing submissions before us do not permit us to conclude that "marriage" in s. 91(26) of the *Constitution Act, 1867,* read expansively, excludes same-sex marriage.

[30] Third, it is submitted that the intention of the framers should be determinative in interpreting the scope of the heads of power enumerated in ss. 91 and 92 given the decision in *R. v. Blais,* [2003] 2 S.C.R. 236, 2003 SCC 44. That case considered the interpretive question in relation to a particular constitu-

tional agreement, as opposed to a head of power which must continually adapt to cover new realities. It is therefore distinguishable and does not apply here....

Section 15(1): Equality

[45] Some interveners submit that the mere legislative recognition of the right of same-sex couples to marry would have the effect of discriminating against (1) religious groups who do not recognize the right of same-sex couples to marry (religiously) and/or (2) opposite-sex married couples. No submissions have been made as to how the *Proposed Act*, in its effect, might be seen to draw a distinction for the purposes of s. 15, nor can the Court surmise how it might be seen to do so. It withholds no benefits, nor does it impose burdens on a differential basis. It therefore fails to meet the threshold requirement of the s. 15(1) analysis laid down in *Law v. Canada (Minister of Employment and Immigration)*, [1999] 1 S.C.R. 497.

[46] The mere recognition of the equality rights of one group cannot, in itself, constitute a violation of the rights of another. The promotion of *Charter* rights and values enriches our society as a whole and the furtherance of those rights cannot undermine the very principles the *Charter* was meant to foster.

RELATED CASES

Attorney-General of Canada v. Lavell [1974] 1 S.C.R. 1349
(In this pre-*Charter* case the Supreme Court of Canada relied on a conception of "formal equality" to uphold a law which treated men and women differently under the federal *Indian Act.*)

Re Ontario Human Rights Commission et. al. and Simpson-Sears Ltd. [1985] 2 S.C.R. 536
(This Supreme Court of Canada case introduced the important distinction between direct and indirect discrimination, as well as the notion of a "duty to accommodate.")

Egan v. The Queen in Right of Canada [1995] 2 S.C.R. 513
(This case helped to establish sexual orientation as "analogous to the enumerated grounds" of section 15 of the *Charter*, namely, those grounds of discrimination which the *Charter* right to equality prohibits.)

R. v. Kapp [2008] 2 S.C.R. 483, and *Withler v. Canada (Attorney-General)* [2011] 1 S.C.R. 396
(These two judgments of the Supreme Court of Canada helped to specify the burden of those making equality claims under section 15 of the *Charter.*)

PART IV

Autonomy and Self-Determination

Traditionally, the law has sought to respect human dignity by preserving personal autonomy, that is, giving each of us sovereignty over decisions about our own lives. The law has recognized that as social life becomes more complicated, more and more occasions arise when our privacy is invaded by "experts" who, in our "best interests," presume to make decisions for us. It should not be surprising that much of the law in this area has arisen from the medical arena. Physicians and other health professionals are perhaps the clearest examples of experts who make decisions in our best interests. In this area of law, respect for autonomy takes the form of the doctrine of informed consent, which is described in *Malette v. Shulman*. The abortion debate has been characterized in terms of a woman's right to be sovereign over her own body (*Morgentaler*), as have cases of physician-assisted suicide (*Carter*). In Canada we have had several dramatic legal cases in this area, some of which are presented in this Part.

Conceptually, to argue that people have the right to make decisions for themselves—however foolish or unreasonable these decisions may seem to others—is to argue that no one should have this power over others. But there is an important exception to this rule, namely, the presumed right that parents have to make decisions for their children. Two cases in which parents insisted on the right to determine their children's fate are included in this Part to suggest how Canadian courts deal with this difficult issue (*B.R.* and *Latimer*), as well as the linked issue of whether and how the interests of a fetus can be legally acknowledged (*Winnipeg Child and Family Services*).

Malette v. Shulman
Ontario Court of Appeal
(1990) 72 O.R. (2d) 417

After a car accident in which her husband was killed, Mrs. Georgette Malette was rushed, unconscious, to the closest hospital. The attending physician, Dr. Shulman, found her to be suffering from incipient shock because of blood loss and decided that a blood transfusion was necessary to preserve her life. Before he did, however, a nurse found in Mrs. Malette's purse a card that said that, as a Jehovah's Witness, she requested that no blood be administered to her under any circumstances. In part, the card read, "I fully realize the implications of this position, but I have resolutely decided to obey the Bible command...." After getting a second opinion and accepting full responsibility, Dr. Shulman administered the transfusions. Mrs. Malette recovered from her injuries, and a few months later sued Dr. Shulman for assault and battery. At trial, she won and was awarded damages of $20,000. Dr. Shulman appealed the ruling.

Justice Robins (for the majority):

I should perhaps underscore the fact that Dr. Shulman was not found liable for any negligence in his treatment of Mrs. Malette. The judge [in the original trial] held that he had acted "promptly, professionally and was well-motivated throughout" and that his management of the case had been "carried out in a competent, careful and conscientious manner" in accordance with the requisite standard of care. His decision to administer blood in the circumstances confronting him was found to be an honest exercise of his professional judgement which did not delay Mrs. Malette's recovery, endanger her life or cause her any bodily harm. Indeed, the judge concluded that the doctor's treatment of Mrs. Malette "may well have been responsible for saving her life." [...]

What then is the legal effect, if any, of the Jehovah's Witness card carried by Mrs. Malette? Was the doctor bound to honour the instructions of his unconscious patient or, given the emergency and his inability to obtain conscious instructions from his patient, was he entitled to disregard the card and act according to his best medical judgement?

To answer these questions and determine the effect to be given to the Jehovah's Witness card, it is first necessary to ascertain what rights a competent patient has to accept or reject medical treatment and to appreciate the nature and extent of those rights.

The right of a person to control his or her own body is a concept that has long been recognized at common law. The tort of battery has traditionally protected the interest in bodily security from unwanted physical interference. Basically, any intentional nonconsensual touching which is harmful or offensive to a person's reasonable sense of dignity is actionable. Of course, a person may choose to waive this protection and consent to the intentional invasion of this interest, in which case an action for battery will not be maintainable. No special exceptions are made for medical care, other than in emergency situations, and the general rules governing actions for battery are applicable to the doctor-patient relationship. Thus, as a matter of common law, a medical intervention in which a doctor touches the body of a patient would constitute a battery if the patient did not consent to the intervention. Patients have the decisive role in the medical decision-making process. [...]

The doctrine of informed consent has developed in the law as the primary means of protecting a patient's right to control his or her medical treatment. Under the doctrine, no medical procedure may be undertaken without the patient's consent obtained after the patient has been provided with sufficient information to evaluate the risks and benefits of the proposed treatment and other available options. The doctrine presupposes the patient's capacity to make a subjective treatment decision based on her understanding of the necessary medical facts provided by the doctor and on her assessment of her own personal circumstances. A doctor who performs a medical procedure without having first furnished the patient with the information needed to obtain an informed consent will have infringed the patient's right to control the course of her medical care, and will be liable in battery even though the procedure was performed with a high degree of skill and actually benefitted the patient.

The right of self-determination which underlies the doctrine of informed consent also obviously encompasses the right to refuse medical treatment. A competent adult is generally entitled to reject a specific treatment or all treatment, or to select an alternate form of treatment, even if the decision may entail risks as serious as death and may appear mistaken in the eyes of the medical profession or of the community. Regardless of the doctor's opinion, it is the patient who has the final say on whether to undergo the treatment. The patient is free to decide, for instance, not to be operated on or not to undergo therapy or, by the same token, not to have a blood transfusion. If a doctor were to proceed in the face of a decision to reject the treatment, he would be civilly liable for his unauthorized conduct notwithstanding his justifiable belief that what he did was necessary to preserve the patient's life or health. The doctrine of informed consent is plainly intended to ensure the freedom of individuals to make choices concerning their medical care. For this freedom to be meaningful, people must have the right to make choices that accord with their own values regardless of how unwise or foolish those choices may appear to others. [...]

The emergency situation is an exception to the general rule requiring a patient's prior consent. When immediate medical treatment is necessary to save the life or preserve the health of a person who, by reason of unconsciousness or extreme illness, is incapable of either giving or withholding consent, the doctor may proceed without the patient's consent. The delivery of medical services is rendered lawful in such circumstances either on the rationale that the doctor has implied consent from the patient to give emergency aid or, more accurately in my view, on the rationale that the doctor is privileged by reason of necessity in giving the aid and is not to be held liable for so doing. On either basis, in an emergency the law sets aside the requirement of consent on the assumption that the patient, as a reasonable person, would want emergency aid to be rendered if she were capable of giving instructions. [...]

On the facts of the present case, Dr. Shulman was clearly faced with an emergency. He had an unconscious, critically ill patient on his hands who, in his opinion, needed blood transfusions to save her life or preserve her health. If there were no Jehovah's Witness card he undoubtedly would have been entitled to administer blood transfusions as part of the emergency treatment and could not have been held liable for so doing. In those circumstances he would have had no indication that the transfusions would have been refused had the patient then been able to make her wishes known and, accordingly, no reason to expect that, as a reasonable person, she would not consent to the transfusions.

However, to change the facts, if Mrs. Malette, before passing into unconsciousness, had expressly instructed Dr. Shulman, in terms comparable to those set forth on the card, that her religious convictions as a Jehovah's Witness were such that she was not to be given a blood transfusion under any circumstances and that she fully realized the implications of this position, the doctor would have been confronted with an obviously different situation. Here, the patient, anticipating an emergency in which she might be unable to make decisions about her health care contemporaneous with the emergency, has given explicit instructions that blood transfusions constitute an unacceptable medical intervention and are not to be administered to her. Once the emergency arises, is the doctor none the less entitled to administer transfusions on the basis of his honest belief that they are needed to save his patient's life?

The answer, in my opinion, is clearly no. A doctor is not free to disregard a patient's advance instructions given at the time of the emergency. The law does not prohibit a patient from withholding consent to emergency medical treatment, nor does the law prohibit a doctor from following his patient's instructions. While the law may disregard the absence of consent in limited emergency circumstances, it otherwise supports the right of competent adults to make decisions concerning their own health care by imposing civil liability on those who perform medical treatment without consent.

The patient's decision to refuse blood in the situation I have posed was made prior to and in anticipation of the emergency. While the doctor would have had the opportunity to dissuade her on the basis of his medical advice, her refusal to accept his advice or her unwillingness to discuss or consider the subject would not relieve him of his obligation to follow her instructions. The principles of self-determination and individual autonomy compel the conclusion that the patient may reject blood transfusions even if harmful consequences may result and even if the decision is generally regarded as foolhardy. Her decision in this instance would be operative after she lapsed into unconsciousness, and the doctor's conduct would be unauthorized. To transfuse a Jehovah's Witness in the face of her explicit instructions to the contrary would, in my opinion, violate her right to control her own body and show disrespect for the religious values by which she has chosen to live her life. [...]

The distinguishing feature of the present case—and the one that makes this a case of first impression—is, of course, the Jehovah's Witness card on the person of the unconscious patient. What then is the effect of the Jehovah's Witness card? [...]

Accepting for the moment that there is no reason to doubt that the card validly expressed Mrs. Malette's desire to withhold consent to blood transfusions, why should her wishes not be respected? Why should she be transfused against her will? The appellant's [Dr. Shulman's] answer, in essence, is that the card cannot be effective when the doctor is unable to provide the patient with the information she would need before making a decision to withhold consent in this specific emergency situation. In the absence of an informed refusal, the appellant submits that Mrs. Malette's right to protection against unwanted infringements of her bodily integrity must give way to countervailing societal interests which limit a person's right to refuse medical treatment. The appellant identifies two such interests as applicable to the unconscious patient in the present situation: first, the interest of the state in preserving life and, second, the interest of the state in safeguarding the integrity of the medical profession.

The state undoubtedly has a strong interest in protecting and preserving the lives and health of its citizens. There clearly are circumstances where this interest may override the individual's right to self-determination. For example, the state may in certain cases require that citizens submit to medical procedures in order to eliminate a health threat to the community or it may prohibit citizens from engaging in activities which are inherently dangerous to their lives. But this interest does not prevent a competent adult from refusing life-preserving medical treatment in general or blood transfusions in particular.

The state's interest in preserving the life or health of a competent patient must generally give way to the patient's stronger interest in directing the course of her own life. As indicated earlier, there is no law prohibiting a patient from declining necessary treatment or prohibiting a doctor from honouring the patient's decision. To the extent that the law reflects the state's interest, it supports the right of individuals to make their own decisions. By imposing civil liability on those who perform medical treatment without consent even though the treatment may be beneficial, the law serves to maximize individual freedom of choice. Recognition of the right to reject medical treatment cannot, in my opinion, be said to depreciate the interest of the state in life or in the sanctity of life. Individual free choice and self-determination are themselves fundamental constituents of life. To deny individuals freedom of choice with respect to their health care can only lessen, and not enhance, the value of life. This state interest, in my opinion, cannot properly be invoked to prohibit Mrs. Malette from choosing for herself whether or not to undergo blood transfusions.

Safeguarding the integrity of the medical profession is patently a legitimate state interest worthy of protection. However, I do not agree that this interest can serve to limit a patient's right to refuse blood transfusions. I recognize, of course, that the choice between violating a patient's private convictions and accepting her decision is hardly an easy one for members of a profession dedicated to aiding the injured and preserving life. The patient's right to determine her own medical treatment is, however, paramount to what might otherwise be the doctor's obligation to provide needed medical care. The doctor is bound in law by the patient's choice even though that choice may be contrary to the mandates of his own conscience and professional judgement. If patient choice were subservient to conscientious medical judgement, the right of the patient to determine her own treatment, and the doctrine of informed consent, would be rendered meaningless. Recognition of a Jehovah's Witness' right to refuse blood transfusions cannot, in my opinion, be seen as threatening the integrity of the medical profession or the state's interest in protecting the same.

In sum, it is my view that the principal interest asserted by Mrs. Malette in this case—the interest in the freedom to reject, or refuse to consent to, intrusions of her bodily integrity—outweighs the interest of the state in the preservation of life and health and the protection of the integrity of the medical profession. While the right to decline medical treatment is not absolute or unqualified, those state interests are not in themselves sufficiently compelling to justify forcing a patient to submit to nonconsensual invasions of her person. The interest of the state in protecting innocent third parties and preventing suicide are, I might note, not applicable to the present circumstances. [...]

One further point should be mentioned. The appellant argues that to uphold the trial decision places a doctor on the horns of a dilemma, in that, on the one hand, if the doctor administers blood in this situation and saves the patient's life, the patient may hold him liable in battery while, on the other hand, if the doctor follows the patient's instructions and, as a consequence, the patient dies, the doctor may face an action by dependants alleging that, notwithstanding the card, the deceased would, if conscious, have accepted blood in the face of imminent death and the doctor was negligent in failing to administer the transfusions. In my view, that result cannot conceivably follow. The doctor cannot be held to have violated either his legal duty or professional responsibility towards the patient or the patient's dependants when he honours the Jehovah's Witness card and respects the patient's right to control her own body in accordance with the dictates of her conscience. The onus is clearly on the patient. When members of the Jehovah's Witness faith choose to carry cards intended to notify doctors and other providers of health care that they reject blood transfusions in an emergency, they must accept the consequences of their decision. Neither they nor their dependants can later be heard to say that the card did not reflect their true wishes. If harmful consequences ensue, the responsibility for those consequences is entirely theirs and not the doctor's. [...]

In the result, for these reasons, I would dismiss the appeal and the cross-appeal, both with costs.

R. v. Morgentaler
Supreme Court of Canada
[1988] 1 S.C.R 30

In this landmark case, a majority of the Supreme Court found Canada's abortion law to be unconstitutional. Section 251 of the *Criminal Code* made it a criminal offence to "procure a miscarriage of a female person" and then outlined a procedure which, if followed, would afford a complete defence to the charge. So, if a pregnant woman's request for an abortion was accepted by a therapeutic abortion committee of an accredited or approved hospital, on the grounds that the continuation of the pregnancy would endanger her health, and if the abortion was performed by a qualified medical practitioner, neither the practitioner nor the woman would be guilty of an indictable offence. Some members of the court felt that this complex procedure, and the unavailability of abortion in parts of the country, violated a woman's right to fair treatment. Justice Wilson, however, in a concurring judgement, took the stronger stand and founded her judgement directly on the value of autonomy.

———————

Justice Wilson (for the majority):

At the heart of this appeal is the question whether a pregnant woman can, as a constitutional matter, be compelled by law to carry the fetus to term. The legislature has proceeded on the basis that she can be so compelled and, indeed, has made it a criminal offence punishable by imprisonment under s. 251 of the *Criminal Code* for her or her physician to terminate the pregnancy unless the procedural requirements of the section are complied with.

My colleagues, the Chief Justice and Justice Beetz, have attacked those requirements in reasons which I have had the privilege of reading. They have found that the requirements do not comport with the principles of fundamental justice in the procedural sense and have concluded that, since they cannot be severed from the provisions creating the substantive offence, the whole of s. 251 must fall.

With all due respect, I think that the court must tackle the primary issue first. [...] If a pregnant woman cannot, as a constitutional matter, be compelled by law to carry the fetus to term against her will, a review of the procedural requirements by which she may be compelled to do so seems pointless. Moreover, it would, in my opinion, be an exercise in futility for the legislature to expend its time and energy in attempting to remedy the defects in the procedural requirements unless it has some assurance that this process will, at the end of the day, result in the creation of a valid criminal offence. [...]

The *Charter* is predicated on a particular conception of the place of the individual in society. An individual is not a totally independent entity disconnected from the society in which he or she lives. Neither, however, is the individual a mere cog in an impersonal machine in which his or her values, goals and aspirations are subordinated to those of the collectivity. The individual is a bit of both. The *Charter* reflects this reality by leaving a wide range of activities and decisions open to legitimate government control while at the same time placing limits on the proper scope of that control. Thus, the rights guaranteed in the *Charter* erect around each individual, metaphorically speaking, an invisible fence over which the state will not be allowed to trespass. The role of the courts is to map out, piece by piece, the parameters of the fence. [...]

The idea of human dignity finds expression in almost every right and freedom guaranteed in the *Charter*. Individuals are afforded the right to choose their own religion and their own philosophy of life, the right to choose with whom they will associate and how they will express themselves, the right to choose where they will live and what occupation they will pursue. These are all examples of the basic theory underlying the *Charter*, namely, that the state will respect choices made by individuals and, to the greatest extent possible, will avoid subordinating these choices to any one conception of the good life.

Thus, an aspect of the respect for human dignity on which the *Charter* is founded is the right to make fundamental personal decisions without interference from the state. This right is a crucial component of the right to liberty. Liberty is a phrase capable of a broad range of meaning. In my view, this right, properly construed, grants the individual a degree of autonomy in making decisions of fundamental personal importance. [...]

In my opinion, the respect for individual decision-making in matters of fundamental personal importance reflected in the American jurisprudence also informs the Canadian *Charter*. Indeed, as the Chief Justice pointed out in *R. v. Big M Drug Mart Ltd.* (1985), beliefs about human worth and dignity "are the *sine qua non* of the political tradition underlying the *Charter*." I would conclude, therefore, that the right to liberty contained in s. 7 guarantees to every individual a degree of personal autonomy over important decisions intimately affecting their private lives.

The question then becomes whether the decision of a woman to terminate her pregnancy falls within this class of protected decisions. I have no doubt that it does. This decision is one that will have profound psychological, economic and social consequences for the pregnant woman. The circumstances giving rise to it can be complex and varied and there may be, and usually are, powerful considerations militating in opposite directions. It is a decision that deeply reflects the way the woman thinks about herself and her relationship to others and to society at large. It is not just a medical decision; it is a profound social and ethical one as well. Her response to it will be the response of the whole person.

It is probably impossible for a man to respond, even imaginatively, to such a dilemma not just because it is outside the realm of his personal experience (although this is, of course, the case) but because he can relate to it only by objectifying it, thereby eliminating the subjective elements of the female psyche which are at the heart of the dilemma. [...] [T]he history of the struggle for human rights from the eighteenth century on has been the history of men struggling to assert their dignity and common humanity against an overbearing state apparatus. The more recent struggle for women's rights has been a struggle to eliminate discrimination, to achieve a place for women in a man's world, to develop a set of legislative reforms in order to place women in the same position as men. It has *not* been a struggle to define the rights of women in relation to their special place in the societal structure and in relation to the biological distinction between the two sexes. Thus, women's needs and aspirations are only now being translated into protected rights. The right to reproduce or not to reproduce which is in issue in this case is one such right and is properly perceived as an integral part of modern woman's struggle to assert *her* dignity and worth as a human being.

Given then that the right to liberty guaranteed by s. 7 of the *Charter* gives a woman the right to decide for herself whether or not to terminate her pregnancy, does s. 251 of the *Criminal Code* violate this right? Clearly it does. The purpose of the section is to take the decision away from the woman and give it to a committee. Furthermore, as the Chief Justice correctly points out, the committee bases its decision on "criteria entirely unrelated to [the pregnant woman's] priorities and aspirations." The fact that the decision whether a woman will be allowed to terminate her pregnancy is in the hands of a committee is just as great a violation of the woman's right to personal autonomy in decisions of an intimate and private nature as it would be if a committee were established to decide whether a woman should be allowed to continue her pregnancy. Both these arrangements violate the woman's right to liberty by deciding for her something that she has the right to decide for herself.

B. (R.) v. Children's Aid Society of Metropolitan Toronto
Supreme Court of Canada
[1995] 1 S.C.R. 315

Sheena B. was a very sick infant who had reached a stage where her physicians believed that she might require a blood transfusion to treat a potentially fatal congestive heart failure. Her parents, who are Jehovah's Witnesses, objected on religious grounds to the blood transfusion. Following an emergency hearing of the Provincial Court, the Children's Aid Society was granted a temporary wardship of Sheena for the purpose of consenting to a blood transfusion, if it should prove medically necessary. Sheena eventually received the transfusion and the wardship order was terminated. Nonetheless, the parents sought to have the Provincial Court's decision overturned on the ground that it constituted an interference with their rights as parents to determine their child's medical treatment. The case made its way to the Supreme Court of Canada, where the issue was broadened, and restated in terms of a general "right of parents to rear their children without undue interference by the state," or parental liberty.

Although the court was unanimous that the Provincial Court was correct to issue the wardship order, on the question of the scope of parental liberty the court dramatically split, in part because of their alternative conceptions of the so-called "liberty interest." Justice La Forest argued that the law must recognize the right of parents to make decisions for their children and interfere only in the rarest case. By contrast, Justice Iacobucci made it clear that parents have no right to risk the life of their child, for whatever reason: although each of us can refuse any medical procedure for ourselves, "it is quite another matter to speak for another separate individual, especially when that individual cannot speak for herself."

Justice La Forest (for the majority):

This appeal raises the constitutionality of state interference with child-rearing decisions. The appellants are parents who argue that the Ontario *Child Welfare Act* infringes their right to choose medical treatment for their infant in accordance with the tenets of their faith. They claim that this right is protected under both ss. 7 and 2(a) of the *Charter*. [...]

Although I am of the view that the principles of fundamental justice have been complied with in the present case, I nonetheless propose to comment on the scope of the protection afforded by the *Charter* as it relates to the right of parents to choose medical treatment for their infant. [...] An examination of the scope of the liberty interest appears warranted, since its formulation may affect the determination of the principles of fundamental justice. I also note that while this case can be disposed of solely on the issue of the right of parents to choose medical treatment for their infant, it is not without consequence for child protection as a whole. Intervention may well be compelling here, but this appeal raises the more general question of the right of parents to rear their children without undue interference by the state.

The appellants claim that parents have the right to choose medical treatment for their infant, relying for this contention on s. 7 of the *Charter*, and more precisely on the liberty interest. They assert that the right enures in the family as an entity, basing this argument on statements made by American courts in the definition of liberty under their Constitution. While, as I will indicate, American experience may be useful in defining the scope of the liberty interest protected under our Constitution, I agree that s. 7 of the *Charter* does not afford protection to the integrity of the family unit as such. The Canadian *Charter*, and s. 7 in particular, protects individuals. It is the individual's right to liberty under the *Charter* with which we are here concerned. The concept of the integrity of the family unit is itself premised, at least in part, on that of parental liberty. [...]

The term "liberty" has yet to be authoritatively defined in this court, although comments have been made on both ends of the spectrum. [...]

In *R. v. Jones*, speaking alone in dissent, Wilson J. gave a broad formulation of the concept of liberty. She stated, at p. 318:

> I believe that the framers of the Constitution in guaranteeing "liberty" as a fundamental value in a free and democratic society had in mind the freedom of the individual to develop and realize his potential to the full, to plan his own life to suit his own character, to make his own choices for good or ill, to be non-conformist, idiosyncratic and even eccentric—to be, in to-day's parlance, "his own person" and accountable as such. John Stuart Mill described it as "pursuing our own good in our own way." This, he believed, we should be free to do "so long as we do not attempt to deprive others of theirs or impede their efforts to obtain it."

While she was of the view that s. 7 protected the right of parents to bring up and educate their children according to their conscientious beliefs, Wilson J. acknowledged that this freedom was not "untrammelled." Some limits could be placed on the interest, as "liberty" did not imply the right to bring up and educate one's children "as one sees fit."

On the other hand, Lamer J. speaking for himself alone in *Reference re ss. 193 and 195. 1(1)(c) of the Criminal Code* rejected the line of American cases pertaining to contractual liberty, noting that such an extension of the liberty interest had also been subject to criticism in the United States. The text of the Canadian *Charter*—which does not mention "property"—and the context of its adoption were sufficiently different to mandate a distinct interpretation. According to him, s. 7, which appears in the *Charter* under the heading "Legal Rights," had to be construed in light of the rights enunciated in ss. 8 to 14, which set out traditional criminal law guarantees. Further, the term "liberty" had to be read in conjunction with its modifier, the principles of fundamental justice. Thus, a restriction on liberty had to occur as a result of an interaction with the justice system. He summarized his position as follows, at pp. 1177–78:

> Put shortly, I am of the view that s. 7 is implicated when the state, by resorting to the justice system, restricts an individual's physical liberty *in any circumstances*. Section 7 is also implicated when the state restricts individuals' security of the person by interfering with, or removing from them, control over their physical or mental integrity. Finally, s. 7 is implicated when the state, either directly or through its agents, restricts certain privileges or liberties by using the threat of punishment in cases of non-compliance.

[…] Lamer J. added, however, that "This is not to say that 'liberty' as a value underlying the *Charter* does not permeate the document in a broader, more general sense, especially as it relates to the maintenance of Canada as a 'free and democratic society.'" (p. 1179) […]

The above-cited cases give us an important indication of the meaning of the concept of liberty. On the one hand, liberty does not mean unconstrained freedom. […] Freedom of the individual to do what he or she wishes must, in any organized society, be subjected to numerous constraints for the common good. The state undoubtedly has the right to impose many types of restraints on individual behaviour, and not all limitations will attract *Charter* scrutiny. On the other hand, liberty does not mean mere freedom from physical restraint. In a free and democratic society, the individual must be left room for personal autonomy to live his or her own life and to make decisions that are of fundamental personal importance. […]

Where to draw the line between interests and regulatory powers falling within the accepted ambit of state authority will often raise difficulty. But much on either side of the line is clear enough. On that basis, I would have thought it plain that the right to nurture a child, to care for its development, and to make decisions for it in fundamental matters such as medical care, are part of the liberty interest of a parent. […] The common law has long recognized that parents are in the best position to take care of their children and make all the decisions necessary to ensure their well-being. […]

Although the philosophy underlying state intervention has changed over time, most contemporary statutes dealing with child protection matters, and in particular the Ontario Act, while focusing on the best interest of the child, favour minimal intervention. In recent years, courts have expressed some reluctance to interfere with parental rights, and state intervention has been tolerated only when necessity was demonstrated. This only serves to confirm that the parental interest in bringing up, nurturing and caring for a child, including medical care and moral upbringing, is an individual interest of fundamental importance to our society.

The respondents have argued that the "parental liberty" asserted by the appellants is an obligation owed to the child which does not fall within the scope of s. 7 of the *Charter*. [...]

While acknowledging that parents bear responsibilities towards their children, it seems to me that they must enjoy correlative rights to exercise them. The contrary view would not recognize the fundamental importance of choice and personal autonomy in our society. [...] [T]he common law has always, in the absence of demonstrated neglect or unsuitability, presumed that parents should make all significant choices affecting their children, and has afforded them a general liberty to do as they choose. This liberty interest is not a parental right tantamount to a right of property in children. (Fortunately, we have distanced ourselves from the ancient juridical conception of children as chattels of their parents.) The state is now actively involved in a number of areas traditionally conceived of as properly belonging to the private sphere.

Nonetheless, our society is far from having repudiated the privileged role parents exercise in the upbringing of their children. This role translates into a protected sphere of parental decision-making which is rooted in the presumption that parents should make important decisions affecting their children both because parents are more likely to appreciate the best interests of their children and because the state is ill equipped to make such decisions itself. Moreover, individuals have a deep personal interest as parents in fostering the growth of their own children. This is not to say that the state cannot intervene when it considers it necessary to safeguard the child's autonomy or health. But such intervention must be justified. In other words, parental decision-making must receive the protection of the *Charter* in order for state interference to be properly monitored by the courts, and be permitted only when it conforms to the values underlying the *Charter*.

The respondents also argued that the infant's rights were paramount to those of the appellants and, on that basis alone, state intervention was justified. Children undeniably benefit from the *Charter*, most notably in its protection of their rights to life and to the security of their person. As children are unable to assert these, our society presumes that parents will exercise their freedom of choice in a manner that does not offend the rights of their children. If one considers the multitude of decisions parents make daily, it is clear that in practice, state interference in order to balance the rights of parents and children will arise only in exceptional cases. In fact, we must accept that parents can, at times, make decisions contrary to their children's wishes—and rights—as long as they do not exceed the threshold dictated by public policy, in its broad conception. For instance, it would be difficult to deny that a parent can dictate to his or her child the place where he or she will live, or which school he or she will attend. However, the state can properly intervene in situations where parental conduct falls below the socially acceptable threshold. But in doing so, the state is limiting the constitutional rights of parents rather than vindicating the constitutional rights of children. [...]

Justice Iacobucci (concurring):

We have read the reasons of Mr. Justice La Forest, and we agree with the result that there has been no unconstitutional violation of the appellants' rights. [...]

However, we respectfully disagree with La Forest J.'s reliance on s. 1 of the *Charter* and the principles of fundamental justice in s. 7 in order to establish the constitutionality of the repealed *Child Welfare Act*. Instead, we conclude that the class of parents caught by [the *Child Welfare Act*] simply cannot benefit from the protection of the liberty interest in s. 7. [...]

We find that the right to liberty embedded in s. 7 does not include a parent's right to deny a child medical treatment that has been adjudged necessary by a medical professional. Although the scope of "liberty" as understood by s. 7 is expansive, it is certainly not all encompassing. [...] Not all individual activity should immediately qualify as an exercise of "liberty" and hence be *prima facie* entitled to constitutional protection, subject only to the limits consonant with fundamental justice or s. 1. [...]

This is clearly a case where Sheena's right to liberty, security of the person, and potentially even to life is deprived. It is important to note that the abridgment of Sheena's s. 7 rights operates independently from the question whether the parents honestly believe that their refusal to consent to the transfusion is in the best interests of the child, since such a refusal shall, according to the appellants, prevent her from being "defiled in the eyes of God." Whether or not her parents' motivations are well-intentioned, the physical effects upon Sheena of the refusal to transfuse blood are equally deleterious.

We note that La Forest J. holds that "liberty" encompasses the right of parents to have input into the education of their child. In fact, "liberty" may very well permit parents to choose among *equally effective* types of medical treatment for their children, but we do not find it necessary to determine this question in the instant case. We say this because, assuming without deciding that "liberty" has such a reach, it certainly does not extend to protect the appellants in the case at bar. There is simply no room within s. 7 for parents to override the child's right to life and security of the person.

In any event, there is an immense difference between sanctioning some input into a child's education and protecting a parent's right to refuse their children medical treatment that a professional adjudges to be necessary and for which there is no legitimate alternative. The child's right to life must not be so completely subsumed to the parental liberty to make decisions regarding that child. In our view, the best way to ensure this outcome is to view an exercise of parental liberty which seriously endangers the survival of the child as falling outside s. 7.

Our colleague's reasons open the door to the possibility that a violation of a guardian's s. 7 rights will be found should the state deny a guardian his or her right to refuse a child in his or her charge medical treatment *and* should that denial fail to conform with fundamental justice. In the case at bar, Sheena's condition, although believed to be serious, was not sufficiently urgent to prevent the Children's Aid Society from seeking a court-ordered wardship, thereby complying with procedural fundamental justice. But what if Sheena were injured in a car accident and required an immediate blood transfusion to save her life? Even if her parents would have been in agreement that the transfusion was necessary and urgently required, their personal convictions would still likely have compelled them to refuse their daughter the treatment. To this end, this exercise of parental liberty can engender the death of an infant.

We find it counter-intuitive that "parental liberty" would permit a parent to deny a child medical treatment felt to be necessary until some element of procedural fundamental justice is complied with. Although an individual may refuse any medical procedures upon his own person, it is quite another matter to speak for another separate individual, especially when that individual cannot speak for herself and, in Sheena's case, has never spoken for herself. The rights enumerated in the *Charter* are individual rights to which children are clearly entitled in their relationships with the state and all persons regardless of their status as strangers, friends, relatives, guardians or parents. [...]

The exercise of parental beliefs that grossly invades the "best interests" of the child is not activity protected by the right to "liberty" in s. 7. To hold otherwise would be to risk undermining the ability of the state to exercise its legitimate *parens patriae* jurisdiction and jeopardize the *Charter*'s goal of protecting the most vulnerable members of society. As society becomes increasingly cognizant of the fact that the family is often a very dangerous place for children, the *parens patriae* jurisdiction assumes greater importance. Although there are times when the family should be shielded from the intrusions of the state, Sheena's situation is one in which the state should be readily able to intervene not only to protect the public interest, but also to preserve the security of infants who cannot yet speak for themselves.

R. v. Latimer
Saskatchewan Court of Appeal
(1995) 128 S.R. 19

At various times, there have been calls to reform Canada's homicide laws to acknowledge that "mercy killing" is morally different from other forms of intentional killing and, if not an innocent act, should still not be subjected to the same level of punishment as first degree murder. If a father intentionally kills his young daughter because he wants to spare her a lifetime of unremitting pain, then it might seem outrageous to punish him like any other first degree murderer. But that is how Mr. Latimer described what he did on October 24, 1993.

Mr. Latimer was convicted of first degree murder, based in part on his confession. He then argued before Saskatchewan's Court of Appeal that the mandatory sentence of life imprisonment without eligibility for parole for ten years was "greater than is warranted or necessary, considering the facts of the case and the accused's background." The jury at trial were unanimous in their recommendation that the Court impose a minimum sentence, with parole as soon as possible. Latimer's lawyer asked for a constitutional exemption from the mandatory sentence. At the Court of Appeal, justices Tallis and Bayda came to opposite conclusions, given below. The case was then sent to the Supreme Court of Canada, which ordered a new trial. Although the new jury convicted Latimer, it once again refused to recommend the mandatory punishment and substituted instead a year in jail and probation.

This decision was appealed and found its way back to the Supreme Court again. This time, in blunt language that reinforced the Canadian legal position on mercy killing, the unanimous Court rejected the argument that this was "cruel and unusual punishment" (as prohibited by *Charter* s. 12) and refused to accept that the minimum sentence of ten years was not deserved.

Justice Tallis (for the majority):

[1] On November 16, 1994, following a jury trial for first degree murder, the appellant Robert Latimer was convicted of second degree murder for the killing of Tracy, his 12-year-old daughter. The presiding judge imposed the mandatory sentence of life imprisonment without eligibility for parole for ten years. [...]

[3] In October 1993, Tracy, who was 12 years old, suffered from severe cerebral palsy—a permanent condition caused by brain damage at birth. She was quadriplegic. Her physical handicaps of palsy and quadriplegia were such that she was bedridden for most of the time. Except for some slight head and facial movements she was immobile. She was physically helpless and unable to care for herself. She was in continual pain. [...]

[5] In February 1990, Tracy underwent surgery for the purpose of balancing the muscles around her pelvis. In August 1992 she underwent further surgery to reduce the abnormal curvature in her back. This surgery was successful but problems then developed in her right hip which became dislocated. This caused considerable pain. [...]

[8] Speaking generally, the Latimer family provided constant care for their daughter Tracy. During the period July to October 1993 she was placed in a group home in North Battleford to provide respite for the family particularly while Mrs. Latimer was pregnant. [...]

[9] After Tracy returned home, Kathleen Johnson, a Social Service worker, learned that an application for permanent placement at the group home had been received from the Latimer family. On October 12, 1993 she spoke to the appellant by phone to ascertain more details of the family's application and wishes. During this discussion the appellant advised her that it was not an urgent matter. If there was any immediate opening at the home he was not sure if they wanted a placement.

[10] While in the appellant's care on Sunday, October 24, 1993 Tracy passed away at her family farm home near Wilkie. [...]

In this statement, the appellant describes how he removed Tracy from her bed and placed her in the cab of a pickup truck in a shed. He then hooked the hose to the exhaust and placed the other end through the back window of the cab. After he left Tracy exposed to carbon monoxide in the cab for a significant period of time, he determined that she was dead and then placed her back in her bed at the house. [...]

[T]he appellant was formally charged with first degree murder. [...]

[72] We think that it is self-evident that the interests involved in the instant case are more substantial, both on an individual and societal level, than those generally involved in the crime of murder.

[73] Section 7 of the *Charter* was enacted for the protection and benefit of all citizens—whether healthy or handicapped. This approach comports with the state's interest in the protection and preservation of human life. Speaking generally, all civilized nations demonstrate their commitment to life by treating homicide as a serious crime. Moreover, many countries including Canada have laws imposing criminal penalties on one who assists another to commit suicide.

[74] But in the context presented here, society has more particular interests at stake. Tracy was not in a position to make an informed and voluntary choice to exercise a hypothetical right to refuse treatment or any other right. Furthermore, this case does not involve medical decisions concerning continuation or

termination of life sustaining treatment. Accordingly such bioethical issues are not before the Court for consideration.

[75] We observe that the choice between life and death is a deeply personal decision of obvious and overwhelming finality. Since Tracy was handicapped there is accordingly no evidence of any desire to terminate her own life by withdrawal of hydration or nutrition.

[76] But this case is not about withdrawal of hydration and nutrition to bring about termination of life. The appellant assumed the role of a surrogate decision-maker and in that role he decided to actively terminate Tracy's life. He first considered shooting her and then successfully pursued the alternative path of carbon monoxide poisoning. In so doing, he decided that her quality of life was of such diminished value that she should not live. In our opinion the learned trial judge was correct in concluding that "[l]ife was not kind to Tracy but it was a life that was hers to make of what she could."

[77] In this situation it is a fair inference that such a decision would never have been suggested or considered if Tracy were not handicapped and in extreme pain. This difference in approach between handicapped and non-handicapped children directly reflects a sense that the life of a handicapped child is of significantly less value than the life of a non-handicapped child in extreme pain. A pivotal question to be considered is, "If the child were not permanently disabled, but in extreme pain, would there be any question about making heroic efforts to sustain and maintain life?" If the answer is no, then the decision would appear to be clearly predicated upon the diminished value assigned to the life of a handicapped child. One would not be so inspired by love and compassion to take the life of the non-handicapped child.

[78] Our law does not authorize such surrogate decision-making based on the assessments of the personal worth or social utility of another's life or the value of that life to the individual involved or to others. Our society, through its criminal law, may properly decline to make judgements about the quality of life that a particular individual may enjoy, and simply assert an unqualified interest in the preservation of human life. Surrogate decision-makers are not entitled to arrogate to themselves the life and death decisions under review in this case. [...]

[80] This homicide involves a significant degree of premeditation. The appellant contemplated taking Tracy's life before performing the act that caused her death. It was "intentional" in every sense of the word. Although he did so to spare her further pain, this approach ignores many other relevant considerations. As a self-appointed surrogate decision-maker, he was not entitled to take the criminal law into his own hands and terminate her life. Furthermore, society, through the operation of the criminal law is entitled to guard against potential abuses in such situations. Accordingly statutory penalties are fashioned to meet the broad objectives and purposes of the criminal law.

[81] In the circumstances of this case we reject the appellant's request for a constitutional exemption from the prescribed sentences for second degree

murder. It is open to Parliament to modify the existing law by appropriate legislation that establishes sentencing criteria for "mercy" killing. In the meantime, it is not for the Court to pass on the wisdom of Parliament with respect to the range of penalties to be imposed on those found guilty of murder. [...]

We dismiss the appellant's application for a constitutional exemption and affirm the sentence imposed by the learned trial judge.

Chief Justice Bayda (dissenting):

[101] The appellant is a typical, salt of the earth, 42-year-old prairie farmer, born and raised on a farm near Wilkie, Saskatchewan. Mrs. Latimer joined the appellant in his farming operation and they lived their entire married lives on the farm. Four children were born to them: Tracy in 1980, a son in 1983, another daughter in 1985 and their youngest in 1993. The appellant is a devoted family man, devoted to his wife and his children. He is a loving, caring, nurturing person who actively participated in the daily care of the children and in particular the caring and nurturing of Tracy. [...]

[110] The appellant has no criminal record. He poses no risk to society and requires no rehabilitation. He enjoys a very healthy and wholesome reputation in the community. [...]

[115] The appellant did not commit an irrational, depraved, brutal, sordid killing having its genesis in and motivated by some base impulse or emotion such as hate, anger, greed, self-gratification, jealousy, selfishness or some combination of those vices, all of which are considered by people to be negative and destructive. On the contrary, the workings of the appellant's intellect and will reveal a mind conditioned day in and day out, week in and week out, month in and month out, year in and year out, for a period of 13 years by his disabled daughter's pain culminating in what appears to be at the very least a severe preoccupation or an obsession with that pain. [...]

[119] [...] It is a fair inference and an important one to keep in mind that she was not put into her father's truck because she was disabled. She was put there because of her pain, something very different from her disability. She was put there because her father loved her too much to watch her suffer. While the killing was a purposeful one, it had its genesis in altruism and was motivated by love, mercy and compassion or a combination of those virtues, generally considered by people to be life-enhancing and affirmative.

[120] As for the physical components of the act, they did not produce a violent, painful killing. The act showed no heinousness or abnormal or aberrant behaviour. Rather, the act was committed in a gentle, painless and compassionate way.

[121] The actor himself was not a murderous thug, devoid of conscience, whose life has been one of violence, greed, contempt for the law and total disrespect for human beings. On the contrary, the actor was a nurturing, caring, giving, respectful, law-abiding responsible parent of the victim. [...]

[195] For the foregoing reasons, I find that the appropriate and just remedy for the violation of the appellant's s. 12 *Charter* right is a constitutional exemp-

tion from the mandatory minimum sentence requirement for second degree murder. [...]

[197] In the result, I would allow the appeal from sentence, set aside the sentence imposed by the trial judge and direct the parties to appear before this Court at a time to be designated to make their submissions respecting the sentence that ought to be imposed without regard to the mandatory minimum sentence requirements.

R. v. Latimer
Supreme Court of Canada
[2001] 1 S.C.R. 3

The Court:

[80] The first factor to consider is the gravity of the offence. [...]

[81] Certainly, in this case one cannot escape the conclusion that Mr. Latimer's actions resulted in the most serious of all possible consequences, namely, the death of the victim, Tracy Latimer.

[82] [Secondly] in considering the character of Mr. Latimer's actions, we are directed to an assessment of the criminal fault requirement or *mens rea* element of the offence rather than the offender's motive or general state of mind. We attach a greater degree of criminal responsibility or moral blameworthiness to conduct where the accused knowingly broke the law. [...]

[84] [...] In this case, the gravest possible consequences resulted from an act of the most serious and morally blameworthy intentionality. It is against this reality that we must weigh the other contextual factors, including and especially the particular circumstances of the offender and the offence.

[85] Turning to the characteristics of the offender and the particular circumstances of the offence we must consider the existence of any aggravating and mitigating circumstances. [...] Specifically, any aggravating circumstances must be weighed against any mitigating circumstances. In this regard, it is possible that prior to gauging the sentence's appropriateness in light of an appreciation of the particular circumstances weighed against the gravity of the offence, the mitigating and aggravating circumstances might well cancel out their ultimate impact. Indeed, this is what occurs in this case. On the one hand, we must give due consideration to Mr. Latimer's initial attempts to conceal his actions, his lack of remorse, his position of trust, the significant degree of planning and premeditation, and Tracy's extreme vulnerability. On the other hand, we are mindful of Mr. Latimer's good character and standing in the community, his tortured anxiety about Tracy's well-being, and his laudable perseverance as a caring and involved parent. Considered together we cannot find that the personal characteristics and particular circumstances of this case displace the serious gravity of this offence. [...]

[87] In summary, the minimum mandatory sentence is not grossly disproportionate in this case. We cannot find that any aspect of the particular circumstances of the case or the offender diminishes the degree of criminal responsibility borne by Mr. Latimer. In addition, although not free of debate, the sentence is not out of step with valid penological goals or sentencing principles. The legislative classification and treatment of this offender meets the requisite standard of proportionality. Where there is no violation of Mr. Latimer's s. 12 right there is no basis for granting a constitutional exemption.

Winnipeg Child and Family Services v. G. (D.F.)
Supreme Court of Canada
[1997] 3 S.C.R. 925

The respondent, pregnant with her fourth child, had been addicted to glue sniffing, which can damage the nervous system of the fetus. Two of her previous children had been born disabled as a result and were now permanent wards of the state. A Manitoba Court had ordered that G.D.F. be detained in a health centre for treatment until the birth of her child, arguing that the unborn child had legal interests worth protecting, and that in any case the Court's inherent *parens patriae* jurisdiction gave it the power to protect children, including unborn children. The Court of Appeal overturned this order and the matter went to the Supreme Court of Canada. (In the meantime, the mother opted to stay in the health centre, controlled her addiction, and gave birth to a healthy child.)

The majority of the Court upheld the "born alive" common law rule that prevents fetuses from possessing legal rights, and insisted that given the huge social consequences of changing that rule, it should be left to Parliament. The dissent equally vigorously argued that the "born alive" rule should be judicially overruled since it merely reflected the low level of medical knowledge of an earlier era. Both sides were mindful, however, that in the end this is an issue in which the autonomy, or potential autonomy, of two individuals are at stake, and deciding between the two forces the court to step into an area it is often reluctant to enter.

Justice McLachlin (for the majority):

[9] This appeal raises two legal issues:

(1) Does tort law, as it exists or may properly be extended by the Court, permit an order detaining a pregnant woman against her will in order to protect her unborn child from conduct that may harm the child?

(2) Alternatively, does the power of a court to make orders for the protection of children (its *parens patriae* jurisdiction), as it exists or may properly be extended by the Court, permit an order detaining a pregnant woman against her will in order to protect her unborn child from conduct that may harm the child?

[10] The appellant agency does not request that the order for mandatory treatment be upheld. At the same time, treatment, at least in the minimal sense of abstention from substance abuse, emerged as the only justification for the order for detention. Without mandatory treatment, the order for detention would lack any foundation. Thus the question of whether a judge may order detention of a pregnant woman at the request of the state encompasses the issue of whether a judge may make an order for mandatory treatment.

Does the Existing Law of Tort Support the Order?

[11] Before dealing with the cases treating the issue in tort law, I turn to the general proposition that the law of Canada does not recognize the unborn child as a legal or juridical person. Once a child is born, alive and viable, the law may recognize that its existence began before birth for certain limited purposes. But the only right recognized is that of the born person. This is a general proposition, applicable to all aspects of the law, including the law of torts.

[12] By way of preamble, two points may be made. First, we are concerned with the common law, not statute. If Parliament or the legislatures wish to legislate legal rights for unborn children or other protective measures, that is open to them, subject to any limitations imposed by the Constitution of Canada. Further, the fact that particular statutes may touch on the interests of the unborn need not concern us. Second, the issue is not one of biological status, nor indeed spiritual status, but of legal status. As this Court put it in *Tremblay v. Daigle*, [1989] 2 S.C.R. 530, at p. 553:

> The task of properly classifying a fetus in law and in science are different pursuits. Ascribing personhood to a fetus in law is a fundamentally normative task. It results in the recognition of rights and duties—a matter which falls outside the concerns of scientific classification. In short, this Court's task is a legal one. Decisions based upon broad social, political, moral and economic choices are more appropriately left to the legislature. [...]

[15] The position is clear. Neither the common law nor the civil law of Quebec recognizes the unborn child as a legal person possessing rights. This principle applies generally, whether the case falls under the rubric of family law, succession law or tort. Any right or interest the fetus may have remains inchoate and incomplete until the birth of the child.

[16] It follows that under the law as it presently stands, the fetus on whose behalf the agency purported to act in seeking the order for the respondent's detention was not a legal person and possessed no legal rights. If it was not a legal person and possessed no legal rights at the time of the application, then there was no legal person in whose interests the agency could act or in whose interests a court order could be made. [...]

Should the Law of Tort Be Extended to Permit the Order?

[18] It is necessary at the outset to consider the principles that govern judicial extension of common law principles. As a general rule, judicial change is confined to incremental change "based largely on the mechanism of extending an existing principle to new circumstances"; courts will not extend the common law "where the revision is major and its ramifications complex": *Watkins v. Olafson*, [1989] 2 S.C.R. 750, at pp. 760–61; approved in *R. v. Salituro*, [1991] 3 S.C.R. 654, at pp. 668–69, *per* Iacobucci J. As I stated in *Watkins*:

> There are sound reasons supporting this judicial reluctance to dramatically recast established rules of law. The court may not be in the best position to assess the deficiencies of the existing law, much less problems which may be associated with the changes it might make. The court has before it a single case; major changes in the law should be predicated on a wider view of how the rule will operate in the broad generality of cases. Moreover, the court may not be in a position to appreciate fully the economic and policy issues underlying the choice it is asked to make. Major changes to the law often involve devising subsidiary rules and procedures relevant to their implementation, a task which is better accomplished through consultation between courts and practitioners than by judicial decree. Finally, and perhaps most importantly, there is the long-established principle that in a constitutional democracy it is the legislature, as the elected branch of government, which should assume the major responsibility for law reform.

Considerations such as these suggest that major revisions of the law are best left to the legislature. Where the matter is one of a small extension of existing rules to meet the exigencies of a new case and the consequences of the change are readily assessable, judges can and should vary existing principles. But where the revision is major and its ramifications complex, the courts must proceed with great caution.

[19] The changes which the agency asks this Court to make to the law of tort may be summarized as follows:

1. Overturn the rule that rights accrue to a person only at birth (the "live-birth" rule);
2. Recognize a fetal right to sue the mother carrying the fetus;
3. Recognize a cause of action for lifestyle choices which may adversely affect others;
4. Recognize an injunctive remedy which deprives a defendant of important liberties, including her involuntary confinement.

[20] The proposed changes to the law of tort are major, affecting the rights and remedies available in many other areas of tort law. They involve moral choices and would create conflicts between fundamental interests and rights.

They would have an immediate and drastic impact on the lives of women as well as men who might find themselves incarcerated and treated against their will for conduct alleged to harm others. And, they possess complex ramifications impossible for this Court to fully assess, giving rise to the danger that the proposed order might impede the goal of healthy infants more than it would promote it. In short, these are not the sort of changes which common law courts can or should make. These are the sort of changes which should be left to the legislature. [...]

[24] This change to the law of tort is fraught with complexities and ramifications, the consequences of which cannot be precisely foretold. At what stage would a fetus acquire rights? Could women who choose to terminate a pregnancy face injunctive relief prohibiting termination, relief which this Court rejected in *Tremblay v. Daigle*? Alternatively, could they face an action for damages brought on behalf of the fetus for its lost life? If a pregnant woman is killed as a consequence of negligence on the highway, may a family sue not only for her death, but for that of the unborn child? If it is established that a fetus can feel discomfort, can it sue its mother (or perhaps her doctor) and claim damages for the discomfort? If the unborn child is a legal person with legal rights, arguments can be made in favour of all these propositions. Some might endorse such changes, others deplore them. The point is that they are major changes attracting an array of consequences that would place the courts at the heart of a web of thorny moral and social issues which are better dealt with by elected legislators than by the courts. Having broken the time-honoured rule that legal rights accrue only upon live birth, the courts would find it difficult to limit application of the new principle to particular cases. By contrast, the legislature, should it choose to introduce a law permitting action to protect unborn children against substance abuse, could limit the law to that precise case.

[25] Two arguments are made in favour of this Court abolishing the rule that no legal rights accrue before live birth. The first is that there is no defensible difference between a born child and an unborn child. This is essentially a biological argument. As noted above, the inquiry before this Court is not a biological one, but a legal one. The common law has always distinguished between an unborn child and a child after birth.

[26] The second argument is that the court should overturn the "live-birth" rule because the present law does not provide a remedy for situations like the case at bar. This argument suffers from two flaws. First, it can be made in every case where a court is asked to make a major and complex change to the law. If there were a remedy, the major change would not be required. Second, the argument begs the questions of whether a remedy is required, and if so, what remedy and how finely tailored a remedy is best able to achieve the desired social consequence. It is not every evil which attracts court action; some evils remain for the legislature to correct. [...]

[33] Behind the refusal of the courts to permit a child to sue its mother for prenatal injuries related to her lifestyle, lies the fear that such suits would take

the courts into the difficult policy issue of the extent to which a mother's lifestyle is actionable. Leaving the special relationship between mother and unborn child aside for the moment, there is little precedent for suing any defendant in tort for damages one has suffered as a consequence of his or her lifestyle. While it is not inconceivable that the courts, proceeding properly in their incremental law-making capacity, may one day recognize such claims, the appellant agency faces the difficulty that on this point too it is asking this Court to break new ground in a controversial area. Once again, the consequences for the law of tort generally might be great. Are children to be permitted to sue their parents for second-hand smoke inhaled around the family dinner table? Could any cohabitant bring such an action? Are children to be permitted to sue their parents for spanking causing psychological trauma or poor grades due to alcoholism or a parent's undue fondness for the office or the golf course? If we permit lifestyle actions, where do we draw the line? [...]

[42] Recognizing a duty of care in relation to the lifestyle of the pregnant woman would also increase the level of outside scrutiny that she would be subjected to. Partners, parents, friends, and neighbours are among the potential classes of people who might monitor the pregnant woman's actions to ensure that they remained within the legal parameters. Difficulty in determining what conduct is and is not permissible might be expected to give rise to conflicts between the interested persons and the pregnant woman or even between the interested persons themselves. This raises the possibility of conflict which may exacerbate the pregnant woman's condition (and thus the fetus') rather than improve it.

[43] If it could be predicted with some certainty that all these negative effects of extending tort liability to the lifestyle choices of pregnant women would in fact diminish the problem of injured infants, the change might nevertheless arguably be justified. But the evidence before this Court fails to establish this. It is far from clear that the proposed tort duty will decrease the incidence of substance-injured children. Indeed, the evidence suggests that such a duty might have negative effects on the health of infants. No clear consensus emerges from the debate on the question of whether ordering women into "places of safety" and mandating medical treatment provide the best solution or, on the contrary, create additional problems.

[44] Indeed, changing tort law to make a pregnant mother liable for lifestyle-related fetal damage may be counterproductive in at least two ways. First, it may tend to drive the problems underground. Pregnant women suffering from alcohol or substance abuse addictions may not seek prenatal care for fear that their problems would be detected and they would be confined involuntarily and/or ordered to undergo mandatory treatment. As a result, there is a real possibility that those women most in need of proper prenatal care may be the ones who will go without and a judicial intervention designed to improve the health of the fetus and the mother may actually put both at serious health risk. Second, changing the law of tort as advocated by the agency might persuade

women who would otherwise choose to continue their pregnancies to undergo an abortion. Women under the control of a substance addiction may be unable to face the prospect of being without their addicting substance and may find terminating the pregnancy a preferable alternative. In the end, orders made to protect a fetus' health could ultimately result in its destruction. [...]

[49] Alternatively, the appellant agency seeks to sustain the order for the detention of the respondent by an extension of the court's *parens patriae* jurisdiction to permit protection of unborn children. Courts have the power to step into the shoes of the parent and make orders in the best interests of the child. [...] The agency argues that this power should be extended to orders on behalf of unborn children.

[50] I would reject this submission for reasons similar to those enunciated in connection with the submission that the law of tort should be extended to the unborn. The submission requires a major change to the law of *parens patriae*. The ramifications of the change would be significant and complex. The change involves conflicts of fundamental rights and interests and difficult policy issues. Not surprisingly these difficulties have led all appellate courts that have considered the extension to reject it. I share their view.

[51] The law as it stands is clear: the courts do not have *parens patriae* or wardship jurisdiction over unborn children. [...]

Conclusion

[59] I conclude that the common law does not clothe the courts with power to order the detention of a pregnant woman for the purpose of preventing harm to her unborn child. Nor, given the magnitude of the changes and their potential ramifications, would it be appropriate for the courts to extend their power to make such an order. The changes to the law sought on this appeal are best left to the wisdom of the elected legislature. I would dismiss the appeal. The respondent is entitled to her costs on a party and party basis in this Court and in the courts below. [...]

Justice Major (dissenting):

[60] I respectfully disagree with the conclusion of McLachlin J. that an order detaining a pregnant woman addicted to glue sniffing for which she has rejected abortion and/or medical treatment and decided to carry her child to term, would require a change to the law which cannot be properly made other than by legislation. [...]

[61] To the extent that a change in the law in the circumstances of this case is required, the much admired flexibility of the common law has proven adaptable enough over centuries to meet exigent circumstances as they arise. That flexibility is surely needed in the appeal. [...]

[91] The law of this country is consistent with the grant of a remedy in this case. The *parens patriae* jurisdiction of the superior courts is of undefined and

undefinable breadth. This Court's decision in *E. (Mrs.) v. Eve.* indicates that inherent power resides in the provincial superior courts to act on behalf of those who cannot act to protect themselves. A fetus suffering from its mother's abusive behaviour is particularly within this class and deserves protection.

[92] It has been submitted, however, that a fetus acquires no actionable rights in our law until it is born alive. In my view, the "born alive" rule, as it is known, is a common law evidentiary presumption rooted in rudimentary medical knowledge that has long since been overtaken by modern science and should be set aside for purpose of this appeal.

[93] This means that a superior court, on proper motion, should be able to exercise its *parens patriae* jurisdiction to restrain a mother's conduct when there is a reasonable probability of that conduct causing serious and irreparable harm to the fetus within her. While the granting of this type of remedy may interfere with the mother's liberty interests, in my view, those interests must bend when faced with a situation where devastating harm and a life of suffering can so easily be prevented. In any event, this interference is always subject to the mother's right to end it by deciding to have an abortion.

[94] The arguments against state intervention are that it improperly interferes with the rights of the mother, that there are innumerable hazards to safe pregnancies, and that the state should not impose health standards on adults without consent. Those arguments are answerable.

[95] Once the mother decides to bear the child the state has an interest in trying to ensure the child's health. What circumstances permit state intervention? The "slippery slope" argument was raised that permitting state intervention here would impose a standard of behaviour on all pregnant women. Questions were raised about women who smoked, who lived with a smoker, who ate unhealthy diets, etc. In response to the query of where a reasonable line should be drawn it was submitted that the pen should not even be lifted. This approach would entail the state to stand idly by while a reckless and/or addicted mother inflicts serious and permanent harm on to a child she had decided to bring into the world. [...]

The "Born-Alive" Rule

[104] The "born alive" rule, as its name suggests, requires a fetus to be born alive before any legal rights of personhood can accrue. The Court of Appeal relied on this rule as one resolution to the present case, but no inquiry was made into the genesis or purpose of the rule. Once the purpose of the rule is known, it becomes more apparent that it should not apply in this case. [...]

[106] Until the early 19th century medical practitioners could not determine with confidence before quickening (the first physical sensation by the mother of the fetus in the womb) whether a woman was pregnant, or further, whether the child *in utero* was alive. Consequently, the common law adopted the presumption that a child was first endowed with life at quickening.

[107] Limited medical knowledge also could not determine whether a child *in utero* was alive at the time it was subjected to an injury unless the child was also born alive, suffering from that injury. [...]

[109] Present medical technology renders the "born alive" rule outdated and indefensible. We no longer need to cling to an evidentiary presumption to the contrary when technologies like real time ultrasound, fetal heart monitors and fetoscopy can clearly show us that a fetus is alive and has been or will be injured by conduct of another. We can gauge fetal development with much more certainty than the common law presumed. How can the sophisticated micro-surgery that is now being performed on fetuses *in utero* be compatible with the "born alive" rule? [...]

[120] The "born alive" rule should be abandoned, for the purposes of this case, as it is medically out-of-date. It may be that the rule has continuing utility in the context of other cases with their own particular facts. The common law boasts that it is adaptable. If so, there is no need to cling for the sake of clinging to notions rooted in rudimentary medical and scientific knowledge of the past. A fetus should be considered within the class of persons whose interests can be protected through the exercise of the *parens patriae* jurisdiction. [...]

[124] Opposition to this intervention has been strenuously argued by the respondent and her supporting interveners. Exercise of the *parens patriae* jurisdiction will necessarily involve an overriding of some rights possessed by the mother in order to protect her fetus. It is acknowledged that these are serious impositions, accordingly, the test is set at such a very high threshold. We are not simply denying the mother her "right" to sniff solvents but also possibly her liberty. That is why a remedy of confinement should be the final option. Before a court takes the severe step of ordering confinement, a condition precedent should be that it is certain on a balance of probabilities that no other solution is workable or effective. The least rights-diminishing option should always be sought. [...]

[131] It is a fundamental precept of our society and justice system that society *can* restrict an individual's right to autonomy where the exercise of that right causes harm to others. Conversely, it would be unjust *not* to restrict one person's right of autonomy when the exercise of that right causes harm to others. In her dissenting opinion in the final report of the Royal Commission on New Reproductive Technologies, *Proceed with Care* (1993), vol. 2, Dr. Suzanne Rozell Scorsone stated, at p. 1131:

> Autonomy is a necessary good, but it is not an absolute. All of us have, as the report says, the right to make our own choices, but rights necessarily entail responsibilities; where our choices may or do harm others, our choices are, in fact, limited, and we are held accountable, whatever our gender. It is the suspension of that accountability with respect to pregnant women which would constitute the setting of a different (and lower) standard of behaviour.

As one American author explained:

> [A] state's compelling interest in potential life outweighs a mother's privacy right to conduct her life as she chooses when state intervention is hardly intrusive. Moreover, a privacy right protecting the daily conduct of a pregnant woman from interference would necessarily be far weaker than her privacy right to decide whether to have an abortion because, although it might not always be in her interest to have a child, it is never in her interest to have a child with birth defects. (C. A. Kyres, "A 'Cracked' Image of My Mother/Myself? The Need for a Legislative Directive Proscribing Maternal Drug Abuse" [1991], 25 *New Eng. L. Rev.* 1325, at p. 1350.) [...]

Conclusion

[138] I do not believe our system, whether legislative or judicial, has become so paralysed that it will ignore a situation where the imposition required in order to prevent terrible harm is so slight. It may be preferable that the legislature act but its failure to do so is not an excuse for the judiciary to follow the same course of inaction. Failure of the court to act should occur where there is no jurisdiction for the court to proceed. Outdated medical assumptions should not provide any licence to permit the damage to continue. Where the harm is so great and the temporary remedy so slight, the law is compelled to act. [...]

[140] It seems fundamentally unfair and inexplicable for this Court to hold that a fetus, upon live birth, can sue for damages to recompense injuries suffered *in utero*, yet have no ability to obtain a remedy preventing that damage from occurring in the first place. This is one of the clearest of cases where monetary damages are a singularly insufficient remedy. If our society is to protect the health and well-being of children, there must exist jurisdiction to order a pre-birth remedy preventing a mother from causing serious harm to her fetus. Someone must speak for those who cannot speak for themselves.

Starson v. Swayze
Supreme Court of Canada
[2003] 1 S.C.R. 722

Under the *Health Care and Consent Act (HCCA)* of Ontario, a person suffering from mental illness may refuse medical treatment if it can be shown that they possess the capacity to understand and appreciate the consequences of their refusal. If it can be shown that a person lacks the requisite capacity, then it may be permissible for medical treatment to be imposed without consent. In this case, Scott Jeffery Schutzman (also known as Scott Starson or "Professor Starson") had initially been found to be incapable of refusing medical treatment for his mental illness. The Supreme Court faced the challenge of examining the appropriate standard of review for findings of capacity or incapacity under the *HCCA*.

The case raises the thorny issue of possible justifications for medical treatment without consent, and the relation of consent to the value of autonomy which must always be presumed even if ultimately overridden by other considerations. The Supreme Court decided by a vote of 6–3 that the initial finding that Starson was incapable of refusing treatment was mistaken.

Justice Major (for the majority):

Factual Background

[65] By all accounts, Professor Starson is an extraordinarily intelligent and unique individual. Although he lacks any formal training in the subject, it is beyond dispute that his driving passion in life is physics. He has published several papers in the field: see a paper co-authored with Professor H. P. Noyes of Stanford University, entitled "Discrete Anti-Gravity" (1991). Professor Noyes is said to have described the respondent's thinking as "ten years ahead of his time." Although the respondent is not by university training a professor, his peers in the academic community allow him to use the title as recognition of his accomplishments.

[66] Unfortunately, since 1985 the respondent has frequently been admitted to mental institutions in the United States and Canada. He has most often been diagnosed as having a bipolar disorder. Professor Starson has never caused physical harm to himself or to others, with the exception of reacting against unwanted forcible medication. His most recent admission to hospital arose after he was found not criminally responsible for making death threats. The Ontario Review Board ("ORB") ordered his detention for 12 months.

[67] The respondent's physicians proposed treatment for his bipolar disorder. It included neuroleptic medication, mood stabilizers, anti-anxiety medication and anti-parkinsonian medication. He refused to consent to this medication. The respondent acknowledges that he has mental health problems, but will not agree that he suffers from an illness. He claims that his full mental functioning is critical to his scientific pursuits. He believes that all previous medication of a similar kind has significantly dulled his thinking and thereby prevented his work as a physicist. Although to him his life is generally very happy, medication has invariably made him miserable in the past.

[68] The attending physician found Professor Starson not capable of deciding whether to reject or accept the proposed medical treatment. Professor Starson applied to the Board for a review of that decision. The Board's confirmation of incapacity was subsequently overturned on judicial review at the Ontario Superior Court of Justice. The Ontario Court of Appeal upheld the findings of the reviewing judge. That decision is appealed by the chief psychiatrist of the hospital in which Professor Starson currently resides. [...]

The Health Care Consent Act, 1996

[75] The right to refuse unwanted medical treatment is fundamental to a person's dignity and autonomy. This right is equally important in the context of treatment for mental illness: see *Fleming v. Reid* (1991), 4 O.R. (3d) 74 (C.A.), *per* Robins J.A., at p. 88:

> Few medical procedures can be more intrusive than the forcible injection
> of powerful mind-altering drugs which are often accompanied by severe
> and sometimes irreversible adverse side effects.

Unwarranted findings of incapacity severely infringe upon a person's right to self-determination. Nevertheless, in some instances the well-being of patients who lack the capacity to make medical decisions depends upon state intervention: see *E. (Mrs.) v. Eve*, [1986] 2 S.C.R. 388, at p. 426. The Act aims to balance these competing interests of liberty and welfare: see B. F. Hoffman, *The Law of Consent to Treatment in Ontario* (2nd ed. 1997), at p. 3. Neither party raised the constitutionality of the Act as an issue in this appeal.

[76] The legislative mandate of the Board is to adjudicate *solely* upon a patient's capacity. The Board's conception of the patient's best interests is irrelevant to that determination. As the reviewing judge observed, "[a] competent patient has the absolute entitlement to make decisions that any reasonable person would deem foolish" (para. 13). This point was aptly stated by Quinn J. in *Koch (Re)* (1997), 33 O.R. (3d) 485 (Gen. Div.), at p. 521:

> The right knowingly to be foolish is not unimportant; the right to volun-
> tarily assume risks is to be respected. The State has no business meddling
> with either. The dignity of the individual is at stake.

In this case, the only issue before the Board was whether Professor Starson was capable of making a decision on the suggested medical treatment. The wisdom of his decision has no bearing on this determination.

[77] The law presumes a person is capable to decide to accept or reject medical treatment: s. 4(2) of the Act. At a capacity hearing, the onus is on the attending physician to prove that the patient is incapable. I agree with the Court of Appeal that proof is the civil standard of a balance of probabilities. As a result, patients with mental disorders are presumptively entitled to make their own treatment decisions. Professor D. N. Weisstub, in his *Enquiry on Mental Competency: Final Report* (1990), at p. 116 ("Weisstub Report"), notes the historical failure to respect this presumption:

> The tendency to conflate mental illness with lack of capacity, which occurs to an even greater extent when involuntary commitment is involved, has deep historical roots, and even though changes have occurred in the law over the past twenty years, attitudes and beliefs have been slow to change. For this reason it is particularly important that autonomy and self determination be given priority when assessing individuals in this group.

The Board must avoid the error of equating the presence of a mental disorder with incapacity. Here, the respondent did not forfeit his right to self-determination upon admission to the psychiatric facility: see *Fleming v. Reid, supra,* at p. 86. The presumption of capacity can be displaced only by evidence that a patient lacks the requisite elements of capacity provided by the Act.

[78] Section 4(1) of the Act describes these elements as follows:

> A person is capable with respect to a treatment, admission to a care facility or a personal assistance service if the person is able to understand the information that is relevant to making a decision about the treatment, admission or personal assistance service, as the case may be, and able to appreciate the reasonably foreseeable consequences of a decision or lack of decision.

Capacity involves two criteria. First, a person must be able to understand the information that is relevant to making a treatment decision. This requires the cognitive ability to process, retain and understand the relevant information. There is no doubt that the respondent satisfied this criterion. Second, a person must be able to appreciate the reasonably foreseeable consequences of the decision or lack of one. This requires the patient to be able to apply the relevant information to his or her circumstances, and to be able to weigh the foreseeable risks and benefits of a decision or lack thereof. The Board's finding of incapacity was based on their perception of Professor Starson's failure in this regard.

[79] Before turning to an analysis of the reviewing judge's decision, two important points regarding this statutory test require comment. First, a patient need not agree with the diagnosis of the attending physician in order to be able to apply the relevant information to his own circumstances. Psychiatry is not

an exact science, and "capable but dissident interpretations of information" are to be expected: see Weisstub Report, *supra*, at p. 229. While a patient need not agree with a particular diagnosis, if it is demonstrated that he has a mental "condition," the patient must be able to recognize the possibility that he is affected by that condition. Professor Weisstub comments on this requirement as follows (at p. 250, note 443):

> Condition refers to the broader manifestations of the illness rather than the existence of a discrete diagnosable pathology. The word condition allows the requirement for understanding to focus on the objectively discernible manifestations of the illness rather than the interpretation that is made of these manifestations.

As a result, a patient is not required to describe his mental condition as an "illness," or to otherwise characterize the condition in negative terms. Nor is a patient required to agree with the attending physician's opinion regarding the cause of that condition. Nonetheless, if the patient's condition results in him being unable to recognize that he is affected by its manifestations, he will be unable to apply the relevant information to his circumstances, and unable to appreciate the consequences of his decision.

[80] Secondly, the Act requires a patient to have the *ability* to appreciate the consequences of a decision. It does not require *actual* appreciation of those consequences. The distinction is subtle but important: see L.H. Roth, A. Meisel and C.W. Lidz, "Tests of Competency to Consent to Treatment" (1977), 134 *Am. J. Psychiatry* 279, at pp. 281–82, and Weisstub Report, *supra*, at p. 249. In practice, the determination of capacity should begin with an inquiry into the patient's actual appreciation of the parameters of the decision being made: the nature and purpose of the proposed treatment; the foreseeable benefits and risks of treatment; the alternative courses of action available; and the expected consequences of not having the treatment. If the patient shows an appreciation of these parameters—regardless of whether he weighs or values the information differently than the attending physician and disagrees with the treatment recommendation—he has the ability to appreciate the decision he makes: see Roth, Meisel, and Lidz, *supra*, at p. 281.

[81] However, a patient's failure to demonstrate actual appreciation does not inexorably lead to a conclusion of incapacity. The patient's lack of appreciation may derive from causes that do not undermine his *ability* to appreciate consequences. For instance, a lack of appreciation may reflect the attending physician's failure to adequately inform the patient of the decision's consequences: see the Weisstub Report, *supra*, at p. 249. Accordingly, it is imperative that the Board inquire into the reasons for the patient's failure to appreciate consequences. A finding of incapacity is justified only if those reasons demonstrate that the patient's mental disorder prevents him from having the *ability* to appreciate the foreseeable consequences of the decision.

Carter v. Canada (Attorney General)
Supreme Court of Canada
[2015] 1 S.C.R. 331

For many years the Criminal Code of Canada prohibited physician-assisted suicide. Historically, this prohibition was most famously applied in *Rodriguez v. British Columbia* [1993] 3 S.C.R. 519. Recently, the Supreme Court had the opportunity to revisit the issues of autonomy and sanctity of life surrounding the debate over physician-assisted suicide. In reaching its decision that the Criminal Code provisions prohibiting physician-assisted suicide unjustifiably infringed section 7 of the *Charter* (the right to life, liberty, and security of the person), the Court found that a new legal issue had arisen and that circumstances and evidence regarding physician-assisted suicide had changed since *Rodriguez*.

———————

The Court:

Does the Law Infringe the Right to Life, Liberty and Security of the Person?

Life

[57] The trial judge found that the prohibition on physician-assisted dying had the effect of forcing some individuals to take their own lives prematurely, for fear that they would be incapable of doing so when they reached the point where suffering was intolerable. On that basis, she found that the right to life was engaged.

[58] We see no basis for interfering with the trial judge's conclusion on this point. The evidence of premature death was not challenged before this Court. It is therefore established that the prohibition deprives some individuals of life.

[59] The appellants and a number of the interveners urge us to adopt a broader, qualitative approach to the right to life. Some argue that the right to life is not restricted to the preservation of life, but protects quality of life and therefore a right to die with dignity. Others argue that the right to life protects personal autonomy and fundamental notions of self-determination and dignity, and therefore includes the right to determine whether to take one's own life.

[60] In dissent at the Court of Appeal, Finch C.J.B.C. accepted the argument that the right to life protects more than physical existence (paras. 84–89). In his view, the life interest is "intimately connected to the way a person values his or her lived experience. The point at which the meaning of life is lost, when life's positive attributes are so diminished as to render life valueless,... is an intensely personal decision which 'everyone' has the right to make for him or herself" (para. 86). Similarly, in his dissent in *Rodriguez*, Cory J. accepted that

the right to life included a right to die with dignity, on the ground that "dying is an integral part of living" (p. 630).

[61] The trial judge, on the other hand, rejected the "qualitative" approach to the right to life. She concluded that the right to life is only engaged when there is a threat of death as a result of government action or laws. In her words, the right to life is limited to a "right not to die" (para. 1322 [emphasis in original]).

[62] This Court has most recently invoked the right to life in *Chaoulli v. Quebec (Attorney General)*, 2005 SCC 35, [2005] 1 S.C.R. 791, where evidence showed that the lack of timely health care could result in death (paras. 38 and 50, per Deschamps J.; para. 123, per McLachlin C.J. and Major J.; and paras. 191 and 200, per Binnie and LeBel JJ.), and in *PHS*, where the clients of Insite were deprived of potentially lifesaving medical care (para. 91). In each case, the right was only engaged by the threat of death. In short, the case law suggests that the right to life is engaged where the law or state action imposes death or an increased risk of death on a person, either directly or indirectly. Conversely, concerns about autonomy and quality of life have traditionally been treated as liberty and security rights. We see no reason to alter that approach in this case.

[63] This said, we do not agree that the existential formulation of the right to life *requires* an absolute prohibition on assistance in dying, or that individuals cannot "waive" their right to life. This would create a "duty to live," rather than a "right to life," and would call into question the legality of any consent to the withdrawal or refusal of lifesaving or life-sustaining treatment. The sanctity of life is one of our most fundamental societal values. Section 7 is rooted in a profound respect for the value of human life. But s. 7 also encompasses life, liberty and security of the person during the passage to death. It is for this reason that the sanctity of life "is no longer seen to require that all human life be preserved at all costs" (*Rodriguez*, at p. 595, per Sopinka J.). And it is for this reason that the law has come to recognize that, in certain circumstances, an individual's choice about the end of her life is entitled to respect. It is to this fundamental choice that we now turn.

Liberty and Security of the Person

[64] Underlying both of these rights is a concern for the protection of individual autonomy and dignity. Liberty protects "the right to make fundamental personal choices free from state interference": *Blencoe v. British Columbia (Human Rights Commission)*, 2000 SCC 44, [2000] 2 S.C.R. 307, at para. 54. Security of the person encompasses "a notion of personal autonomy involving...control over one's bodily integrity free from state interference" (*Rodriguez*, at pp. 587–88, per Sopinka J., referring to *R. v. Morgentaler*, [1988] 1 S.C.R. 30) and it is engaged by state interference with an individual's physical or psychological integrity, including any state action that causes physical or serious psychological suffering...While liberty and security of the person are distinct interests, for the purpose of this appeal they may be considered together.

[65] The trial judge concluded that the prohibition on assisted dying limited Ms. Taylor's s. 7 right to liberty and security of the person, by interfering with "fundamentally important and personal medical decision-making" (para. 1302), imposing pain and psychological stress and depriving her of control over her bodily integrity (paras. 1293–94). She found that the prohibition left people like Ms. Taylor to suffer physical or psychological pain and imposed stress due to the unavailability of physician-assisted dying, impinging on her security of the person. She further noted that seriously and irremediably ill persons were "denied the opportunity to make a choice that may be very important to their sense of dignity and personal integrity" and that is "consistent with their life-long values and that reflects their life's experience" (para. 1326).

[66] We agree with the trial judge. An individual's response to a grievous and irremediable medical condition is a matter critical to their dignity and autonomy. The law allows people in this situation to request palliative sedation, refuse artificial nutrition and hydration, or request the removal of life-sustaining medical equipment, but denies them the right to request a physician's assistance in dying. This interferes with their ability to make decisions concerning their bodily integrity and medical care and thus trenches on liberty. And, by leaving people like Ms. Taylor to endure intolerable suffering, it impinges on their security of the person.

[67] The law has long protected patient autonomy in medical decision-making. In *A.C. v. Manitoba (Director of Child and Family Services)*, 2009 SCC 30, [2009] 2 S.C.R. 181, a majority of this Court, per Abella J. (the dissent not disagreeing on this point), endorsed the "tenacious relevance in our legal system of the principle that competent individuals are—and should be—free to make decisions about their bodily integrity" (para. 39). This right to "decide one's own fate" entitles adults to direct the course of their own medical care (para. 40): it is this principle that underlies the concept of "informed consent" and is protected by s. 7's guarantee of liberty and security of the person (para. 100; see also *R. v. Parker* [2000], 49 O.R. [3d] 481 [C.A.]). As noted in *Fleming v. Reid* (1991), 4 O.R. (3d) 74 (C.A.), the right of medical self-determination is not vitiated by the fact that serious risks or consequences, including death, may flow from the patient's decision. It is this same principle that is at work in the cases dealing with the right to refuse consent to medical treatment, or to demand that treatment be withdrawn or discontinued....

[68] In *Blencoe*, a majority of the Court held that the s. 7 liberty interest is engaged "where state compulsions or prohibitions affect important and fundamental life choices" (para. 49). In *A.C.*, where the claimant sought to refuse a potentially lifesaving blood transfusion on religious grounds, Binnie J. noted that we may "instinctively recoil" from the decision to seek death because of our belief in the sanctity of human life (para. 219). But his response is equally relevant here: it is clear that anyone who seeks physician-assisted dying because they are suffering intolerably as a result of a grievous and irremediable medical condition "does so out of a deeply personal and fundamental belief about how

they wish to live, or cease to live" (*ibid.*). The trial judge, too, described this as a decision that, for some people, is "very important to their sense of dignity and personal integrity, that is consistent with their lifelong values and that reflects their life's experience" (para. 1326). This is a decision that is rooted in their control over their bodily integrity; it represents their deeply personal response to serious pain and suffering. By denying them the opportunity to make that choice, the prohibition impinges on their liberty and security of the person. As noted above, s. 7 recognizes the value of life, but it also honours the role that autonomy and dignity play at the end of that life. We therefore conclude that ss. 241 (*b*) and 14 of the *Criminal Code*, insofar as they prohibit physician-assisted dying for competent adults who seek such assistance as a result of a grievous and irremediable medical condition that causes enduring and intolerable suffering, infringe the rights to liberty and security of the person. [...]

Section 1

[94] In order to justify the infringement of the appellants' s. 7 rights under s. 1 of the *Charter*, Canada must show that the law has a pressing and sub-stantial object and that the means chosen are proportional to that object. A law is proportionate if (1) the means adopted are rationally connected to that objective; (2) it is minimally impairing of the right in question; and (3) there is proportionality between the deleterious and salutary effects of the law. [...]

Rational Connection

[99] The government must show that the absolute prohibition on physician-assisted dying is rationally connected to the goal of protecting the vulnerable from being induced to take their own lives in times of weakness. The question is whether the means the law adopts are a rational way for the legislature to pursue its objective. If not, rights are limited for no good reason. To establish a rational connection, the government need only show that there is a causal connection between the infringement and the benefit sought "on the basis of reason or logic": *RJR-MacDonald*, at para. 153.

[100] We agree with Finch C.J.B.C. in the Court of Appeal that, where an activity poses certain risks, prohibition of the activity in question is a rational method of curtailing the risks (para. 175). We therefore conclude that there is a rational connection between the prohibition and its objective.

[101] The appellants argue that the *absolute* nature of the prohibition is not logically connected to the object of the provision. This is another way of saying that the prohibition goes too far. In our view, this argument is better dealt with in the inquiry into minimal impairment. It is clearly rational to conclude that a law that bars all persons from accessing assistance in suicide will protect the vulnerable from being induced to commit suicide at a time of weakness. The means here are logically connected with the objective.

Minimal Impairment

[102] At this stage of the analysis, the question is whether the limit on the right is reasonably tailored to the objective. The inquiry into minimal impairment asks "whether there are less harmful means of achieving the legislative goal" (*Hutterian Brethren*, at para. 53). The burden is on the government to show the absence of less drastic means of achieving the objective "in a real and substantial manner" (*ibid.*, at para. 55). The analysis at this stage is meant to ensure that the deprivation of *Charter* rights is confined to what is reasonably necessary to achieve the state's object.

[103] The question in this case comes down to whether the absolute prohibition on physician-assisted dying, with its heavy impact on the claimants' s. 7 rights to life, liberty and security of the person, is the least drastic means of achieving the legislative objective. It was the task of the trial judge to determine whether a regime less restrictive of life, liberty and security of the person could address the risks associated with physician-assisted dying, or whether Canada was right to say that the risks could not adequately be addressed through the use of safeguards.

[104] This question lies at the heart of this case and was the focus of much of the evidence at trial. In assessing minimal impairment, the trial judge heard evidence from scientists, medical practitioners, and others who were familiar with end-of-life decision-making in Canada and abroad. She also heard extensive evidence from each of the jurisdictions where physician-assisted dying is legal or regulated. In the trial judge's view, an absolute prohibition would have been necessary if the evidence showed that physicians were unable to reliably assess competence, voluntariness, and non-ambivalence in patients; that physicians fail to understand or apply the informed consent requirement for medical treatment; or if the evidence from permissive jurisdictions showed abuse of patients, carelessness, callousness, or a slippery slope, leading to the casual termination of life (paras. 1365–66).

[105] The trial judge, however, expressly rejected these possibilities. After reviewing the evidence, she concluded that a permissive regime with properly designed and administered safeguards was capable of protecting vulnerable people from abuse and error. While there are risks, to be sure, a carefully designed and managed system is capable of adequately addressing them:

> My review of the evidence in this section, and in the preceding section on the experience in permissive jurisdictions, leads me to conclude that the risks inherent in permitting physician-assisted death can be identified and very substantially minimized through a carefully-designed system imposing stringent limits that are scrupulously monitored and enforced. [para. 883]

[106] The trial judge found that it was feasible for properly qualified and experienced physicians to reliably assess patient competence and voluntariness, and that coercion, undue influence, and ambivalence could all be reliably

assessed as part of that process (paras. 795–98, 815, 837, and 843). In reaching this conclusion, she particularly relied on the evidence on the application of the informed consent standard in other medical decision-making in Canada, including end-of-life decision-making (para. 1368). She concluded that it would be possible for physicians to apply the informed consent standard to patients who seek assistance in dying, adding the caution that physicians should ensure that patients are properly informed of their diagnosis and prognosis and the range of available options for medical care, including palliative care interventions aimed at reducing pain and avoiding the loss of personal dignity (para. 831).

[107] As to the risk to vulnerable populations (such as the elderly and disabled), the trial judge found that there was no evidence from permissive jurisdictions that people with disabilities are at heightened risk of accessing physician-assisted dying (paras. 852 and 1242). She thus rejected the contention that unconscious bias by physicians would undermine the assessment process (para. 1129). The trial judge found there was no evidence of inordinate impact on socially vulnerable populations in the permissive jurisdictions, and that in some cases palliative care actually improved post-legalization (para. 731). She also found that while the evidence suggested that the law had both negative and positive impacts on physicians, it did support the conclusion that physicians were better able to provide overall end-of-life treatment once assisted death was legalized (para. 1271). Finally, she found no compelling evidence that a permissive regime in Canada would result in a "practical slippery slope" (para. 1241).

RELATED CASES

Attorney-General of B.C. v. Astaforoff [1983] 6 W.W.R. 322
(In this case the British Columbia Supreme Court had to consider whether the state has the authority or the obligation to prevent a suicide, by force-feeding someone on a hunger strike.)

Rodriguez v. Attorney-General of B.C. [1992] 4 W.W.R. 109
(While the section of the *Criminal Code* making physician-assisted suicide an offence was upheld by the Supreme Court of Canada at the time, this decision of the British Columbia Court of Appeal is notable for its suggested safeguards of a practice that would allow physician-assisted suicide.)

Arsenault-Cameron v. Prince Edward Island [2000] 1 S.C.R. 3
(This case raises an issue of group self-determination, in which the right of a linguistic minority in Summerside, PE, to educate its children in French was upheld.)

PART V

Procedural Justice

Since ancient times judges and their courts have been associated with a particular kind of process: courts operate using procedural rules knowable to all and designed to support the court's reaching a well-informed yet impartial judgement in a particular dispute. "Procedural justice" as an ideal and body of practices ensures that judges hear each side advancing its case in a deliberate way, guided by court processes applied in the same way to similar cases. Readers will already be familiar with many of the principles associated with procedural justice and implemented in different ways in different legal systems: "Everyone has the right to hear claims against them and to defend themselves." "Everyone has the right to hear evidence against them." "Everyone has a right to trial without undue delay." These are some of the principles that Canadian lawyers have historically called the "rules of natural justice," often called "due process" in the United States.

With the arrival of the *Charter*, the importance of procedural fairness has been given a different character. Section 7 of the *Charter* guarantees everyone a right to life, liberty, and security of the person—and "the right not to be deprived thereof except in accordance with the principles of fundamental justice." The principles of fundamental justice require the state to proceed fairly when it limits or deprives individuals of their rights in order to pursue the interests of the state and, indirectly, of all its citizens. What fairness requires, is, however, often a matter requiring reflection on more than whether rules of procedure have been followed in ways required by natural justice. The Supreme Court is increasingly willing to assert that rules of procedure must be interpreted and applied in ways which recognize that procedures have substantive effects, and fundamental justice requires not just following the rules but doing so in a way which ensures that the intentions motivating adoption of the rules are respected. Some of the cases excerpted in this Part treat familiar issues in criminal trial, such as the way evidence is heard and how the Crown must prove guilt beyond reasonable doubt. Other cases take up civil matters including the role of administrative officials and administrative tribunals, examining procedural justice in circumstances involving the way legal authority is wielded and limited. All demonstrate the deep connection between justice in process and justice in outcome. A final document, a UN report from the Committee on Torture, shows the broader context and implications of procedural justice as practised by Canadian courts. The Committee argues that the Supreme Court decision in *Suresh*, excerpted here, misunderstands the implications of its decision, and so arrives via a defensible process at a conclusion which does not satisfy the demands of substantive justice.

Roncarelli v. Duplessis
Supreme Court of Canada
[1959] S.C.R. 121

In this very famous case, the Supreme Court of Canada was asked whether there are any implicit, legal limitations on the exercise of what appears to be the absolute discretion of an administrative official. In particular, if a statute gives an official the absolute power to grant, refuse or cancel liquor licences as he or she sees fit, and then proceeds to peremptorily cancel someone's licence on dubious grounds, does the victim of this treatment have any legal recourse? In arguing, for the majority, that discretion is never so absolute that it can be exercised arbitrarily, capriciously, or for purposes irrelevant to the nature of the legislation, Justice Rand helped to define the scope of procedural justice in Canadian law.

Justice Rand (for the majority):

The material facts from which my conclusion is drawn are these. The appellant was the proprietor of a restaurant in a busy section of Montreal which in 1946 through its transmission to him from his father had been continuously licensed for the sale of liquor for approximately 34 years; he is of good education and repute and the restaurant was of a superior class. On December 4th of that year, while his application for annual renewal was before the Liquor Commission, the existing licence was cancelled and his application for renewal rejected, to which was added a declaration by the respondent [Mr. Maurice Duplessis, then Premier and Attorney-General of Quebec] that no future licence would ever issue to him. These primary facts took place in the following circumstances.

For some years the appellant [Mr. Frank Roncarelli] had been an adherent of a rather militant Christian religious sect known as the Witnesses of Jehovah. Their ideology condemns the established church institutions and stresses the absolute and exclusive personal relation of the individual to the Deity without human intermediation or intervention.

The first impact of their proselytizing zeal upon the Roman Catholic Church and community in Quebec, as might be expected, produced a violent reaction. Meetings were forcibly broken up, property damaged, individuals ordered out of communities, in one case out of the Province, and generally, within the cities and towns, bitter controversy aroused. The work of the Witnesses was carried on both by word of mouth and by the distribution of printed matter, the latter including two periodicals known as "The Watch Tower" and "Awake," sold at a small price.

In 1945 the provincial authorities began to take steps to bring an end to what was considered insulting and offensive to the religious beliefs and feelings of the Roman Catholic population. Large scale arrests were made of young men and women, by whom the publications mentioned were being held out for sale, under local by-laws requiring a licence for peddling any kind of wares. Altogether almost one thousand of such charges were laid. The penalty involved in Montreal, where most of the arrests took place, was a fine of $40, and as the Witnesses disputed liability, bail was in all cases resorted to.

The appellant, being a person of some means, was accepted by the Recorder's Court as bail without question, and up to November 12, 1946 he had gone security in about 380 cases, some of the accused being involved in repeated offences. [...]

At no time did [Roncarelli] take any part in the distribution of the tracts: he was an adherent of the group but nothing more. [...] Beyond the giving of bail and being an adherent, the appellant is free from any relation that could be tortured into a badge of character pertinent to his fitness or unfitness to hold a liquor licence. [...]

Admittedly an adherent, [Roncarelli] was enabling these protagonists to be at large to carry on their campaign of publishing what they believed to be the Christian truth as revealed by the Bible; he was also the holder of a liquor licence, a "privilege" granted by the Province, the profits from which, as it was seen by the authorities, he was using to promote the disturbance of settled beliefs and arouse community disaffection generally. Following discussions between the then Mr. Archambault, as the personality of the Liquor Commission, and the chief prosecuting officer in Montreal, the former, on or about November 21st, telephoned to the respondent, advised him of those facts, and queried what should be done. Mr. Duplessis answered that the matter was serious and that the identity of the person furnishing bail and the liquor licensee should be put beyond doubt. A few days later, that identity being established through a private investigator, Mr. Archambault again communicated with the respondent and, as a result of what passed between them, the licence, as of December 4, 1946, was revoked.

In the meantime, about November 25, 1946, a blasting answer had come from the Witnesses. In an issue of one of the periodicals, under the heading "Quebec's Burning Hate," was a searing denunciation of what was alleged to be the savage persecution of Christian believers. Immediately instructions were sent out from the department of the Attorney-General ordering the confiscation of the issue and proceedings were taken against one Boucher charging him with publication of a seditious libel. [...]

The complementary state of things is equally free from doubt. From the evidence of Mr. Duplessis and Mr. Archambault alone, it appears that the action taken by the latter as the General Manager and sole member of the Commission was dictated by Mr. Duplessis as Attorney-General and Prime Minister of the Province; that that step was taken as a means of bringing to a halt the activities of the Witnesses, to punish the appellant for the part he had played not only by revoking the existing licence but in declaring him barred from one "forever," and to warn others that they similarly would be stripped of provincial "privileges" if they persisted in any activity directly or indirectly related to the Witnesses and to the objectionable campaign. [...]

In these circumstances, when the *de facto* power of the Executive over its appointees at will to such a statutory public function is exercised deliberately and intentionally to destroy the vital business interests of a citizen, is there any legal redress by him against the person so acting? [...]

The field of licensed occupations and businesses of this nature is steadily becoming of greater concern to citizens generally. It is a matter of vital importance that a public administration that can refuse to allow a person to enter or continue a calling which, in the absence of regulation, would be free and legitimate, should be conducted with complete impartiality and integrity; and that the grounds for refusing or cancelling a permit should unquestionably be such and such only as are incompatible with the purposes envisaged by the statute: the duty of a Commission is to serve those purposes and those only. A decision to deny or cancel such a privilege lies within the "discretion" of the Commission; but that means that decision is to be based upon a weighing of considerations pertinent to the object of the administration.

In public regulation of this sort there is no such thing as absolute and untrammelled "discretion," that is that action can be taken on any ground or for any reason that can be suggested to the mind of the administrator; no legislative Act can, without express language, be taken to contemplate an unlimited arbitrary power, exercisable for any purpose, however capricious or irrelevant, regardless of the nature or purpose of the statute. Fraud and corruption in the Commission may not be mentioned in such statutes but they are always implied as exceptions. "Discretion" necessarily implies good faith in discharging public duty; there is always a perspective within which a statute is intended to operate; and any clear departure from its lines or objects is just as objectionable as fraud or corruption. Could an applicant be refused a permit because he had been born in another Province, or because of the colour of his hair? The ordinary language of the Legislature cannot be so distorted.

To deny or revoke a permit because a citizen exercises an unchallengeable right totally irrelevant to the sale of liquor in a restaurant is equally beyond the scope of the discretion conferred. There was here not only revocation of the existing permit but a declaration of a future, definitive disqualification of the appellant to obtain one: it was to be "forever." This purports to divest his citizenship status of its incident of membership in the class of those of the public to whom such a privilege could be extended. Under the statutory language here, that is not competent to the Commission and *a fortiori* to the Government or the respondent. [...]

It was urged by Mr. Beaulieu that the respondent, as the incumbent of an office of state, so long as he was proceeding in "good faith," was free to act in a matter of this kind virtually as he pleased. The office of Attorney-General traditionally and by statute carries duties that relate to advising the Executive, including here, administrative bodies, enforcing the public law and directing the administration of justice. In any decision of the statutory body in this case, he had no part to play beyond giving advice on legal questions arising. In that role his action should have been limited to advice on the validity of a revocation for such a reason or purpose and what that advice should have been does not seem to me to admit of any doubt. To pass from this limited scope of action to that of bringing about a step by the Commission beyond the bounds prescribed by the Legislature for its exclusive action converted what was done into his personal act.

"Good faith" in this context, applicable both to the respondent and the General Manager, means carrying out the statute according to its intent and for its purpose; it means good faith in acting with a rational appreciation of that intent and purpose and not with an improper intent and for an alien purpose; it does not mean for the purposes of punishing a person for exercising an unchallengeable right; it does not mean arbitrarily and illegally attempting to divest a citizen of an incident of his civil status.

Re B.C. Motor Vehicle Act
Supreme Court of Canada
[1985] 2 S.C.R. 486

British Columbia's *Motor Vehicle Act* made it an offence, punishable by fine or imprisonment, to drive when one's licence was suspended or when one was otherwise prohibited from driving. The problem was that this was an "absolute liability" offence, which meant that to prove guilt the Crown did not have to show that the driver actually knew of the suspension or prohibition (for more on these kinds of offences see *R. v. City of Sault Ste. Marie* in Part VI). Did such an offence offend the "principles of fundamental justice" guaranteed by section 7 of the *Charter*? Along the way the majority and Justice Wilson's concurring judgement debate the issue whether the "principles" referred to in section 7 are purely procedural, or whether potentially go beyond these to more substantive principles.

Justice Lamer (for the majority):

[62] The term "principles of fundamental justice" is not a right, but a qualifier of the right not to be deprived of life, liberty and security of the person; its function is to set the parameters of that right.

[63] Sections 8 to 14 address specific deprivations of the "right" to life, liberty and security of the person in breach of the principles of fundamental justice, and as such, violations of s. 7. They are therefore illustrative of the meaning, in criminal or penal law, of "principles of fundamental justice"; they represent principles which have been recognized by the common law, the international conventions and by the very fact of entrenchment in the *Charter*, as essential elements of a system for the administration of justice which is founded upon a belief in the dignity and worth of the human person and the rule of law.

[64] Consequently, the principles of fundamental justice are to be found in the basic tenets and principles, not only of our judicial process, but also of the other components of our legal system.

[65] We should not be surprised to find that many of the principles of fundamental justice are procedural in nature. Our common law has largely been a law of remedies and procedures and, as Frankfurter J. wrote in *McNabb v. U.S.* 318 U.S. 332 (1942), at p. 347 "the history of liberty has largely been the history of observance of procedural safeguards." This is not to say, however, that the principles of fundamental justice are limited solely to procedural guarantees. Rather, the proper approach to the determination of the principles of fundamental justice is quite simply one in which, as Professor L. Tremblay has

written, "future growth will be based on historical roots" ("Section 7 of the Charter: Substantive Due Process?" [1984], 18 *U.B.C.L. Rev.* 201, at p. 254).

[66] Whether any given principle may be said to be a principle of fundamental justice within the meaning of s. 7 will rest upon an analysis of the nature, sources, *rationale* and essential role of that principle within the judicial process and in our legal system, as it evolves.

[67] Consequently, those words cannot be given any exhaustive content or simple enumerative definition, but will take on concrete meaning as the courts address alleged violations of s. 7.

[68] I now turn to such an analysis of the principle of *mens rea* and absolute liability offences in order to determine the question which has been put to the Court in the present Reference.

Absolute Liability and Fundamental Justice in Penal Law

[69] It has from time immemorial been part of our system of laws that the innocent not be punished. This principle has long been recognized as an essential element of a system for the administration of justice which is founded upon a belief in the dignity and worth of the human person and on the rule of law. It is so old that its first enunciation was in Latin *actus non facit reum nisi mens sit rea.* [...]

[74] In my view, it is because absolute liability offends the principles of fundamental justice that this Court created presumptions against legislatures having intended to enact offences of a regulatory nature falling within that category. This is not to say, however, that, as a result, absolute liability *per se* offends s. 7 of the *Charter.*

[75] A law enacting an absolute liability offence will violate s. 7 of the *Charter* only if and to the extent that it has the potential of depriving of life, liberty or security of the person.

[76] Obviously, imprisonment (including probation orders) deprives persons of their liberty. An offence has the potential as of the moment it is open to the judge to impose imprisonment. There is no need that punishment, as in s. 94(2) [of the B.C. *Motor Vehicle Act*], be made mandatory.

[77] I am therefore of the view that the combination of imprisonment and of absolute liability violates s. 7 of the *Charter* and can only be salvaged if the authorities demonstrate under s. 1 that such a deprivation of liberty in breach of those principles of fundamental justice is, in a free and democratic society, under the circumstances, a justified reasonable limit to one's rights under s. 7. [...]

[Mr. Justice Lamer went on to conclude the *Motor Vehicle Act* was not saved by s. 1.]

Justice Wilson (concurring):

[121] Unlike my colleague, I do not think that ss. 8 to 14 of the *Charter* shed much light on the interpretation of the phrase "in accordance with the principles of fundamental justice" as used in s. 7. I find them very helpful as illus-

trating facets of the right to life, liberty and security of the person. I am not ready at this point, however, to equate unreasonableness or arbitrariness or tardiness as used in some of these sections with a violation of the principles of fundamental justice as used in s. 7. Delay, for example, may be explained away or excused or justified on a number of grounds under s. 1. I prefer, therefore, to treat these sections as self-standing provisions, as indeed they are.

[122] I approach the interpretive problem raised by the phrase "the principles of fundamental justice" on the assumption that the legislature was very familiar with the concepts of "natural justice" and "due process" and the way in which those phrases had been judicially construed and applied. Yet they chose neither. Instead, they chose the phrase "the principles of fundamental justice." What is "fundamental justice"? We know what "fundamental principles" are. They are the basic, bedrock principles that underpin a system. What would "fundamental principles of justice" mean? And would it mean something different from "principles of fundamental justice"? I am not entirely sure. We have been left by the legislature with a conundrum. I would conclude, however, that if the citizen is to be guaranteed his right to life, liberty and security of the person—surely one of the most basic rights in a free and democratic society—then he certainly should not be deprived of it by means of a violation of a fundamental tenet of our justice system.

[123] It has been argued very forcefully that s. 7 is concerned only with procedural injustice but I have difficulty with that proposition. There is absolutely nothing in the section to support such a limited construction. Indeed, it is hard to see why one's life and liberty should be protected against procedural injustice and not against substantive injustice in a *Charter* that opens with the declaration:

> Whereas Canada is founded upon principles that recognize the supremacy of God and the rule of law;

and sets out the guarantee in broad and general terms as follows:

> 1. The *Canadian Charter of Rights and Freedoms* guarantees the rights and freedoms set out in it subject only to such reasonable limits prescribed by law as can be demonstrably justified in a free and democratic society.

I cannot think that the guaranteed right in s. 7 which is to be subject *only* to limits which are reasonable and justifiable in a free and democratic society can be taken away by the violation of a principle considered fundamental to our justice system. Certainly, the rule of law acknowledged in the preamble as one of the foundations on which our society is built is more than mere procedure. It will be for the courts to determine the principles which fall under the rubric "the principles of fundamental justice." Obviously, not all principles of law are covered by the phrase; only those which are basic to our system of justice.

[124] I have grave doubts that the dichotomy between substance and procedure which may have served a useful purpose in other areas of the law such as

administrative law and private international law should be imported into s. 7 of the *Charter*. In many instances the line between substance and procedure is a very narrow one. For example, the presumption of innocence protected by s. 11(d) of the *Charter* may be viewed as a substantive principle of fundamental justice but it clearly has both a substantive and a procedural aspect. Indeed, any rebuttable presumption of fact may be viewed as procedural, as going primarily to the allocation of the burden of proof. Nevertheless, there is also an interest of substance to be protected by the presumption, namely, the right of an accused to be treated as innocent until proved otherwise by the Crown. This right has both a societal and an individual aspect and is clearly fundamental to our justice system. I see no particular virtue in isolating its procedural from its substantive elements or *vice versa* for purposes of s. 7.

R. v. Carosella
Supreme Court of Canada
[1997] 1 S.C.R. 80

A major part of our body of law on procedural justice has arisen from the criminal law, where "following proper procedures" in criminal investigation, arrest, detention, and trial is taken very seriously. In order to defend oneself against a criminal charge one needs relevant evidence. It has long been held that the Crown cannot keep evidence that it has in its possession from the accused's lawyers, especially if that evidence tends to exculpate. A failure of "disclosure" by the Crown could result in a stay of proceedings which, in practice, could mean that the accused is set free. Generally speaking, for centuries courts have insisted that no obstacles should be placed before the accused that might hinder his or her right to "make full answer and defence." But does the duty to disclose potential evidence apply to someone other than the Crown, especially someone who has independent reasons for not making that evidence available?

In this case, the accused was charged with gross indecency. Shortly before laying the charge, the victim sought counselling from a social worker at a government-funded sexual assault crisis centre. When the defence made an application to have the notes of that interview released to them as evidence, it was found that the centre, in order to maintain the privacy of its clients and to ensure that women are not dissuaded from seeking their help, routinely shred notes of such interviews. The accused then brought this action claiming that his trial is procedurally unjust because, without those notes, he could not adequately defend himself. In this 5 to 4 decision, the Supreme Court of Canada tips the balance in favour of the accused's procedural rights.

Justice Sopinka (for the majority):

[1] This appeal requires the court to determine the appropriate response of a trial court to the deliberate destruction of evidence which may be relevant to the defence of an accused person. The trial judge found that notes of interviews with the complainant conducted before she laid a charge of gross indecency were relevant material and that this destruction deprived the appellant of the right to make full answer and defence in breach of his constitutional rights.

The trial judge ordered a stay of proceedings. The Court of Appeal reversed the trial judge and the appeal to this court is, therefore, as of right. [...]

Was There a Breach of the Right to Full Answer and Defence?

[26] [...] The entitlement of an accused person to production [of documents] either from the Crown or third parties is a constitutional right. Breach of this right entitles the accused person to a remedy under s. 24(1) of the *Charter*. Remedies range from one or several adjournments to a stay of proceedings. To require the accused to show that the conduct of his or her defence was prejudiced would foredoom any application for even the most modest remedy where the material has not been produced. It would require the accused to show how the defence would be affected by the absence of material which the accused has not seen. [...]

[38] It is immaterial that the right to disclosure is not explicitly listed as one of the components of the principles of fundamental justice. That is true as well of the right to make full answer and defence and other rights. The components of the right cannot be separated from the right itself. An analogy can be made to the s. 10(b) right to counsel. Although s. 10(b) of the *Charter* makes no mention of the right to be informed of the availability of legal aid (or its equivalent), we have treated this requirement as a component of the s. 10(b) guarantee. As a result, an accused can satisfy the court that he or she was denied his or her s. 10(b) right to counsel as a result of the failure of the police to inform him or her as to the availability of legal aid. There is no further onus imposed on the accused to show that, in addition to the fact that his corollary right to be informed of the availability of legal aid was breached, this resulted in prejudice of such a magnitude that his right to counsel as a whole was also breached. [...]

[40] It follows from the foregoing that if the material which was destroyed meets the threshold test for disclosure or production, the appellant's *Charter* rights were breached without the requirement of showing additional prejudice. The Court of Appeal accepted the submission that the propriety of the order for production was not in issue by reason of the fact that both the Crown and the complainants consented to the application for production. As between the [Sexual Assault Crisis] centre and the complainant, it was the latter's consent that was required. The high-handed policy adopted by the centre appears to ignore the fact that the right to confidentiality resides in the complainant and that destruction of records without the consent of the complainant is a violation of that right. Some complainants may wish to waive any right to confidentiality for a variety of reasons including the fact that the records may tend to support the complainant's claim. [...]

[45] In my view, it is clear that the appellant could have made use of the information in the notes even though it is difficult to specify the precise manner in which the information could have been used without knowing the contents of the notes. The classic use of such evidence is, of course, to cross-examine the witness on inconsistent statements. Although in this case the complainant

could not have been cross-examined on the notes themselves as the notes were not statements of the complainant, they could have afforded a foundation for cross-examination. If the notes indicated an inconsistency with evidence in the witness box, the witness could have been confronted with this inconsistency, and if denied, the statement could have been proved by calling the note-taker. [...]

[47] I conclude from the foregoing that there was abundant evidence before the trial judge to enable him to conclude that there was a reasonable possibility that the information contained in the notes that were destroyed was logically probative to an issue at the trial as to the credibility of the complainant. This information, therefore, would have satisfied the test for disclosure. The destruction of this material and its consequent non-disclosure resulted in a breach of the appellant's constitutional right to full answer and defence. [...]

Justice L'Heureux-Dubé (dissenting):

[65] I disagree with the result reached by my colleague [Justice Sopinka] and would dismiss the appeal. I also take a very different approach to the issues raised. For this reason, it seems appropriate at this point to clarify a few matters, in light of the assertions about this case made by Sopinka J.

[66] First, in my view, this case has absolutely nothing to do with disclosure. While Sopinka J. speaks at great length of the "right to disclosure" and the obligation which rests to disclose, I feel constrained to point out that disclosure is a concept which is binding *solely* upon the Crown, and not upon the public at large. [...] Nor does [the duty to disclose] impose an obligation upon the Crown to comb the world for information which might be of possible relevance to the defence. [...]

[67] It is crucial to recall, therefore, that in the case at bar, the centre is a third party, a party which has no obligation to preserve evidence for prosecutions or otherwise. Its policy decisions are for itself to determine and not for the Crown, the accused or the courts to interfere with, so long as it acts within the confines of the law. In this case, when the notes were destroyed, the centre had not received any subpoena or court order to produce such notes. Whether its policy of destruction was appropriate is not for us to decide. [...]

Lost Evidence

[71] Does an accused automatically have the right to every piece of potentially relevant evidence in the world? My colleague suggests this is in fact the case. He suggests that there will be a breach of the right to full answer and defence and therefore an unfair trial anytime material is unavailable that would have been disclosed if in the hands of the Crown. Therefore, whenever information in the hands of a third party has the reasonable possibility of being of some use to the defence the fact that it is unavailable immediately causes a violation of the *Charter*. In my view, the adoption of this rationale could quite possibly lead one

to the conclusion that there has never been a fair trial in this country. It goes against the grain of this court's *Charter* jurisprudence and is contrary to basic underlying notions of how the criminal justice system actually operates. [...]

[74] The *Charter* does not entitle an accused to a "perfect" trial, in which every piece of relevant information which might or might not affect the defence is diligently piled at the defence's door. An accused is entitled to a fair trial, where relevant, unprivileged material gathered by the Crown is disclosed, while evidence in the hands of third parties, after a balancing of considerations, is produced in appropriate cases. Where evidence is unavailable, the accused must demonstrate that a fair trial, and not a perfect one, cannot be had as a result of the loss.

[75] In my view, for the appellant to suggest that he is unable to receive a fair trial because of the destroyed notes, he must be able to demonstrate that there was actually some harm to his position. It is not enough to speculate, as my colleague proposes, that there is the *potential* for harm, as the notes might somehow have proved useful. [...]

Application to the Case at Bar

[114] In my view, the request [for the centre's notes] made here amounted to no more than what I stated should not be permitted: a fishing expedition in the hopes of uncovering a prior inconsistent statement. Despite the finding of the trial judge, there is absolutely nothing on the record to suggest that there was any discussion between the complainant and the counselor about the actual details of the events themselves. [...]

Centre's Conduct

[141] In any event, I am not convinced that the crisis centre's conduct was "manifestly inappropriate" so as to meet the standard of an abuse of process.

[142] The Centre was not acting out of *animus* against this appellant; nor was it acting out of generalized *animus* against persons accused of sexual assault, or at the instigation of the Crown. Rather, the record indicates that the crisis centre was implementing a general policy designed to protect its clients' privacy and ensure that women would not be dissuaded from seeking assistance for fear that their private discussions will be communicated to the defence. The fact that this particular complainant had, to a certain extent, waived confidentiality does not affect the validity of the crisis centre's general policy. It is entirely legitimate and understandable for a centre to warn its clients that their files could be subpoenaed, and to obtain their consent to release the records in such an eventuality, while at the same time taking steps to defend the confidentiality of the records.

[143] According to Sopinka J., the conduct of the crisis centre is an affront to the justice system and the crisis centre is flouting the authority of the courts. In my view, it is important to keep the actions of the centre in their proper

perspective. First, this is not a case where a person shredded documents in respect of which a subpoena or court order had been issued. On the contrary, the Centre's policy on shredding states that "[W]e cannot shred a document if it has been subpoenaed or there is an application requesting a Court Order."

[144] It is also highly significant that the Centre was under no obligation whatsoever to create or maintain records. My colleague appears to suggest that an independent agency cannot destroy materials which *might* one day be required to be produced to the court. In my view, this type of obligation is completely inappropriate. The Centre created notes for its own purposes. It was under no obligation to do so. Once it did, it had a legitimate property interest in them which it was able to do with as it saw fit. To suggest that the court should be able to enforce a maintenance obligation to property which *might one day be needed* by the courts is a hefty burden indeed. [...]

[147] Finally, I must comment upon the fact that these agencies have even felt it necessary to go to such lengths. From a quick perusal of lower court judgements, it would appear as if a request for therapeutic records in cases of sexual assault is becoming virtually automatic, with little regard to the actual relevancy of the documents. We have now come to a situation where people trying to help victims have resorted to forgoing the taking of notes or destroying them *en masse* in order to prevent what they see as a grave injustice. It is extremely likely that the therapeutical process for which these notes are actually created is being harmed in their absence.

Suresh v. Canada (Minister of Citizenship and Immigration)
Supreme Court of Canada
[2002] 1 S.C.R. 3

Balancing the rights of the individual against fundamental interests of the state is a basic role of our courts. Nowhere is this balancing more difficult than when the security of the country, in
the form of perceived threats of terrorism, conflicts with the basic
rights and freedoms of individuals. Surely, unless our security
is protected, these rights are meaningless; yet, if in the cause of
security our rights are abrogated, have not some of the goals of
terrorism been achieved?

In this case, Mr. Suresh, a refugee from Sri Lanka, appeals
a decision of the Minister of Citizenship and Immigration to
deport him on the grounds that he is, or was, a terrorist and as
such a threat to the security of Canada. The Minister has the
discretion to do so under s. 53 of the *Immigration Act*, but Mr.
Suresh insisted that if he went back he would be tortured. The
Supreme Court of Canada had no problem saying that being
tortured is a fundamental violation of rights. But the Court also
argued that there was nothing unconstitutional about s. 53 which
gives the Minister the right to decide that Canada's security is
more important than Mr. Suresh's rights. The Court insisted
that courts must be deferential to these decisions, and overturn
them only if utterly unreasonable. After all of this, however, the
Court still ordered a new deportation hearing. It did so by relying on what may be the most important legal tool for balancing
individual rights and the demands of security: procedural justice.

The Court:

[2] The appeal requires us to consider a number of issues: the standard to be
applied in reviewing a ministerial decision to deport; whether the *Charter*
precludes deportation to a country where the refugee faces torture or death;
whether deportation on the basis of mere membership in an alleged terrorist
organization unjustifiably infringes the *Charter* rights of free expression and
free association; whether "terrorism" and "danger to the security of Canada"
are unconstitutionally vague; and whether the deportation scheme contains
adequate procedural safeguards to ensure that refugees are not expelled to a
risk of torture or death.

[3] The issues engage concerns and values fundamental to Canada and indeed the world. On the one hand stands the manifest evil of terrorism and the random and arbitrary taking of innocent lives, rippling out in an ever-widening spiral of loss and fear. Governments, expressing the will of the governed, need the legal tools to effectively meet this challenge.

[4] On the other hand stands the need to ensure that those legal tools do not undermine values that are fundamental to our democratic society—liberty, the rule of law, and the principles of fundamental justice—values that lie at the heart of the Canadian constitutional order and the international instruments that Canada has signed. In the end, it would be a Pyrrhic victory if terrorism were defeated at the cost of sacrificing our commitment to those values. Parliament's challenge is to draft laws that effectively combat terrorism and conform to the requirements of our Constitution and our international commitments. [...]

Analysis

[41] [I]n reviewing ministerial decisions to deport under the Act, courts must accord deference to those decisions. If the Minister has considered the correct factors, the courts should not reweigh them. Provided the s. 53(1)(b) decision is not patently unreasonable—unreasonable on its face, unsupported by evidence, or vitiated by failure to consider the proper factors or apply the appropriate procedures—it should be upheld. At the same time, the courts have an important role to play in ensuring that the Minister has considered the relevant factors and complied with the requirements of the Act and the Constitution. [...]

[47] Determining whether deportation to torture violates the principles of fundamental justice requires us to balance Canada's interest in combatting terrorism and the Convention refugee's interest in not being deported to torture. Canada has a legitimate and compelling interest in combatting terrorism. But it is also committed to fundamental justice. The notion of proportionality is fundamental to our constitutional system. Thus we must ask whether the government's proposed response is reasonable in relation to the threat. [...]

[77] In Canada, the balance struck by the Minister must conform to the principles of fundamental justice under s. 7 of the *Charter*. It follows that insofar as the *Immigration Act* leaves open the possibility of deportation to torture, the Minister should generally decline to deport refugees where on the evidence there is a substantial risk of torture.

[78] [Yet] we do not exclude the possibility that in exceptional circumstances, deportation to face torture might be justified, either as a consequence of the balancing process mandated by s. 7 of the *Charter* or under s. 1. We may predict that it will rarely be struck in favour of expulsion where there is a serious risk of torture. However, as the matter is one of balance, precise prediction is elusive. The ambit of an exceptional discretion to deport to torture, if any, must await future cases. [...]

The Required Evidence

[87] Whatever the historic validity of insisting on direct proof of specific danger to the deporting country, as matters have evolved, we believe courts may now conclude that the support of terrorism abroad raises a possibility of adverse repercussions on Canada's security. International conventions must be interpreted in the light of current conditions. It may once have made sense to suggest that terrorism in one country did not necessarily implicate other countries. But after the year 2001, that approach is no longer valid.

[88] First, the global transport and money networks that feed terrorism abroad have the potential to touch all countries, including Canada, and to thus implicate them in the terrorist activity. Second, terrorism itself is a worldwide phenomenon. The terrorist cause may focus on a distant locale, but the violent acts that support it may be close at hand. Third, preventive or precautionary state action may be justified; not only an immediate threat but also possible future risks must be considered. Fourth, Canada's national security may be promoted by reciprocal cooperation between Canada and other states in combating international terrorism. These considerations lead us to conclude that to insist on direct proof of a specific threat to Canada as the test for "danger to the security of Canada" is to set the bar too high. There must be a real and serious possibility of adverse effect to Canada. But the threat need not be direct; rather it may be grounded in distant events that indirectly have a real possibility of harming Canadian security. [...]

[121] We are of the opinion that the procedural protections required by s. 7 in this case do not extend to the level of requiring the Minister to conduct a full oral hearing or a complete judicial process. However, they require more than the procedure required by the Act under s. 53(1)(b)—that is, none—and they require more than Suresh received.

[122] We find that a person facing deportation to torture under s. 53(1) (b) must be informed of the case to be met. Subject to privilege or similar valid reasons for reduced disclosure, such as safeguarding confidential public security documents, this means that the material on which the Minister is basing her decision must be provided to the individual. Furthermore, fundamental justice requires that an opportunity be provided to respond to the case presented to the Minister. While the Minister accepted written submissions from the appellant in this case, in the absence of access to the material she was receiving from her staff and on which she based much of her decision, Suresh and his counsel had no knowledge of which factors they specifically needed to address, nor any chance to correct any factual inaccuracies or mischaracterizations. Fundamental justice requires that written submissions be accepted from the subject of the order after the subject has been provided with an opportunity to examine the material being used against him or her. The Minister must then consider these submissions along with the submissions made by the Minister's staff.

[123] Not only must the refugee be informed of the case to be met, the refugee must also be given an opportunity to challenge the information of the Minister where issues as to its validity arise. Thus the refugee should be permitted to present evidence pursuant to s. 19 of the Act showing that his or her continued presence in Canada will not be detrimental to Canada, notwithstanding evidence of association with a terrorist organization. The same applies to the risk of torture on return. Where the Minister is relying on written assurances from a foreign government that a person would not be tortured, the refugee must be given an opportunity to present evidence and make submissions as to the value of such assurances. [...]

[126] The Minister must provide written reasons for her decision. These reasons must articulate and rationally sustain a finding that there are no substantial grounds to believe that the individual who is the subject of a s. 53(1)(b) declaration will be subjected to torture, execution or other cruel or unusual treatment, so long as the person under consideration has raised those arguments. The reasons must also articulate why, subject to privilege or valid legal reasons for not disclosing detailed information, the Minister believes the individual to be a danger to the security of Canada as required by the Act. [...]

[127] These procedural protections need not be invoked in every case, as not every case of deportation of a Convention refugee under s. 53(1)(b) will involve risk to an individual's fundamental right to be protected from torture or similar abuses. It is for the refugee to establish a threshold showing that a risk of torture or similar abuse exists before the Minister is obliged to consider fully the possibility. This showing need not be *proof* of the risk of torture to that person, but the individual must make out a *prima facie* case that there *may* be a risk of torture upon deportation. If the refugee establishes that torture is a real possibility, the Minister must provide the refugee with all the relevant information and advice she intends to rely on, provide the refugee an opportunity to address that evidence in writing, and after considering all the relevant information, issue responsive written reasons. This is the minimum required to meet the duty of fairness and fulfill the requirements of fundamental justice under s. 7 of the *Charter*. [...]

[5] We conclude that to deport a refugee to face a substantial risk of torture would generally violate s. 7 of the *Charter*. The Minister of Citizenship and Immigration must exercise her discretion to deport under the *Immigration Act* accordingly. Properly applied, the legislation conforms to the *Charter*. We reject the arguments that the terms "danger to the security of Canada" and "terrorism" are unconstitutionally vague and that ss. 19 and 53(1)(b) of the Act violate the *Charter* guarantees of free expression and free association, and conclude that the Act's impugned procedures, properly followed, are constitutional. We believe these findings leave ample scope to Parliament to adopt new laws and devise new approaches to the pressing problem of terrorism. [...]

[6] Applying these conclusions in the instant case, we find that the appellant Suresh made a *prima facie* case showing a substantial risk of torture if deported to Sri Lanka, and that his hearing did not provide the procedural safeguards required to protect his right not to be expelled to a risk of torture or death. This means that the case must be remanded to the Minister for reconsideration. The immediate result is that Suresh will remain in Canada until his new hearing is complete. Parliament's scheme read in light of the Canadian Constitution requires no less.

Report of the Committee against Torture
United Nations
**[2005] General Assembly Official Records, Sixtieth Session,
Supplement No. 44 (A/60/44)**

While there is no higher court of appeal in Canada beyond the Supreme Court, it is still possible for Supreme Court decisions to be scrutinized by international organizations in light of Canada's international obligations. The excerpt below is taken from the 2005 report of the United Nations (UN) Committee Against Torture, in which the committee criticized, among other things, the Supreme Court's decision in *Suresh*. In *Suresh* the Supreme Court held that while Canada had an obligation not to deport persons back to their home countries where there are substantial grounds for believing a threat of torture exists, under section 1 of the Canadian constitution this obligation could be balanced against the interests of a free and democratic society.

The UN Committee observed that the decision in *Suresh* was a failure to uphold the right against torture contained in the Convention against Torture and Other Cruel, Inhuman or Degrading Treatment or Punishment, of which Canada is a state party. The UN Committee noted that the right against torture is absolute, and so is not subject to limitations or balancing of any kind.

UN Committee against Torture:

CANADA

Positive Aspects

[56] The Committee notes:

(a) The definition of torture in the Canadian Criminal Code that is in accordance with the definition contained in article 1 of the Convention and the exclusion in the Criminal Code of the defences of superior orders or exceptional circumstances, including in armed conflict, as well as the inadmissibility of evidence obtained by torture;

(b) The direct application of the criminal norms cited in subparagraph (a) above to the State party's military personnel wherever they are located, by means of the National Defence Act;

(c) The general inclusion in the Immigration and Refugee Protection Act 2002 of torture within the meaning of article 1 of the Convention as an independent ground qualifying a person as in need of protection (sect. 97, subsect. 1 of the Act) and as a basis for non-refoulement (sect. 115, subsect. 1), where there are substantial grounds for believing that the threat of torture exists;

(d) The careful constitutional scrutiny of the powers conferred by the Anti-Terrorism Act 2001;

(e) The recognition of the Supreme Court of Canada that enhanced procedural guarantees have to be made available, even in national security cases, and the State party's subsequent decision to extend enhanced procedural protections to all cases of persons challenging on grounds of risk of torture, Ministerial expulsion decisions;

(f) The changes to Corrections policy and practice implemented to give effect to the recommendations of the Arbour Report on the treatment of female offenders in the federal prison system;

(g) The requirement that body cavity searches be carried out by medical rather than correctional staff in a non-emergency situation and after written consent and access to legal advice have been provided;

(h) The efforts made by the State party, in response to the issue of over-representation of indigenous offenders in the correctional system previously identified by the Committee, to develop innovative and culturally sensitive alternative criminal justice mechanisms, such as the use of healing lodges.

Subjects of Concern

[57] The Committee expresses its concern at:

(a) The failure of the Supreme Court of Canada, in *Suresh v. Minister of Citizenship and Immigration*, to recognize at the level of domestic law the absolute nature of the protection of article 3 of the Convention, which is not subject to any exception whatsoever;

(b) The alleged roles of the State party's authorities in the expulsion of Canadian national Mr. Maher Arar, expelled from the United States of America to the Syrian Arab Republic where torture was reported to be practised;

(c) The blanket exclusion by the Immigration and Refugee Protection Act 2002 (sect. 97) of the status of refugee or person in need of protection for persons falling within the security exceptions set out in the Convention relating to the Status of Refugees and its Protocol; as a result, such persons' substantive claims are not considered by the Refugee Protection Division or reviewed by the Refugee Appeal Division;

(d) The explicit exclusion of certain categories of persons posing security or criminal risks from the protection against refoulement provided by the Immigration and Refugee Protection Act 2002 (sect. 115, subsect. 2);

(e) The State party's apparent willingness, in the light of the low number of prosecutions for terrorism and torture offences, to resort in the first instance to immigration processes to remove or expel individuals from its territory, thus implicating issues of article 3 of the Convention more readily, rather than subject him or her to the criminal process;

(f) The State party's reluctance to comply with all requests for interim measures of protection, in the context of individual complaints presented under article 22 of the Convention;

(g) The absence of effective measures to provide civil compensation to victims of torture in all cases;

(h) The still substantial number of "major violent incidents," defined by the State party as involving serious bodily harm and/or hostage-taking, in the State party's federal corrections facilities; and

(i) Continued allegations of inappropriate use of chemical, irritant, incapacitating and mechanical weapons by law enforcement authorities in the context of crowd control.

Recommendations

[58] The Committee recommends that:

(a) The State party unconditionally undertake to respect the absolute nature of article 3 in all circumstances and fully to incorporate the provision of article 3 into the State party's domestic law;

(b) The State party remove the exclusions in the Immigration and Refugee Protection Act 2002 described in paragraph 57, subparagraphs (c) and (d) above, thereby extending to currently excluded persons entitlement to the status of protected person, and protection against refoulement on account of a risk of torture;

(c) The State party should provide for judicial review of the merits, rather than merely of the reasonableness, of decisions to expel an individual where there are substantial grounds for believing that the person faces a risk of torture;

(d) The State party should insist on unrestricted consular access to its nationals who are in detention abroad, with facility for unmonitored meetings and, if required, of appropriate medical expertise;

(e) Given the absolute nature of the prohibition against refoulement contained in article 3 of the Convention, the State party should provide the

Committee with details on how many cases of extradition or removal subject to receipt of "diplomatic assurances" or guarantees have occurred since 11 September 2001, what the State party's minimum requirements are for such assurances or guarantees, what measures of subsequent monitoring it has undertaken in such cases and the legal enforceability of the assurances or guarantees given;

(f) The State party should review its position under article 14 of the Convention to ensure the provision of compensation through its civil jurisdiction to all victims of torture;

(g) The State party should take steps to ensure that the frequency of "major violent incidents" in its federal corrective facilities decreases progressively;

(h) The State party should conduct a public and independent study and a policy review of the crowd control methods, at federal and provincial levels, described in paragraph 57, subparagraph (i) above;

(i) The State party should fully clarify, if necessary through the adoption of legislation, the competence of the Commission for Public Complaints Against the RCMP (Royal Canadian Mounted Police) to investigate and report on all activities of the Royal Canadian Mounted Police falling within its complaint mandate; and

(j) The State party should consider becoming party to the Optional Protocol to the Convention.

Dunsmuir v. New Brunswick
Supreme Court of Canada
[2008] 1 S.C.R. 190

In this case the Supreme Court took important steps to clarify the relations of courts to administrative tribunals established to bring special expertise to application of law, and to relieve courts of the day to day burden of addressing matters better handled by expert bodies. The Court recognized the inadequacy of its previous reasoning on the question of the conditions under which a court ought to review the reasonableness of an administrative tribunal's decision, and introduced a simpler approach explained in this excerpt. The Court articulates a new, reasonableness standard together with a correctness standard, each to be applied under specific conditions when considering whether a court ought to review an administrative tribunal's decision, with possible outcomes including replacement of the tribunal's reasoning and decision with the reasoning and decision of a court. In articulating these standards, the Court reflects on the meaning of "reasonableness" and the relation of both administrative tribunals and courts to legislators. The Court leaves to administrative tribunals those matters where tribunals have special expertise and legislation requires special respect for that expertise, yet reserves to judicial review those matters where a tribunal's jurisdiction and authority is in question, or where a matter goes beyond the expertise of the tribunal. Careful consideration should be given as to whether the Court's attempt to improve upon prior law offers a standard likely to be applicable in ways ensuring that neither courts nor tribunals stray into matters for which the other is properly intended and suited.

Justices Bastarache and Lebel (for the majority):

Defining the Concepts of Reasonableness and Correctness

[46] Reasonableness is one of the most widely used and yet most complex legal concepts. In any area of the law we turn our attention to, we find ourselves dealing with the reasonable, reasonableness or rationality. But what is a reasonable decision? How are reviewing courts to identify an unreasonable decision in the context of administrative law and, especially, of judicial review?

[47] Reasonableness is a deferential standard animated by the principle that underlies the development of the two previous standards of reasonableness: certain questions that come before administrative tribunals do not lend themselves to one specific, particular result. Instead, they may give rise to a number of possible, reasonable conclusions. Tribunals have a margin of appreciation within the range of acceptable and rational solutions. A court conducting a review for reasonableness inquires into the qualities that make a decision reasonable, referring both to the process of articulating the reasons and to outcomes. In judicial review, reasonableness is concerned mostly with the existence of justification, transparency and intelligibility within the decision-making process. But it is also concerned with whether the decision falls within a range of possible, acceptable outcomes which are defensible in respect of the facts and law.

[48] The move towards a single reasonableness standard does not pave the way for a more intrusive review by courts and does not represent a return to pre-*Southam* formalism. In this respect, the concept of deference, so central to judicial review in administrative law, has perhaps been insufficiently explored in the case law. What does deference mean in this context? Deference is both an attitude of the court and a requirement of the law of judicial review. It does not mean that courts are subservient to the determinations of decision makers, or that courts must show blind reverence to their interpretations, or that they may be content to pay lip service to the concept of reasonableness review while in fact imposing their own view. Rather, deference imports respect for the decision-making process of adjudicative bodies with regard to both the· facts and the law. The notion of deference "is rooted in part in a respect for governmental decisions to create administrative bodies with delegated powers" (*Canada (Attorney General) v. Mossop*, 1993 CanLII 164 (SCC), [1993] 1 S.C.R. 554, at p. 596, *per* L'Heureux-Dubé J., dissenting). We agree with David Dyzenhaus where he states that the concept of "deference as respect" requires of the courts "not submission but a respectful attention to the reasons offered or which could be offered in support of a decision": "The Politics of Deference: Judicial Review and Democracy," in M. Taggart, ed., *The Province of Administrative Law* (1997), 279, at p. 286 (quoted with approval in *Baker*, at para. 65, *per* L'Heureux-Dubé J.; *Ryan*, at para. 49).

[49] Deference in the context of the reasonableness standard therefore implies that courts will give due consideration to the determinations of decision makers. As Mullan explains, a policy of deference "recognizes the reality that, in many instances, those working day to day in the implementation of frequently complex administrative schemes have or will develop a considerable degree of expertise or field sensitivity to the imperatives and nuances of the legislative regime": D. J. Mullan, "Establishing the Standard of Review: The Struggle for Complexity?" (2004), 17 *C.J.A.L.P.* 59, at p. 93. In short, deference requires respect for the legislative choices to leave some matters in the hands of administrative decision makers, for the processes and determinations that draw on particular expertise and experiences, and for the different roles of the courts and administrative bodies within the Canadian constitutional system.

[50] As important as it is that courts have a proper understanding of reasonableness review as a deferential standard, it is also without question that the standard of correctness must be maintained in respect of jurisdictional and some other questions of law. This promotes just decisions and avoids inconsistent and unauthorized application of law. When applying the correctness standard, a reviewing court will not show deference to the decision maker's reasoning process; it will rather undertake its own analysis of the question. The analysis will bring the court to decide whether it agrees with the determination of the decision maker; if not, the court will substitute its own view and provide the correct answer. From the outset, the court must ask whether the tribunal's decision was correct.

Determining the Appropriate Standard of Review

[51] Having dealt with the nature of the standards of review, we now turn our attention to the method for selecting the appropriate standard in individual cases. As we will now demonstrate, questions of fact, discretion and policy as well as questions where the legal issues cannot be easily separated from the factual issues generally attract a standard of reasonableness while many legal issues attract a standard of correctness. Some legal issues, however, attract the more deferential standard of reasonableness.

[52] The existence of a privative or preclusive clause gives rise to a strong indication of review pursuant to the reasonableness standard. This conclusion is appropriate because a privative clause is evidence of Parliament or a legislature's intent that an administrative decision maker be given greater deference and that interference by reviewing courts be minimized. This does not mean, however, that the presence of a privative clause is determinative. The rule of law requires that the constitutional role of superior courts be preserved and, as indicated above, neither Parliament nor any legislature can completely remove the courts' power to review the actions and decisions of administrative bodies. This power is constitutionally protected. Judicial review is necessary to ensure that the privative clause is read in its appropriate statutory context and that administrative bodies do not exceed their jurisdiction.

[53] Where the question is one of fact, discretion or policy, deference will usually apply automatically (*Mossop*, at pp. 599–600; *Dr. Q*, at para. 29; *Suresh*, at paras. 29–30). We believe that the same standard must apply to the review of questions where the legal and factual issues are intertwined with and cannot be readily separated.

[54] Guidance with regard to the questions that will be reviewed on a reasonableness standard can be found in the existing case law. Deference will usually result where a tribunal is interpreting its own statute or statutes closely connected to its function, with which it will have particular familiarity: *Canadian Broadcasting Corp. v. Canada (Labour Relations Board)*, 1995 CanLII 148 (SCC), [1995] 1 S.C.R. 157, at para. 48; *Toronto (City) Board of Education v. O.S.S.T.F., District 15*, 1997 CanLII 378 (SCC), [1997] 1 S.C.R. 487, at para. 39.

Deference may also be warranted where an administrative tribunal has developed particular expertise in the application of a general common law or civil law rule in relation to a specific statutory context: *Toronto (City) v. C.U.P.E.*, at para. 72. Adjudication in labour law remains a good example of the relevance of this approach. The case law has moved away considerably from the strict position evidenced in *McLeod v. Egan*, 1974 CanLII 12 (SCC), [1975] 1 S.C.R. 517, where it was held that an administrative decision maker will always risk having its interpretation of an external statute set aside upon judicial review.

[55] A consideration of the following factors will lead to the conclusion that the decision maker should be given deference and a reasonableness test applied:

- A privative clause: this is a statutory direction from Parliament or a legislature indicating the need for deference.
- A discrete and special administrative regime in which the decision maker has special expertise (labour relations for instance).
- The nature of the question of law. A question of law that is of "central importance to the legal system...and outside the...specialized area of expertise" of the administrative decision maker will always attract a correctness standard (*Toronto (City) v. C.U.P.E.*, at para. 62). On the other hand, a question of law that does not rise to this level may be compatible with a reasonableness standard where the two above factors so indicate.

[56] If these factors, considered together, point to a standard of reasonableness, the decision maker's decision must be approached with deference in the sense of respect discussed earlier in these reasons. There is nothing unprincipled in the fact that some questions of law will be decided on the basis of reasonableness. It simply means giving the adjudicator's decision appropriate deference in deciding whether a decision should be upheld, bearing in mind the factors indicated.

[57] An exhaustive review is not required in every case to determine the proper standard of review. Here again, existing jurisprudence may be helpful in identifying some of the questions that generally fall to be determined according to the correctness standard (*Cartaway Resources Corp. (Re)*, [2004] 1 S.C.R. 672, 2004 SCC 26 (CanLII)). This simply means that the analysis required is already deemed to have been performed and need not be repeated.

[58] For example, correctness review has been found to apply to constitutional questions regarding the division of powers between Parliament and the provinces in the *Constitution Act, 1867: Westcoast Energy Inc. v. Canada (National Energy Board)*, 1998 CanLII 813 (SCC), [1998] 1 S.C.R. 322. Such questions, as well as other constitutional issues, are necessarily subject to correctness review because of the unique role of s. 96 courts as interpreters of the Constitution: *Nova Scotia (Workers' Compensation Board) v. Martin*, [2003] 2 S.C.R. 504, 2003 SCC 54 (CanLII); Mullan, *Administrative Law*, at p. 60.

[59] Administrative bodies must also be correct in their determinations of true questions of jurisdiction or *vires*. We mention true questions of *vires*

to distance ourselves from the extended definitions adopted before *CUPE*. It is important here to take a robust view of jurisdiction. We neither wish nor intend to return to the jurisdiction/preliminary question doctrine that plagued the jurisprudence in this area for many years. "Jurisdiction" is intended in the narrow sense of whether or not the tribunal had the authority to make the inquiry. In other words, true jurisdiction questions arise where the tribunal must explicitly determine whether its statutory grant of power gives it the authority to decide a particular matter. The tribunal must interpret the grant of authority correctly or its action will be found to be *ultra vires* or to constitute a wrongful decline of jurisdiction: D.J.M. Brown and J.M. Evans, *Judicial Review of Administrative Action in Canada* (looseleaf), at pp. 14–3 to 14–6. An example may be found in *United Taxi Drivers' Fellowship of Southern Alberta v. Calgary (City)*, [2004] 1 S.C.R. 485, 2004 SCC 19 (CanLII). In that case, the issue was whether the City of Calgary was authorized under the relevant municipal acts to enact bylaws limiting the number of taxi plate licences (para. 5, *per* Bastarache J.). That case involved the decision-making powers of a municipality and exemplifies a true question of jurisdiction or *vires*. These questions will be narrow. We reiterate the caution of Dickson J. in *CUPE* that reviewing judges must not brand as jurisdictional issues that are doubtfully so.

[60] As mentioned earlier, courts must also continue to substitute their own view of the correct answer where the question at issue is one of general law "that is both of central importance to the legal system as a whole and outside the adjudicator's specialized area of expertise" (*Toronto (City) v. C.U.P.E.*, at para. 62, *per* LeBel J.). Because of their impact on the administration of justice as a whole, such questions require uniform and consistent answers. Such was the case in *Toronto (City) v. C.U.P.E.*, which dealt with complex common law rules and conflicting jurisprudence on the doctrines of *res judicata* and abuse of process—issues that are at the heart of the administration of justice (see para. 15, *per* Arbour J.).

[61] Questions regarding the jurisdictional lines between two or more competing specialized tribunals have also been subject to review on a correctness basis: *Regina Police Assn. Inc. v. Regina (City) Board of Police Commissioners*, [2000] 1 S.C.R. 360, 2000 SCC 14 (CanLII); *Quebec (Commission des droits de la personne et des droits de la jeunesse) v. Quebec (Attorney General)*, [2004] 2 S.C.R. 185, 2004 SCC 39 (CanLII).

[62] In summary, the process of judicial review involves two steps. First, courts ascertain whether the jurisprudence has already determined in a satisfactory manner the degree of deference to be accorded with regard to a particular category of question. Second, where the first inquiry proves unfruitful, courts must proceed to an analysis of the factors making it possible to identify the proper standard of review.

[63] The existing approach to determining the appropriate standard of review has commonly been referred to as "pragmatic and functional." That name is unimportant. Reviewing courts must not get fixated on the label at

the expense of a proper understanding of what the inquiry actually entails. Because the phrase "pragmatic and functional approach" may have misguided courts in the past, we prefer to refer simply to the "standard of review analysis" in the future.

[64] The analysis must be contextual. As mentioned above, it is dependent on the application of a number of relevant factors, including: (1) the presence or absence of a privative clause; (2) the purpose of the tribunal as determined by interpretation of enabling legislation; (3) the nature of the question at issue, and; (4) the expertise of the tribunal. In many cases, it will not be necessary to consider all of the factors, as some of them may be determinative in the application of the reasonableness standard in a specific case.

R. v. J.H.S.
Supreme Court of Canada
[2008] 2 S.C.R. 152

Criminal cases often involve matters where the credibility of the accused and the credibility of witnesses are in question. In this case, the Court revisits the question of the relation of credibility to the standard of criminal proof—proof beyond reasonable doubt, as established by the Crown. Two aspects of this decision are of particular interest. The first is the Court's insistence on the correctness of prior jurisprudence on the principle in question. Here the Court reaffirms the principle that the Crown must prove guilt beyond reasonable doubt, and a lack of credibility on the part of the accused cannot relieve the Crown of its burden. The second aspect of interest is seen in the Court's sharp reminder that its decisions must be interpreted with attention to the principles they advance, not as formulae reducible to processes operated like a "magic incantation."

Procedural justice, the Court demonstrates, is not a matter of rigid adherence to an established practice. Rather, it is a matter of ensuring that a principle is actually implemented in practice. The Court's decision acknowledges that while a lower court may have varied from precise imitation of the steps a preceding Supreme Court decision established for instruction of a jury as to the difference between reasonable doubt and credibility, that lower court nonetheless achieved in substance what was required, so the demands of procedural justice were satisfied.

Justice Binnie (for the majority):

[1] The Crown appeals the decision of the Nova Scotia Court of Appeal setting aside the conviction of the respondent for the sexual assault of his stepdaughter. The complainant and the accused were the principal witnesses. The majority judgement of the Court of Appeal concluded that the trial judge had insufficiently instructed the jury on their duty, even if they disbelieved the accused, to determine whether the Crown had proved on the whole of the evidence every element of the charge against him to the criminal standard of proof. In other words, the majority concluded that the jury was not clearly instructed that lack of credibility on the part of the accused does not equate to proof of his guilt beyond a reasonable doubt as required by *R. v. W. (D.)*, [1991] 1 S.C.R. 742. The dissenting judge in the Court of Appeal, Saunders J.A., was of the view that

the jury instruction on this point left no room for misunderstanding about the correct burden and standard of proof to apply. That is the bottom line. I agree with him and would allow the appeal.

[...]

[8] A series of decisions over at least the past 20 years has affirmed and reaffirmed the proposition that where credibility is a central issue in a jury trial, the judge must explain the relationship between the assessment of credibility and the Crown's ultimate burden to prove the guilt of the accused to the criminal standard. A general instruction on reasonable doubt without adverting to its relationship to the credibility (or lack of credibility) of the witnesses leaves open too great a possibility of confusion or misunderstanding. [...]

[9] The passage from *W. (D.)* at issue in this case, as in so many others, is found at pp. 757–58, where Cory J. explained:

> Ideally, appropriate instructions on the issue of credibility should be given, not only during the main charge, but on any recharge. A trial judge might well instruct the jury on the question of credibility along these lines:
>
> > First, if you believe the evidence of the accused, obviously you must acquit.
> >
> > Second, if you do not believe the testimony of the accused but you are left in reasonable doubt by it, you must acquit.
> >
> > Third, even if you are not left in doubt by the evidence of the accused, you must ask yourself whether, on the basis of the evidence which you do accept, you are convinced beyond a reasonable doubt by that evidence of the guilt of the accused.
>
> If that formula were followed, the oft repeated error which appears in the recharge in this case would be avoided. The requirement that the Crown prove the guilt of the accused beyond a reasonable doubt is fundamental in our system of criminal law. Every effort should be made to avoid mistakes in charging the jury on this basic principle.
>
> Nonetheless, the failure to use such language is not fatal if the charge, when read as a whole, makes it clear that the jury could not have been under any misapprehension as to the correct burden and standard of proof to apply. [...]

Essentially, *W. (D.)* simply unpacks for the benefit of the lay jury what reasonable doubt means in the context of evaluating conflicting testimonial accounts. It alerts the jury to the "credibility contest" error. It teaches that trial judges are required to impress on the jury that the burden never shifts from the Crown to prove every element of the offence beyond a reasonable doubt.

[10] The precise formulation of the *W. (D.)* questions has been criticized. As to the first question, the jury may believe inculpatory elements of the state-

ments of an accused but reject the exculpatory explanation. In *R. v. Latimer*, [2001] 1 S.C.R. 3, 2001 SCC 1, the accused did not testify, but his description of the killing of his daughter was put into evidence by way of statements to the police. His description of the event itself was obviously believed. The exculpatory explanation did not amount to a defence at law. He was convicted. The principle that a jury may believe some, none, or all of the testimony of any witness, including that of an accused, suggests to some critics that the first *W. (D.)* question is something of an oversimplification.

[11] As to the second question, some jurors may wonder how, if they believe *none* of the evidence of the accused, such rejected evidence may nevertheless *of itself* raise a reasonable doubt. Of course, some elements of the evidence of an accused may raise a reasonable doubt, even though the bulk of it is rejected. Equally, the jury may simply conclude that they do not know whether to believe the accused's testimony or not. In either circumstance the accused is entitled to an acquittal.

[12] The third question, again, is taken by some critics as failing to contemplate a jury's acceptance of inculpatory bits of the evidence of an accused but not the exculpatory elements. In light of these possible sources of difficulty, Wood J.A. in *H. (C.W.)* suggested an additional instruction:

> I would add one more instruction in such cases, which logically ought to be second in the order, namely: "If, after a careful consideration of all the evidence, you are unable to decide whom to believe, you must acquit." [p. 155]

[13] In short the *W. (D.)* questions should not have attributed to them a level of sanctity or immutable perfection that their author never claimed for them. *W. (D.)*'s message that it must be made crystal clear to the jury that the burden *never* shifts from the Crown to prove *every* element of the offence beyond a reasonable doubt is of fundamental importance but its application should not result in a triumph of form over substance. In *R. v. S. (W.D.)*, [1994] 3 S.C.R. 521, Cory J. reiterated that the *W. (D.)* instructions need not be given "word for word as some magic incantation" (p. 533). In *R. v. Avetysan*, [2000] 2 S.C.R. 745, 2000 SCC 56, Major J. for the majority pointed out that in any case where credibility is important "[t]he question is really whether, in substance, the trial judge's instructions left the jury with the impression that it had to choose between the two versions of events" (para. 19). The main point is that lack of credibility on the part of the accused does not equate to proof of his or her guilt beyond a reasonable doubt.

[14] In the present case Oland J.A. agreed that the trial judge did not "call upon the jury to simply decide which of the complainant or [the accused] it believed" (para. 20). Nevertheless, in her view:

> The charge only instructed that probable guilt was not enough to meet the standard of proof beyond a reasonable doubt, that the appellant was to be given the benefit of the doubt, and they did not have to accept or

reject all of the testimony of any witness including his, and that they were to consider all of the evidence. Nowhere did it provide any guidance as to how, in the event they were uncertain or unable to resolve the issue of credibility, they were to proceed with their deliberations. *The charge failed to direct that if the jury did not believe the testimony of the accused but were left in a reasonable doubt by that evidence, they must acquit.* [Emphasis added; para. 21.]

In my view, with respect, the reasoning of the majority brushes uncomfortably close to the "magic incantation" error. At the end of the day, reading the charge as a whole, I believe the instruction to this jury satisfied the ultimate test formulated by Cory J. in *W. (D.)* as being whether "the jury could not have been under any misapprehension as to the correct burden and standard of proof to apply" (p. 758).

[15] Here the trial judge explained that any reasonable doubt must be resolved in favour of the accused. She also explained that even if they did not accept all of the accused's testimony, they could still accept some of it. She also explained to the jury that they should *not* see their task as that of deciding between two versions of events. She told them that they could not decide the case simply by choosing between the evidence of the complainant and that of the accused. She reminded them, in that context, that they must consider *all* of the evidence when determining reasonable doubt. She stated:

> You do not decide whether something happened simply by comparing one version of events with another, or choosing one of them. You have to consider all the evidence and decide whether you have been satisfied beyond a reasonable doubt that the events that form the basis of the crime charged, in fact, took place. [A.R., at p. 54]

> [...] Again, you do not decide whether something happened simply by comparing one version of events with the other, or by choosing one of them. You have to consider all of the evidence and decide whether you have been satisfied beyond a reasonable doubt that the events that form the basis of the crimes charges, in fact, took place. [A.R., at p. 55]

[16] In my view, the trial judge got across the point of the second *W. (D.)* question without leaving any realistic possibility of misunderstanding. As stated, she told the jury:

> It is for the Crown counsel to prove beyond a reasonable doubt that the events alleged in fact occurred. It is not for [the accused] to prove that these events never happened. If you have a reasonable doubt whether the events alleged ever took place, you *must* find him not guilty. [Emphasis added; A.R., at p. 54.]

[17] There was much discussion at the hearing about defence counsel's failure to object. In my view, he correctly ascertained that the jury had been adequately instructed on the relationship between the assessment of credibility

and the ultimate determination of guilt beyond a reasonable doubt. Before the recharge was given he told the trial judge he would "feel more comfortable if simply the wording that was read previously was re-read to the jury again" (A.R., at p. 77). He discharged his duty to the respondent.

Disposition

[18] I would allow the appeal, set aside the judgement of the Court of Appeal, and restore the conviction.

RELATED CASES

Re Singh and Minister of Employment and Immigration [1985] 1 S.C.R. 177
(This Supreme Court of Canada case sets out important procedural mechanisms for application of the "convention refugee" status under Canada's *Immigration Act, 1976.*)

Baker v. Canada (Minister of Citizenship and Immigration) [1999] 2 S.C.R. 817
(At issue for the Supreme Court in this case was whether decisions of immigration officers, which had discretionary elements, were subject to judicial review, and what the principles of procedural fairness required for persons facing deportation orders.)

R. v. Heywood [1994] 174 N.R. 81
(In this case the Supreme Court held that overly broad language in criminal prohibitions can amount to procedural unfairness.)

PART VI

Responsibility

Much of this textbook is concerned with the rights citizens hold against state intrusion into their lives. This part turns to the responsibility of citizens to the state, and to the responsibility of citizens to one another. The basics of these two relations are deceptively simple.

Our most basic responsibilities to the state are expressed in criminal laws. The association of criminal offences with punishment including loss of liberty by imprisonment marks the seriousness of the matters addressed by criminal law. In criminal law, the state acts as the representative of our collective interests, treating a crime against one as an attack on us all and the value we place in maintaining agreed standards of conduct. Murder, kidnapping, sexual assault, theft, arson, and cruelty to animals are just a few of the diverse matters included in criminal law in Canada and similar jurisdictions.

Other socially important responsibilities of citizens to one another are considered matters of private law. Calling these matters "private" signals not secrecy but instead the sense that the actions of one person affecting another person are limited to those persons, and there is no greater public interest at stake. Disputes regarding contracts and property are generally matters of private law, as is the realm of torts, a legal term capturing acts and omissions of one person with negative affects on legally protected interests of another person. Familiar examples of torts include trespassing, damage to reputation, and sale of defective goods. Resolution of disputes subject to private law is usually accomplished by a judgement awarding financial compensation to a person whose interests have been wrongly set back by the person who caused the damage. Sometimes judges do more than put the disputing persons back to their position prior to their dispute, adding to an award of compensation further "punitive" damages meant to serve as a warning or deterrent to the person causing damage to others' interests.

This quick sketch of the central differences between criminal law and private law is helpful as an introduction to understanding the difference between actions which might leave a person in jail rather than paying for damage they have done. It is, however, just an introduction, and you will soon find that the distinction between criminal and civil acts and responsibility is very difficult to draw, with significant overlap in practice. One famous example of this overlap is found in the American legal system. Former football player OJ Simpson was found not guilty of the crime of murder, yet in a separate civil trial, was found responsible for wrongful death and other civil matters. He was ordered by the court to pay both compensatory and punitive damages to the persons bringing a lawsuit against him. This result was possible in part because both criminal and civil law were applicable to the facts of the case, and because the legal system did not require any choice to be made as to whether the facts should be regarded as an exclusively criminal or an exclusively civil matter. The result was also possible because criminal and civil law may address different dimensions of the same set of actions, with different standards of proof. Criminal conviction generally requires that the accused be shown to be guilty "beyond reasonable doubt." In civil matters a lower standard of proof is required—phrases like "more probable than not" are used to capture the much less demanding civil standard. One of the questions facing legislators and judges is whether this overlap ought to be removed from our system of law, since it appears to be very close to violating the motivation of the principle of "double jeopardy," which says that no one should be tried twice for the same criminal wrongdoing. A system where the state has one opportunity to bring a person to trial, and fellow citizens have another opportunity, even if at a lower standard of proof with less serious consequences, may amount to allowing double jeopardy and double punishment for the same act. Or perhaps this double trial of different kinds and double punishment is exactly what is required in order to ensure that all dimensions of a particular instance of wrongdoing are named, measured, and given the response appropriate to each.

The reasoning of the Supreme Court of Canada, before and after the arrival of the *Charter*, shows how the distinction between criminal and civil wrongdoing has been developed, and shows additionally how our understanding of punishment and compensation are evolving. In order to understand that reasoning as it is found in the cases excerpted here, it will be helpful to examine in more detail some of the aspects of criminal responsibility, civil wrongdoing, and punishment. As you read each case excerpted in each of these three areas, you will see the extent to which the law in this area changes with our society and stands in need of constant attention to ensure against serious injustice to both wrongdoers and those who suffer wrongdoing.

The most serious crimes, for which we reserve our strongest punishments, are those in which the legally prohibited action is accompanied by the actor's having meant to take that action. More technically, these crimes are composed of an act referred to by the Latin term *actus reus*, and a particular mental state referred to by the Latin term *mens rea*. It is up to the prosecutor to show that the accused both committed the prohibited action, and did so with the kind of mental state that poses a threat to the state and us all. There is no shortage of easy examples of this sort of crime. Murder is the most familiar: one person kills another, perhaps having shouted aloud "I'm going to kill you" before using a weapon to commit the murder, all in plain view of others. There is a long history of viewing this situation as one in which the state acts for us all in seeking to identify and punish the willingness to commit murder—we find even the mere intention to commit such a crime to be deeply morally wrong. The beliefs motivating this approach to crimes can be seen in our handling of criminal attempts. In many jurisdictions, attempted crimes are evaluated and punished in the same way as completed crimes, marking our sense that what matters in the crime and deserves punishment is the intention to commit the crime, even if some stroke of luck means the act is not completed. It would seem very odd if, for example, the fact that a police officer is wearing a protective vest might mean that shooting the police officer is a less serious crime simply because the vest reduces the seriousness of the harm likely to be suffered by the police officer. What matters to most of us, our culture and our legal history show, is the intention to use deadly force against the police officer.

The example of murder just used is a deliberate simplification of what is often a very complex situation. The example said nothing about the situation of the killer beneath the expression of the intention to kill. Inquiry into that situation might begin with assessment of the killer's mental state. We might ask whether the killer was capable of understanding the difference between right and wrong or whether the killer was affected by some condition leaving the killer unable to understand the meaning and implications of his or her actions, so deserving to be excused from criminal liability and given medical treatment instead. Further inquiry might look into the situation to see whether there was an acceptable justification available to the killer—a matter of self-defence, for example. Other inquiries might investigate the context to determine the full meaning of the intention shown by the killer's shouting "I'm going to kill you!" Investigation might find that the killer intended not to kill but to play a practical joke with an unloaded weapon—but in fact the gun was loaded. In that situation the killer might be seen as reckless or negligent while falling short of the *mens rea* required for conviction of the crime of murder, deserving instead punishment for a different crime, such as negligent homicide. The nature of the *mens rea* requirement is explored in several cases here, including *R. v. Hundal* and *Perka v. The Queen*. Other cases excerpted here, including *R. v. Lavallee, R. v. Mallot, R. v. Ewanchuk,* and *R. v. JA* examine the *mens rea* requirement in relation to defences and excuses available to the accused.

The preceding example begins to show just how difficult it can be to assess *mens rea*, a process which at trial may cost a great deal of court time, jury time, and further resources devoted to prosecution and defence. Legislators and courts have long been aware of these costs and have sought to avoid them via simpler ways of handling less serious offences. A solution to this situation has been developed in the form of criminal laws which do not require demonstration of both an *actus reus* and *mens rea* for conviction—demonstration of the *actus reus* is enough. In a strict liability criminal offence, the mere fact of having committed the act is regarded as warranting conviction, and defence against these claims is usually limited to demonstration that the accused exercised due diligence, doing all possible to avoid committing the offence. In absolute liability offences, no defence is available beyond leaving the prosecutor to show beyond reasonable doubt that the accused did indeed commit the offence. Absolute and strict liability offences are viewed as less serious offences and are not punished by jail sentences—many are punished by fines. *R. v. City of Sault Ste. Marie,* excerpted here, is a famous pre-*Charter* examination of criminal offences without a *mens rea* requirement.

The existence of crimes punished by fines may seem odd, since we began examination of responsibility by distinguishing responsibility to the state from responsibility to others, and we observed that responsibility to others is generally viewed as generating disputes reasonably resolved by the wrongdoer paying the sufferer for damage done. Here we arrive at the border between criminal and civil law, and see in civil law much of the same kind of reasoning regarding actions and consequences, but with much more emphasis on the value of consequences rather than the nature of intentions. Many issues in private law concern the distinction between what some person or persons has caused to happen in a sense that can be traced back to their action, and what in a chain of action and consequence should be regarded as their responsibility. Courts have developed a number of doctrines enabling judges to isolate an individual person's actions from a surrounding context, and to identify which consequences should be attributed to that person and which should not. In *Cook v. Lewis*, excerpted here, you will see the Supreme Court of Canada explore the question of whether we ought to be responsible for all consequences of our actions, or just reasonably foreseeable consequences. In these excerpts you will also find exploration of the question of whether the law should view us all as equals in our interactions with one another, or whether special roles bring with them special responsibilities. This is a familiar notion as we are used to expecting specific high standards of conduct from persons in positions of authority, such as teachers and coaches. But what exactly ought those high standards to be, and what counts as appropriate compensation for failure to meet those standards? These issues are examined in excerpts provided here from *Norberg v. Wynrib* and *Crocker v. Sundance Northwest Resorts Ltd.*

Questions we have just explored in the context of private law, and particularly the question of compensation for wrong done, quite naturally bring us to this part's final topic: punishment for crime. Cases excerpted here demonstrate many of the questions explored in great depth in the philosophy of criminal law. It is easy enough to say what punishment is believed to do, but it is somewhat more difficult to see how the various claimed purposes of punishment are associated with the ways we think about crimes. One of the immediate purposes of punishment is *denunciation*, denouncing and stating for the world—via a finding of guilt and often via a permanent criminal record—that a person has been convicted of a crime so "named and shamed." Denunciation begins to *separate* those convicted of crimes from the remainder of society, and additional forms of punishment running from house arrest to jail sentences further separate those who are convicted of crimes. Denunciation and separation may individually or together tend to *deter* others from committing the same crime, and convicted criminals may themselves be punished in ways which support their *rehabilitation*, and sometimes their sincere expression of *repentance*. Some forms of punishment may involve *restitution*, typically financial payment to victims. More holistic approaches to punishment may conceive of the convicted criminal as a member of a community which can benefit from *restorative* justice reconciling offender and community.

It is sometimes very difficult to relate these diverse, possibly consistent and possibly competing dimensions of punishment to the forms of criminal offence we have examined. Crimes requiring both *actus reus* and *mens rea* elements raise a fundamental question: what, exactly, is being punished? It is the mere intention or mental state, the willingness to violate shared standards? Or is it the actual consequences of a criminal act? Or some of each? If what is punished is the mental state, as seems necessary to make sense of why we punish criminal attempts, we are then left with further questions regarding just what is punished—and left unpunished—in strict and absolute liability criminal offences. Courts continue to refine the answers to these questions in ways seen in an excerpt included here from *R. v. Proulx*.

Good answers to the questions of what is being punished lead to further questions regarding amounts of punishment and limits to punishment. Here you will see the Supreme Court's reasoning in *Sauve v. Canada (Chief Electoral Officer)* regarding an attempt by Parliament to restrict the voting right of prisoners serving sentences of two years or more. This Part also includes excerpts from two cases regarding the constitutional permissibility of sending someone convicted of a crime committed in another country back to that country for punishment, when that punishment may extend to the death penalty. Is that punishment incompatible with *Charter* guarantees to security of the person, or is it part of a reasonable limit on that guarantee? In *Kindler v. Canada (Minister of Justice)*, and *United States v. Burns*, we see the Supreme Court wrestle with this question.

A: CRIMINAL RESPONSIBILITY AND DEFENCE

R. v. City of Sault Ste. Marie
Supreme Court of Canada
[1978] 2 S.C.R. 1299

What makes a wrongdoing a *criminal* offence? For centuries, crimes have been distinguished from other wrongs, illegalities and delicts in terms of the quality of responsibility involved, and to a certain extent, the potential for the action to undermine the fabric of society. Traditionally, the common law has rejected the view that the purpose of the criminal law is merely to regulate behaviour: the intrinsic blameworthiness of the behaviour is thought to be an essential feature of a crime. As such, a determination of criminal responsibility requires more than proof that the accused performed some action or other; he or she must have possessed at the time the "guilty mind" (*mens rea*) involved in acting intentionally, on purpose, or with "malice aforethought." Over the years, courts have come to the conclusion that one's mind can be sufficiently guilty merely if one *knew* of the consequences of one's actions. Nonetheless, that the state is required to prove that the accused had some level of a guilty mind before it convicts is traditionally thought to be a fundamental principle of justice. (See *Re B.C. Motor Vehicle Act* in Part V.)

Since it is a subjective state, it is not always easy to prove that someone had the required *mens rea*. Officials and legislators are therefore often tempted to fudge the question and create offences that either do not require the prosecutor to prove *mens rea*, or else allow the prosecutor to infer *mens rea* from objective behaviour. In the following case, the Supreme Court of Canada explored the problem raised by one very important class of such offences— the so-called "public welfare" offences that are concerned with pressing social problems (pollution, for example), but which do require the proving of *mens rea*.

Justice Dickson (for the majority):

In the present appeal the Court is concerned with offences variously referred to as "statutory," "public welfare," "regulatory," "absolute liability," or "strict responsibility," which are not criminal in any real sense, but are prohibited in the public interest. [...] Although enforced as penal laws through the utilization of the machinery of the criminal law, the offences are in substance of a civil nature and might well be regarded as a branch of administrative law to which traditional principles of criminal law have but limited application. They relate to such everyday matters as traffic infractions, sales of impure food, violations of liquor laws, and the like. In this appeal we are concerned with pollution.

The doctrine of the guilty mind expressed in terms of intention or reckless-ness, but not negligence, is at the foundation of the law of crimes. In the case of true crimes there is a presumption that a person should not be held liable for the wrongfulness of his act if that act is without *mens rea*. [...] Blackstone made the point over two hundred years ago in words still apt: "...to constitute a crime against human laws, there must be, first, a vicious will; and secondly, an unlawful act consequent upon such vicious will." 4 Comm. 21. I would emphasize at the outset that nothing in the discussion which follows is intended to dilute or erode that basic principle. [...]

To relate briefly the facts, the City on November 18, 1970, entered into an agreement with Cherokee Disposal and Construction Co. Ltd., for the disposal of all refuse originating in the City. Under the terms of the agreement, Cherokee became obligated to furnish a site and adequate labour, material and equip-ment. The site selected bordered Cannon Creek which, it would appear, runs into the Root River. The method of disposal adopted is known as the "area," or "continuous slope" method of sanitary land fill, whereby garbage is compacted in layers which are covered each day by natural sand or gravel.

Prior to 1970, the site had been covered with a number of freshwater springs that flowed into Cannon Creek. Cherokee dumped material to cover and sub-merge these springs and then placed garbage and wastes over such material. The garbage and wastes in due course formed a high mound sloping steeply toward, and within twenty feet of, the creek. Pollution resulted. Cherokee was convicted of a breach of s. 32(1) of the *Ontario Water Resources Act*, the section under which the City has been charged. The question now before the Court is whether the City is also guilty of an offence under that section.

In dismissing the charge at first instance, the judge found that the City had had nothing to do with the actual disposal operations, that Cherokee was an independent contractor and its employees were not employees of the City. On the appeal *de novo* Judge Vannini found the offence to be one of strict liability and he convicted. The Divisional Court in setting aside the judgement found that the charge was duplicitous. As a secondary point, the Divisional Court also held that the charge required *mens rea* with respect to causing or permitting a discharge. When the case reached the Court of Appeal that Court held that the conviction could not be quashed on the ground of duplicity, because there had been no challenge to the information at trial. The Court of Appeal agreed, however, that the charge was one requiring proof of *mens rea*. A majority of the Court (Brooke and Howland JJ.A.) held there was not sufficient evidence to establish *mens rea* and ordered a new trial. In the view of Mr. Justice Lacourcière, dissenting, the inescapable inference to be drawn from the findings of fact of Judge Vannini was that the City had known of the potential impairment of waters of Cannon Creek and Root River and had failed to exercise its clear powers of control. [...]

The Mens Rea *Point*

The distinction between the true criminal offence and the public welfare offence is one of prime importance. Where the offence is criminal, the Crown must establish a mental element, namely, that the accused who committed the prohibited act did so intentionally or recklessly, with knowledge of the facts constituting the offence, or with wilful blindness toward them. Mere negligence is excluded from the concept of the mental element required for conviction. Within the context of a criminal prosecution a person who fails to make such inquiries as a reasonable and prudent person would make, or who fails to know facts he should have known, is innocent in the eyes of the law.

In sharp contrast, "absolute liability" entails conviction on proof merely that the defendant committed the prohibited act constituting the *actus reus* of the offence. There is no relevant mental element. It is no defence that the accused was entirely without fault. He may be morally innocent in every sense, yet be branded as a malefactor and punished as such.

Public welfare offences obviously lie in a field of conflicting values. It is essential for society to maintain, through effective enforcement, high standards of public health and safety. Potential victims of those who carry on latently pernicious activities have a strong claim to consideration. On the other hand, there is a generally held revulsion against punishment of the morally innocent.

Public welfare offences evolved in mid-19th century Britain [...] as a means of doing away with the requirement of *mens rea* for petty policy offences. The concept was a judicial creation, founded on expediency. That concept is now firmly embedded in the concrete of Anglo-American and Canadian jurisprudence, its importance heightened by the ever-increasing complexities of modern society.

Various arguments are advanced in justification of absolute liability in public welfare offences. Two predominate. Firstly, it is argued that the protection of social interests requires a high standard of care and attention on the part of those who follow certain pursuits and such persons are more likely to be stimulated to maintain those standards if they know that ignorance or mistake will not excuse them. The removal of any possible loophole acts, it is said, as an incentive to take precautionary measures beyond what would otherwise be taken, in order that mistakes and mishaps be avoided. The second main argument is one based on administrative efficiency. Having regard to both the difficulty of proving mental culpability and the number of petty cases which daily come before the Courts, proof of fault is just too great a burden in time and money to place upon the prosecution. To require proof of each person's individual intent would allow almost every violator to escape. This, together with the glut of work entailed in proving *mens rea* in every case, would clutter the docket and impede adequate enforcement as virtually to nullify the regulatory statutes. In further justification, it is urged that slight penalties are usually imposed and that conviction for breach of a public welfare offence does not carry the stigma associated with conviction for a criminal offence.

Arguments of greater force are advanced against absolute liability. The most telling is that it violates fundamental principles of penal liability. It also rests upon assumptions which have not been, and cannot be, empirically established. There is no evidence that a higher standard of care results from absolute liability. If a person is already taking every reasonable precautionary measure, is he likely to take additional measures, knowing that however much care he takes, it will not serve as a defence in the event of breach? If he has exercised care and skill, will conviction have a deterrent effect upon him or others? Will the injustice of conviction lead to cynicism and disrespect for the law, on his part and on the part of others? These are among the questions asked. The argument that no stigma attaches does not withstand analysis, for the accused will have suffered loss of time, legal costs, exposure to the processes of the criminal law at trial and, however one may downplay it, the opprobrium of conviction. It is not sufficient to say that the public interest is engaged and, therefore, liability may be imposed without fault. In serious crimes, the public interest is involved and *mens rea* must be proven. The administrative argument has little force. In sentencing, evidence of due diligence is admissible and therefore the evidence might just as well be heard when considering guilt. [...]

Public welfare offences involve a shift of emphasis from the protection of individual interests to the protection of public and social interests. [...] The unfortunate tendency in many past cases has been to see the choice as between two stark alternatives: (i) full *mens rea*; or (ii) absolute liability. In respect of public welfare offences (within which category pollution offences fall) where full *mens rea* is not required, absolute liability has often been imposed. English jurisprudence has consistently maintained this dichotomy. [...] There has, however, been an attempt in Australia, in many Canadian Courts, and indeed in England, to seek a middle position, fulfilling the goals of public welfare offences while still not punishing the entirely blameless. There is an increasing and impressive stream of authority which holds that where an offence does not require full *mens rea*, it is nevertheless a good defence for the defendant to prove that he was not negligent. [...]

The correct approach, in my opinion, is to relieve the Crown of the burden of proving *mens rea*, having regard to the virtual impossibility in most regulatory cases of proving wrongful intention. In a normal case, the accused alone will have knowledge of what he has done to avoid the breach and it is not improper to expect him to come forward with the evidence of due diligence. This is particularly so when it is alleged, for example, that pollution was caused by the activities of a large and complex corporation. Equally, there is nothing wrong with rejecting absolute liability and admitting the defence of reasonable care.

In this doctrine it is not up to the prosecution to prove negligence. Instead, it is open to the defendant to prove that all due care has been taken. This burden falls upon the defendant as he is the only one who will generally have the means of proof. This would not seem unfair as the alternative is absolute liability which denies an accused any defence whatsoever. While the prosecution must prove beyond a reasonable doubt that the defendant committed the prohibited act, the defendant must only establish on the balance of probabilities that he has a defence of reasonable care.

I conclude, for the reasons which I have sought to express, that there are compelling grounds for the recognition of three categories of offences rather than the traditional two:

1. Offences in which *mens rea*, consisting of some positive state of mind such as intent, knowledge, or recklessness, must be proved by the prosecution either as an inference from the nature of the act committed, or by additional evidence.

2. Offences in which there is no necessity for the prosecution to prove the existence of *mens rea*; the doing of the prohibited act *prima facie* imports the offence, leaving it open to the accused to avoid liability by proving that he took all reasonable care. This involves consideration of what a reasonable man would have done in the circumstances. The defence will be available if the accused reasonably believed in a mistaken set of facts which, if true, would render the act or omission innocent, or if he took all reasonable steps to avoid the particular event. These offences may properly be called offences of strict liability. [...]

3. Offences of absolute liability where it is not open to the accused to exculpate himself by showing that he was free of fault.

Offences which are criminal in the true sense fall in the first category. Public welfare offences would, *prima facie*, be in the second category. They are not subject to the presumption of full *mens rea*. An offence of this type would fall in the first category only if such words as "wilfully," "with intent," "knowingly," or "intentionally" are contained in the statutory provision creating the offence. On the other hand, the principle that punishment should in general not be inflicted on those without fault applies. Offences of absolute liability would be those in respect of which the Legislature had made it clear that guilt would follow proof merely of the proscribed act. The over-all regulatory pattern adopted by the Legislature, the subject matter of the legislation, the importance of the penalty, and the precision of the language used will be primary considerations in determining whether the offence falls into the third category.

R. v. Hundal
Supreme Court of Canada
[1993] 1 S.C.R. 867

The requirement of *mens rea* may be an essential feature of criminal offences, but what does the requirement mean? Are we really looking into the soul of the offender to determine his or her blameworthiness? Does criminal guilt require an investigation into the actual thoughts and beliefs of the accused at the time of the offence? Or can we dispense with mind-reading, and just infer from the harm that was done what the accused had in mind? Criminal lawyers label these two approaches investigations into "subjective" and "objective" *mens rea*, and for centuries it was assumed that only the subjective approach, despite its problems, could satisfy the requirements of justice.

But increasingly, prosecutors and courts have expressed their frustration with the subjective approach: surely, since we can never know what really went on inside the accused's head, why should we dwell on this issue at all? The Supreme Court of Canada in 1993 took a small, but important step in the direction of an "objective *mens rea*" in a case involving a fatal motor vehicle accident (the law of which the Court admits has long been "in a mess").

Justice Cory (for the majority):

At issue on this appeal is whether there is a subjective element in the requisite *mens rea* which must be established by the Crown in order to prove the offence of dangerous driving described in s. 233 of the *Criminal Code*.

Factual Background

The accident occurred at about 3:40 in the afternoon in downtown Vancouver. The streets were wet at the time, a situation not uncommon to that city. The downtown traffic was heavy. The appellant was driving his dump truck eastbound on Nelson Street, a four lane road, approaching its intersection with Cambie Street. At the time, his truck was overloaded. It exceeded by 1160 kilograms the maximum gross weight permitted for the vehicle. He was travelling in the passing lane for eastbound traffic. The deceased was travelling southbound on Cambie Street. He had stopped for a red light at the intersection with Nelson Street. When the light turned green, the deceased proceeded into the intersection through a cross-walk, continued south across the two lanes for westbound traffic on Nelson Street and reached the passing lane for eastbound traffic. At that moment his car was struck on the right side by the dump truck killing him instantly.

The appellant stated that when he approached the intersection of Nelson and Cambie Streets he observed that the light had turned amber. He thought that he could not stop in time so he simply honked his horn and continued through the intersection when the impact occurred. Several witnesses observed the collision. They testified that the appellant's truck entered the intersection after the Nelson Street traffic light had turned red. It was estimated that at least one second had passed between the end of the amber light and the time when the dump truck first entered the intersection. A Vancouver police officer gave evidence that the red light for Nelson at this intersection is preceded by a three second amber light and there is a further one-half second delay before the Cambie light turned green. One witness observed that the deceased's vehicle had travelled almost the entire width of the intersection before it was struck by the truck. Another witness, Mr. Mumford, had been travelling close to the appellant's truck through some twelve intersections. He testified that on an earlier occasion, the appellant went through an intersection as the light turned red. He estimated the speed of the truck at the time of the collision was between 50 to 60 kilometres per hour. [...]

Analysis

The relevant portions of s. 233 read as follows:

> 233(1) Every one commits an offence who operates (a) a motor vehicle on a street, road, highway or other public place in a manner that is dangerous to the public, having regard to all the circumstances, including the nature, condition and use of such place and the amount of traffic that at the time is or might reasonably be expected to be on such place;

> (4) Every one who commits an offence under subsection (1) and thereby causes the death of any other person is guilty of an indictable offence and is liable to imprisonment for a term not exceeding fourteen years.

At the outset it must be admitted that the cases dealing with driving offences are not models of clarity. Professor Stuart in his book *Canadian Criminal Law* (2nd ed. 1987), at p. 202, states quite frankly that the law with regard to driving offences is a mess. He writes:

> As a matter of theory the law of driving offences has long been in a mess. The offence of careless driving may require simple or gross negligence; the more serious offence of dangerous driving involves simple negligence although sometimes the courts talk about an "advertence" requirement; and the most serious offence of negligent driving required on one view, advertent recklessness and on another gross inadvertent negligence. The

law has been so confused that it has almost certainly been ignored. There is a fairyland quality to the esoteric analysis involved. Statistics indicate that most prosecutors have been content to rely on the provincial careless driving offence.

[…]

The Constitutional Requirement of Mens Rea

The appellant contends that the prison sentence which may be imposed for a breach of s. 233 makes it evident that an accused cannot be convicted without proof beyond a reasonable doubt of a subjective mental element of an intention to drive dangerously. Certainly every crime requires proof of an act or failure to act, coupled with an element of fault which is termed the *mens rea*. This Court has made it clear that s. 7 of the *Charter* prohibits the imposition of imprisonment in the absence of proof of that element of fault. See *Re B. C. Motor Vehicle Act* (1985). [...]

Depending on the provisions of the particular section and the context in which it appears, the constitutional requirement of *mens rea* may be satisfied in different ways. The offence can require proof of a positive state of mind such as intent, recklessness or wilful blindness. Alternatively, the *mens rea* or element of fault can be satisfied by proof of negligence whereby the conduct of the accused is measured on the basis of an objective standard without establishing the subjective mental state of the particular accused. In the appropriate context, negligence can be an acceptable basis of liability which meets the fault requirement of s. 7 of the *Charter*. [...] Thus, the intent required for a particular offence may be either subjective or objective.

A truly subjective test seeks to determine what was actually in the mind of the particular accused at the moment the offence is alleged to have been committed. Professor Stuart puts it in this way in *Canadian Criminal Law* (2nd ed.), at pp. 123–24 and at p. 125:

> What is vital is that *this accused* given his personality, situation and circumstances, actually intended, knew or foresaw the consequence and/or circumstance as the case may be. Whether he "could," "ought" or "should" have foreseen or whether a reasonable person would have foreseen is not the relevant criterion of liability.
>
> In trying to ascertain what was going on in the accused's mind, as the subjective approach demands, the trier of fact may draw reasonable inferences from the accused's actions or words at the time of his act or in the witness box. The accused may or may not be believed. To conclude that, considering all the evidence, the Crown has proved beyond a reasonable doubt that the accused "must" have thought in the penalized way is no departure from the subjective substantive standard. Resort to an objective substantive standard would only occur if the reasoning became that the accused "must have realized it if he had thought about it." [Emphasis in original]

On the other hand, the test for negligence is an objective one requiring a marked departure from the standard of care of a reasonable person. There is no need to establish the intention of the particular accused. The question to be answered under the objective test concerns what the accused "should" have known. The potential harshness of the objective standard may be lessened by the consideration of certain personal factors as well as the consideration of a defence of mistake of fact. [...] Nevertheless, there should be a clear distinction in the law between one who was aware (pure subjective intent) and one who should have taken care irrespective of awareness (pure objective intent).

What Is the Mens Rea Required to Prove the Offence of Dangerous Driving?

The nature of driving offences suggests that an objective test, or more specially a modified objective test, is particularly appropriate to apply to dangerous driving. I say that for a number of reasons.

(a) The Licensing Requirement

First, driving can only be undertaken by those who have a licence. The effect of the licensing requirement is to demonstrate that those who drive are mentally and physically capable of doing so. Moreover, it serves to confirm that those who drive are familiar with the standards of care which must be maintained by all drivers. There is a further aspect that must be taken into consideration in light of the licensing requirement for drivers. Licensed drivers choose to engage in the regulated activity of driving. They place themselves in a position of responsibility to other members of the public who use the roads.

As a result, it is unnecessary for a court to establish that the particular accused intended or was aware of the consequences of his or her driving. The minimum standard of physical and mental well-being coupled with the basic knowledge of the standard of care required of licensed drivers obviate that requirement. As a general rule, a consideration of the personal factors, so essential in determining subjective intent, is simply not necessary in light of the fixed standards that must be met by licensed drivers.

(b) The Automatic and Reflexive Nature of Driving

Second, the nature of driving itself is often so routine, so automatic that it is almost impossible to determine a particular state of mind of a driver at any given moment. Driving motor vehicles is something that is familiar to most adult Canadians. It cannot be denied that a great deal of driving is done with little conscious thought. It is an activity that is primarily reactive and not contemplative. It is every bit as routine and familiar as taking a shower or going to work. Often it is impossible for a driver to say what his or her specific intent was at any moment during a drive other than the desire to go from A to B.

It would be a denial of common sense for a driver, whose conduct was objectively dangerous, to be acquitted on the ground that he was not thinking of his manner of driving at the time of the accident.

(c) The Wording of Section 233

Third, the wording of the section itself which refers to the operation of a motor vehicle "in a manner that is dangerous to the public, having regard to all the circumstances" suggests that an objective standard is required. The "manner of driving" can only be compared to a standard of reasonable conduct. That standard can be readily judged and assessed by all who would be members of juries.

Thus, it is clear that the basis of liability for dangerous driving is negligence. The question to be asked is not what the accused subjectively intended but rather whether, viewed objectively, the accused exercised the appropriate standard of care. It is not overly difficult to determine when a driver has fallen markedly below the acceptable standard of care. There can be no doubt that the concept of negligence is well understood and readily recognized by most Canadians. Negligent driving can be thought of as a continuum that progresses, or regresses, from momentary lack of attention giving rise to civil responsibility through careless driving under a provincial Highway Traffic Act to dangerous driving under the *Criminal Code*.

(d) Statistics

Fourth, the statistics which demonstrate that all too many tragic deaths and disabling injuries flow from the operation of motor vehicles indicate the need to control the conduct of drivers. The need is obvious and urgent. Section 233 seeks to curb conduct which is exceedingly dangerous to the public. The statistics on car accidents in Canada indicate with chilling clarity the extent of the problem. The number of people killed and injured each year in traffic accidents is staggering. Data from Transport Canada shows that, in 1991, the number of deaths related to traffic accidents in Canada was 3,654. In 1990, there were 178,423 personal injury traffic accidents, 630,000 property damage accidents and 3,442 fatal accidents. These figures highlight the tragic social cost which can and does arise from the operation of motor vehicles. There is therefore a compelling need for effective legislation which strives to regulate the manner of driving vehicles and thereby lessen the carnage on our highways. It is not only appropriate but essential in the control of dangerous driving that an objective standard be applied.

In my view, to insist on a subjective mental element in connection with driving offences would be to deny reality. It cannot be forgotten that the operation of a motor vehicle is, as I have said so very often, automatic and with little conscious thought. It is simply inappropriate to apply a subjective test in determining whether an accused is guilty of dangerous driving.

(e) Modified Objective Test

Although an objective test must be applied to the offence of dangerous driving it will remain open to the accused to raise a reasonable doubt that a reasonable person would have been aware of the risks in the accused's conduct. The test must be applied with some measure of flexibility. That is to say the objective test should not be applied in a vacuum but rather in the context of the events surrounding the incident.

There will be occasions when the manner of driving viewed objectively will clearly be dangerous yet the accused should not be convicted. Take for example a driver who, without prior warning, suffers a totally unexpected heart attack, epileptic seizure or detached retina. As a result of the sudden onset of a disease or physical disability the manner of driving would be dangerous yet those circumstances could provide a complete defence despite the objective demonstration of dangerous driving. Similarly, a driver who, in the absence of any warning or knowledge of its possible effects, takes a prescribed medication which suddenly and unexpectedly affects the driver in such a way that the manner of driving was dangerous to the public, could still establish a good defence to the charge although it had been objectively established. These examples, and there may well be others, serve to illustrate the aim and purpose of the modified objective test. It is to enable a court to take into account the sudden and unexpected onset of disease and similar human frailties as well as the objective demonstration of dangerous driving. [...]

In summary, the *mens rea* for the offence of dangerous driving should be assessed objectively but in the context of all the events surrounding the incident. That approach will satisfy the dictates both of common sense and fairness. As a general rule, personal factors need not be taken into account. This flows from the licensing requirement for driving which assures that all who drive have a reasonable standard of physical health and capability, mental health and a knowledge of the reasonable standard required of all licensed drivers.

In light of the licensing requirement and the nature of driving offences, a modified objective test satisfies the constitutional minimum fault requirement for s. 233 of the *Criminal Code* and is eminently well-suited to that offence.

It follows then that a trier of fact may convict if satisfied beyond a reasonable doubt that, viewed objectively, the accused was, in the words of the section, driving in a manner that was "dangerous to the public, having regard to all the circumstances, including the nature, condition and use of such place and the amount of traffic that at the time is or might reasonably be expected to be on such place." In making the assessment, the trier of fact should be satisfied that the conduct amounted to a marked departure from the standard of care that a reasonable person would observe in the accused's situation.

Next, if an explanation is offered by the accused, such as a sudden and unexpected onset of illness, then in order to convict, the trier of fact must be satisfied that a reasonable person in similar circumstances ought to have been aware of the risk and of the danger involved in the conduct manifested by the accused. If a jury is determining the fact, they may be instructed with regard to dangerous driving along the lines set out above. There is no necessity for a long or complex charge. Neither the section nor the offence requires it. Certainly the instructions should not be unnecessarily confused by any references to advertent or inadvertent negligence. The offence can be readily assessed by jurors who can arrive at a conclusion based on common sense and their own everyday experiences.

Application of These Principles to the Facts

Let us now consider whether the modified objective test was properly applied in this case. The trial judge carefully examined the circumstances of the accident. He took into account the busy downtown traffic, the weather conditions, and the mechanical conditions of the accused vehicle. He concluded, in my view very properly, that the appellant's manner of driving represented a gross departure from the standard of a reasonably prudent driver. No explanation was offered by the accused that could excuse his conduct. There is no reason for interfering with the trial judge's finding of fact and application of the law.

In the result the appeal must be dismissed.

Perka v. The Queen
Supreme Court of Canada
[1984] 2 S.C.R. 232

This Supreme Court of Canada case explores the philosophically rich part of the criminal law that deals with defences. Roughly, in defence, one can either argue that one has an excuse inasmuch as, at the time of the offence, one did not have the required *mens rea*, or one can argue that one's criminal conduct was justified under the (special) circumstances. Excuses excuse the actor; justifications justify (or at least decriminalize) the action. Courts are far more comfortable with excuses, not only because of their general adherence to the principle of *mens rea*, but also because the action (and its consequences) remain socially sanctioned. When justifications are successful, the judgement seems to be made that, sometimes, a crime is not the wrong thing to do: not a message that courts are eager to send to the public.

Here the accused tried to make a case for the defence of necessity, one of the most difficult and contentious defences recognized in our law (perhaps because it is most naturally understood as a justification rather than an excuse). The Court took the opportunity to decide, in what it hoped would be once and for all, what the defence of necessity means and when it applies.

Chief Justice Dickson (for the majority):

Facts

The appellants are drug smugglers. At trial, they led evidence that in early 1979 three of the appellants were employed, with sixteen crew members, to deliver, by ship (the *Samarkanda*) a load of cannabis (marihuana) worth $6,000,000 or $7,000,000 from a point in international waters off the coast of Colombia, South America, to a drop point in international waters 200 miles off the coast of Alaska. [...]

En route, according to the defence evidence, the vessel began to encounter a series of problems; engine breakdowns, overheating generators and malfunctioning navigation devices, aggravated by deteriorating weather. In the meantime the fourth appellant, Nelson, part owner of the illicit cargo, and three other persons left Seattle in a small boat, the *Whitecap*, intending to rendezvous with the *Samarkanda* at the drop point in Alaska. The problems of the *Samarkanda* intensified as fuel was consumed. The vessel became lighter, the intakes in the hull for sea water, used as a coolant, lost suction and took in air instead, causing the generators to overheat. At this point the vessel was 180 miles from the Canadian coastline. The weather worsened. There were eight-to-ten-foot swells and a rising wind. It was finally decided for the safety of ship and crew to seek refuge on the Canadian shoreline for the purpose of making temporary repairs. The *Whitecap* found a sheltered cove on the west coast of Vancouver Island, "No Name Bay." The *Samarkanda* followed the *Whitecap* into the Bay but later grounded amidships on a rock because the depth sounder was not working. The tide ran out. The vessel listed severely to starboard, to the extent that the Captain, fearing the vessel was going to capsize, ordered the men to offload the cargo. That is a brief summary of the defence evidence.

Early on the morning of May 22, 1979 police officers entered No Name Bay in a marked police boat with siren sounding. The *Samarkanda* and the *Whitecap* were arrested, as were all the appellants except Perka and Nelson, the same morning. The vessels and 33.49 tons of cannabis marihuana were seized by the police officers.

Charged with importing cannabis into Canada and with possession for the purpose of trafficking, the appellants claimed they did not plan to import into Canada or to leave their cargo of cannabis in Canada. They had planned to make repairs and leave. Expert witnesses on marine matters called by the defence testified that the decision to come ashore was, in the opinion of one witness, expedient and prudent and in the opinion of another, essential. At trial, counsel for the Crown alleged that the evidence of the ship's distress was a recent fabrication. Crown counsel relied on the circumstances under which the appellants were arrested to belie the "necessity" defence; when the police arrived on the scene most of the marihuana was already onshore, along with plastic ground sheets, battery operated lights, liquor, food, clothing, camp stoves, and sleeping bags. Nevertheless, the jury believed the appellants and acquitted them.

The acquittal was reversed on appeal. [...]

The Necessity Defence

(a) History and Background

From earliest times it has been maintained that in some situations the force of circumstances makes it unrealistic and unjust to attach criminal liability to actions which, on their face, violate the law. Aristotle, in the *Nicomachean Ethics*, Book III, 1110a (trans. D. Ross, 1975, at p. 49), discusses the jettisoning of cargo from a ship in distress and remarks that "any sensible man does so" to secure the safety of himself and his crew. [...]

In *Leviathan* (Pelican ed. 1968), at p. 157, Hobbes writes:

> If a man by the terrour of present death, be compelled to doe a fact against the Law, he is totally Excused; because no Law can oblige a man to abandon his own preservation. And supposing such a Law were obligatory: yet a man would reason thus, if I doe it not, I die presently: if I doe

it, I die afterwards; therefore by doing it, there is time of life gained;
Nature therefore compells him to the fact.

To much the same purpose Kant, in *The Metaphysical Elements of Justice* (trans.
Ladd, 1965), discussing the actions of a person who, to save his own life sacri-
fices that of another, says at p. 41:

> A penal law applying to such a situation could never have the effect
> intended, for the threat of an evil that is still uncertain (being condemned
> to death by a judge) cannot outweigh the fear of an evil that is certain
> (being drowned). Hence, we must judge that, although an act of self-
> preservation through violence is not inculpable, it still is unpunishable ...

In those jurisdictions in which such a general principle has been recognized
or codified it is most often referred to by the term "necessity." Classic and har-
rowing instances which have been cited to illustrate the arguments both for
and against this principle include the mother who steals food for her starving
child, the shipwrecked mariners who resort to cannibalism (*R. v. Dudley and
Stephens* [1884], 14 Q.B.D. 273) or throw passengers overboard to lighten a
sinking lifeboat (*United States v. Holmes*, 26 Fed. Cas. 360 [1842]), and the more
mundane case of the motorist who exceeds the speed limit taking an injured
person to the hospital. [...]

In England, opinion as to the existence of a general defence of necessity
has varied. Blackstone in his *Commentaries on the Law* (abridged edition of
Wm. Hardcastle Browne, edited by Bernard C. Gavit, 1941) mentioned two
principles capable of being read as underlying such a defence. In Book 4, chap.
2, at p. 761, he says:

> As punishments are only inflicted for the abuse of that free will, which
> God has given to man, it is just that a man should be excused for those
> acts, which are done through unavoidable force and compulsion.

Then under the rubric "Choice Between Two Evils" he writes:

> *Choice Between Two Evils.* This species of necessity is the result of reason
> and reflection and obliges a man to do an act, which, without such obli-
> gation, would be criminal. This occurs, when a man has his choice of
> two evils set before him, and chooses the less pernicious one. He rejects
> the greater evil and chooses the less. As where a man is bound to arrest
> another for a capital offence, and being resisted, kills the offender, rather
> than permit him to escape. [...]

In Canada the existence and the extent of a general defence of necessity was
discussed by this Court in *Morgentaler v. The Queen*, [1976] 1 S.C.R. 616. As to
whether or not the defence exists at all I had occasion to say at p. 678:

> On the authorities it is manifestly difficult to be categorical and state that
> there is a law of necessity, paramount over other laws, relieving obedience

from the letter of the law. If it does exist, it can go no further than to justify non-compliance in urgent situations of clear and imminent peril when compliance with the law is demonstrably impossible.

[...]

(b) The Conceptual Foundation of the Defence

[T]he "defence" of necessity in fact is capable of embracing two different and distinct notions. As Mr. Justice Macdonald observed succinctly but accurately in the *Salvador* case, *supra*, at p. 542:

> Generally speaking, the defence of necessity covers all cases where non-compliance with law is excused by an emergency or justified by the pursuit of some greater good. [...]

Criminal theory recognizes a distinction between "justifications" and "excuses." A "justification" challenges the wrongfulness of an action which technically constitutes a crime. The police officer who shoots the hostage-taker, the innocent object of an assault who uses force to defend himself against his assailant, the Good Samaritan who commandeers a car and breaks the speed laws to rush an accident victim to the hospital, these are all actors whose actions we consider *rightful*, not wrongful. For such actions people are often praised, as motivated by some great or noble object. The concept of punishment often seems incompatible with the social approval bestowed on the doer.

In contrast, an "excuse" concedes the wrongfulness of the action but asserts that the circumstances under which it was done are such that it ought not to be attributed to the actor. The perpetrator who is incapable, owing to a disease of the mind, of appreciating the nature and consequences of his acts, the person who labours under a mistake of fact, the drunkard, the sleepwalker: these are all actors of whose "criminal" actions we disapprove intensely, but whom, in appropriate circumstances, our law will not punish. [...]

I retain the skepticism I expressed in *Morgentaler, supra*, at p. 678. It is still my opinion that, "[n]o system of positive law can recognize any principle which would entitle a person to violate the law because on his view the law conflicted with some higher social value." The *Criminal Code* has specified a number of identifiable situations in which an actor is justified in committing what would otherwise be a criminal offence. To go beyond that and hold that ostensibly illegal acts can be validated on the basis of their expediency, would import an undue subjectivity into the criminal law. It would invite the courts to second-guess the legislature and to assess the relative merits of social policies underlying criminal prohibitions. Neither is a role which fits well with the judicial function. Such a doctrine could well become the last resort of scoundrels and in the words of Edmund Davies L.J. in *Southwark London Borough Council v. Williams*, [1971] Ch. 734, it could "very easily become simply a mask for anarchy."

Conceptualized as an "excuse," however, the residual defence of necessity is, in my view, much less open to criticism. It rests on a realistic assessment of human weakness, recognizing that a liberal and humane criminal law cannot hold people to the strict obedience of laws in emergency situations where normal human instincts, whether of self-preservation or of altruism, overwhelmingly impel disobedience. The objectivity of the criminal law is preserved; such acts are still wrongful, but in the circumstances they are excusable. Praise is indeed not bestowed, but pardon is, when one does a wrongful act under pressure which, in the words of Aristotle in the *Nicomachean Ethics, supra,* at p. 49, "overstrains human nature and which no one could withstand."

George Fletcher, *Rethinking Criminal Law* (1978), describes this view of necessity as "compulsion of circumstance" which description points to the conceptual link between necessity as an excuse and the familiar criminal law requirement that in order to engage criminal liability, the actions constituting the *actus reus* of an offence must be voluntary. Literally this voluntariness requirement simply refers to the need that the prohibited physical acts must have been under the conscious control of the actor. Without such control, there is, for purposes of the criminal law, no act. The excuse of necessity does not go to voluntariness in this sense. The lost alpinist who on the point of freezing to death breaks open an isolated mountain cabin is not literally behaving in an involuntary fashion. He has control over his actions to the extent of being physically capable of abstaining from the act. Realistically, however, his act is not a "voluntary" one. His "choice" to break the law is no true choice at all; it is remorselessly compelled by normal human instincts. This sort of involuntariness is often described as "moral or normative involuntariness." Its place in criminal theory is described by Fletcher at pp. 804–05 as follows:

> The notion of voluntariness adds a valuable dimension to the theory of excuses. That conduct is involuntary—even in the normative sense—explains why it cannot fairly be punished. Indeed, H.L.A. Hart builds his theory of excuses on the principle that the distribution of punishment should be reserved for those who voluntarily break the law. Of the arguments he advances for this principle of justice, the most explicit is that it is preferable to live in a society where we have the maximum opportunity to choose whether we shall become the subject of criminal liability. In addition, Hart intimates that it is ideologically desirable for the government to treat its citizens as self-actuating, choosing agents. This principle of respect for individual autonomy is implicitly confirmed whenever those who lack an adequate choice are excused for their offenses.

I agree with this formulation of the rationale for excuses in the criminal law. In my view this rationale extends beyond specific codified excuses and embraces the residual excuse known as the defence of necessity. At the heart of this defence is the perceived injustice of punishing violations of the law in circumstances in which the person had no other viable or reasonable choice available; the act was wrong but it is excused because it was realistically unavoidable. [...]

Relating necessity to the principle that the law ought not to punish involuntary acts leads to a conceptualization of the defence that integrates it into the normal rules for criminal liability rather than constituting it as a *sui generis* exception and threatening to engulf large portions of the criminal law. Such a conceptualization accords with our traditional legal, moral and philosophic views as to what sorts of acts and what sorts of actors ought to be punished. In this formulation it is a defence which I do not hesitate to acknowledge and would not hesitate to apply to relevant facts capable of satisfying its necessary prerequisites.

(c) Limitations on the Defence

If the defence of necessity is to form a valid and consistent part of our criminal law it must, as has been universally recognized, be strictly controlled and scrupulously limited to situations that correspond to its underlying rationale. That rationale, as I have indicated, is the recognition that it is inappropriate to punish actions which are normatively "involuntary." The appropriate controls and limitations on the defence of necessity are, therefore, addressed to ensuring that the acts for which the benefit of the excuse of necessity is sought are truly "involuntary" in the requisite sense.

In *Morgentaler, supra*, I was of the view that any defence of necessity was restricted to instances of non-compliance "in urgent situations of clear and imminent peril when compliance with the law is demonstrably impossible." In my opinion this restriction focuses directly on the "involuntariness" of the purportedly necessitous behaviour by providing a number of tests for determining whether the wrongful act was truly the only realistic reaction open to the actor or whether he was in fact making what in fairness could be called a choice. If he was making a choice, then the wrongful act cannot have been involuntary in the relevant sense. [...]

At a minimum the situation must be so emergent and the peril must be so pressing that normal human instincts cry out for action and make a counsel of patience unreasonable.

The requirement that compliance with the law be "demonstrably impossible" takes this assessment one step further. Given that the accused had to act, could he nevertheless realistically have acted to avoid the peril or prevent the harm, without breaking the law? *Was there a legal way out?* [...] The question to be asked is whether the agent had any real choice: could he have done otherwise? If there is a reasonable legal alternative to disobeying the law, then the decision to disobey becomes a voluntary one, impelled by some consideration beyond the dictates of "necessity" and human instincts.

The importance of this requirement that there be no reasonable legal alternative cannot be overstressed.

Even if the requirements for urgency and "no legal way out" are met, there is clearly a further consideration. There must be some way of assuring proportionality. No rational criminal justice system, no matter how humane or liberal, could excuse the infliction of a greater harm to allow the actor to avert a lesser evil. In such circumstances we expect the individual to bear the harm and refrain from acting illegally. If he cannot control himself we will not excuse him. [...]

I would therefore add to the preceding requirements a stipulation of proportionality expressable, as it was in *Morgentaler*, by the proviso that the harm inflicted must be less than the harm sought to be avoided.

(d) Illegality or Contributory Fault

The Crown submits that there is an additional limitation on the availability of the defence of necessity. Citing *R. v. Salvador, supra*, it argues that because the appellants were committing a crime when their necessitous circumstances arose, they should be denied the defence of necessity as a matter of law. [...]

[...] I have considerable doubt as to the cogency of such a limitation. If the conduct in which an accused was engaging at the time the peril arose was illegal, then it should clearly be punished, but I fail to see the relevance of its illegal character to the question of whether the accused's subsequent conduct in dealing with this emergent peril ought to be excused on the basis of necessity. At most the illegality—or if one adopts Jones J.A.'s approach, the immorality—of the preceding conduct will colour the subsequent conduct in response to the emergency as also wrongful. But that wrongfulness is never in any doubt. Necessity goes to *excuse* conduct, not to *justify* it. Where it is found to apply it carries with it no implicit vindication of the deed to which it attaches. That cannot be over-emphasized. Were the defence of necessity to succeed in the present case, it would not in any way amount to a vindication of importing controlled substances nor to a critique of the law prohibiting such importation. It would also have nothing to say about the comparative social utility of breaking the law against importing as compared to obeying the law. The question, as I have said, is never whether what the accused has done is wrongful. It is always and by definition, wrongful. The question is whether what he has done is voluntary. Except in the limited sense I intend to discuss below, I do not see the relevance of the legality or even the morality of what the accused was doing at the time the emergency arose to this question of the voluntariness of the subsequent conduct. [...]

In my view the accused's fault in bringing about the situation later invoked to excuse his conduct *can* be relevant to the availability of the defence of necessity, but not in the sweeping way suggested by some of the commentators and in some of the statutory formulations. Insofar as the accused's "fault" reflects on the moral quality of the action taken to meet the emergency, it is irrelevant to the issue of the availability of the defence on the same basis as the illegality or immorality of the actions preceding the emergency are irrelevant. If this fault is capable of attracting criminal or civil liability in its own right, the culprit should be appropriately sanctioned. I see no basis, however, for "transferring" such liability to the actions taken in response to the emergency, especially where to do so would result in attaching criminal consequences on the basis of negligence to actions which would otherwise be excused.

In my view the better approach to the relationship of fault to the availability of necessity as a defence is based once again on the question of whether the actions sought to be excused were truly "involuntary." If the necessitous situation was clearly foreseeable to a reasonable observer, if the actor contemplated or ought to have contemplated that his actions would likely give rise to an emergency requiring the breaking of the law, then I doubt whether what confronted the accused was in the relevant sense an emergency. His response was in that sense not "involuntary." "Contributory fault" of this nature, but only of this nature, is a relevant consideration to the availability of the defence.

If the accused's "fault" consists of actions whose clear consequences were in the situation that actually ensued, then he was not "really" confronted with an emergency which compelled him to commit the unlawful act he now seeks to have excused. In such situations the defence is unavailable. Mere negligence, however, or the simple fact that he was engaged in illegal or immoral conduct when the emergency arose will not disentitle an individual to rely on the defence of necessity.

(e) Onus of Proof

Although necessity is spoken of as a defence, in the sense that it is raised by the accused, the Crown always bears the burden of proving a voluntary act. The prosecution must prove every element of the crime charged. One such element is the voluntariness of the act. Normally, voluntariness can be presumed, but if the accused places before the Court, through his own witnesses or through cross-examination of Crown witnesses, evidence sufficient to raise an issue that the situation created by external forces was so emergent that failure to act could endanger life or health and upon any reasonable view of the facts, compliance with the law was impossible, then the Crown must be prepared to meet that issue. There is no onus of proof on the accused. [...]

(f) Preliminary Conclusions as to the Defence of Necessity

It is now possible to summarize a number of conclusions as to the defence of necessity in terms of its nature, basis and limitations: (1) the defence of necessity could be conceptualized as either a justification or an excuse; (2) it should be recognized in Canada as an excuse, operating by virtue of s. 7(3) of the *Criminal Code*; (3) necessity as an excuse implies no vindication of the deeds of the actor; (4) the criterion is the moral involuntariness of the wrongful action; (5) this involuntariness is measured on the basis of society's expectation of appropriate and normal resistance to pressure; (6) negligence or involvement in criminal or immoral activity does not disentitle the actor to the excuse of necessity; (7) actions or circumstances which indicate that the wrongful deed was not truly involuntary do disentitle; (8) the existence of a reasonable legal alternative similarly disentitles; to be involuntary the act must be inevitable, unavoidable and afford no reasonable opportunity for an alternative course of action that does not involve a breach of the law; (9) the defence only applies in circumstances of imminent risk where the action was taken to avoid a direct and immediate peril; (10) where the accused places before the Court sufficient evidence to raise the issue, the onus is on the Crown to meet it beyond a reasonable doubt.

R. v. Lavallee
Supreme Court of Canada
[1990] 1 S.C.R. 852

Lyn Lavallee was acquitted of murdering her common law spouse by a jury who had heard expert evidence from a psychiatrist who described Lavallee's actions in terms of the "battered wife syndrome." Lavallee had convinced the jury that she fatally shot Kevin Rust out of self-defence. The Manitoba Court of Appeal overturned the acquittal on the grounds that the psychiatric evidence should not have been admitted, since it was based on unsworn and hearsay evidence, and without the expert evidence the jury would not have accepted the plea of self-defence.

In rejecting this argument, and reinstating the acquittal, the Supreme Court of Canada found it necessary to look carefully at the requirements for self-defence as well as the conditions that can be imposed on exculpatory expert evidence. Along the way, Justice Bertha Wilson also considered the role of juries in cases, such as this, in which it cannot be presumed that ordinary, reasonable people can fully appreciate or understand the circumstances some accused people were in at the time of the offence. What would the "reasonable man" do when, in fact, she is a woman in an abusive relationship?

Several years later, in 1998, the Supreme Court in *Malott* reaffirmed the reasoning in *Lavallee*, before adding the subtle, but very important, remark that the syndrome is not a defence at all, but rather a matter of evidence of the accused's mental state.

———————

Justice Wilson (for the majority):

The expert evidence which forms the subject matter of the appeal came from Dr. Fred Shane, a psychiatrist with extensive professional experience in the treatment of battered wives. [...] The substance of Dr. Shane's opinion was that the appellant had been terrorized by Rust to the point of feeling trapped, vulnerable, worthless and unable to escape the relationship despite the violence. At the same time, the continuing pattern of abuse put her life in danger. In Dr. Shane's opinion the appellant's shooting of the deceased was a final desperate act by a woman who sincerely believed that she would be killed that night. [...]

Relevant Legislation: Criminal Code

34(2) Every one who is unlawfully assaulted and who causes death or grievous bodily harm in repelling the assault is justified if...

(a) he causes it under reasonable apprehension of death or grievous bodily harm from the violence with which the assault was originally made or with which the assailant pursues his purposes, and

(b) he believes on reasonable and probable grounds, that he cannot otherwise preserve himself from death or grievous bodily harm. [...]

Analysis

(i) Admissibility of Expert Evidence

[...] The bare facts of this case, which I think are amply supported by the evidence, are that the appellant was repeatedly abused by the deceased but did not leave him (although she twice pointed a gun at him), and ultimately shot him in the back of the head as he was leaving her room. The Crown submits that these facts disclose all the information a jury needs in order to decide whether or not the appellant acted in self-defence. I have no hesitation in rejecting the Crown's submission.

Expert evidence on the psychological effect of battering on wives and common law partners must, it seems to me, be both relevant and necessary in the context of the present case. How can the mental state of the appellant be appreciated without it? The average member of the public (or of the jury) can be forgiven for asking: Why would a woman put up with this kind of treatment? Why should she continue to live with such a man? How could she love a partner who beat her to the point of requiring hospitalization? We would expect the woman to pack her bags and go. Where is her self-respect? Why does she not cut loose and make a new life for herself? Such is the reaction of the average person confronted with the so-called "battered wife syndrome." We need help to understand it and help is available from trained professionals.

The gravity, indeed, the tragedy of domestic violence can hardly be overstated. Greater media attention to this phenomenon in recent years has revealed both its prevalence and its horrific impact on women from all walks of life. Far from protecting women from it the law historically sanctioned the abuse of women within marriage as an aspect of the husband's ownership of his wife and his "right" to chastise her. One need only recall the centuries old law that a man is entitled to beat his wife with a stick "no thicker than his thumb."

Laws do not spring out of a social vacuum. The notion that a man has a right to "discipline" his wife is deeply rooted in the history of our society. The woman's duty was to serve her husband and to stay in the marriage at all costs "till death do us part" and to accept as her due any "punishment" that was meted out for failing to please her husband. One consequence of this attitude was that "wife battering" was rarely spoken of, rarely reported, rarely prosecuted, and even more rarely punished. Long after society abandoned its formal approval of spousal abuse tolerance of it continued and continues in some circles to this day.

Fortunately, there has been a growing awareness in recent years that no man has a right to abuse any woman under any circumstances. Legislative initiatives designed to educate police, judicial officers and the public, as well as more aggressive investigation and charging policies all signal a concerted effort by the criminal justice system to take spousal abuse seriously. However, a woman who comes before a judge or jury with the claim that she has been battered and suggests that this may be a relevant factor in evaluating her subsequent actions still faces the prospect of being condemned by popular mythology about domestic violence. Either she was not as badly beaten as she claims or she would have left the man long ago. Or, if she was battered that severely, she must have stayed out of some masochistic enjoyment of it. [...]

(ii) The Relevance of Expert Testimony to the Elements of Self-Defence

In my view, there are two elements of the defence. The first is the temporal connection in s. 34(2)(a) between the apprehension of death or grievous bodily harm and the act allegedly taken in self-defence. Was the appellant "under reasonable apprehension of death or grievous bodily harm" from Rust as he was walking out of the room? The second is the assessment in s. 34(2)(b) of the magnitude of the force used by the accused. Was the accused's belief that she could not "otherwise preserve herself from death or grievous bodily harm" except by shooting the deceased based on "reasonable grounds"?

The feature common to both s. 34(2)(a) and (b) is the imposition of an objective standard of reasonableness on the apprehension of death and the need to repel the assault with deadly force. In *Reilly v. The Queen* [1984] 2 S.C.R. 396, this Court considered the interaction of the objective and subjective components of s. 34(2), at p. 404:

Subsection (2) of s. 34 places in issue the accused's state of mind at the time he caused death. The subsection can only afford protection to the accused if he apprehended death or grievous bodily harm from the assault he was repelling and if he believed he could not preserve himself from death or grievous bodily harm otherwise than by the force he used. Nonetheless, his apprehension must be a *reasonable* one and his belief must *be based upon reasonable and probable grounds*. The subsection requires that the jury consider, and be guided by, what they decide on the evidence was the accused's appreciation of the situation and his belief as to the reaction it required, so long as there exists an objectively verifiable basis for his perception.

> Since s. 34(2) places in issue the accused's perception of the attack upon and the response required to meet it, the accused may still be found to have acted in self-defence even if he was mistaken in his perception. Reasonable and probable grounds must still exist for this mistaken perception in the sense that the mistake must have been one which an ordinary man using ordinary care could have made in the same circumstances. [Emphasis in original]

If it strains credulity to imagine what the "ordinary man" would do in the position of a battered spouse, it is probably because men do not typically find themselves in that situation. Some women do, however. The definition of what is reasonable must be adapted to circumstances which are, by and large, foreign to the world inhabited by the hypothetical "reasonable man." [...]

[...] In the present case, the assault precipitating the appellant's alleged defensive act was Rust's threat to kill her when everyone else was gone.

It will be observed that s. 34(2)(a) does not actually stipulate that the accused apprehend *imminent* danger when he or she acts. Case law has, however, read that requirement into the defence. [...] The sense in which "imminent" is used conjures up the image of "an uplifted knife" or a pointed gun. The rationale for the imminence rule seems obvious. The law of self-defence is designed to ensure that the use of defensive force is really necessary. It justifies the act because the defender reasonably believed that he or she had no alternative but to take the attacker's life. If there is a significant time interval between the original unlawful assault and the accused's response, one tends to suspect that the accused was motivated by revenge rather than self-defence. [...]

[The appellant] was routinely beaten over the course of her relationship with the man she ultimately killed. According to the testimony of Dr. Shane these assaults were not entirely random in their occurrence. [...]

Dr. Walker defines a battered woman as a woman who has gone through the battering cycle at least twice. As she explains in the introduction to *The Battered Woman* (1979), at p. xv "Any woman may find herself in an abusive relationship with a man once. If it occurs a second time, and she remains in the situation, she is defined as a battered woman."

Given the relational context in which the violence occurs, the mental state of an accused at the critical moment she pulls the trigger cannot be understood except in terms of the cumulative effect of months or years of brutality. As Dr. Shane explained in his testimony, the deterioration of the relationship between the appellant and Rust in the period immediately preceding the killing led to feelings of escalating terror on the part of the appellant. [...]

Another aspect of the cyclical nature of the abuse is that it begets a degree of predictability to the violence that is absent in an isolated violent encounter between two strangers. This also means that it may in fact be possible for a battered spouse to accurately predict the onset of violence before the first blow is struck, even if an outsider to the relationship cannot. Indeed it has been suggested that a battered woman's knowledge of her partner's violence is so heightened that she is able to anticipate the nature and extent (though not the onset) of the violence by his conduct beforehand. [...]

Where evidence exists that an accused is in a battering relationship, expert testimony can assist the jury in determining whether the accused had a "reasonable" apprehension of death when she acted by explaining the heightened sensitivity of a battered woman to her partner's acts. Without such testimony I am skeptical that the average fact-finder would be capable of appreciating why her subjective fear may have been reasonable in the context of the relationship. After all, the hypothetical "reasonable man" observing only the final incident may have been unlikely to recognize the batterer's threat as potentially lethal. Using the case at bar as an example the "reasonable man" might have thought, as the majority of the Court of Appeal seemed to, that it was unlikely that Rust would make good on his threat to kill the appellant that night because they had guests staying overnight.

The issue is not, however, what an outsider would have reasonably perceived but what the accused reasonably perceived, given her situation and her experience.

Even accepting that a battered woman may be uniquely sensitized to danger from her batterer, it may yet be contended that the law ought to require her to wait until the knife is uplifted, the gun pointed or the fist clenched before her apprehension is deemed reasonable. This would allegedly reduce the risk that the woman is mistaken in her fear, although the law does not require her fear to be correct, only reasonable. In response to this contention, I need only point to the observation made by Huband J.A. that the evidence showed that when the appellant and Rust physically fought the appellant "invariably got the worst of it." I do not think it is an unwarranted generalization to say that due to their size, strength, socialization and lack of training, women are typically no match for men in hand-to-hand combat. The requirement that a battered woman wait until the physical assault is "underway" before her apprehensions can be validated in law would, in the words of an American court, be tantamount to sentencing her to "murder by installment." [...]

Lack of Alternatives to Self-Help

Section 34(2) requires an accused who pleads self-defence to believe "on reasonable grounds" that it is not possible to otherwise preserve him or herself from death or grievous bodily harm. The obvious question is if the violence was so intolerable, why did the appellant not leave her abuser long ago? This question does not really go to whether she had an alternative to killing the deceased at the critical moment. Rather, it plays on the popular myth already referred to that a woman who says she was battered yet stayed with her batterer was either not as badly beaten as she claimed or else she liked it. Nevertheless, to the extent that her failure to leave the abusive relationship earlier may be used in support of the proposition that she was free to leave at the final moment, expert testimony can provide useful insights. [...]

I emphasize at this juncture that it is not for the jury to pass judgement on the fact that an accused battered woman stayed in the relationship. Still less is it entitled to conclude that she forfeited her right to self-defence for having done so. I would also point out that traditional self-defence doctrine does not require a person to retreat from her home instead of defending herself. A man's home may be his castle but it is also the woman's home even if it seems to her more like a prison in the circumstances.

If, after hearing the evidence (including the expert testimony), the jury is satisfied that the accused had a reasonable apprehension of death or grievous bodily harm and felt incapable of escape, it must ask itself what the "reasonable person" would do in such a situation. The situation of the battered woman as described by Dr. Shane strikes me as somewhat analogous to that of a hostage. If the captor tells her that he will kill her in three days time, is it potentially reasonable for her to seize an opportunity presented on the first day to kill the captor or must she wait until he makes the attempt on the third day? I think the question the jury must ask itself is whether, given the history, circumstances and perceptions of the appellant, her belief that she could not preserve herself from being killed by Rust that night except by killing him first was reasonable. To the extent that expert evidence can assist the jury in making that determination, I would find such testimony to be both relevant and necessary. [...]

I would accordingly allow the appeal, set aside the order of the Court of Appeal, and restore the acquittal.

R. v. Malott
Supreme Court of Canada
[1998] 1 S.C.R. 123

Justice Major (for the majority):

[36] A crucial implication of the admissibility of expert evidence in *Lavallee* is the legal recognition that historically both the law and society may have treated women in general, and battered women in particular, unfairly. *Lavallee* accepted that the myths and stereotypes which are the products and the tools of this unfair treatment interfere with the capacity of judges and juries to justly determine a battered woman's claim of self-defence, and can only be dispelled by expert evidence designed to overcome the stereotypical thinking. The expert evidence is admissible, and necessary, in order to understand the reasonableness of a battered woman's perceptions, which in *Lavallee* were the accused's perceptions that she had to act with deadly force in order to preserve herself from death or grievous bodily harm. [...]

[37] It is clear [...] that "battered woman syndrome" is not a legal defence in itself such that an accused woman need only establish that she is suffering from the syndrome in order to gain an acquittal. As Wilson J. commented in *Lavallee*, "Obviously the fact that the appellant was a battered woman does not entitle her to an acquittal. Battered women may well kill their partners other than in self-defence." Rather, "battered woman syndrome" is a psychiatric explanation of the mental state of women who have been subjected to continuous battering by their male intimate partners, which can be relevant to the legal inquiry into a battered woman's state of mind.

[38] Second, the majority of the Court in *Lavallee* also implicitly accepted that women's experiences and perspectives may be different from the experiences and perspectives of men. It accepted that a woman's perception of what is reasonable is influenced by her gender, as well as by her individual experience, and both are relevant to the legal inquiry. This legal development was significant, because it demonstrated a willingness to look at the whole context of a woman's experience in order to inform the analysis of the particular events. But it is wrong to think of this development of the law as merely an example where an objective test—the requirement that an accused claiming self-defence must *reasonably* apprehend death or grievous bodily harm—has been modified to admit evidence of the subjective perceptions of a battered woman. More important, a majority of the Court accepted that the perspectives of women, which have historically been ignored, must now equally inform the "objective" standard of the reasonable person in relation to self-defence. [...]

[43] How should these principles be given practical effect in the context of a jury trial of a woman accused of murdering her abuser? To fully accord with the spirit of *Lavallee*, where the reasonableness of a battered woman's belief is at issue in a criminal case, a judge and jury should be made to appreciate that a battered woman's experiences are both individualized, based on her

own history and relationships, as well as shared with other women, within the context of a society and a legal system which has historically undervalued women's experiences. A judge and jury should be told that a battered woman's experiences are generally outside the common understanding of the average judge and juror, and that they should seek to understand the evidence being presented to them in order to overcome the myths and stereotypes which we all share. Finally, all of this should be presented in such a way as to focus on the reasonableness of the woman's actions, without relying on old or new stereotypes about battered women.

R. v. Ewanchuk
Supreme Court of Canada
[1999] 1 S.C.R. 330

Under the criminal law in Canada, as in many other jurisdictions, sexual advances or activity without consent can constitute a criminal offence of sexual assault. What are the conditions under which consent can be considered given, and is there any such thing under Canadian law as "implied consent" to sexual touching? In this case the Supreme Court had to consider whether someone accused of sexual assault could rely on the defense that consent could be inferred or implied from the absence of active resistance to a sexual advance.

This case raises the theoretical issue about whether consent is to be understood objectively or subjectively, and how such an understanding might vary depending on whether it is being assessed from the perspective of the accused for the purposes of determining *mens rea*, or from the perspective of the complainant for the purposes of determining his or her mental state.

The Court found that there is no defence of "implied consent" to sexual assault in Canadian law, and found the accused in this case guilty of sexual assault.

―――――――

Justice Major (for the majority):

The Components of Sexual Assault

[23] A conviction for sexual assault requires proof beyond reasonable doubt of two basic elements, that the accused committed the *actus reus* and that he had the necessary *mens rea*. The *actus reus* of assault is unwanted sexual touching. The *mens rea* is the intention to touch, knowing of, or being reckless of or wilfully blind to, a lack of consent, either by words or actions, from the person being touched.

(1) Actus Reus

[24] The crime of sexual assault is only indirectly defined in the Criminal Code, R.S.C., 1985, c. C-46. The offence is comprised of an assault within any one of the definitions in s. 265(1) of the *Code*, which is committed in circumstances of a sexual nature, such that the sexual integrity of the victim is violated: see *R. v. S. (P.L.)*, [1991] 1 S.C.R. 909. Section 265 provides that:

265. (1) A person commits an assault when

(*a*) without the consent of another person, he applies force intentionally to that other person, directly or indirectly;

(*b*) he attempts or threatens, by an act or a gesture, to apply force to another person, if he has, or causes that other person to believe on reasonable grounds that he has, present ability to effect his purpose ...

(2) This section applies to all forms of assault, including sexual assault, sexual assault with a weapon, threats to a third party or causing bodily harm and aggravated sexual assault.

[25] The *actus reus* of sexual assault is established by the proof of three elements: (i) touching, (ii) the sexual nature of the contact, and (iii) the absence of consent. The first two of these elements are objective. It is sufficient for the Crown to prove that the accused's actions were voluntary. The sexual nature of the assault is determined objectively; the Crown need not prove that the accused had any *mens rea* with respect to the sexual nature of his or her behaviour: see *R. v. Litchfield*, [1993] 4 S.C.R. 333, and *R. v. Chase*, [1987] 2 S.C.R. 293.

[26] The absence of consent, however, is subjective and determined by reference to the complainant's subjective internal state of mind towards the touching, at the time it occurred. [...]

[27] Confusion has arisen from time to time on the meaning of consent as an element of the *actus reus* of sexual assault. Some of this confusion has been caused by the word "consent" itself. A number of commentators have observed that the notion of consent connotes active behaviour: see, for example, N. Brett, "Sexual Offenses and Consent" (1998), 11 *Can. J. Law& Jur.* 69, at p. 73. While this may be true in the general use of the word, for the purposes of determining the absence of consent as an element of the *actus reus*, the actual state of mind of the complainant is determinative. At this point, the trier of fact is only concerned with the complainant's perspective. The approach is purely subjective.

[28] The rationale underlying the criminalization of assault explains this. Society is committed to protecting the personal integrity, both physical and psychological, of every individual. Having control over who touches one's body, and how, lies at the core of human dignity and autonomy. The inclusion of assault and sexual assault in the *Code* expresses society's determination to protect the security of the person from any non-consensual contact or threats of force. The common law has recognized for centuries that the individual's right to physical integrity is a fundamental principle, "every man's person being sacred, and no other having a right to meddle with it, in any the slightest manner": see Blackstone's *Commentaries on the Laws of England* (4th ed. 1770), Book III, at p. 120. It follows that any intentional but unwanted touching is criminal.

[29] While the complainant's testimony is the only source of direct evidence as to her state of mind, credibility must still be assessed by the trial judge, or jury, in light of all the evidence. It is open to the accused to claim that the

complainant's words and actions, before and during the incident, raise a reasonable doubt against her assertion that she, in her mind, did not want the sexual touching to take place. If, however, as occurred in this case, the trial judge believes the complainant that she subjectively did not consent, the Crown has discharged its obligation to prove the absence of consent.

[30] The complainant's statement that she did not consent is a matter of credibility to be weighed in light of all the evidence including any ambiguous conduct. The question at this stage is purely one of credibility, and whether the totality of the complainant's conduct is consistent with her claim of non-consent. The accused's perception of the complainant's state of mind is not relevant. That perception only arises when a defence of honest but mistaken belief in consent is raised in the *mens rea* stage of the inquiry.

(a) "Implied Consent"

[31] Counsel for the respondent submitted that the trier of fact may believe the complainant when she says she did not consent, but still acquit the accused on the basis that her conduct raised a reasonable doubt. Both he and the trial judge refer to this as "implied consent." It follows from the foregoing, however, that the trier of fact may only come to one of two conclusions: the complainant either consented or not. There is no third option. If the trier of fact accepts the complainant's testimony that she did not consent, no matter how strongly her conduct may contradict that claim, the absence of consent is established and the third component of the *actus reus* of sexual assault is proven. The doctrine of implied consent has been recognized in our common law jurisprudence in a variety of contexts but sexual assault is not one of them. There is no defence of implied consent to sexual assault in Canadian law. [...]

(c) Effect of the Complainant's Fear

[36] To be legally effective, consent must be freely given. Therefore, even if the complainant consented, or her conduct raises a reasonable doubt about her non-consent, circumstances may arise which call into question what factors prompted her apparent consent. The *Code* defines a series of conditions under which the law will deem an absence of consent in cases of assault, notwithstanding the complainant's ostensible consent or participation. As enumerated in s. 265(3), these include submission by reason of force, fear, threats, fraud or the exercise of authority, and codify the longstanding common law rule that consent given under fear or duress is ineffective: see G. Williams, *Textbook of Criminal Law* (2nd ed. 1983), at pp. 551–61. This section reads as follows:

> **265.** ... (3) For the purposes of this section, no consent is obtained where the complainant submits or does not resist by reason of
>
> (*a*) the application of force to the complainant or to a person other than the complainant;

(*b*) threats or fear of the application of force to the complainant or to a person other than the complainant ...

[37] The words of Fish J.A. in *Saint-Laurent v. Hétu*, [1994] R.J.Q. 69 (C.A.), at p. 82, aptly describe the concern which the trier of fact must bear in mind when evaluating the actions of a complainant who claims to have been under fear, fraud or duress:

> "Consent" is ... stripped of its defining characteristics when it is applied to the submission, non-resistance, non-objection, or even the apparent agreement, of a deceived, unconscious or compelled will.

[38] In these instances the law is interested in a complainant's reasons for choosing to participate in, or ostensibly consent to, the touching in question. In practice, this translates into an examination of the choice the complainant believed she faced. The courts' concern is whether she *freely* made up her mind about the conduct in question. The relevant section of the *Code* is s. 265(3) (*b*), which states that there is no consent as a matter of law where the complainant believed that she was choosing between permitting herself to be touched sexually or risking being subject to the application of force.

[39] The question is not whether the complainant would have preferred not to engage in the sexual activity, but whether she believed herself to have only two choices: to comply or to be harmed. If a complainant agrees to sexual activity solely because she honestly believes that she will otherwise suffer physical violence, the law deems an absence of consent, and the third component of the *actus reus* of sexual assault is established. The trier of fact has to find that the complainant did not want to be touched sexually and made her decision to permit or participate in sexual activity as a result of an honestly held fear. The complainant's fear need not be reasonable, nor must it be communicated to the accused in order for consent to be vitiated. While the plausibility of the alleged fear, and any overt expressions of it, are obviously relevant to assessing the credibility of the complainant's claim that she consented out of fear, the approach is subjective. [...]

(a) Meaning of "Consent" in the Context of an Honest but Mistaken Belief in Consent

[45] As with the *actus reus* of the offence, consent is an integral component of the *mens rea*, only this time it is considered from the perspective of the accused. Speaking of the *mens rea* of sexual assault in *Park, supra*, at para. 39, L'Heureux-Dubé J. (in her concurring reasons) stated that:

> ... the *mens rea* of sexual assault is not only satisfied when it is shown that the accused knew that the complainant was essentially saying "no," but is also satisfied when it is shown that the accused knew that the complainant was essentially not saying "yes."

[46] In order to cloak the accused's actions in moral innocence, the evidence must show that he believed that the complainant *communicated consent to engage in the sexual activity in question*. A belief by the accused that the complainant, in her own mind wanted him to touch her but did not express that desire, is not a defence. The accused's speculation as to what was going on in the complainant's mind provides no defence.

[47] For the purposes of the *mens rea* analysis, the question is whether the accused believed that he had obtained consent. What matters is whether the accused believed that the complainant effectively said "yes" through her words and/or actions. The statutory definition added to the *Code* by Parliament in 1992 is consistent with the common law:

> **273.1** (1) Subject to subsection (2) and subsection 265(3), "consent" means, for the purposes of sections 271, 272, and 273, the voluntary agreement of the complainant to engage in the sexual activity in question.

[48] There is a difference in the concept of "consent" as it relates to the state of mind of the complainant *vis-à-vis* the *actus reus* of the offence and the state of mind of the accused in respect of the *mens rea*. For the purposes of the *actus reus*, "consent" means that the complainant in her mind wanted the sexual touching to take place.

[49] In the context of *mens rea*—specifically for the purposes of the honest but mistaken belief in consent—"consent" means that the complainant had affirmatively communicated by words or conduct her agreement to engage in sexual activity with the accused. This distinction should always be borne in mind and the two parts of the analysis kept separate.

(b) Limits on Honest but Mistaken Belief in Consent

[50] Not all beliefs upon which an accused might rely will exculpate him. Consent in relation to the *mens rea* of the accused is limited by both the common law and the provisions of ss. 273.1(2) and 273.2 of the *Code*, which provide that:

> **273.1** ... (2) No consent is obtained, for the purposes of sections 271, 272 and 273, where
>
> (*a*) the agreement is expressed by the words or conduct of a person other than the complainant;
>
> (*b*) the complainant is incapable of consenting to the activity;
>
> (*c*) the accused induces the complainant to engage in the activity by abusing a position of trust, power or authority;
>
> (*d*) the complainant expresses, by words or conduct, a lack of agreement to engage in the activity; or
>
> (*e*) the complainant, having consented to engage in sexual activity, expresses, by words or conduct, a lack of agreement to continue to engage in the activity.

273.2 It is not a defence to a charge under section 271, 272 or 273 that the accused believed that the complainant consented to the activity that forms the subject-matter of the charge, where

(*a*) the accused's belief arose from the accused's

    (i) self-induced intoxication, or

    (ii) recklessness or wilful blindness; or

(*b*) the accused did not take reasonable steps, in the circumstances known to the accused at the time, to ascertain that the complainant was consenting.

[51] For instance, a belief that silence, passivity or ambiguous conduct constitutes consent is a mistake of law, and provides no defence: see *R. v. M. (M.L.)*, [1994] 2 S.C.R. 3. Similarly, an accused cannot rely upon his purported belief that the complainant's expressed lack of agreement to sexual touching in fact constituted an invitation to more persistent or aggressive contact. An accused cannot say that he thought "no meant yes." As Fraser C.J. stated at p. 272 of her dissenting reasons below:

> One "No" will do to put the other person on notice that there is then a problem with "consent." *Once a woman says "No" during the course of sexual activity, the person intent on continued sexual activity with her must then obtain a clear and unequivocal "Yes" before he again touches her in a sexual manner.* [Emphasis in original.]

I take the reasons of Fraser C.J. to mean that an unequivocal "yes" may be given by either the spoken word or by conduct.

[52] Common sense should dictate that, once the complainant has expressed her unwillingness to engage in sexual contact, the accused should make certain that she has truly changed her mind before proceeding with further intimacies. The accused cannot rely on the mere lapse of time or the complainant's silence or equivocal conduct to indicate that there has been a change of heart and that consent now exists, nor can he engage in further sexual touching to "test the waters." Continuing sexual contact after someone has said "No" is, at a minimum, reckless conduct which is not excusable. [...]

R. v. JA
Supreme Court of Canada
[2011] 2 S.C.R. 440

Similar to *Ewanchuk,* this case raises the question of the conditions of consent to sexual touching. At issue before the court is whether there is any such thing as "advance consent," and in particular whether such consent can exist for sexual activity when one is unconscious.

By a vote of 6 to 3, the court determined that consent to sexual activity can only be given and present while one is conscious; once one becomes unconscious, even by one's own decision, consent is extinguished.

Chief Justice McLachlin (for the majority):

[27] The *Criminal Code* defines sexual assault as an assault that is committed in circumstances of a sexual nature. Section 265 provides that:

265. (1) A person commits an assault when

(*a*) without the consent of another person, he applies force intentionally to that other person, directly or indirectly;

(*b*) he attempts or threatens, by an act or a gesture, to apply force to another person, if he has, or causes that other person to believe on reasonable grounds that he has, present ability to effect his purpose ...

(2) This section applies to all forms of assault, including sexual assault, sexual assault with a weapon, threats to a third party or causing bodily harm and aggravated sexual assault....

[28] Parliament has enacted provisions that specifically define consent for the purpose of sexual assault. In particular, s. 273.1 establishes as follows:

273.1 (1) Subject to subsection (2) and subsection 265(3), "consent" means, for the purposes of sections 271, 272 and 273, the voluntary agreement of the complainant to engage *in the sexual activity in question.*

(2) *No consent is obtained,* for the purposes of sections 271, 272 and 273, where

(*a*) the agreement is expressed by the words or conduct of a person other than the complainant;

(*b*) *the complainant is incapable of consenting to the activity* ...

(*d*) *the complainant expresses, by words or conduct, a lack of agreement to engage in the activity*; or

(*e*) *the complainant, having consented to engage in sexual activity, expresses, by words or conduct, a lack of agreement to continue to engage in the activity.*

(3) Nothing in subsection (2) shall be construed as limiting the circumstances in which no consent is obtained.

[29] The definition of consent for the purposes of sexual assault is found in s. 273.1(1). In order to clarify this broad definition, Parliament provides a nonexhaustive list of circumstances in which no consent is obtained in s. 273.1(2). Section 273.1(3) authorizes the courts to identify additional cases in which no consent is obtained, in a manner consistent with the policies underlying the provisions of the *Criminal Code*.

[30] The defence of honest but mistaken belief in consent was recognized and limited by Parliament in s. 273.2 of the *Criminal Code*:

273.2 It is not a defence to a charge under section 271, 272 or 273 that the accused believed that the complainant consented to the activity that forms the subject-matter of the charge, where

(*a*) the accused's belief arose from the accused's

(i) self-induced intoxication, or

(ii) recklessness or wilful blindness; or

(*b*) the accused did not take reasonable steps, in the circumstances known to the accused at the time, to ascertain that the complainant was consenting.

C. The Concept of Consent Under the Criminal Code

[31] The foregoing provisions of the *Criminal Code* indicate that Parliament viewed consent as the conscious agreement of the complainant to engage in every sexual act in a particular encounter. [...]

[37] The provisions of the *Criminal Code* that relate to the *mens rea* of sexual assault confirm that individuals must be conscious throughout the sexual activity. Before considering these provisions, however, it is important to keep in mind the differences between the meaning of consent under the *actus reus* and under the *mens rea*: *Ewanchuk*, at paras. 48–49. Under the *mens rea* defence, the issue is whether the accused believed that the complainant *communicated consent*. Conversely, the only question for the *actus reus* is whether the complainant was subjectively consenting in her mind. The complainant is not required to *express* her lack of consent or her revocation of consent for the *actus reus* to be established.

[38] With this caution in mind, I come to the three provisions that relate to the *mens rea* that are relevant to the issue in this case: s. 273.1(2) (*d*), s. 273.1(2) (*e*) and s. 273.2 (*b*).

[39] Section 273.1(2) (*d*) provides that there can be no consent if the "complainant expresses, by words or conduct, a lack of agreement to engage in the activity." Since this provision refers to the expression of consent, it is clear that it can only apply to the accused's *mens rea*. The point here is the linking of lack of consent to any "activity." This suggests a present, ongoing conception of consent, rather than advance consent to a suite of activities.

[40] Section 273.1(2) (*e*) establishes that it is an error of law for the accused to believe that the complainant is still consenting after she "expresses...a lack of agreement to continue to engage in the activity." Since this provision refers to the expression of consent, it is clear that it can only apply to the accused's *mens rea*. Nonetheless, it indicates that Parliament wanted people to be capable of revoking their consent at any time during the sexual activity. This in turn supports the view that Parliament viewed consent as the product of a conscious mind, since a person who has been rendered unconscious cannot revoke her consent. As a result, the protection afforded by s. 273.1(2) (*e*) would not be available to her.

[41] According to my colleague, Fish J., s. 273.1(2) (*e*) "suggests that the complainant's consent *can* be given in advance, and remains operative unless and until it is subsequently revoked" (para. 104 [emphasis in original]). With respect, I cannot accept this interpretation. The provision in question establishes that the accused must halt all sexual contact once the complainant expresses that she no longer consents. This does not mean that a failure to tell the accused to stop means that the complainant must have been consenting. As this Court has repeatedly held, the complainant is not required to express her lack of consent for the *actus reus* to be established. Rather, the question is whether the complainant subjectively consented in her mind: *Ewanchuk*; *R. v. M. (M.L.)*, [1994] 2 S.C.R. 3.

[42] Section 273.2 sheds further light on Parliament's conception of consent. Section 273.2 (*b*) states that a person wishing to avail himself of the *mens rea* defence must not only believe that the complainant communicated her consent (or in French, "*l'accusé croyait que le plaignant avait consenti*" [s. 273.2]), but must also have taken reasonable steps to ascertain whether she "was consenting" to engage in the sexual activity in question at the time it occurred. How can one take reasonable steps to ascertain whether a person is consenting to sexual activity while it is occurring if that person is unconscious? Once again, the provision is grounded in the assumption that the complainant must consciously consent to each and every sexual act. Further, by requiring the accused to take reasonable steps to ensure that the complainant "was consenting," Parliament has indicated that the consent of the complainant must be an ongoing state of mind.

[43] The question in this case is whether Parliament defined consent in a way that extends to advance consent to sexual acts committed while the complainant

is unconscious. In my view, it did not. J.A.'s contention that advance consent can be given to sexual acts taking place during unconsciousness is not in harmony with the provisions of the *Code* and their underlying policies. These provisions indicate that Parliament viewed consent as requiring a "capable" or operating mind, able to evaluate each and every sexual act committed. To hold otherwise runs counter to Parliament's clear intent that a person has the right to consent to particular acts and to revoke her consent at any time. Reading these provisions together, I cannot accept the respondent's contention that an individual may consent in advance to sexual activity taking place while she is unconscious. [...]

Justice Fish (dissenting):
[68] It is a fundamental principle of the law governing sexual assault in Canada that no means "no" and only yes means "yes."

[69] K.D., the complainant in this case, said yes, not no. She consented to her erotic asphyxiation by the respondent, J.A., her partner at the time. Their shared purpose was to render K.D. unconscious and to engage in sexual conduct while she remained in that state. It is undisputed that K.D.'s consent was freely and voluntarily given—in advance and while the conduct was still in progress. Immediately afterward, K.D. had intercourse with J.A., again consensually.

[70] K.D. first complained to the police nearly two months later when J.A. threatened to seek sole custody of their two-year-old child. She later recanted.

[71] We are nonetheless urged by the Crown to find that the complainant's *yes in fact* means *no in law*. With respect for those who are of a different view, I would decline to do so.

[72] The provisions of the Criminal Code, R.S.C. 1985, c. C-46, regarding consent to sexual contact and the case law (including *R. v. Ewanchuk*, [1999] 1 S.C.R. 330) relied on by the Crown were intended to protect women against abuse by others. Their mission is not to "protect" women *against themselves* by limiting their freedom to determine autonomously when and with whom they will engage in the sexual relations of their choice. Put differently, they aim to safeguard and enhance the sexual autonomy of women, and not to make choices for them.

[73] The Crown's position, if adopted by the Court, would achieve exactly the opposite result. It would deprive women of their freedom to engage by choice in sexual adventures that involve no proven harm to them or to others. That is what happened here.

[74] Adopting the Crown's position would also require us to find that cohabiting partners across Canada, including spouses, commit a sexual assault when either one of them, *even with express prior consent*, kisses or caresses the other while the latter is asleep. The absurdity of this consequence makes plain that it is the product of an unintended and unacceptable extension of the *Criminal Code* provisions upon which the Crown would cause this appeal to rest.

[75] Lest I be misunderstood to suggest otherwise, I agree that consent will be vitiated where the contemplated sexual activity involves a degree of bodily harm or risk of fatal injury that cannot be condoned under the common law, or on grounds of public policy. Asphyxiation to the point of unconsciousness may well rise to that level, but the contours of this limitation on consent have not been addressed by the parties. Nor has the matter been previously considered by the Court. For procedural reasons as well, the issue of bodily harm must be left for another day.

[76] I agree as well that prior consent affords no defence where it is later revoked or where the ensuing conduct does not comply with the consent given. [...]

[79] According to the Chief Justice, the question is "whether an unconscious person can qualify as consenting [to sexual activity]" (para. 33). With respect, that is not the question at all: *No one* has suggested in this case that an unconscious person can validly consent to sexual activity.

[80] Rather, the question is whether a *conscious* person can freely and voluntarily consent in advance to agreed sexual activity that will occur while he or she is briefly and consensually rendered unconscious. My colleague would answer that question in the negative; I would answer that question in the affirmative, absent a clear prohibition in the *Criminal Code*, absent proven bodily harm that would vitiate consent at common law, and absent any evidence that the conscious partner subjected the unconscious partner to sexual activity beyond their agreement.

B: LIABILITY IN PRIVATE LAW

Cook v. Lewis
Supreme Court of Canada
[1952] S.C.R. 830

In order to prove liability for the tort of negligence the plaintiff must prove that the defendant acted carelessly in circumstances in which there was a duty to be more careful and that this conduct caused the plaintiff to be harmed in some way. On the face of it one might suspect that the element of causation would be the least difficult to prove, and this is usually true. The general rule for causation in torts (or "cause-in-fact") is the so-called "but for" test: the plaintiff must show that, but for the defendant's negligent conduct, the plaintiff would not have suffered harm. What could be more straightforward? *Cook v. Lewis* shows cause-in-fact to be anything but straightforward.

Stripped to its essentials, the situation was this: plaintiff Lewis was struck by birdshot in the face immediately after defendants Cook and Akenhead, who were hunting in the vicinity, had discharged their guns at the same moment. One of these shots hit Lewis, but it was not possible to tell which one. The jury found that since Lewis could not prove which of Cook and Akenhead caused his injury, neither was liable. The Court of Appeal said this was perverse and the case made its way up to the Supreme Court of Canada. That Court strove to find a way out of the causal conundrum.

Justice Rand (for the majority):

I agree with the Court of Appeal that the finding of the jury exculpating both defendants from negligence was perverse and it is unnecessary to examine the facts on which that conclusion is based.

There remains the answer that, although shots from one of the two guns struck the respondent [Lewis], the jury could not determine from which they came. This is open to at least four interpretations: first, believing that only one discharge could have inflicted the injuries, they found it difficult to decide which testimony, whether that of Cook or Akenhead, was to be accepted, the evidence of each, taken at its face, excluding guilt; or that the shots from both guns having been fired so nearly at the same time and to have been aimed so nearly at the same target, it was impossible for them to say which struck the eye; or that they were unable to say whether the situation was either of those two alternatives; or finally, that they were not unanimous on anyone or more of these views.

It will be seen that there is one feature common to the first three: having found that either A or B had been the cause of injury to C, the jury declare that C has not satisfied them which of the two it was. It is then a problem in proof and must be considered from that standpoint.

A cause may be said to be an operating element which in *de facto* co-operation with what may be called environment is considered the factor of culpability in determining legal responsibility for damage or loss done to person or property. But in that determination the practical difficulty turns on the allocation of elements to the one or other of these two divisions of data. In considering the second and third possibilities in this case, the essential obstacle to proof is the fact of multiple discharges so related as to confuse their individual effects: it is the fact that bars final proof. But if the victim, having brought guilt down to one or both of the two persons before the Court, can bring home to either of them a further wrong done him in relation to his remedial right of making that proof, then I should say that on accepted principles, the barrier to it can and should be removed.

The Court of Appeal of England has laid down this principle: that if A is guilty of a negligent act toward B, the total direct consequences of that act are chargeable against A notwithstanding that they arise from reactions unforeseeable by the ordinary person acting reasonably; *Polemis v. Furness Withy*. [...]

Similarly would that result follow where, instead of an unforeseen potentiality, an element is introduced into the scene at the critical moment of which or its probability the negligent actor knows or ought to have known. That element becomes, then, one of the circumstances in reaction with which the consequences of his act manifest themselves, among which, here, is the confusion of consequences. If the new element is innocent, no liability results to the person who introduces it; if culpable, its effect in law remains to be ascertained.

What, then, the culpable actor has done by his initial negligent act is, first, to have set in motion a dangerous force which embraces the injured person within the scope of its probable mischief; and next, in conjunction with circumstances which he must be held to contemplate, to have made more difficult if not impossible the means of proving the possible damaging results of his own act or the similar results of the act of another. He has violated not only the victim's substantive right to security, but he has also culpably impaired the latter's remedial right of establishing liability. By confusing his act with environmental conditions, he has, in effect, destroyed the victim's power of proof.

The legal consequences of that is, I should say, that the onus is then shifted to the wrongdoer to exculpate himself; it becomes in fact a question of proof between him and the other and innocent member of the alternatives, the burden of which he must bear. The onus attaches to culpability, and if both acts bear that taint, the onus or *prima facie* transmission of responsibility attaches to both, and the question of the sole responsibility of one is a matter between them.

On the first interpretation, the answer of the jury was insufficient as a return. Their duty was to determine the facts from the evidence laid before them as best they could on the balance of probabilities, and it could not be evaded in the face of such divergent testimony either because of a tender regard for distasteful implications or for any other reason. The jury might have reached a deadlock from which there was no escape: but with the proper direction as to onus, that would have been obviated. The result is that there has been no verdict on an essential question, and the judgement based upon the answer cannot stand. [...]

If, next, the answer means, as it may, that lack of unanimity was the frustrating factor, there is again a fatal incompleteness of findings, because of which, likewise, the judgement cannot stand.

The remaining interpretations fall within the considerations already expressed. The dominating fact is a confusion of causal factors and consequences resulting in what was, in substance, a small shower of flying shot. In dealing with such a situation, we must keep in mind that the task of the Court is to determine responsibility, not cause, but obviously for that purpose cause as ordinarily conceived is a controlling factor. Ultimately, it is cause in a juridical sense that we are to find. In the judicial process also, auxiliary mechanisms have been adopted which experience has vindicated, such as, for example, onus, estoppel, presumption. Although the facts here, in their precise form, have not, then, previously been presented to the courts of either this country or England, they are such as to which onus is properly invoked.

The risks arising from these sporting activities by increased numbers of participants and diminishing opportunity for their safe exercise, as the facts here indicate, require appropriate refinements in foresight. Against the private and public interests at stake, is the privilege of the individual to engage in a sport not inherently objectionable. As yet, certainly, the community is not ready to assume the burden of such a mishap. The question is whether a victim is to be told that such a risk, not only in substantive right but in remedy, is one he must assume. When we have reached the point where, as here, shots are considered spent at a distance of between 150 feet and 200 feet and the woods are "full" of hunters, a somewhat stringent regard to conduct seems to me to be obvious. It would be a strange commentary on its concern toward personal safety, that the law, although forbidding the victim any other mode of redress, was powerless to accord him any in its own form of relief. I am unable to assent to the view that there is any such helplessness.

Liability would, *a fortiori*, be the legal result if the acts of several were intended to be co-operative for a common object or if the act of one was so aided or abetted or induced by the act or conduct of another that it could be said to have had the will and the influence of that other behind it; and in determining that fact, the usual understandings between hunters in relation to the existence of conditions that would make shooting in a particular situation dangerous, are relevant.

Assuming, then, that the jury have found one or both of the defendants here negligent, as on the evidence I think they must have, and at the same time have found that the consequences of the two shots, whether from a confusion in time or in area, cannot be segregated, the onus on the guilty person arises. This is a case where each hunter would know of or expect the shooting by the other and the negligent actor has culpably participated in the proof-destroying fact, the multiple shooting and its consequences. No liability will, in any event, attach to an innocent act of shooting, but the culpable actor, as against innocence, must bear the burden of exculpation.

These views of the law were not as adequately presented to the jury as I think they should have been. I would, therefore, dismiss the appeal with costs.

Marconato and Marconato v. Franklin
British Columbia Supreme Court
[1974] 6 W.W.R. 676

Should people who negligently harm others be responsible for *all* the damage that actually results, even if it is unforeseeable? Suppose you have a very rare condition—a thin skull—and I, negligently, hit your head causing you far greater injury than a similar blow would have caused anyone else, and certainly far greater injury than I thought was possible when I did the hitting. Should I be liable for all of this harm or only the reasonably foreseeable part of it? Generally speaking the law's answer is the former: tortfeasors must take their victims as they find them. In this case, this rule is applied to a different kind of "thin skull."

Justice Aikins:

The plaintiffs are husband and wife. On 1st February 1971 Mrs. Marconato was driving her car in Vancouver; a car driven by the defendant collided with the left side of her car. Mrs. Marconato was injured. The left side of her head and body was thrown against some part of her car. Mrs. Marconato sues for damages for personal injury and her husband sues for damages for loss of consortium and servitium. Liability is admitted. The parties have agreed on special damages.

I shall first consider the amount of general damages that should be awarded to Mrs. Marconato. Her physical injuries were fortunately not of major severity. However, assessment of damages presents some difficulty because it is asserted that because of the collision, caused by the admitted negligence of the defendant, Mrs. Marconato suffered psychiatric injury referred to in the statement of claim as "traumatic neurosis" and "conversion hysteria."

I propose to review Mrs. Marconato's evidence and the evidence of the two doctors at length because much of the difficulty in the case stems from somewhat bizarre symptoms of which Mrs. Marconato complained from time to time after she was hurt and to which she testified. Many of her complaints cannot be explained by straightforward physical causation. That is to say, clinical examination does not reveal any physiological line of causation running from the force to which she was subjected in the collision to many of the aches, pains and disabilities of which she has complained over the following years. Mrs. Marconato's doctors cannot clinically find any physiological reasons for many of Mrs. Marconato's complaints. In the face of this, it might be thought that Mrs. Marconato was malingering. I think it convenient at this point to state plainly that I thought Mrs. Marconato to be an honest witness. I do not think that she lied to her doctors and I do not think she lied to me. I found some support for Mrs. Marconato's evidence in the evidence given by her husband and I add that I thought him to be an honest witness.

I find that Mrs. Marconato had a paranoid type personality. She was not, however, mentally ill before she was hurt. I accept Dr. Whitman's diagnosis: a neurotic or psychoneurotic reaction with mixed anxiety and depression. Indeed I am satisfied that Mrs. Marconato has suffered great anxiety and great depression. She has had to cope with a great deal of pain. I find that the main cause of her continued pain and disability has been anxiety and tension but that, as well, conversion hysteria has played some part. She has developed unfounded mistrust of her medical advisers. She has shown some characteristics of paranoia. She has undergone what can best be described, I suppose, as a personality change; she was a happy and contented woman in her role in life and she has become a very unhappy woman. She has given up hobbies and activities which gave her pleasure.

I turn to the question of causation. One would not ordinarily anticipate, using reasonable foresight, that a moderate cervical strain with soft tissue damage would give rise to the consequences which followed for Mrs. Marconato. These arose, however, because of her pre-existing personality traits. She had a peculiar susceptibility or vulnerability to suffer much greater consequences from a moderate physical injury than the average person. The consequences for Mrs. Marconato could no more be foreseen than it could be foreseen by a tortfeasor that his victim was thin-skulled and that a minor blow to the head would cause very serious injury. It is plain enough that the defendant could foresee the probability of physical injury. It is implicit, however, in the principle that a wrongdoer takes his victim as he finds him, that he takes his victim with all the victim's peculiar susceptibilities and vulnerabilities. The consequences of Mrs. Marconato's injuries were unusual but arose involuntarily. Granted her type of personality they arose as night follows day because of the injury and the circumstances in which she found herself because of the injury.

As to the argument that the damage suffered is too remote because not reasonably foreseeable, I refer first to an English case *Smith v. Leech Brain & Co. Ltd.* (1962). In this case the plaintiff widow claimed damages for the death of her husband under the Fatal Accidents Acts. The defendant was the deceased's employer. The deceased suffered a burn on his lip; as a result cancer developed at that site, from which the injured man died some three years later. Remoteness on the ground of lack of foreseeability was argued. I cite two passages from the judgement of Lord Parker C.J.:

> It has always been the law of this country that a tortfeasor takes his victim as he finds him. It is unnecessary to do more than refer to the short passage in the decision of Kennedy J. in *Dulieu v. White & Sons*, (1901) where he said: "If a man is negligently run over or otherwise negligently injured in his body, it is no answer to the sufferer's claim for damages that he would have suffered less injury, or no injury at all, if he had not had an unusually thin skull or an unusually weak heart."

The second passage is:

> The test is not whether these employers could reasonably have foreseen that a burn would cause cancer and that he would die. The question is whether these employers could reasonably foresee the type of injury he suffered, namely, the burn. What, in the particular case, is the amount of damage which he suffers as a result of that burn, depends upon the characteristics and constitution of the victim.

What I have cited might well be transposed in the present case to go as follows: Mrs. Marconato was predisposed by her personality to suffer the consequences which she did suffer as a result of the modest physical injury caused by the accident and it was that predisposition which brought on the unusual consequences of the injury. The defendant must pay damages for all the consequences of his negligence.

Norberg v. Wynrib
Supreme Court of Canada
[1992] 2 S.C.R. 226

Laura Norberg became addicted to pain killers and maintained her supply by "double doctoring"—obtaining narcotic prescriptions from several doctors without telling them that she already had other prescriptions. She eventually went to Dr. Morris Wynrib who confronted her about her addiction. But instead of recommending treatment, Dr. Wynrib made it clear that he would provide her with the drug in exchange for sexual intercourse. She gave in to his demands, and soon Dr. Wynrib was directly giving her the narcotic after each sexual encounter. Not long after, Norberg was charged criminally for double doctoring and went to a rehabilitation centre on her own initiative. Then she sued Dr. Wynrib.

The Supreme Court of Canada split three ways, not on the question of *whether* Dr. Wynrib had done something wrong and so was liable to Laura Norberg for damages, but on the issue of *what* duty he owed her and which he failed to live up to. The debate here comes down to what, precisely, is the essence or core of Dr. Wynrib's civil wrong against Norberg. Two of the justices sought to capture this duty in a highly innovative way, one which signals a change in our understanding of the patient-physician and other professional relationships.

Justice McLachlin (for the majority):

The relationship of physician and patient can be conceptualized in a variety of ways. It can be viewed as a creature of contract, with the physician's failure to fulfil his or her obligations giving rise to an action for breach of contract. It undoubtedly gives rise to a duty of care, the breach of which constitutes the tort of negligence. In common with all members of society, the doctor owes the patient a duty not to touch him or her without his or her consent; if the doctor breaches this duty he or she will have committed the tort of battery. But perhaps the most fundamental characteristic of the doctor-patient relationship is *its fiduciary* nature. All the authorities agree that the relationship of physician to patient also falls into that special category of relationships which the law calls fiduciary. [...]

[...] I think it is readily apparent that the doctor-patient relationship shares the peculiar hallmark of the fiduciary relationship—trust, the trust of a person with inferior power that another person who has assumed superior power and responsibility will exercise that power for his or her good and only for his or her good and in his or her best interests. Recognizing the fiduciary nature of the doctor-patient relationship provides the law with an analytic model by which physicians can be held to the high standards of dealing with their patient which the trust accorded them requires. [...]

The foundation and ambit of the fiduciary obligation are conceptually distinct from the foundation and ambit of contract and tort. Sometimes the doctrines may overlap in their application, but that does not destroy their conceptual and functional uniqueness. In negligence and contract the parties are taken to be independent and equal actors, concerned primarily with their own self-interest. Consequently, the law seeks a balance between enforcing obligations by awarding compensation when those obligations are breached, and preserving optimum freedom for those involved in the relationship in question. The essence of a fiduciary relationship, by contrast, is that one party exercises power on behalf of another and pledges himself or herself to act in the best interests of the other. [...]

The fiduciary relationship has trust, not self-interest, at its core, and when breach occurs, the balance favours the person wronged. The freedom of the fiduciary is limited by the obligation he or she has undertaken—an obligation which "betokens loyalty, good faith and avoidance of a conflict of duty and self-interest": *Canadian Aero Service Ltd. v. O'Malley* [1974] S.C.R. 592, at p. 606. To cast a fiduciary relationship in terms of contract or tort (whether negligence or battery) is to diminish this obligation. If a fiduciary relationship is shown to exist, then the proper legal analysis is one based squarely on the full and fair consequences of a breach of that relationship.

As La Forest J. went on to note in *McInerney v. MacDonald* (1992) at p. 149, characterizing the doctor-patient relationship as fiduciary is not the end of the analysis: "not all fiduciary relationships and not all fiduciary obligations are the same; these are shaped by the demands of the situation. A relationship may properly be described as 'fiduciary' for some purposes, but not for others." So the question must be asked, did a fiduciary relationship exist between Dr. Wynrib and Ms. Norberg? And assuming that such relationship did exist, is it properly described as fiduciary for the purposes relevant to this appeal?

Wilson J. in *Frame v. Smith*, [1987] 2 S.C.R. 99, at p. 136, (approved by Sopinka and La Forest JJ. in *Lac Minerals Ltd. v. International Corona Resources Ltd.*, [1989] 2 S.C.R. 574, at pp. 598 and 646, and by McLachlin J., Lamer C.J. and L'Heureux-Dubé J. concurring, in *Canson Enterprises Ltd. v. Boughton & Co.*, [1991] 3 S.C.R. 534, at pp. 543–44), attributed the following characteristics to a fiduciary relationship: "(1) [t]he fiduciary has scope for the exercise of some discretion or power; (2) the fiduciary can unilaterally exercise that power or discretion so as to affect the beneficiary's legal or practical interests; (3) the beneficiary is peculiarly vulnerable to or at the mercy of the fiduciary holding the discretion or power."

Dr. Wynrib was in a position of power vis-à-vis the plaintiff; he had scope for the exercise of power and discretion with respect to her. He had the power to advise her, to treat her, to give her the drug or to refuse her the drug. He could unilaterally exercise that power or discretion in a way that affected her interests. And her status as a patient rendered her vulnerable and at his mercy, particularly in light of her addiction. So Wilson J.'s test appears to be met. All the classic characteristics of a fiduciary relationship were present. Dr. Wynrib and Ms. Norberg were on an unequal footing. He pledged himself—by the act of hanging out his shingle as a medical doctor and accepting her as his patient—to act in her best interests and not permit any conflict between his duty to act only in her best interests and his own interests—including his interest in sexual gratification—to arise. As a physician, he owed her the classic duties associated with a fiduciary relationship—the duties of "loyalty, good faith and avoidance of a conflict of duty and self-interest."

Closer examination of the principles enunciated by Wilson J. in *Frame* confirms the applicability of the fiduciary analysis in this case. The possession of power or discretion needs little elaboration. That one party in a fiduciary relationship holds such power over the other is not in and of itself wrong; on the contrary, "the fiduciary must be entrusted with power in order to perform his function": Frankel, *supra* at p. 809. What will be a wrong is if the risk inherent in entrusting the fiduciary with such power is realized and the fiduciary abuses the power which has been entrusted to him or her. As Wilson J. noted in *Frame*, at p. 136, in the absence of such a discretion or power and the possibility of abuse of power which it entails, "there is no need for a superadded obligation to restrict the damaging use of the discretion or power."

As to the second characteristic, it is, as Wilson J. put it at p. 136, "the fact that the power or discretion may be used to affect the beneficiary in a damaging way that makes the imposition of a fiduciary duty necessary." Wilson J. went on to state that fiduciary duties are not confined to the exercise of power which can affect the legal interests of the beneficiary, but extend to the beneficiary's "vital non-legal or 'practical' interests." This negates the suggestion inherent in some of the other judgements which this case has engendered that the fiduciary obligation should be confined to legal rights such as confidentiality and conflict of interest and undue influence in the business sphere.

The case at bar is not concerned with the protection of what has traditionally been regarded as a legal interest. It is, however, concerned with the protection of interests, both societal and personal, of the highest importance. Society has an abiding interest in ensuring that the power entrusted to physicians by us, both collectively and individually, not be used in corrupt ways, to borrow the language of *Reading v. Attorney-General*, [1951] A.C. 507 (H.L.). On the other side of the coin, the plaintiff, as indeed does every one of us when we put ourselves in the hands of a physician, has a striking personal interest in obtaining professional medical care free of exploitation for the physician's private purposes. These are not collateral duties and rights created at the whim of an aggrieved patient. They are duties universally recognized as essential to the physician-patient relationship. The Hippocratic Oath reflects this universal concern that physicians not exploit their patients for their own ends, and in particular, not for their own sexual ends. [...]

To the extent that the law requires that physicians who breach them be disciplined, these duties have legal force. The interests which the enforcement of these duties protect are, to be sure, different from the legal and economic interests which the law of fiduciary relationships has traditionally been used to safeguard. But as Wilson J. said in *Frame v. Smith* at p. 143, "[t]o deny relief because of the nature of the interest involved, to afford protection to material interests but not to human or personal interests would, it seems to me, be arbitrary in the extreme." At the very least, the societal and personal interests at issue here constitute "a vital and substantial 'practical' interest" (at p. 137), within the meaning of the second characteristic of a fiduciary duty set out in *Frame v. Smith*.

The third requirement is that of vulnerability. This is the other side of the differential power equation which is fundamental to all fiduciary relationships. In order to be the beneficiary of a fiduciary relationship a person need not be *per se* vulnerable. [...] It is only where there is a material discrepancy, in the circumstances of the relationship in question, between the power of one person and the vulnerability of the other that the fiduciary relationship is recognized by the law. Where the parties are on a relatively equal footing, contract and tort provide the appropriate analysis. [...]

In the case at bar, this requirement too is fulfilled. A physician holds great power over the patient. The recent decision of the Ontario Court (General Division) in *College of Physicians and Surgeons of Ontario v. Gillen* (1990), 1 O.R. (3d) 710, contains a reminder that a patient's vulnerability may be as much physical as emotional, given the fact that a doctor (at p. 713) "has the right to examine the patient in any state of dress or undress and to administer drugs to render the patient unconscious." Visits to doctors occur in private: the door is closed, there is rarely a third party present, everything possible is done to encourage the patient to feel that the patient's privacy will be respected. This is essential to the meeting of the patient's medical and emotional needs; the unfortunate concomitant is that it also creates the conditions under which the patient may be abused without fear of outside intervention. Whether physically vulnerable or not, however, the patient, by reason of lesser expertise, the "submission" which is essential to the relationship, and sometimes, as in this case, by reason of the nature of the illness itself, is typically in a position of comparative powerlessness. The fact that society encourages us to trust our doctors, to believe that they will be persons worthy of our trust, cannot be ignored as a factor inducing a heightened degree of vulnerability: see Feldman-Summers, "Sexual Contact in Fiduciary Relationships," in Gabbard, ed., *Sexual Exploitation in Professional Relationships*, at pp. 204–05.

Women, who can so easily be exploited by physicians for sexual purposes, may find themselves particularly vulnerable. That female patients are disproportionately the targets of sexual exploitation by physicians is borne out by the [College of Physicians and Surgeons of Ontario, *Final Report of the Task Force on Sexual Abuse of Patients*]. Of the 303 reports they received of sexual exploitation at the hands of those in a position of trust (the vast majority of whom were physicians), 287 were by female patients, 16 by males. [...]

The principles outlined by Wilson J. in *Frame v. Smith* may apply with varying force depending on the nature of the particular doctor-patient relationship. For example, the uniquely intimate nature of the psychotherapist-patient relationship, the potential for transference, and the emotional fragility of many psychotherapy patients make the argument for a fiduciary obligation resting on psychotherapists, and in particular an obligation to refrain from any sexualizing of the relationship, especially strong in that context. [...]

But, it is said, there are a number of reasons why the doctrine of breach of fiduciary relationship cannot apply in this case. I turn then to these alleged conditions of defeasibility.

The first factor which is said to prevent application of the doctrine of breach of fiduciary duty is Ms. Norberg's conduct. Two terms have been used to raise this consideration to the status of a legal or equitable bar—the equitable maxim that he who comes into equity must come with clean hands and the tort doctrine of *ex turpi causa non orbitur actio*. For our purposes, one may think of the two respectively as the equitable and legal formulations of the same type of bar to recovery. The trial judge found that although Dr. Wynrib was under a trust obligation to Ms. Norberg, she was barred from claiming damages against him because of her "immoral" and "illegal" conduct. [...]

The short answer to the arguments based on wrongful conduct of the plaintiff is that she did nothing wrong in the context of this relationship. She was not a sinner, but a sick person, suffering from an addiction which proved to be uncontrollable in the absence of a professional drug rehabilitation program. She went to Dr. Wynrib for relief from that condition. She hoped he would give her relief by giving her the drug; "hustling" doctors for drugs is a recognized symptom of her illness: Wilford, *Drug Abuse, A Guide for the Primary Care Physician* (1981), at pp. 280–82. Such behaviour is commonly seen by family physicians. Patients may, as did Ms. Norberg, feign physical problems which, if *bona fide*, would require analgesic relief. They may, as Ms. Norberg also did, specify the drug they wish to receive. Once a physician has diagnosed a patient as an addict who is "hustling" him for drugs the recommended response is to "(1) maintain control of the doctor-patient relationship, (2) remain professional in the face of ploys for sympathy or guilt and (3) regard the drug seeker as a patient with a serious illness": Wilford, at p. 282. [...]

The law might accuse Ms. Norberg of "double doctoring" and moralists might accuse her of licentiousness; but she did no wrong because not she but the doctor was responsible for this conduct. He had the power to cure her of her addiction, as her successful treatment after leaving his "care" demonstrated; instead he chose to use his power to keep her in her addicted state and to use her for his own sexual purposes.

It is difficult not to see the attempt to bar Ms. Norberg from obtaining redress for the wrong she has suffered through the application of the clean hands maxim as anything other than "blaming the victim." [...]

[Another] objection raised to viewing the relationship between Dr. Wynrib and Ms. Norberg as fiduciary is that it will open the floodgates to unfounded claims based on the abuse of real or perceived inequality of power. The spec- tre is conjured up of a host of actions based on exploitation—children suing parents, wives suing husbands, mistresses suing lovers, all for abuse of superior power. The answer to this objection lies in defining the ambit of the fiduciary obligation in a way that encompasses meritorious claims while excluding those without merit. The prospect of the law's recognizing [un]meritorious claims by the powerless and exploited against the powerful and exploitive should not alone serve as a reason for denying just claims. This Court has an honourable tradi- tion of recognizing new claims of the disempowered against the exploitive. [...]

The criteria for the imposition of a fiduciary duty already enunciated by this Court in cases such as *Frame, Lac Minerals* and *Guerin* provide a good starting point for the task of defining the general principles which determine whether such a relationship exists. As we have seen, an imbalance of power is not enough to establish a fiduciary relationship. It is a necessary but not sufficient condi- tion. There must also be the potential for interference with a legal interest or a non-legal interest of "vital and substantial 'practical' interest." And I would add this. Inherent in the notion of fiduciary duty, inherent in the judgements of this Court in *Guerin* and *Canson,* is the requirement that the fiduciary have assumed or undertaken to "look after" the interest of the beneficiary. As I put it in *Canson* at p. 543, quoting from this Court's decision in *Canadian Aero Service Ltd. v. O'Malley, supra,* at p. 606, "[t]he freedom of the fiduciary is diminished by the nature of the obligation he or she has undertaken—an obligation which 'betokens loyalty, good faith and avoidance of a conflict of duty and self-interest.'" It is not easy to bring relationships within this rubric. Generally people are deemed by the law to be motivated in their relationships by mutual self-interest. The duties of trust are special, confined to the exceptional case where one person assumes the power which would normally reside with the other and undertakes to exercise that power solely for the other's benefit. It is as though the fiduciary has taken the power which rightfully belongs to the beneficiary on the condition that the fiduciary exercise the power entrusted exclusively for the good of the beneficiary. Thus the trustee of an estate takes the financial power that would normally reside with the beneficiaries and must exercise those powers in their stead and for their exclusive benefit. Similarly, a physician takes the power which a patient normally has over her body, and which she cedes to him for purposes of treatment. The physician is pledged by the nature of his calling to use the power the patient cedes to him exclusively for her benefit. If he breaks that pledge, he is liable.

In summary, the constraints inherent in the principles governing fiduciary relationships belie the contention that the recognition of a fiduciary obligation in this case will open the floodgates to unmeritorious claims. Taking the case at its narrowest, it is concerned with a relationship which has long been recognized as fiduciary—the physician-patient relationship; it represents no extension of the law. Taking the case more broadly, with reference to the general principles governing fiduciary obligations, it is seen to fall within principles previously recognized by this court, and again represents no innovation. In so far as application of those principles in this case might be argued to give encouragement to new categories of claims, the governing principles offer assurance against unlimited liability while at the same time promising a great measure of justice for the exploited.

Crocker v. Sundance Northwest Resorts Ltd.
Supreme Court of Canada
[1988] 1 S.C.R. 1186

Should our law recognize a private "duty to rescue"—a duty to help others when they get into trouble, even if they are to blame for putting themselves into harm's way? A long-standing tort doctrine says no: *volenti non fit injuria*—if you consent to a risk, then you can't complain of the foreseeable injuries you sustain. But should the law allow us to stand by and let harm happen to others, or should it require us to be, if not good, then at least minimally decent Samaritans? In this case Crocker joined a competition run by the Sundance resort involving two-person teams sliding down a mogulled portion of a snow-covered hill in oversized inner tubes. Crocker paid his entry fee and signed, but did not read, a waiver form. Unfortunately, as the competition progressed, he got increasingly more drunk. The owner and manager of the resort both told him he should not continue, but Crocker insisted and on the next run broke his neck and became a quadriplegic. He now sues the resort for not rescuing him from his imprudence.

Justice Wilson (for the Court):

The Facts

[5] Crocker and his friend were the winners of their first heat. During the race the two were thrown from their tube and Crocker suffered a cut above his eye. Between the first and second heats Crocker drank two large swallows of brandy offered to him by the driver of a Molson beer van and was sold two more drinks at the bar.

[6] The owner of Sundance, Beals, saw Crocker between the first and second heats. Noting Crocker's condition Beals asked him whether he was in any condition to compete in another heat. Crocker responded that he was. Beals did nothing more to dissuade him.

[7] At the top of the hill Crocker fell down and his inner tube slid down the hill. The competition organizers obtained a new inner tube for him and his friend. Crocker was visibly drunk and Durno, the manager of Sundance, suggested that it would be a good idea if he did not continue in the competition. But Crocker insisted on competing and Durno took no further steps to restrain him.

[8] Crocker and his friend hit a mogul on the way down the hill. The two were flipped out of their inner tube. Crocker injured his neck in the fall and was rendered a quadriplegic. [...]

Ontario Court of Appeal

[12] Finlayson J.A. (Arnup J.A. concurring) overturned the trial judge's finding that the defendant was liable: see (1985), 51 O.R. (2d) 608. He concluded that the plaintiff could not establish that the resort breached its duty to warn him of the risks involved. Finlayson J.A. stated at p. 621:

> In my view there are two distinct factual situations here. The first relates to the plaintiff entering the race. As to that, it is my view that the defendant corporation took all reasonable steps to make the plaintiff aware of the risks of harm associated with the race. The plaintiff introduced a further and perhaps inevitable risk of harm in deliberately getting drunk. This created a second factual situation. I do not believe that this latter circumstance is the responsibility of the defendant corporation. Once it was brought to the attention of its president and manager they did all that could reasonably be expected of them in warning the plaintiff that he should not continue.

[13] Further, he held that the defendant did not bear any affirmative duty to rescue the plaintiff that extended beyond the duty to warn him of the risks involved. [...]

The Issue

[15] People engage in dangerous sports every day. They scale sheer cliffs and slide down the sides of mountains. They jump from airplanes and float down white water rivers in rubber rafts. Risk hangs almost palpably over these activities. Indeed, the element of risk seems to make the sports more attractive to many. Occasionally, however, the risk materializes and the result is usually tragic.

[16] In general, when someone is injured in a sporting accident the law does not hold anyone else responsible. The injured person must rely on private insurance and on the public health care system. The broad issue in the present appeal is whether there is something to distinguish the situation here from the run of the mill sports accident. [...]

Duty of Care

[17] The common law has generally distinguished between negligent conduct (misfeasance) and failure to take positive steps to protect others from harm (nonfeasance). The early common law was reluctant to recognize affirmative duties to act. Limited exceptions were carved out where the parties were in a special relationship (e.g., parent and child) or where the defendant had a statutory or contractual obligation to intervene. The philosophy underlying this reluctance to extend legal obligation is described in Fleming, *The Law of Torts* (6th ed. 1983), at p. 137:

The reluctance to extend the reach of legal obligation beyond this point drew sustenance from the long fashionable philosophy of individualism.... The *laissez faire* approach of the common law restrained men from committing affirmative acts of injury, but shrank from converting the courts into an agency for forcing men to help each other. Obviously, it involves a more serious restraint on individual liberty to require a person to act than it is to place limits on his freedom to act. Besides, the plaintiff's loss is unequal in the two situations. In the case of commission, the defendant has positively made his position worse: he has *created* a risk; in the case of inaction, he has merely failed to benefit him by not interfering in his affairs. Yet today, though far from defunct, the strength of these sentiments is steadily being sapped by an increasing sense of heightened social obligation and other collectivist tendencies in our midst. Accordingly, the legal doctrine which they once sustained is itself under retreat.

[18] Canadian courts have become increasingly willing to expand the number and kind of special relationships to which a positive duty to act attaches. As Linden notes in his text on *Canadian Tort Law* (3rd ed. 1982), at p. 304:

There is a growing group of special relations which import an obligation to engage in positive conduct for the benefit of another. Normally, there is some element of control or some economic benefit inuring to the person as a result of the relation, which justifies the creation of the duty. For example, if there is a contract or a bailment, a failure to act may be actionable. It is not enough, however, if the contract is with a third person, as where a doctor agreed with the husband to attend his wife at childbirth. Carriers, innkeepers, warehousemen and public utilities, who hold themselves out to the public as being prepared to give service, are subject to this responsibility. So too, a master may be obliged to provide aid to one of his servants in peril, a shopkeeper to his invitee, a school to a pupil, and a shipmaster to a passenger. Obligations to take positive action are also imposed upon occupiers of premises to make their property safe for the reception of certain entrants and for passersby on the highway. A policeman may owe a civil duty to report dangerous road conditions. Institutions which have custody over people, such as hospitals, jails, and the like, may be obliged to take reasonable steps to protect those under their care. There will undoubtedly be additions to this list of special situations in the years ahead. [...]

[20] The trial judge's decision was upheld by the Ontario Court of Appeal, *sub nom. Menow v. Honsberger*, [1971] 1 O.R. 129, 14 D.L.R. (3d) 545, and by this Court. Laskin J. commenced his analysis by summarizing at p. 247 the general common law position on liability in tort:

I return to the main issue. The common law assesses liability for negligence on the basis of breach of a duty of care arising from a foreseeable and unreasonable risk of harm to one person created by the act or omission of another. This is the generality which exhibits the flexibility of the common law; but since liability is predicated upon fault, the guiding principle assumes a nexus or relationship between the injured person and the injuring person which makes it reasonable to conclude that the latter owes a duty to the former not to expose him to an unreasonable risk of harm. Moreover, in considering whether the risk of injury to which a person may be exposed is one that he should not reasonably have to run, it is relevant to relate the probability and the gravity of injury to the burden that would be imposed upon the prospective defendant in taking avoiding measures. [...]

[22] The trial judge concluded that it did. He characterized this duty alternatively as a "duty to warn" or a "duty to rescue." I find Dubin J.A.'s approach to the issue analytically clearer. The question, in his view, was (p. 623):

> ...whether Sundance Northwest Resorts Limited, the defendant, owed a duty of care to take all reasonable measures to prevent the plaintiff from continuing to participate in the very dangerous activity which was under its full control and supervision and promoted by it for commercial gain when it became apparent that the plaintiff was drunk and injured....

He concluded that such a duty of care did arise. I agree with Dubin J.A. that the relationship between Crocker and Sundance gave rise to such a duty.

[23] Sundance set up an inherently dangerous competition in order to promote its resort and improve its financial future. Sundance employees were in charge of the way in which the event was to be conducted. Sundance provided liquor to Crocker during the event and knew of Crocker's inebriated and injured condition before the start of the second heat. Sundance officials were well aware that Crocker's condition heightened the chance of injury. Both Beals and Durno questioned Crocker's ability to continue. It is clearly not open to Sundance to characterize itself as a stranger to Crocker's misfortune. The nexus between Sundance and Crocker is much too close for that. Sundance must accept the responsibility as the promoter of a dangerous sport for taking all reasonable steps to prevent a visibly incapacitated person from participating.

[24] The jurisprudence in this area seems to me to make this conclusion inevitable. When a railway company removes a drunken passenger from one of its trains it owes a duty of care to this passenger to take reasonable steps to see that the passenger does not come to harm (*Dunn v. Dominion Atlantic Railway Co.* [1920], 60 S.C.R. 310). Likewise, when a hotel ejects a drunken patron, it owes a duty of care to the patron to take certain steps to ensure that the patron arrives home safely (*Jordan House*). It would seem a fortiori that when a ski resort establishes a competition in a highly dangerous sport and runs the competition for profit, it owes a duty of care towards visibly intoxicated participants. The risk of calamity in the latter case is even more obvious than in the two preceding cases. I would conclude, therefore, that Sundance was subject to a

duty to Crocker to take all reasonable steps to prevent him from entering such a competition. The question that must now be decided is whether Sundance took sufficient steps to discharge that duty. [...]

Conclusion

[39] Sundance put on a dangerous event to draw people to its resort and enhance its profits. It allowed, and indeed aided, Crocker, a visibly intoxicated person, to participate in the event. In so doing it breached the duty of care it owed him. It is, accordingly, liable for the damage that resulted from its negligence.

C. PUNISHMENT

Kindler v. Canada (Minister of Justice)
Supreme Court of Canada
[1991] 2 S.C.R. 779

Is capital punishment, always and by its nature, "cruel and unusual"? Does it violate our "fundamental principles of justice"? Although there has not been an execution in Canada since 1962 and Parliament voted against reinstating capital punishment in 1987, *Kindler* shows why the legal question is still debatable. Our courts are often called upon to determine whether people, accused or convicted of offenses in other countries should be extradited back to those jurisdictions to face trial or punishment. Kindler, the appellant, had been convicted of murder in Pennsylvania and sentenced to death there. He escaped to Canada and the United States sought his extradition. Under the terms of a bilateral extradition treaty, Canada had the option of refusing to extradite if it failed to get assurances that the death penalty would not be carried out. To bolster his argument that that option should be exercised in his case, Kindler argued that capital punishment violated both sections 7 and 12 of the *Charter*. Although a majority of the Court rejected Kindler's argument, the Court was still dramatically divided on the question of capital punishment: Justice McLachlin appeared to think that the lack of a clear consensus about capital punishment in Canada was determinative, whereas Justices Cory and Lamer in dissent insisted that as capital punishment "is the annihilation of the very essence of human dignity" it is, *a priori*, a violation of *Charter* s. 12.

Ten years later, in the case of *U.S. v. Burns*, the extradition to the state of Washington (where capital punishment is practised) of Canadian citizens convicted of first degree murder was under consideration by the same court. Though the unanimous Court reaffirmed the weighing approach set out in *Kindler*, it felt that Kindler's argument, unsuccessful for him, should now be successful for Burns. Clearly, the Court has not finished with this issue.

———————

Justice McLachlin (for the majority):

This appeal, and the companion case, *Reference Re Ng Extradition (Canada)*, raise the issue of whether the Minister of Justice can order the extradition of fugitives to the United States without obtaining an assurance from that country's authorities that the death penalty will not be imposed. Canadian law does not impose the death penalty, except for certain military offences. The question is whether our government is obliged, in all cases, to obtain assurances from the state requesting extradition that the death penalty will not be carried out by them. [...]

The Minister's orders of extradition are attacked on two grounds: (1) that section 25 of the *Extradition Act*, R.S.C., 1985, c. E-23, under which they are made is unconstitutional; and (2) that the Minister's exercise of his discretion under the order was unconstitutional.

For the reasons that follow, I conclude that it is not contrary to the *Canadian Charter of Rights and Freedoms* to give the minister discretion on the question of whether to seek assurances from the requesting state that the death penalty will not be carried out. I further conclude that the Minister did not err in the way he exercised his discretion in the cases of Ng and Kindler. [...]

Applying Section 7 Test to Section 25 of the Extradition Act

Section 25 of the *Extradition Act* is attacked because it permits the Minister to order the extradition of a fugitive to a state where he or she may, if convicted, face capital punishment. To allow this, it is said, is to offend the principles of fundamental justice.

I do not agree. The question is not whether the death penalty is constitutional, or even desirable in this country, but whether returning a fugitive to face it in another jurisdiction offends the Canadian sense of what is fair and right. The answer to this question turns on attitudes in this country toward the death penalty, and toward extradition, considered along with other factors such as the need to preserve an effective extradition policy and to deter American criminals fleeing to Canada as a "safe haven."

The practice of extradition has deep roots in this country, and the practice *per se* has never been controversial. This reflects a strong belief that crime must not go unpunished. Fairness requires that alleged criminals be brought to justice and extradition is the normal means by which this is achieved when the offence was committed in a foreign jurisdiction.

When an accused person is to be tried in Canada there will be no conflict between our desire to see an accused face justice, and our desire that the justice he or she faces conforms to the most exacting standards which have emerged from our judicial system. However, when a fugitive must face trial in a foreign jurisdiction if he or she is to face trial at all, the two desires may come into conflict. In some cases the social consensus may clearly favour one of these values above the other, and the resolution of the conflict will be straightforward.

This would be the case if, for instance, the fugitive faced torture on return to his or her country. In many cases, though, neither value will be able to claim absolute priority; rather, one will serve to temper the other. There may be less unfairness in requiring an accused to face a judicial process which may be less than perfect according to our standards, than in having him or her escape the judicial process entirely.

For this reason, in considering the attitude of Canadians toward the death penalty we must consider not only whether Canadians consider it unacceptable, but whether they consider it to be so absolutely unacceptable that it is better that a fugitive not face justice at all rather than face the death penalty.

With this in mind I turn to consider Canadian attitudes to the death penalty. Much has been said and written in this country on the death penalty. While it is difficult to generalize about a subject so controversial, this much can be ventured. There is no clear consensus in this country that capital punishment is morally abhorrent and absolutely unacceptable.

Capital punishment was a component of Canadian criminal law from this country's colonial beginnings until it was abolished by Parliament in 1976. For most of that period the penalty was accepted with little question, although executions became increasingly rare in the latter years of its existence in Canada. The last execution in Canada was in 1962. Yet, while the death penalty has been formally abolished in this country, its possible return continues to be debated. In 1987, in response to persistent calls to bring back the death penalty, Members of Parliament conducted a free vote on a resolution to reinstate capital punishment. The result was a defeat of the motion, but the vote—148 to 127—fell far short of reflecting a broad consensus even among Parliamentarians.

To this day, capital punishment continues to apply to certain military offences. At the same time, public opinion polls continue to show considerable support among Canadians for the return of the death penalty for certain offences. Can it be said, in light of such indications as these, that the possibility that a fugitive might face the death penalty in California or Pennsylvania "shocks" the Canadian conscience or leads Canadians to conclude that the situation the fugitive faces is "simply unacceptable"? The case is far from plain.

When other considerations are brought into the picture, the matter becomes even less clear. In some cases, the unconditional surrender of a fugitive to face the death penalty may "sufficiently shock" the national conscience as to render it mandatory that the minister seek an assurance that the penalty will not be imposed. But in other cases, this may not be so. [...]

Another relevant consideration in determining whether surrender without assurances regarding the death penalty would be a breach of fundamental justice is the danger that if such assurances were mandatory, Canada might become a safe haven for criminals in the United States seeking to avoid the death penalty. This is not a new concern. The facility with which American offenders can flee to Canada has been recognized since the nineteenth century. [...]

The fugitives, in suggesting that s. 25 should be struck down, in effect urge that the only constitutional law is one which absolutely forbids extradition in the absence of assurances that the death penalty will not be imposed. The foregoing discussion suggests that such a law might well prove too inflexible to permit the government of Canada to deal with particular situations in a way which maintains the required comity with other nations, while at the same time going beyond what is required to conform to our fundamental sense of fairness. What is required is a law which permits the minister, in the particular case before her, to act in a way which preserves the effectiveness of the extradition process, while conforming to the Canadian sense of what is fundamentally just. Section 25 does this; the less flexible alternative proposed by the fugitives would not.

I conclude that the fugitives have not established that the law which permits their extradition without assurances that the death penalty will not be applied in the requesting states offends the fundamental principles of justice enshrined in s. 7 of the *Charter*.

Justice Cory (dissenting):

Early History of the Death Penalty

At the very heart of this appeal is a conflict between two concepts. On one side is the concept of human dignity and the belief that this concept is of paramount importance in a democratic society. On the other side is the concept of retributive justice and the belief that capital punishment is necessary to deter murderers. An historical review reveals an increasing tendency to resolve this tension in favour of human dignity. [...]

[...] [F]rom the 12th century forward there was a reluctance on the part of jurors to impose the death sentence. The jurors, the very people who might have been expected to be most interested in enforcing the criminal law particularly with regard to property offences, were loath to condemn the accused to death. Their verdicts gave early recognition to the fundamental importance of human dignity and of the need to accord that dignity to all. As well, reformers for over 300 years advocated not only the reduction but the total abolition of the death penalty. Opposition to the imposition of the death penalty has a long and honoured history. [...]

Canada's International Commitment

The international community has affirmed its commitment to the principle of human dignity through various international instruments. Except for the United States, the western world has reinforced this commitment to human dignity, both internationally and nationally, through the express abolition of the death penalty. Canada's action in the international forum affirms its own commitment to the preservation and enhancement of human dignity and to the abolition of the death penalty. [...]

The Position under the Charter

What then is the constitutional status of the death penalty under s. 12 of the *Charter*?

The American experience provides no guidance. Cases dealing with the constitutional validity of the death penalty were decided on very narrow bases unique to the wording of the American *Constitution* and rooted in early holdings of the United States Supreme Court. Canadian courts should articulate a distinct Canadian approach with respect to cruel and unusual punishment based on Canadian traditions and values.

The approach to be taken by this Court in determining whether capital punishment contravenes s. 12 of the *Charter* should, in my view, be guided by two central considerations. First is the principle of human dignity which lies at the heart of s. 12. It is the dignity and importance of the individual which is the essence and the cornerstone of democratic government. Second is the decision of this court in *R. v. Smith* (1987). [...]

Does the Death Penalty Violate Section 12 of the Charter?

In my view, there can be no doubt that it does. A consideration of the effect of the imposition of the death penalty on human dignity is enlightening. Descriptions of executions demonstrate that it is state-imposed death which is so repugnant to any belief in the importance of human dignity. The methods utilized to carry out the execution serve only to compound the indignities inflicted upon the individual. [...]

The death penalty not only deprives the prisoner of all vestiges of human dignity, it is the ultimate desecration of the individual as a human being. It is the annihilation of the very essence of human dignity.

Let us now consider the principles set out in *R. v. Smith* to determine whether the death penalty is of the same nature as corporal punishment, lobotomy or castration which were designated as cruel and unusual punishment.

What is acceptable as punishment to a society will vary with the nature of that society, its degree of stability and its level of maturity. The punishments of lashing with the cat-o-nine tails and keel-hauling were accepted forms of punishment in the 19th century in the British navy. Both of those punishments could, and not infrequently, did result in death to the recipient. By the end of the 19th century, however, it was unthinkable that such penalties would be inflicted. A more sensitive society had made such penalties abhorrent.

Similarly, corporal punishment is now considered cruel and unusual yet it was an accepted form of punishment in Canada until it was abolished in 1973. The explanation, it seems to me, is that a maturing society has recognized that the imposition of the lash would now be a cruel and intolerable punishment.

If corporal punishment, lobotomy and castration are no longer acceptable and contravene s. 12, then the death penalty cannot be considered to be anything other than cruel and unusual punishment. It is the supreme indignity to the individual, the ultimate corporal punishment, the final and complete lobotomy and the absolute and irrevocable castration.

As the ultimate desecration of human dignity, the imposition of the death penalty in Canada is a clear violation of the protection afforded by s. 12 of the *Charter*. Capital punishment is *per se* cruel and unusual. [...]

The Responsibility of the Extraditing State

Notwithstanding the fact that it is the United States and not Canada which would impose the death penalty, Canada has the obligation not to extradite a person to face a cruel and unusual treatment or punishment. To surrender a fugitive who may be subject to the death penalty violates s. 12 of the *Charter* just as surely as would the execution of the fugitive in Canada. Therefore, the Minister's decision to extradite Kindler without obtaining Article 6 assurances violates Kindler's s. 12 rights. [...]

[I]t must be remembered that, no matter how vile the killing, Kindler would not be executed in Canada had he committed the murder in this country. Further, Canada has committed itself in the international community to the recognition and support of human dignity and to the abolition of the death penalty. These commitments were not lightly made. They reflect Canadian values and principles. Canada cannot, on the one hand, give an international commitment to support the abolition of the death penalty and at the same time extradite a fugitive without seeking the very assurances contemplated by the Treaty. To do so would mean that Canada either was not honouring its international commitments or was applying one standard to the United States and another to other nations. Neither alternative is acceptable; both would contravene Canadian values and commitments.

United States v. Burns
Supreme Court of Canada
[2001] 1 S.C.R. 283

The Court:

[127] International experience, particularly in the past decade, has shown the death penalty to raise many complex problems of both a philosophic and pragmatic nature. While there remains the fundamental issue of whether the state can ever be justified in taking the life of a human being within its power, the present debate goes beyond arguments over the effectiveness of deterrence and the appropriateness of vengeance and retribution. It strikes at the very ability of the criminal justice system to obtain a uniformly correct result even where death hangs in the balance.

[128] International experience thus confirms the validity of concerns expressed in the Canadian Parliament about capital punishment. It also shows that a rule requiring that assurances be obtained prior to extradition in death penalty cases not only accords with Canada's principled advocacy on the international level, but is also consistent with the practice of other countries with whom Canada generally invites comparison, apart from the retentionist jurisdictions in the United States.

[129] The "balancing process" mandated by *Kindler* and *Ng* remains a flexible instrument. The difficulty in this case is that the Minister proposes to send the respondents without assurances into the death penalty controversy at a time when the legal system of the requesting country is under such sustained and authoritative internal attack. Although rumblings of this controversy in Canada, the United States and the United Kingdom pre-dated *Kindler* and *Ng*, the concern has grown greatly in depth and detailed proof in the intervening years. The imposition of a moratorium (*de facto* or otherwise) in some of the retentionist states of the United States attests to this concern, but a moratorium itself is not conclusive, any more than the lifting of a moratorium would be. What is important is the recognition that despite the best efforts of all concerned, the judicial system is and will remain fallible and reversible whereas the death penalty will forever remain final and irreversible.

[130] The arguments in favour of extradition without assurances would be as well served by extradition with assurances. There was no convincing argument that exposure of the respondents to death in prison by execution advances Canada's public interest in a way that the alternative, eventual death in prison by natural causes, would not. This is perhaps corroborated by the fact that other abolitionist countries do not, in general, extradite without assurances.

[131] The arguments against extradition without assurances have grown stronger since this Court decided *Kindler* and *Ng* in 1991. Canada is now abolitionist for all crimes, even those in the military field. The international

trend against the death penalty has become clearer. The death penalty controversies in the requesting State—the United States—are based on pragmatic, hard-headed concerns about wrongful convictions. None of these factors is conclusive, but taken together they tilt the s. 7 balance against extradition without assurances.

R. v. Proulx
Supreme Court of Canada
[2000] 1 S.C.R. 61

After a night of partying and heavy drinking, teenager Proulx, who had only been driving for seven weeks, decided to drive his friends home. Driving erratically and dangerously, he drove his car into an oncoming lane of traffic and hit another car, killing a passenger in the car and seriously injuring the driver. Proulx himself was in a near-death coma for several days, although he ultimately recovered. Proulx pleaded guilty to dangerous driving causing death and was sentenced to 18 months in jail.

Since 1996 sentencing judges have, under s. 742 of the *Criminal Code*, discretion to impose a "conditional sentence" that allows the accused to serve his sentence in the community, rather than jail. Unlike probation (the aim of which is rehabilitation), a conditional sentence was meant to retain explicit punitive objectives. Though Parliament's likely aim in amending Canada's sentencing law was to relieve strain on Canadian jails, conditional sentences had to be consistent with the legal objectives of punishment, which s. 718 explicitly sets out as: (a) to denounce unlawful conduct; (b) to deter the offender and other persons from committing offences; (c) to separate offenders from society, where necessary; (d) to assist in rehabilitating offenders; (e) to provide reparations for harm done to victims or to the community; and (f) to promote a sense of responsibility in offenders, and acknowledgement of the harm done to victims and to the community. ((e) and (f) are the so-called "restorative" objectives.)

In this case, the sentencing judge exercised her discretion by refusing to grant Proulx a conditional sentence; the Court of Appeal disagreed but, at the end of the day the Supreme Court reaffirmed the sentencing judge's decision. Along the way, the Supreme Court found itself debating the objectives of punishment (a perennial philosophical puzzle) and the extent to which either incarceration or a conditional sentence can meet those objectives.

Chief Justice Lamer (for the majority):

[1] By passing the *Act to amend the Criminal Code (sentencing) and other Acts in consequence thereof*, S.C. 1995, c. 22 ("Bill C-41"), Parliament has sent a clear message to all Canadian judges that too many people are being sent to prison. In an attempt to remedy the problem of over incarceration, Parliament has introduced a new form of sentence, the conditional sentence of imprisonment. […]

Issues

[12] Since it came into force on September 3, 1996, the conditional sentence has generated considerable debate. With the advent of s. 742.1, Parliament has clearly mandated that certain offenders who used to go to prison should now serve their sentences in the community. Section 742.1 makes a conditional sentence available to a subclass of non-dangerous offenders who, prior to the introduction of this new regime, would have been sentenced to a term of incarceration of less than two years for offences with no minimum term of imprisonment. […]

Reducing the Use of Prison as a Sanction

[16] Bill C-41 is in large part a response to the problem of over incarceration in Canada. […] Canada's incarceration rate of approximately 130 inmates per 100,000 population places it second or third highest among industrialized democracies. In their reasons, Cory and Iacobucci JJ. reviewed numerous studies that uniformly concluded that incarceration is costly, frequently unduly harsh and "ineffective, not only in relation to its purported rehabilitative goals, but also in relation to its broader public goals" (para. 54). See also Report of the Canadian Committee on Corrections, *Toward Unity: Criminal Justice and Corrections* (1969); Canadian Sentencing Commission, *Sentencing Reform: A Canadian Approach* (1987), at pp. xxiii–xxiv; Standing Committee on Justice and Solicitor General, *Taking Responsibility* (1988), at p. 75. Prison has been characterized by some as a finishing school for criminals and as ill-preparing them for reintegration into society: see generally Canadian Committee on Corrections, *supra*, at p. 314; Correctional Service of Canada, *A Summary of Analysis of Some Major Inquiries on Corrections—1938 to 1977* (1982), at p. iv. In *Gladue*, at para. 57, Cory and Iacobucci JJ. held:

> Thus, it may be seen that although imprisonment is intended to serve the traditional sentencing goals of separation, deterrence, denunciation, and rehabilitation, there is widespread consensus that imprisonment has not been successful in achieving some of these goals. Overincarceration is a longstanding problem that has been many times publicly acknowledged but never addressed in a systematic manner by Parliament. In recent years, compared to other countries, sentences of imprisonment in Canada have increased at an alarming rate. *The 1996 sentencing reforms*

embodied in Part XXIII, and s. 718.2(e) in particular, must be understood
as a reaction to the overuse of prison as a sanction, and must accordingly be
given appropriate force as remedial provisions. [Emphasis added.]

[...]

Expanding the Use of Restorative Justice Principles in Sentencing

[18] Restorative justice is concerned with the restoration of the parties that
are affected by the commission of an offence. Crime generally affects at least
three parties: the victim, the community, and the offender. A restorative
justice approach seeks to remedy the adverse effects of crime in a manner
that addresses the needs of all parties involved. This is accomplished, in part,
through the rehabilitation of the offender, reparations to the victim and to the
community, and the promotion of a sense of responsibility in the offender and
acknowledgment of the harm done to victims and to the community.

[19] Canadian sentencing jurisprudence has traditionally focussed on the
aims of denunciation, deterrence, separation, and rehabilitation, with rehabilitation a relative late-comer to the sentencing analysis: see *Gladue*, at para.
42. With the introduction of Bill C-41, however, Parliament has placed new
emphasis upon the goals of restorative justice. Section 718 sets out the fundamental purpose of sentencing, as well as the various sentencing objectives that
should be vindicated when sanctions are imposed. In *Gladue, supra*, Cory and
Iacobucci JJ. stated (at para. 43):

> Clearly, s. 718 is, in part, a restatement of the basic sentencing aims,
> which are listed in paras. (*a*) through (*d*). What are new, though, are
> paras. (*e*) and (*f*), which along with para. (*d*) focus upon the restor-
> ative goals of repairing the harms suffered by individual victims and by
> the community as a whole, promoting a sense of responsibility and an
> acknowledgment of the harm caused on the part of the offender, and
> attempting to rehabilitate or heal the offender. The concept of restor-
> ative justice which underpins paras. (*d*), (*e*), and (*f*) is briefly discussed
> below, *but as a general matter restorative justice involves some form of*
> *restitution and reintegration into the community. The need for offenders*
> *to take responsibility for their actions is central to the sentencing process....*
> *Restorative sentencing goals do not usually correlate with the use of prison as*
> *a sanction. In our view, Parliament's choice to include (e) and (f) alongside*
> *the traditional sentencing goals must be understood as evidencing an inten-*
> *tion to expand the parameters of the sentencing analysis for all offenders.*
> [Emphasis added; citation omitted.]

[20] Parliament has mandated that expanded use be made of restorative
principles in sentencing as a result of the general failure of incarceration to reha-
bilitate offenders and reintegrate them into society. By placing a new emphasis
on restorative principles, Parliament expects both to reduce the rate of incarceration and improve the effectiveness of sentencing. [...]

The Nature of the Conditional Sentence

[22] The conditional sentence incorporates some elements of non-custodial measures and some others of incarceration. Because it is served in the community, it will generally be more effective than incarceration at achieving the restorative objectives of rehabilitation, reparations to the victim and community, and the promotion of a sense of responsibility in the offender. However, *it is also a punitive sanction capable of achieving the objectives of denunciation and deterrence.* [...]

Conditional Sentences Must Be More Punitive Than Probation

[32] [Unlike conditional sentences] probation has traditionally been viewed as a rehabilitative sentencing tool. Recently, the rehabilitative nature of the probation order was explained by the Saskatchewan Court of Appeal in *R. v. Taylor* (1997), 122 C.C.C. (3d) 376. Bayda C.J.S. wrote, at p. 394:

> Apart from the wording of the provision, the innate character of a probation order is such that it seeks to influence the future behaviour of the offender. More specifically, it seeks to secure "the good conduct" of the offender and to deter him from committing other offences. *It does not particularly seek to reflect the seriousness of the offence or the offender's degree of culpability. Nor does it particularly seek to fill the need for denunciation of the offence or the general deterrence of others to commit the same or other offences. Depending upon the specific conditions of the order there may well be a punitive aspect to a probation order but punishment is not the dominant or an inherent purpose. It is perhaps not even a secondary purpose but is more in the nature of a consequence of an offender's compliance with one or more of the specific conditions with which he or she may find it hard to comply.* [Emphasis added.]

[...]

[36] Accordingly, conditional sentences should generally include punitive conditions that are restrictive of the offender's liberty. Conditions such as house arrest or strict curfews should be the norm, not the exception. As the Minister of Justice said during the second reading of Bill C-41 (*House of Commons Debates, supra*, at p. 5873), "[t]his sanction is obviously aimed at offenders who would otherwise be in jail but who could be in the community under *tight* controls" (emphasis added).

[37] There must be a reason for failing to impose punitive conditions when a conditional sentence order is made. Sentencing judges should always be mindful of the fact that conditional sentences are only to be imposed on offenders who would otherwise have been sent to jail. If the judge is of the opinion that punitive conditions are unnecessary, then probation, rather than a conditional sentence, is most likely the appropriate disposition. [...]

Conditional Sentences and Incarceration

[41] This is not to say that the conditional sentence is a lenient punishment or that it does not provide significant denunciation and deterrence, or that a conditional sentence can never be as harsh as incarceration. As this Court stated in *Gladue, supra*, at para. 72:

> ...in our view a sentence focussed on restorative justice is not necessarily a "lighter" punishment. Some proponents of restorative justice argue that when it is combined with probationary conditions it may in some circumstances impose a greater burden on the offender than a custodial sentence.

A conditional sentence may be as onerous as, or perhaps even more onerous than, a jail term, particularly in circumstances where the offender is forced to take responsibility for his or her actions and make reparations to both the victim and the community, all the while living in the community under tight controls. [...]

Application of Section 742.1 of the Criminal Code

[45] For convenience, I will reproduce here s. 742.1 :

> **742.1** Where a person is convicted of an offence, except an offence that is punishable by a minimum term of imprisonment, and the court
>
> (*a*) imposes a sentence of imprisonment of less than two years, and
>
> (*b*) is satisfied that serving the sentence in the community would not endanger the safety of the community and would be consistent with the fundamental purpose and principles of sentencing set out in sections 718 to 718.2,
>
> the court may, for the purpose of supervising the offender's behaviour in the community, order that the offender serve the sentence in the community, subject to the offender's complying with the conditions of a conditional sentence order made under section 742.3.

[46] This provision lists four criteria that a court must consider before deciding to impose a conditional sentence:

(1) the offender must be convicted of an offence that is not punishable by a minimum term of imprisonment;

(2) the court must impose a term of imprisonment of less than two years;

(3) the safety of the community would not be endangered by the offender serving the sentence in the community; and

(4) a conditional sentence would be consistent with the fundamental purpose and principles of sentencing set out in ss. 718 to 718.2.

[...]

A Purposive Interpretation of Section 742.1 (a)

[61] This purposive interpretation of s. 742.1 (a) avoids the pitfalls of the literal interpretation discussed above, while at all times taking into account the principles and objectives of sentencing. As I stressed in *M. (C.A.)*, *supra*, at para. 82.

> In the final analysis, the overarching duty of a sentencing judge is to draw upon all the legitimate principles of sentencing to determine a "just and appropriate" sentence which reflects the gravity of the offence committed and the moral blameworthiness of the offender.

[...]

[101] I turn now to the question of when a conditional sentence may be appropriate having regard to the six sentencing objectives set out in s. 718.

(i) Denunciation

[102] Denunciation is the communication of society's condemnation of the offender's conduct. In *M. (C.A.)*, *supra*, at para. 81, I wrote:

> In short, a sentence with a denunciatory element represents a symbolic, collective statement that the offender's conduct should be punished for encroaching on our society's basic code of values as enshrined within our substantive criminal law. As Lord Justice Lawton stated in *R. v. Sargeant* (1974), 60 Cr. App. R. 74, at p. 77: "society, through the courts, must show its abhorrence of particular types of crime, and the only way in which the courts can show this is by the sentences they pass."

Incarceration will usually provide more denunciation than a conditional sentence, as a conditional sentence is generally a more lenient sentence than a jail term of equivalent duration. That said, a conditional sentence can still provide a significant amount of denunciation. This is particularly so when onerous conditions are imposed and the duration of the conditional sentence is extended beyond the duration of the jail sentence that would ordinarily have been imposed in the circumstances. [...]

[105] The stigma of a conditional sentence with house arrest should not be underestimated. Living in the community under strict conditions where fellow residents are well aware of the offender's criminal misconduct can provide ample denunciation in many cases. In certain circumstances, the shame of encountering members of the community may make it even more difficult for the offender to serve his or her sentence in the community than in prison. [...]

(ii) Deterrence

[107] Incarceration, which is ordinarily a harsher sanction, may provide more deterrence than a conditional sentence. Judges should be wary, however, of placing too much weight on deterrence when choosing between a conditional

sentence and incarceration: see *Wismayer, supra*, at p. 36. The empirical evidence suggests that the deterrent effect of incarceration is uncertain: see generally *Sentencing Reform: A Canadian Approach, supra*, at pp. 136–37. Moreover, a conditional sentence can provide significant deterrence if sufficiently punitive conditions are imposed and the public is made aware of the severity of these sentences. There is also the possibility of deterrence through the use of community service orders, including those in which the offender may be obliged to speak to members of the community about the evils of the particular criminal conduct in which he or she engaged, assuming the offender were amenable to such a condition. Nevertheless, there may be circumstances in which the need for deterrence will warrant incarceration. This will depend in part on whether the offence is one in which the effects of incarceration are likely to have a real deterrent effect, as well as on the circumstances of the community in which the offences were committed.

(iii) Separation

[108] The objective of separation is not applicable in determining whether a conditional sentence would be consistent with the fundamental purpose and principles of sentencing because it is a prerequisite of a conditional sentence that the offender not pose a danger to the community. Accordingly, it is not necessary to completely separate the offender from society. To the extent that incarceration, which leads to the complete separation of offenders, is warranted in circumstances where the statutory prerequisites are met, it is as a result of the objectives of denunciation and deterrence, not the need for separation as such.

(iv) Restorative Objectives

[109] While incarceration may provide for more denunciation and deterrence than a conditional sentence, a conditional sentence is generally better suited to achieving the restorative objectives of rehabilitation, reparations, and promotion of a sense of responsibility in the offender. As this Court held in *Gladue, supra*, at para. 43, "[r]estorative sentencing goals do not usually correlate with the use of prison as a sanction." The importance of these goals is not to be underestimated, as they are primarily responsible for lowering the rate of recidivism. Consequently, when the objectives of rehabilitation, reparation, and promotion of a sense of responsibility may realistically be achieved in the case of a particular offender, a conditional sentence will likely be the appropriate sanction, subject to the denunciation and deterrence considerations outlined above. [...]

(v) Summary

[113] In sum, in determining whether a conditional sentence would be consistent with the fundamental purpose and principles of sentencing, sentencing judges should consider which sentencing objectives figure most prominently in

the factual circumstances of the particular case before them. Where a combination of both punitive and restorative objectives may be achieved, a conditional sentence will likely be more appropriate than incarceration. In determining whether restorative objectives can be satisfied in a particular case, the judge should consider the offender's prospects of rehabilitation, including whether the offender has proposed a particular plan of rehabilitation; the availability of appropriate community service and treatment programs; whether the offender has acknowledged his or her wrongdoing and expresses remorse; as well as the victim's wishes as revealed by the victim impact statement (consideration of which is now mandatory pursuant to s. 722 of the *Code*). This list is not exhaustive.

[114] Where punitive objectives such as denunciation and deterrence are particularly pressing, such as cases in which there are aggravating circumstances, incarceration will generally be the preferable sanction. This may be so notwithstanding the fact that restorative goals might be achieved by a conditional sentence. Conversely, a conditional sentence may provide sufficient denunciation and deterrence, even in cases in which restorative objectives are of diminished importance, depending on the nature of the conditions imposed, the duration of the conditional sentence, and the circumstances of the offender and the community in which the conditional sentence is to be served. [...]

Application to the Case at Hand

[128] In the case at hand, [the sentencing judge] considered that a term of imprisonment of 18 months was appropriate and declined to permit the respondent to serve his term in the community. She found that, while the respondent would not endanger the safety of the community by serving a conditional sentence, such a sentence would not be in conformity with the objectives of s. 718. In her view, even if incarceration was not necessary to deter the respondent from similar future conduct or necessary for his rehabilitation, incarceration was necessary to denounce the conduct of the respondent and to deter others from engaging in similar conduct.

[129] [...] I am not convinced that an 18-month sentence of incarceration was demonstrably unfit for these offences and this offender. I point out that the offences here were very serious, and that they had resulted in a death and in severe bodily harm. Moreover, dangerous driving and impaired driving may be offences for which harsh sentences plausibly provide general deterrence. These crimes are often committed by otherwise law-abiding persons, with good employment records and families. Arguably, such persons are the ones most likely to be deterred by the threat of severe penalties. [...]

Disposition

[132] I would allow the appeal. Accordingly, the 18-month sentence of incarceration imposed by the trial judge should be restored. However, given that

the respondent has already served the conditional sentence imposed by the Court of Appeal in its entirety, and that the Crown stated in oral argument that it was not seeking any further punishment, I would stay the service of the sentence of incarceration.

Sauve v. Canada (Chief Electoral Officer)
Supreme Court of Canada
[2002] 3 S.C.R. 519

This case adjudicates the constitutionality of s. 51(e) of the *Canada Elections Act* that denies the right to vote to "[e]very person who is imprisoned in a correctional institution serving a sentence of two years or more." It is a 5 to 4 decision that accepts the claim that s. 51 violates *Charter* sections 3 (the democratic right to vote) and 15(1). The bulk of the case concerns whether, on the *Oakes* test, there is a rational, and proportional, connection between this provision and the government's aims of "enhancing civic responsibility and respect for the rule of law" by providing additional punishment to "enhance the general purposes of the criminal sanction."

The majority, led by Chief Justice McLachlin, insists that the right to vote is so important that the government has to provide strong evidence and persuasive argument that denying the right to vote plausibly serves its stated objectives. By contrast, the dissent, led by Justice Gonthier, argues that since the issue rests on "philosophical, political and social considerations" the government must meet a minimal test of reasonableness, but no more: the *Charter* does not authorize Courts "to prioritize one reasonable social or political philosophy over reasonable others."

Justice Gonthier (dissenting):

[67] My disagreement with the reasons of the Chief Justice is at a more fundamental level. This case rests on philosophical, political and social considerations which are not capable of "scientific proof." It involves justifications for and against the limitation of the right to vote which are based upon axiomatic arguments of principle or value statements. I am of the view that when faced with such justifications, this Court ought to turn to the text of s. 1 of the *Charter* and to the basic principles which undergird both s. 1 and the relationship that provision has with the rights and freedoms protected within the *Charter*. Particularly, s. 1 of the *Charter* requires that this Court look to the fact that there may be different social or political philosophies upon which justifications for or against the limitations of rights may be based. In such a context, where this Court is presented with competing social or political philosophies relating to the right to vote, it is not by merely approving or preferring one that the other is necessarily disproved or shown not to survive *Charter* scrutiny. If

the social or political philosophy advanced by Parliament reasonably justifies a limitation of the right in the context of a free and democratic society, then it ought to be upheld as constitutional. I conclude that this is so in the case at bar. [...]

[92] As emerges from the submissions before this Court, there seem generally to be two options available for dealing with the issue at hand. The first, that chosen by the Chief Justice, is to prefer an inclusive approach to democratic participation for serious criminal offenders incarcerated for two years or more. This view locates democratic participation as a central dimension of rehabilitation, insofar as the incarcerated offenders remain citizens with the fullest exercise of their democratic rights. By the same token, the unrestricted franchise enhances democratic legitimacy of government, and confirms or enhances the citizenship or standing of prisoners in society. To do otherwise, it is suggested, undermines the "dignity" or "worth" of prisoners. The alternative view, adopted by Parliament, considers that the temporary suspension of the prisoner's right to vote, in fact, enhances the general purposes of the criminal sanction, including rehabilitation. It does so by underlining the importance of civic responsibility and the rule of law. This approach sees the temporary removal of the vote as a deterrent to offending or re-offending and the return of the vote as an inducement to reject further criminal conduct. In withdrawing for a time one expression of political participation concurrently with personal freedom, the significance of both are enhanced. Rather than undermine the dignity or worth of prisoners, the removal of their vote takes seriously the notion that they are free actors and attaches consequences to actions that violate certain core values as expressed in the *Criminal Code*.

[93] Both of these approaches, however, entail accepting logically prior political or social philosophies about the nature and content of the right to vote. The former approach, that accepted by the reasons of the Chief Justice, entails accepting a philosophy that preventing criminals from voting does damage to both society and the individual, and undermines prisoners' inherent worth and dignity. The latter approach also entails accepting a philosophy, that not permitting serious incarcerated criminals to vote is a social rejection of serious crime which reflects a moral line which safeguards the social contract and the rule of law and bolsters the importance of the nexus between individuals and the community. Both of these social or political philosophies, however, are aimed at the same goal: that of supporting the fundamental importance of the right to vote itself. Further, both of these social or political philosophies are supported by the practices of the various Canadian provinces, the practices of other liberal democracies, and academic writings. Finally, neither position can be proven empirically—rather, the selection of one over the other is largely a matter of philosophical preference. What is key to my approach is that the acceptance of one or the other of these social or political philosophies dictates much of the constitutional analysis which ensues, since the reasonableness of any limitation upon the right to vote and the appropriateness of particular

penal theories and their relation to the right to vote will logically be related to whether or not the justification for that limitation is based upon an "acceptable" social or political philosophy. [...]

[95] The reasons of the Chief Justice apply something seemingly more onerous than the "justification" standard referred to just above. She describes the right to vote as a "core democratic right" and suggests that its exemption from the s. 33 override somehow raises the bar for the government in attempting to justify its restriction. This altering of the justification standard is problematic in that it seems to be based upon the view that there is only one plausible social or political philosophy upon which to ground a justification for or against the limitation of the right. This approach, however, is incorrect on a basic reading of s. 1 of the *Charter*, which clearly does not constrain Parliament or authorize this Court to prioritize one reasonable social or political philosophy over reasonable others, but only empowers this Court to strike down those limitations which are not reasonable and which cannot be justified in a free and democratic society. [...]

[97] There is a flaw in an analysis which suggests that because one social or political philosophy can be justified, it necessarily means that another social or political philosophy is not justified: in other words, where two social or political philosophies exist, it is not by approving one that you disprove the other. Differences in social or political philosophy, which result in different justifications for limitations upon rights, are perhaps inevitable in a pluralist society. That having been said, it is only those limitations which are not reasonable or demonstrably justified in a free and democratic society which are unconstitutional. Therefore, the most significant analysis in this case is the examination of the social or political philosophy underpinning the justification advanced by the Crown. This is because it will indicate whether the limitation of the right to vote is reasonable and is based upon a justification which is capable of being demonstrated in a free and democratic society. If the choice made by Parliament is such, then it ought to be respected. The range of choices made by different legislatures in different jurisdictions supports the view that there are many resolutions to the particular issue at bar which are reasonable; it demonstrates that there are many possible rational balances.

[98] The role of this Court, when faced with competing social or political philosophies and justifications dependent on them, is therefore to define the parameters within which the acceptable reconciliation of competing values lies. The decision before this Court is therefore not whether or not Parliament has made a proper policy decision, but whether or not the policy position chosen is an acceptable choice amongst those permitted under the *Charter*. [...]

[99] A subject that is related to and follows from the above discussion concerning the evaluation of competing social or political philosophies is the role of symbolic arguments in *Charter* adjudication. In the context of the *Charter* analysis, it is important not to downplay the importance of symbolic or abstract arguments. Symbolic or abstract arguments cannot be dismissed outright by

virtue of their symbolism: many of the great principles, the values upon which society rests, could be said to be symbolic. In fact, one of the more important dimensions of s. 3 of the *Charter* is clearly its symbolism: the affirmation of political equality reflected in all citizens being guaranteed the right to vote, subject only to reasonable limits prescribed by law that can be demonstrably justified in a free and democratic society. The case at bar concerns debates about symbolism, as the arguments involved relate to abstract concepts such as democracy, rights, punishment, the rule of law and civic responsibility. To choose a narrow reading of rights over the objectives advanced by Parliament is to choose one set of symbols over another.

[100] In her reasons, the Chief Justice claims at para. 16 that Parliament is relying on "lofty objectives," and suggests that the presence of "symbolic and abstract" objectives is problematic. However, the reasons of the Chief Justice have the very same objective—to protect the value of the right to vote and the rule of law—and rely on equally vague concepts. Breaking down the meaning and value of the right to vote, one is unavoidably led to abstract and symbolic concepts such as the rule of law, the legitimacy of law and government, and the meaning of democracy. The Chief Justice discusses these concepts at length, along with theories of individual motivation. For instance, relying on the philosopher J.S. Mill, she suggests at para. 38 that "[t]o deny prisoners the right to vote is to lose an important means of teaching them democratic values and social responsibility." This type of statement is as symbolic, abstract and philosophical as the government's claim that denying serious incarcerated criminals the right to vote will strengthen democratic values and social responsibility.

Chief Justice McLachlin (for the majority):

[8] My colleague Justice Gonthier proposes a deferential approach to infringement and justification. He argues that there is no reason to accord special importance to the right to vote, and that we should thus defer to Parliament's choice among a range of reasonable alternatives. He further argues that in justifying limits on the right to vote under s. 1, we owe deference to Parliament because we are dealing with "philosophical, political and social considerations," because of the abstract and symbolic nature of the government's stated goals, and because the law at issue represents a step in a dialogue between Parliament and the courts.

[9] I must, with respect, demur. The right to vote is fundamental to our democracy and the rule of law and cannot be lightly set aside. Limits on it require not deference, but careful examination. This is not a matter of substituting the Court's philosophical preference for that of the legislature, but of ensuring that the legislature's proffered justification is supported by logic and common sense. [...]

[12] At the [*Charter*] s. 1 stage, the government argues that denying the right to vote to penitentiary inmates is a matter of social and political philosophy,

requiring deference. Again, I cannot agree. This Court has repeatedly held that the "general claim that the infringement of a right is justified under s. 1" does not warrant deference to Parliament. Section 1 does not create a presumption of constitutionality for limits on rights; rather, it requires the state to justify such limitations.

[13] The core democratic rights of Canadians do not fall within a "range of acceptable alternatives" among which Parliament may pick and choose at its discretion. Deference may be appropriate on a decision involving competing social and political policies. It is not appropriate, however, on a decision to limit fundamental rights. This case is not merely a competition between competing social philosophies. It represents a conflict between the right of citizens to vote—one of the most fundamental rights guaranteed by the *Charter*—and Parliament's denial of that right. Public debate on an issue does not transform it into a matter of "social philosophy," shielding it from full judicial scrutiny. It is for the courts, unaffected by the shifting winds of public opinion and electoral interests, to safeguard the right to vote guaranteed by s. 3 of the *Charter*. [...]

[18] While deference to the legislature is not appropriate in this case, legislative justification does not require empirical proof in a scientific sense. While some matters can be proved with empirical or mathematical precision, others, involving philosophical, political and social considerations, cannot. In this case, it is enough that the justification be convincing, in the sense that it is sufficient to satisfy the reasonable person looking at all the evidence and relevant considerations, that the state is justified in infringing the right at stake to the degree it has. However, one must be wary of stereotypes cloaked as common sense, and of substituting deference for the reasoned demonstration required by s. 1.

[19] Keeping in mind these basic principles of *Charter* review, I approach the familiar stages of the *Oakes* test. I conclude that the government's stated objectives of promoting civic responsibility and respect for the law and imposing appropriate punishment, while problematically vague, are capable in principle of justifying limitations on *Charter* rights. However, the government fails to establish proportionality, principally for want of a rational connection between denying the vote to penitentiary inmates and its stated goals. [...]

[52] When the facade of rhetoric is stripped away, little is left of the government's claim about punishment other than that criminals are people who have broken society's norms and may therefore be denounced and punished as the government sees fit, even to the point of removing fundamental constitutional rights. Yet, the right to punish and to denounce, however important, is constitutionally constrained. It cannot be used to write entire rights out of the Constitution, it cannot be arbitrary, and it must serve the constitutionally recognized goals of sentencing. On all counts, the case that s. 51(e) furthers lawful punishment objectives fails.

RELATED CASES

Canadian Dredge and Dock Co. v. *The Queen* [1985] 1 S.C.R. 662
(This is the leading case in Canada on corporate criminal liability.)

R. v. Jacob [1996] 31 O.R. (3d) 350
(In this case the Ontario Court of Appeal examined whether a community's standard of tolerance, long used in characterization of obscenity and indecency, can serve as a reliable guide to what conduct should be criminal.)

R. v. Smith [1987] 1 S.C.R. 1047
(In this case the Supreme Court of Canada decided on whether a disproportionate sentence can be, in virtue of being disproportionate, "cruel and unusual.")

R. v. M (CA) [1996] 1 S.C.R. 500
(In this case the Supreme Court of Canada found that there is no upper limit to fixed-term sentences for persons convicted of multiple crimes but where none of the crimes carry a potential maximum sentence of life imprisonment. In reaching its decision the court reflected on the nature and purpose of sentencing and punishment for criminal wrongdoing.)

PART VII

Indigenous Issues

The place of Aboriginal people in Canadian law is simultaneously old and new. There can be no denying the status of Aboriginal peoples as founding partners alongside French and British settlers in the formation of Canada. The Royal Proclamation of 1763 asserted sovereignty over all of Canada, yet it recognized a range of pre-existing rights of First Nations. Yet it is only in Canada's recent history that such partnership has begun to be recognized in Canada's legal and constitutional practices and commitments. Section 35(1) of the *Constitution Act, 1982*, entrenches and puts beyond easy change the inclusion of Aboriginal rights in the legal foundation of Canada: "The existing aboriginal and treaty rights of the aboriginal peoples of Canada are hereby recognized and affirmed." Prior to this recognition and affirmation, relations between settlers and Aboriginal peoples were dominated by British and French legal concepts and practices, and the promises of the Royal Proclamation of 1763 lay dormant. A gradual process of sometimes contentious dialogue led to inclusion of Aboriginal and treaty rights in Canada's constitution, and since that time several Supreme Court decisions have begun to shape the meaning of those rights.

The cases excerpted in this part begin with a nineteenth-century Ontario Court of Appeal decision demonstrating the very tentative accommodation of Aboriginal perspectives prevailing at that time, in the context of the application of the concept of *mens rea*. We then turn to post-*Constitution Act, 1982* cases, beginning with examination of the content of pre-existing Aboriginal rights in *Mitchell v. MNR*. In the next case, *R v. Sparrow*, the Supreme Court explores related issues regarding the relationship between Indian, Inuit, and Metis peoples and the Crown. The reasoning expressed in this case goes a long way to explaining what the Crown's fiduciary relationship to Aboriginal peoples must mean as the Crown's claim to sovereignty interacts with both pre-existing Aboriginal rights and treaties, and treaties yet to be negotiated. This Part continues with *Tsilhqot'in Nation v. British Columbia*, a decision upholding an appeal court's recognition of an Aboriginal title claim in British Columbia. This decision, which may yet come to be regarded as a landmark in Canadian law, set the conditions for the *Letter of Understanding between the Tsilhqot'in Nation and Canada* reproduced here. The *Letter* commits the two parties to working in a "nation-to-nation" partnership to achieve the so far elusive goal of reconciliation. The final case in this Part shows the complexity of the interactions between two legal cultures in the Supreme Court's decision in *Ktunaxa Nation v. British Columbia (Forests, Lands and Natural Resource Operations)*. What appears to be a question of freedom of religion from one perspective is from another perspective a more fundamental matter of human relations to land and other beings. We leave for your evaluation the question of whether the Court's reasoning gives each perspective its due within the constraints of constitutional adjudication.

R. v. Machekequonabe
Ontario Court of Appeal
(1897) 28 O.R. 309

In this criminal case, an old one by Canadian standards, the problem of bridging a cultural gap was at issue, although it was clearly not given much consideration by the Court. A "pagan Indian" (his nation or tribe is never mentioned) was charged with manslaughter for killing what, from his cultural and religious perspective, was a dangerous evil spirit, a Wendigo. The question here is (obviously) not whether Wendigos exist or not, but whether a person's sincere belief that they exist, are dangerous to the group and must be killed, should figure in some way into our assessment of the "guilty mind" or *mens rea*. (In the style of the day, the argument of the defence counsel is presented after the facts have been set out and before the court's actual judgement, which is starkly brief.)

It appeared from the evidence that the prisoner was a member of a tribe of pagan Indians who believed in the existence of an evil spirit clothed in human flesh, or in human form, called a Wendigo which would eat a human being.

That it was reported that a Wendigo had been seen and it was supposed was in the neighbourhood of their camp desiring to do them harm. That among other precautions to protect themselves, guards and sentries, the prisoner being one, were placed out in pairs armed with firearms (the prisoner having a rifle); that the prisoner saw what appeared to be a tall human being running in the distance, which he supposed was the Wendigo; that he and another Indian gave chase, and after challenging three times and receiving no answer fired and shot the object, when it was discovered to be his own foster father, who died soon afterward.

The jury found affirmative answers to the following questions:

Are you satisfied the prisoner did kill the Indian?
Did the prisoner believe the object he shot at to be a Wendigo or spirit?
Did he believe the spirit to be embodied in human flesh?
   Was it the prisoner's belief that the Wendigo could be killed by a bullet shot from a rifle?
   Was the prisoner sane apart from the delusion or belief in the existence of a Wendigo?

The learned trial Judge then proceeded with his charge as follows: "Assuming these facts to be found by you, I think I must direct you as a matter of law that there is no justification in manslaughter so that unless you can suggest to yourselves something stated in the evidence, or drawn from the evidence to warrant a different conclusion, I think it will be your duty to return a verdict of manslaughter. You may confer among yourselves if you please, and if you take that view, I will reserve a case for consideration by the Court of Appeal as to whether he was properly convicted upon this evidence."

The jury found the prisoner guilty of manslaughter recommending him to mercy, and the learned Judge reserved a case for consideration whether upon the findings of the jury in answer to the questions he had submitted the prisoner was properly found guilty of manslaughter.

This case was argued on February 8th, 1897, before a Divisional Court composed of Armour, C.J., and Falconbridge, and Street, JJ.

J.K. Kerr, Q.C., for the prisoner. The evidence shews the Indian tribe were pagans, and believed in an evil spirit clothed in human form which they called a Wendigo, and which attacked, killed and ate human beings. The man that was shot was thought to be a Wendigo, a spirit as distinguished from a human being. It is true there was a mistake, but there was no intention even to harm a human being much less to kill. The evidence shews the mistake was not unreasonable. At common law the following of a religious belief would be an excuse. The trial Judge wrongly directed the jury to find the prisoner guilty. There should be a new trial at least. [...]

The judgement of the Court was delivered by Armour, C.J.:

Upon the case reserved if there was evidence upon which the jury could find the prisoner guilty of manslaughter it is not open to us to reverse that finding, and the question we have to decide is whether there was such evidence.

We think there was, and therefore do not see how we can say that the prisoner was not properly convicted of manslaughter.

Mitchell v. MNR
Supreme Court of Canada
[2001] 1 S.C.R. 911

Grand Chief Michael Mitchell is a Mohawk of Akwesasne, a descendant of the Mohawk nation that formed part of the Iroquois Confederacy prior to "first contact" with Europeans in 1609. Akwesasne lies at the jurisdictional centre of the St. Lawrence River and straddles the Canada-United States border, as well as provincial and state borders, a fact that has made life complex, and often frustrating, for Chief Mitchell and his people. In 1988, after a ceremonial visit to the historic capital of the Iroquois Confederacy in New York, Chief Mitchell crossed the border with symbolic gifts of blankets, bibles, motor oil, bread, butter, milk, and a washing machine, destined for the Mohawk community of Tyendinaga near Kingston. At the border he declared the goods to Canadian customs agents but asserted an Aboriginal right to be exempt from paying duty. His claim was that north-south trading was an essential and integral part of the Mohawk culture, which was recognised and preserved by treaty, and further protected, centuries later, by section 35 of the *Charter*.

The Supreme Court of Canada rejected the claim on the grounds that—even if we are careful to acknowledge traditional oral histories and other non-European sources of information— there was simply not enough evidence to support the claim that trading across the St. Lawrence River was an important feature of the Mohawk culture. Two other justices, however, explored the deeper issue implied by multiculturalism: what exactly is entailed by the official government policy of a "shared" or "merged" sovereignty between First Nations or other minorities and the country Canada in which these minorities are embedded.

Chief Justice McLachlin (for the majority):

What Is the Nature of Aboriginal Rights?

[9] Long before Europeans explored and settled North America, aboriginal peoples were occupying and using most of this vast expanse of land in organized, distinctive societies with their own social and political structures. The part of North America we now call Canada was first settled by the French and the British who, from the first days of exploration, claimed sovereignty over the

land on behalf of their nations. English law, which ultimately came to govern aboriginal rights, accepted that the aboriginal peoples possessed pre-existing laws and interests, and recognized their continuance in the absence of extinguishment, by cession, conquest, or legislation: see, e.g., the *Royal Proclamation of 1763*, R.S.C. 1985, App. II, No. 1, and *R. v. Sparrow*, [1990] 1 S.C.R. 1075, at p. 1103. At the same time, however, the Crown asserted that sovereignty over the land, and ownership of its underlying title, vested in the Crown: *Sparrow, supra*. With this assertion arose an obligation to treat aboriginal peoples fairly and honourably, and to protect them from exploitation, a duty characterized as "fiduciary" in *Guerin v. The Queen*, [1984] 2 S.C.R. 335.

[10] Accordingly, European settlement did not terminate the interests of aboriginal peoples arising from their historical occupation and use of the land. To the contrary, aboriginal interests and customary laws were presumed to survive the assertion of sovereignty, and were absorbed into the common law as rights, unless (1) they were incompatible with the Crown's assertion of sovereignty, (2) they were surrendered voluntarily via the treaty process, or (3) the government extinguished them: see B. Slattery, "Understanding Aboriginal Rights" (1987), 66 *Can. Bar Rev.* 727. Barring one of these exceptions, the practices, customs and traditions that defined the various aboriginal societies as distinctive cultures continued as part of the law of Canada: see *Calder v. Attorney-General of British Columbia*, [1973] S.C.R. 313, and *Mabo v. Queensland* (1992), 175 C.L.R. 1, at p. 57 (*per* Brennan J.), pp. 81–82 (*per* Deane and Gaudron JJ.), and pp. 182–83 (*per* Toohey J.).

[11] The common law status of aboriginal rights rendered them vulnerable to unilateral extinguishment, and thus they were "dependent upon the good will of the Sovereign": see *St. Catherine's Milling and Lumber Co. v. The Queen* (1888), 14 App. Cas. 46 (P.C.), at p. 54. This situation changed in 1982, when Canada's constitution was amended to entrench existing aboriginal and treaty rights: *Constitution Act, 1982*, s. 35(1). The enactment of s. 35(1) elevated existing common law aboriginal rights to constitutional status (although, it is important to note, the protection offered by s. 35(1) also extends beyond the aboriginal rights recognized at common law: *Delgamuukw v. British Columbia*, [1997] 3 S.C.R. 1010, at para. 136). Henceforward, aboriginal rights falling within the constitutional protection of s. 35(1) could not be unilaterally abrogated by the government. However, the government retained the jurisdiction to limit aboriginal rights for justifiable reasons, in the pursuit of substantial and compelling public objectives: see *R. v. Gladstone*, [1996] 2 S.C.R. 723, and *Delgamuukw, supra*.

[12] In the seminal cases of *R. v. Van der Peet*, [1996] 2 S.C.R. 507, and *Delgamuukw, supra*, this Court affirmed the foregoing principles and set out the test for establishing an aboriginal right. Since s. 35(1) is aimed at reconciling the prior occupation of North America by aboriginal societies with the Crown's assertion of sovereignty, the test for establishing an aboriginal right focuses on identifying the integral, defining features of those societies. Stripped to

essentials, an aboriginal claimant must prove a modern practice, tradition or custom that has a reasonable degree of continuity with the practices, traditions or customs that existed prior to contact. The practice, custom or tradition must have been "integral to the distinctive culture" of the aboriginal peoples, in the sense that it distinguished or characterized their traditional culture and lay at the core of the peoples' identity. It must be a "defining feature" of the aboriginal society, such that the culture would be "fundamentally altered" without it. It must be a feature of "central significance" to the peoples' culture, one that "truly *made the society what it was*" (*Van der Peet, supra,* at paras. 54–59 [emphasis in original]). This excludes practices, traditions and customs that are only marginal or incidental to the aboriginal society's cultural identity, and emphasizes practices, traditions and customs that are vital to the life, culture and identity of the aboriginal society in question. [...]

What Is the Aboriginal Right Claimed?

[20] It may be tempting for a claimant or a court to tailor the right claimed to the contours of the specific act at issue. In this case, for example, Chief Mitchell seeks to limit the scope of his claimed trading rights by designating specified trading partners. Originally, he claimed the right to trade with other First Nations in Canada. After the Federal Court of Appeal decision, he further limited his claim to trade with First Nations in Quebec and Ontario. These self-imposed limitations may represent part of Chief Mitchell's commendable strategy of negotiating with the government and minimizing the potential effects on its border control. However, narrowing the claim cannot narrow the aboriginal practice relied upon, which is what defines the right. The essence of the alleged Mohawk tradition was not to bring goods across the St. Lawrence River to trade with designated communities, but rather to simply bring goods to trade. As a matter of necessity, pre-contact trading partners were confined to other First Nations, but this historical fact is incidental to the claim—the right to cross the St. Lawrence River with goods for personal use and trade. For example, in *Gladstone, supra,* the majority of this Court found an aboriginal right to engage in the commercial trade of herring spawn, but did not then proceed to restrict the Heiltsuk to their pre-contact First Nations trading partners. Moreover, it is difficult to imagine how limitations on trading partners would operate in practice. If Chief Mitchell trades goods to First Nations in Ontario and Quebec, there is nothing to prevent them from trading the goods with anyone else in Canada, aboriginal or not. Thus, the limitations placed on the trading right by Chief Mitchell and the courts below artificially narrow the claimed right and would, at any rate, prove illusory in practice. [...]

[23] The Attorney General of Manitoba raises two additional points about the characterization of the right. First, he argues that the claim should not be characterized in the negative. The original claim was to bring goods across the border "without having to pay any duty or taxes whatsoever to any Canadian

government or authority." Manitoba argues that the right should be characterized simply as a right to bring goods, without qualification. I agree. As in the
fishing and hunting cases, once an existing right is established, any restriction
on that right through the imposition of duties or taxes should be considered
at the infringement stage: see, e.g., *R. v. Adams*, [1996] 3 S.C.R. 101; *Côté,
supra*; *R. v. Nikal*, [1996] 1 S.C.R. 1013; *Gladstone, supra*; see also *R. v. Badger,*
[1996] 1 S.C.R. 771. The right claimed in those cases was not the right "to fish
(or hunt) without restriction." Similarly, here the right is not "to bring trade
goods without having to pay duty"; properly defined, the right claimed is to
bring trade goods *simpliciter*.

[24] Manitoba also argues that the right should not be construed as a right
to cross the border. Technically this argument is correct, as the border is a
construction of newcomers. Aboriginal rights are based on aboriginal practices,
customs and traditions, not those of newcomers. This objection can be dealt
with simply: the right claimed should be to bring goods across the St. Lawrence
River (which always existed) rather than across the border. In modern terms,
the two are equivalent. [...]

Evidentiary Concerns—Proving Aboriginal Rights

[27] Aboriginal right claims give rise to unique and inherent evidentiary difficulties. Claimants are called upon to demonstrate features of their pre-contact
society, across a gulf of centuries and without the aid of written records. Recognizing these difficulties, this Court has cautioned that the rights protected
under s. 35(1) should not be rendered illusory by imposing an impossible burden of proof on those claiming this protection (*Simon v. The Queen*, [1985] 2
S.C.R. 387, at p. 408). Thus in *Van der Peet, supra*, the majority of this Court
stated that "a court should approach the rules of evidence, and interpret the
evidence that exists, with a consciousness of the special nature of aboriginal
claims, and of the evidentiary difficulties in proving a right which originates
in times where there were no written records of the practices, customs and
traditions engaged in" (para. 68). [...]

Admissibility of Evidence in Aboriginal Right Claims

[32] Aboriginal oral histories may meet the test of usefulness on two grounds.
First, they may offer evidence of ancestral practices and their significance that
would not otherwise be available. No other means of obtaining the same evidence may exist, given the absence of contemporaneous records. Second, oral
histories may provide the aboriginal perspective on the right claimed. Without
such evidence, it might be impossible to gain a true picture of the aboriginal
practice relied on or its significance to the society in question. Determining
what practices existed, and distinguishing central, defining features of a culture from traits that are marginal or peripheral, is no easy task at a remove of
400 years. Cultural identity is a subjective matter and not easily discerned: see

R. L. Barsh and J. Y. Henderson, "The Supreme Court's *Van der Peet* Trilogy: Naive Imperialism and Ropes of Sand" (1997), 42 *McGill L.J.* 993, at p. 1000, and J. Woodward, *Native Law* (loose-leaf), at p. 137. Also see *Sparrow, supra*, at p. 1103; *Delgamuukw, supra*, at paras. 82–87, and J. Borrows, "The Trickster: Integral to a Distinctive Culture" (1997), 8 *Constitutional Forum* 27.

[33] The second factor that must be considered in determining the admissibility of evidence in aboriginal cases is reliability: does the witness represent a reasonably reliable source of the particular people's history? The trial judge need not go so far as to find a special guarantee of reliability. However, inquiries as to the witness's ability to know and testify to orally transmitted aboriginal traditions and history may be appropriate both on the question of admissibility and the weight to be assigned the evidence if admitted.

[34] In determining the usefulness and reliability of oral histories, judges must resist facile assumptions based on Eurocentric traditions of gathering and passing on historical facts and traditions. Oral histories reflect the distinctive perspectives and cultures of the communities from which they originate and should not be discounted simply because they do not conform to the expectations of the non-aboriginal perspective. Thus, *Delgamuukw* cautions against facilely rejecting oral histories simply because they do not convey "historical" truth, contain elements that may be classified as mythology, lack precise detail, embody material tangential to the judicial process, or are confined to the community whose history is being recounted.

[35] In this case, the parties presented evidence from historians and archaeologists. The aboriginal perspective was supplied by oral histories of elders such as Grand Chief Mitchell. Grand Chief Mitchell's testimony, confirmed by archaeological and historical evidence, was especially useful because he was trained from an early age in the history of his community. The trial judge found his evidence credible and relied on it. He did not err in doing so and we may do the same.

The Interpretation of Evidence in Aboriginal Right Claims

[...]

[38] Again, however, it must be emphasized that a consciousness of the special nature of aboriginal claims does not negate the operation of general evidentiary principles. While evidence adduced in support of aboriginal claims must not be undervalued, neither should it be interpreted or weighed in a manner that fundamentally contravenes the principles of evidence law, which, as they relate to the valuing of evidence, are often synonymous with the "general principles of common sense" (Sopinka and Lederman, *supra*, at p. 524). As Lamer C.J. emphasized in *Delgamuukw, supra*, at para. 82:

> [A]boriginal rights are truly *sui generis*, and demand a unique approach to the treatment of evidence which accords due weight to the perspective of aboriginal peoples. *However, that accommodation must be done in a*

manner which does not strain "the Canadian legal and constitutional struc-ture" [Van der Peet at para. 49]. Both the principles laid down in *Van der Peet*—first, that trial courts must approach the rules of evidence in light of the evidentiary difficulties inherent in adjudicating aboriginal claims, and second, that trial courts must interpret that evidence in the same spirit—must be understood against this background. [Emphasis added.]

[...]

Does the Evidence Show an Ancestral Mohawk Practice of Trading North of the St. Lawrence River?

[41] While the ancestral home of the Mohawks lay in the Mohawk Valley of present-day New York State, the evidence establishes that, before the arrival of Europeans, they travelled north on occasion across the St. Lawrence River. We may assume they travelled with goods to sustain themselves. There was also ample evidence before McKeown J. to support his finding that trade was a central, distinguishing feature of the Iroquois in general and the Mohawks in particular. This evidence indicates the Mohawks were well situated for trade, and engaged in small-scale exchange with other First Nations. A critical question in this case, however, is whether these trading practices and northerly travel *coincided* prior to the arrival of Europeans; that is, does the evidence establish an ancestral Mohawk practice of transporting goods across the St. Lawrence River for the purposes of trade? Only if this ancestral practice is established does it become necessary to determine whether it is an integral feature of Mohawk culture with continuity to the present day.

[42] With respect, the trial judge's affirmative response to this question finds virtually no support in the evidentiary record. [...]

[51] As discussed in the previous section, claims must be proven on the basis of cogent evidence establishing their validity on the balance of probabilities. Sparse, doubtful and equivocal evidence cannot serve as the foundation for a successful claim. With respect, this is exactly what has occurred in the present case. The contradiction between McKeown J.'s statement that little direct evidence supports a cross-river trading right and his conclusion that such a right exists suggests the application of a very relaxed standard of proof (or, perhaps more accurately, an unreasonably generous weighing of tenuous evidence). The *Van der Peet* approach, while mandating the equal and due treatment of evidence supporting aboriginal claims, does not bolster or enhance the cogency of this evidence. The relevant evidence in this case—a single knife, treaties that make no reference to pre-existing trade, and the mere fact of Mohawk involvement in the fur trade—can only support the conclusion reached by the trial judge if strained beyond the weight they can reasonably hold. Such a result is not contemplated by *Van der Peet* or s. 35(1). While appellate courts grant considerable deference to findings of fact made

by trial judges, I am satisfied that the findings in the present case represent a "palpable and overriding error" warranting the substitution of a different result (*Delgamuukw, supra,* at paras. 78–80). I conclude that the claimant has not established an ancestral practice of transporting goods across the St. Lawrence River for the purposes of trade. [...]

Does the Evidence Establish that the Alleged Practice of Trading Across the St. Lawrence River Was Integral to Mohawk Culture and Continuous to the Present Day?

[54] Even if deference were granted to the trial judge's finding of pre-contact trade relations between the Mohawks and First Nations north of the St. Lawrence River, the evidence does not establish this northerly trade as a defining feature of the Mohawk culture. As discussed earlier, the *Van der Peet* test identifies as aboriginal rights only those activities that represent "an element of a practice, custom or tradition integral to the distinctive culture of the aboriginal group claiming the right" (para. 46). It is therefore incumbent upon Chief Mitchell in this case to demonstrate not only that personal and community goods were transported across the St. Lawrence River for trade purposes prior to contact, but also that this practice is integral to the Mohawk people.

[55] The importance of trade—in and of itself—to Mohawk culture is *not* determinative of the issue. It is necessary on the facts of this case to demonstrate the integrality of this practice to the Mohawk *in the specific geographical region* in which it is alleged to have been exercised (i.e., north of the St. Lawrence River), rather than in the abstract. This Court has frequently considered the geographical reach of a claimed right in assessing its centrality to the aboriginal culture claiming it. [...]

[60] The claimed right in the present case implicates an international boundary and, consequently, imports a geographical element into the inquiry. Instead of asking whether the right to trade—in the abstract—is integral to the Mohawk people, this Court must ask whether the right to trade *across the St. Lawrence River* is integral to the Mohawks. The evidence establishes that it is not. Even if the trial judge's generous interpretation of the evidence were accepted, it discloses negligible transportation and trade of goods by the Mohawks north of the St. Lawrence River prior to contact. If the Mohawks did transport trade goods across the St. Lawrence River for trade, such occasions were few and far between. Certainly it cannot be said that the Mohawk culture would have been "fundamentally altered" without this trade, in the language of *Van der Peet, supra,* at para. 59. It was not vital to the Mohawks' collective identity. It was not something that "truly *made the society what it was*" (*Van der Peet,* at para. 55 [emphasis in original]). Participation in northerly trade was therefore not a practice integral to the distinctive culture of the Mohawk people. It follows that no aboriginal right to bring goods across the border for the purposes of trade has been established. [...]

Justice Binnie (concurring):

[73] In terms of traditional aboriginal law, the issue, as I see it, is whether trading/mobility activities asserted by the respondent not as a Canadian citizen but as an heir of the Mohawk regime that existed prior to the arrival of the Europeans, created a *legal right* to cross international boundaries under succeeding sovereigns. This aspect of the debate, to be clear, is not at the level of *fact* about the effectiveness of border controls in the 18th century. (Nor is it about the compatibility of internal aboriginal self-government with Canadian sovereignty.) The issue is at the level of *law* about the alleged incompatibility between European (now Canadian) sovereignty and mobility rights across non-aboriginal borders said by the trial judge to have been acquired by the Mohawks of Akwesasne by reason of their conduct prior to 1609. [...]

The Sovereignty Objection

[111] The unusual aspect of this case is that not only the value but the very *purpose* of the claimed trading/mobility right depends on a boundary that is itself an expression of non-aboriginal sovereignties on the North American continent.

[112] The respondent is understandably proud of the Mohawk heritage. The Iroquois Confederacy is thought to have been formed around 1450. The evidence accepted by the trial judge at p. 26 was that at their height

> ...the Iroquois had achieved for themselves the most remarkable civil organization in the New World excepting only Mexico and Peru.

The respondent's 17th century ancestors were no doubt unaware that some of the Kings in distant Europe were laying claim to sovereignty over Mohawk territory. As Marshall C.J. of the United States Supreme Court observed in *Worcester v. Georgia*, 31 U.S. (6 Pet.) 515 (1832), at p. 543:

> It is difficult to comprehend the proposition, that the inhabitants of either quarter of the globe could have rightful original claims of dominion over the inhabitants of the other, or over the lands they occupied....

[113] Nevertheless, this is what happened. From the aboriginal perspective, moreover, those early claims to European "dominion" grew to reality in the decades that followed. Counsel for the respondent does not dispute Canadian sovereignty. He seeks Mohawk autonomy within the broader framework of Canadian sovereignty. [...]

[118] Fundamentally, the respondent views his aboriginal rights as a shield against non-aboriginal laws, including what he sees as the imposition of a border that "wasn't meant for [the] Kanienkehaka or the Mohawk Nation or any of the Six Nations." He thus testified at trial:

Even though my grandfather didn't speak any English he was able to explain to me, as other elders have, that the promises made by the English to the Haudenosaunee that they would continue to recognize our nation as free and independent peoples. At one meeting they would recite it, what exactly were those words and the gist that we had to understand it.

So, when our people in Akwesasne today say this border was not intended for us, they have an understanding in historical terms of the interpretation of those promises. In our language and the way it is passed down, the line of what is now known as the International Border belongs to somebody else. It wasn't meant for Kanienkehaka or the Mohawk Nation or any of the Six Nations. We understand that much.

[...]

The Substance of the Claim Disclosed by the Evidence

[127] In the constitutional framework envisaged by the respondent, the claimed aboriginal right is simply a manifestation of the more fundamental relationship between the aboriginal and non-aboriginal people. In the Mohawk tradition this relationship is memorialized by the "two-row" wampum, referred to by the respondent in Exhibit D-13, at pp. 109–10, and in his trial evidence (trans., vol. 2, at pp. 191–92), and described in the Haudenosaunee presentation to the Parliamentary Special Committee on Indian Self-Government in 1983 as follows:

> When the Haudenosaunee first came into contact with the European nations, treaties of peace and friendship were made. Each was symbolized by the Gus-Wen-Tah or Two Row Wampum. There is a bed of white wampum which symbolizes the purity of the agreement. There are two rows of purple, and those two rows have the spirit of your ancestors and mine. There are three beads of wampum separating the two rows and they symbolize peace, friendship and respect.
>
> These two rows will symbolize two paths or two vessels, travelling down the same river together. One, a birch bark canoe, will be for the Indian people, their laws, their customs and their ways. The other, a ship, will be for the white people and their laws, their customs and their ways. We shall each travel the river together, side by side, but in our own boat. Neither of us will try to steer the other's vessel. (*Indian Self-Government in Canada: Report of the Special Committee* [1983], back cover)

[128] Thus, in the "two-row" wampum there are two parallel paths. In one path travels the aboriginal canoe. In the other path travels the European ship. The two vessels co-exist but they never touch. Each is the sovereign of its own destiny.

[129] The modern embodiment of the "two-row" wampum concept, modified to reflect some of the realities of a modern state, is the idea of a "merged" or "shared" sovereignty. "Merged sovereignty" asserts that First Nations were

not wholly subordinated to non-aboriginal sovereignty but over time became merger partners. The final *Report of the Royal Commission on Aboriginal Peoples*, vol. 2 (*Restructuring the Relationship* [1996]), at p. 214, says that "Aboriginal governments give the constitution [of Canada] its deepest and most resilient roots in the Canadian soil." This updated concept of Crown sovereignty is of importance. Whereas historically the Crown may have been portrayed as an entity across the seas with which aboriginal people could scarcely be expected to identify, this was no longer the case in 1982 when the s. 35(1) reconciliation process was established. The Constitution was patriated and all aspects of our sovereignty became firmly located within our borders. If the principle of "merged sovereignty" articulated by the Royal Commission on Aboriginal Peoples is to have any true meaning, it must include at least the idea that aboriginal and non-aboriginal Canadians *together* form a sovereign entity with a measure of common purpose and united effort. It is this new entity, as inheritor of the historical attributes of sovereignty, with which existing aboriginal and treaty rights must be reconciled.

[130] The final *Report of the Royal Commission on Aboriginal Peoples*, vol. 2, goes on to describe "shared" sovereignty at pp. 240–41 as follows:

> Shared sovereignty, in our view, is a hallmark of the Canadian federation and a central feature of the three-cornered relations that link Aboriginal governments, provincial governments and the federal government. These governments are sovereign within their respective spheres and hold their powers by virtue of their constitutional status rather than by delegation. Nevertheless, many of their powers are shared in practice and may be exercised by more than one order of government.

On this view, to return to the nautical metaphor of the "two-row" wampum, "merged" sovereignty is envisaged as a single vessel (or ship of state) composed of the historic elements of wood, iron and canvas. The vessel's components pull together as a harmonious whole, but the wood remains wood, the iron remains iron and the canvas remains canvas. Non-aboriginal leaders, including Sir Wilfrid Laurier, have used similar metaphors. It represents, in a phrase, partnership without assimilation.

[...]

[134] The Royal Commission does not explain precisely how "shared sovereignty" is expected to work in practice, although it recognized as a critical issue how "60 to 80 historically based nations in Canada at present, comprising a thousand or so local Aboriginal communities" would "interact with the jurisdictions of the federal and provincial governments" in cases of operational conflict (Final Report, vol. 2, *supra*, at pp. 166 and 216). It also recognized the challenge aboriginal self-government poses to the orthodox view that constitutional powers in Canada are wholly and exhaustively distributed between the federal and provincial governments: see, e.g., *Attorney-General for Ontario*

v. Attorney-General for Canada, [1912] A.C. 571 (P.C.), at p. 581; P.W. Hogg and M.E. Turpel, "Implementing Aboriginal Self-Government: Constitutional and Jurisdictional Issues" (1995), 74 *Can. Bar Rev.* 187, at p. 192; this issue is presently before the courts in British Columbia in *Campbell v. British Columbia (Attorney General)* (2000), 79 B.C.L.R. (3d) 122, 2000 BCSC 1123. There are significant economic and funding issues. Some aboriginal people who live off reserves, particularly in urban areas, have serious concerns about how self-government would affect them, as discussed in part in *Corbiere v. Canada (Minister of Indian and Northern Affairs)*, [1999] 2 S.C.R. 203. With these difficulties in mind perhaps, the Royal Commission considered it to be "essential that any steps toward self-government be initiated by the aboriginal group in question" and "respond to needs identified by its members" (*Partners in Confederation: Aboriginal Peoples, Self-Government and the Constitution* [1993], at p. 41). It rejected the "one size fits all" approach to First Nations' self-governing institutions in favour of a negotiated treaty model. The objective, succinctly put, is to create sufficient "constitutional space for aboriginal peoples to be aboriginal": D. Greschner, "Aboriginal Women, the Constitution and Criminal Justice," [1992] *U.B.C. L. Rev. (Sp. ed.)* 338, at p. 342. See also J. Borrows, "Uncertain Citizens: Aboriginal Peoples and the Supreme Court" (2001), 80 *Can. Bar Rev.* 15, at p. 34. The Royal Commission Final Report, vol. 2, states at p. 214 that:

> Section 35 does not warrant a claim to unlimited governmental powers or to complete sovereignty, such as independent states are commonly thought to possess. As with the federal and provincial governments, Aboriginal governments operate within a sphere of sovereignty defined by the constitution. In short, the Aboriginal right of self-government in section 35(1) involves circumscribed rather than unlimited powers.

[...]

The Legal Basis of the Respondent's Claim

[148] I am far from suggesting that the key to s. 35(1) reconciliation is to be found in the legal archives of the British Empire. The root of the respondent's argument nevertheless is that the Mohawks of Akwesasne acquired under the legal regimes of 18th century North America, a positive *legal right* as a group to continue to come and go across any subsequent international border dividing their traditional homelands with whatever goods they wished, just as they had in pre-contact times. In other words, Mohawk autonomy in this respect was continued but not as a mere custom or practice. It emerged in the new European-based constitutional order as a *legal* trading and mobility *right*. By s. 35(1) of the *Constitution Act, 1982*, it became a constitutionally protected right. That is the respondent's argument.

The Limitation of "Sovereign Incompatibility"

[149] Care must be taken not to carry forward doctrines of British colonial law into the interpretation of s. 35(1) without careful reflection. In *R. v. Eninew* (1984), 12 C.C.C. (3d) 365 (Sask. C.A.), and *R. v. Hare* (1985), 20 C.C.C. (3d) 1 (Ont. C.A.), for example, it was held by two provincial courts of appeal that s. 35(1) "recognized and affirmed" (and thus set in constitutional concrete) the traditional frailties of common law aboriginal rights, including their vulnerability to unilateral extinguishment by governments. This was rejected in *Sparrow, supra*, where the Court construed s. 35(1) as affirming the promise of a new commitment by Canadians to resolve some of the ancient grievances that have exacerbated relations between aboriginal and non-aboriginal communities.

[150] Yet the language of s. 35(1) cannot be construed as a wholesale repudiation of the common law. The subject matter of the constitutional provision is "existing" aboriginal and treaty rights and they are said to be "recognized and affirmed" not wholly cut loose from either their legal or historical origins. One of the defining characteristics of sovereign succession and therefore a limitation on the scope of aboriginal rights, as already discussed, was the notion of incompatibility with the new sovereignty. Such incompatibility seems to have been accepted, for example, as a limitation on the powers of aboriginal self-government in the 1993 working report of the Royal Commission on Aboriginal Peoples, *Partners in Confederation: Aboriginal Peoples, Self-Government and the Constitution, supra*, at p. 23:

> ...Aboriginal nations did not lose their inherent rights when they entered into a confederal relationship with the Crown. Rather, they retained their ancient constitutions *so far as these were not inconsistent with the new relationship.* [Emphasis added.]

[...]

[153] However, important as they may have been to the Mohawk identity as a people, it could not be said, in my view, that pre-contact warrior activities gave rise under successor regimes to a *legal right* under s. 35(1) to engage in military adventures on Canadian territory. Canadian sovereign authority has, as one of its inherent characteristics, a monopoly on the *lawful* use of military force within its territory. I do not accept that the Mohawks *could* acquire under s. 35(1) a legal right to deploy a military force in what is now Canada, as and when they choose to do so, even if the warrior tradition was to be considered a defining feature of pre-contact Mohawk society. Section 35(1) should not be interpreted to throw on the Crown the burden of demonstrating subsequent extinguishment by "clear and plain" measures (*Gladstone, supra*, at para. 31) of a "right" to organize a private army, or a requirement to justify such a limitation after 1982 under the *Sparrow* standard. This example, remote as it is from the particular claim advanced in this case, usefully illus-

trates the principled limitation flowing from sovereign incompatibility in the s. 35(1) analysis. [...]

The Alleged Incompatibility between the Aboriginal Right Disclosed by the Evidence and Canadian Sovereignty

[163] Similar views were expressed by scholars writing before the Canada-United States border was ever established. E. de Vattel, whose treatise *The Law of Nations* was first published in 1758, said this:

> The sovereign may forbid the entrance of his territory either to foreigners in general, or in particular cases, or to certain persons, or for certain particular purposes, according as he may think it advantageous to the state. There is nothing in all this that does not flow from the rights of domain and sovereignty: every one is obliged to pay respect to the prohibition; and whoever dares to violate it, incurs the penalty decreed to render it effectual. (*The Law of Nations* [Chitty ed. 1834], Book II, at pp. 169–70)

To the same effect is Blackstone, *supra*, at p. 259:

> Upon exactly the same reason stands the prerogative of granting safe-conducts, without which by the law of nations no member of one society has a right to intrude into another.

In my view, therefore, the international trading/mobility right claimed by the respondent as a citizen of the Haudenosaunee (Iroquois) Confederacy is incompatible with the historical attributes of Canadian sovereignty.

[164] The question that then arises is whether this conclusion is at odds with the purpose of s. 35(1), i.e. the reconciliation of the interests of aboriginal peoples with Crown sovereignty? In addressing this question it must be remembered that aboriginal people are themselves part of Canadian sovereignty as discussed above. I agree with Borrows, *supra*, at p. 40, that accommodation of aboriginal rights should *not* be seen as "a zero-sum relationship between minority rights and citizenship; as if every gain in the direction of accommodating diversity comes at the expense of promoting citizenship" (quoting W. Kymlicka and W. Norman, eds., *Citizenship in Diverse Societies* [2000], at p. 39). On the other hand, the reverse is also true. Affirmation of the sovereign interest of Canadians as a whole, including aboriginal peoples, should not necessarily be seen as a loss of sufficient "constitutional space for aboriginal peoples to be aboriginal" (Greschner, *supra*, at p. 342). A finding of distinctiveness is a judgement that to fulfill the purpose of s. 35, a measure of constitutional space is required to accommodate particular activities (traditions, customs or practices) rooted in the aboriginal peoples' prior occupation of the land. In this case, a finding against "distinctiveness" is a conclusion that the respondent's claim does not relate to a "defining feature" that makes Mohawk "culture what it is" (*Van der Peet*, at paras. 59 and 71 [emphasis in original deleted]); it is a conclusion that to extend constitutional protection to the respondent's claim finds no

support in the pre-1982 jurisprudence and would overshoot the purpose of s. 35(1). In terms of sovereign incompatibility, it is a conclusion that the respondent's claim relates to national interests that all of us have in common rather than to distinctive interests that for some purposes differentiate an aboriginal community. In my view, reconciliation of these interests in this particular case favours an affirmation of our collective sovereignty.

R. v. Sparrow
Supreme Court of Canada
[1990] 1 S.C.R. 1075

In this case the Supreme Court had to consider whether aboriginal rights recognized in section 35(1) of the *Constitution Act, 1982*
invalidated a restriction on the length of fishing nets used by
persons of the Musqueam band in British Columbia. In reaching
its decision the Supreme Court had to set out an analysis of the
nature of Aboriginal rights under the Canadian constitution, and
more generally articulate the relationship between the government of Canada and Aboriginal peoples in Canada.

While the Supreme Court did not offer a conclusion on the
constitutionality of the restriction on the length of fishing nets,
it re-ordered a trial to be decided on the basis of the reasons and
analysis elaborated in its judgement.

———————

Chief Justice Dickson and Justice Lamer (for the majority):

It is worth recalling that while British policy towards the native population was
based on respect for their right to occupy their traditional lands, a proposition to which the Royal Proclamation of 1763 bears witness, there was from
the outset never any doubt that sovereignty and legislative power, and indeed
the underlying title, to such lands vested in the Crown. [...] And there can be
no doubt that over the years the rights of the Indians were often honoured in
the breach. [...]

For many years, the rights of the Indians to their aboriginal lands—certainly
as *legal* rights—were virtually ignored. The leading cases defining Indian rights
in the early part of the century were directed at claims supported by the Royal
Proclamation or other legal instruments, and even these cases were essentially
concerned with settling legislative jurisdiction or the rights of commercial
enterprises. For fifty years after the publication of Clement's *The Law of the
Canadian Constitution* (3rd ed. 1916), there was a virtual absence of discussion
of any kind of Indian rights to land even in academic literature. By the late
1960s, aboriginal claims were not even recognized by the federal government
as having any legal status. Thus the *Statement of the Government of Canada on
Indian Policy* (1969), although well meaning, contained the assertion (at p. 11)
that "aboriginal claims to land...are so general and undefined that it is not
realistic to think of them as specific claims capable of remedy except through
a policy and program that will end injustice to the Indians as members of the
Canadian community." In the same general period, the James Bay development by Quebec Hydro was originally initiated without regard to the rights

of the Indians who lived there, even though these were expressly protected by a constitutional instrument; see *The Quebec Boundaries Extension Act, 1912*, S.C. 1912, c. 45. It took a number of judicial decisions and notably the *Calder* case in this Court (1973) to prompt a reassessment of the position being taken by government.

In the light of its reassessment of Indian claims following *Calder*, the federal Government on August 8, 1973 issued "a statement of policy" regarding Indian lands. By it, it sought to "signify the Government's *recognition and acceptance* of its continuing responsibility under the British North America Act for Indians and lands reserved for Indians," which it regarded "as an historic evolution dating back to the Royal Proclamation of 1763, which, whatever differences there may be about its judicial interpretation, stands as a basic declaration of the Indian people's interests in land in this country." (Emphasis added.) See *Statement made by the Honourable Jean Chrétien, Minister of Indian Affairs and Northern Development on Claims of Indian and Inuit People*, August 8, 1973. The remarks about these lands were intended "as an expression of acknowledged responsibility." But the statement went on to express, for the first time, the government's willingness to negotiate regarding claims of aboriginal title, specifically in British Columbia, Northern Quebec, and the Territories, and this without regard to formal supporting documents. "The Government," it stated, "is now ready to negotiate with authorized representatives of these native peoples on the basis that where their traditional interest in the lands concerned can be established, an agreed form of compensation or benefit will be provided to native peoples in return for their interest."

It is obvious from its terms that the approach taken towards aboriginal claims in the 1973 statement constituted an expression of a policy, rather than a legal position; see also *In All Fairness: A Native Claims Policy—Comprehensive Claims* (1981), pp. 11–12; Slattery, "Understanding Aboriginal Rights" op. cit., at p. 730. As recently as *Guerin v. The Queen*, [1984] 2 S.C.R. 335, the federal government argued in this Court that any federal obligation was of a political character.

It is clear, then, that s. 35(1) of the *Constitution Act, 1982* represents the culmination of a long and difficult struggle in both the political forum and the courts for the constitutional recognition of aboriginal rights. The strong representations of native associations and other groups concerned with the welfare of Canada's aboriginal peoples made the adoption of s. 35(1) possible and it is important to note that the provision applies to the Indians, the Inuit and the Métis. Section 35(1), at the least, provides a solid constitutional base upon which subsequent negotiations can take place. It also affords aboriginal peoples constitutional protection against provincial legislative power. We are, of course, aware that this would, in any event, flow from the *Guerin* case, *supra*, but for a proper understanding of the situation, it is essential to remember that the *Guerin* case was decided after the commencement of the *Constitution Act, 1982*. In addition to its effect on aboriginal rights, s. 35(1) clarified other issues regarding the enforcement of treaty rights (see Sanders, "Preexisting Rights: The Aboriginal Peoples of Canada," in Beaudoin and Ratushny, eds., *The Canadian Charter of Rights and Freedoms*, 2nd ed., especially at p. 730).

In our opinion, the significance of s. 35(1) extends beyond these fundamental effects. Professor Lyon in "An Essay on Constitutional Interpretation" (1988), 26 *Osgoode Hall L.J.* 95, says the following about s. 35(1), at p. 100:

> ...the context of 1982 is surely enough to tell us that this is not just a codification of the case law on aboriginal rights that had accumulated by 1982. Section 35 calls for a just settlement for aboriginal peoples. It renounces the old rules of the game under which the Crown established courts of law and denied those courts the authority to question sovereign claims made by the Crown.

The approach to be taken with respect to interpreting the meaning of s. 35(1) is derived from general principles of constitutional interpretation, principles relating to aboriginal rights, and the purposes behind the constitutional provision itself. Here, we will sketch the framework for an interpretation of "recognized and affirmed" that, in our opinion, gives appropriate weight to the constitutional nature of these words.

In *Reference re Manitoba Language Rights*, [1985] 1 S.C.R. 721, this Court said the following about the perspective to be adopted when interpreting a constitution, at p. 745:

> The Constitution of a country is a statement of the will of the people to be governed in accordance with certain principles held as fundamental and certain prescriptions restrictive of the powers of the legislature and government. It is, as s. 52 of the *Constitution Act, 1982* declares, the "supreme law" of the nation, unalterable by the normal legislative process, and unsuffering of laws inconsistent with it. The duty of the judiciary is to interpret and apply the laws of Canada and each of the provinces, and it is thus our duty to ensure that the constitutional law prevails.

The nature of s. 35(1) itself suggests that it be construed in a purposive way. When the purposes of the affirmation of aboriginal rights are considered, it is clear that a generous, liberal interpretation of the words in the constitutional provision is demanded. When the Court of Appeal below was confronted with the submission that s. 35 has no effect on aboriginal or treaty rights and that it is merely a preamble to the parts of the *Constitution Act, 1982*, which deal with aboriginal rights, it said the following, at p. 322:

> This submission gives no meaning to s. 35. If accepted, it would result in denying its clear statement that existing rights are hereby recognized and affirmed, and would turn that into a mere promise to recognize and affirm those rights sometime in the future.... To so construe s. 35(1) would be to ignore its language and the principle that the Constitution should be interpreted in a liberal and remedial way. We cannot accept

that that principle applies less strongly to aboriginal rights than to the rights guaranteed by the *Charter*, particularly having regard to the history and to the approach to interpreting treaties and statutes relating to Indians required by such cases as *Nowegijick v. R.*, [1983] 1 S.C.R. 29. [...]

In *Nowegijick v. The Queen*, [1983] 1 S.C.R. 29, at p. 36, the following principle that should govern the interpretation of Indian treaties and statutes was set out:

... treaties and statutes relating to Indians should be liberally construed and doubtful expressions resolved in favour of the Indians.

[...]

In *Guerin, supra*, the Musqueam Band surrendered reserve lands to the Crown for lease to a golf club. The terms obtained by the Crown were much less favourable than those approved by the Band at the surrender meeting. This Court found that the Crown owed a fiduciary obligation to the Indians with respect to the lands. The *sui generis* nature of Indian title, and the historic powers and responsibility assumed by the Crown constituted the source of such a fiduciary obligation. In our opinion, *Guerin*, together with *R. v. Taylor and Williams* (1981), 34 O.R. (2d) 360, ground a general guiding principle for s. 91(24). That is, the Government has the responsibility to act in a fiduciary capacity with respect to aboriginal peoples. The relationship between the Government and aboriginals is trustlike, rather than adversarial, and contemporary recognition and affirmation of aboriginal rights must be defined in light of this historic relationship.

[...]

There is no explicit language in the provision that authorizes this Court or any court to assess the legitimacy of any government legislation that restricts aboriginal rights. Yet, we find that the words "recognition and affirmation" incorporate the fiduciary relationship referred to earlier and so import some restraint on the exercise of sovereign power. Rights that are recognized and affirmed are not absolute. Federal legislative powers continue, including, of course, the right to legislate with respect to Indians pursuant to s. 91(24) of the *Constitution Act, 1867*. These powers must, however, now be read together with s. 35(1). In other words, federal power must be reconciled with federal duty and the best way to achieve that reconciliation is to demand the justification of any government regulation that infringes upon or denies aboriginal rights. Such scrutiny is in keeping with the liberal interpretive principle enunciated in *Nowegijick, supra*, and the concept of holding the Crown to a high standard of honourable dealing with respect to the aboriginal peoples of Canada as suggested by *Guerin v. The Queen, supra*.

We refer to Professor Slattery's "Understanding Aboriginal Rights," *supra*, with respect to the task of envisioning a s. 35(1) justificatory process. Professor Slattery, at p. 782, points out that a justificatory process is required as a compromise between a "patchwork" characterization of aboriginal rights whereby past regulations would be read into a definition of the rights, and a characterization that would guarantee aboriginal rights in their original form unrestricted by subsequent regulation. We agree with him that these two extreme positions must be rejected in favour of a justificatory scheme.

Section 35(1) suggests that while regulation affecting aboriginal rights is not precluded, such regulation must be enacted according to a valid objective. Our history has shown, unfortunately all too well, that Canada's aboriginal peoples are justified in worrying about government objectives that may be superficially neutral but which constitute *de facto* threats to the existence of aboriginal rights and interests. By giving aboriginal rights constitutional status and priority, Parliament and the provinces have sanctioned challenges to social and economic policy objectives embodied in legislation to the extent that aboriginal rights are affected. Implicit in this constitutional scheme is the obligation of the legislature to satisfy the test of justification. The way in which a legislative objective is to be attained must uphold the honour of the Crown and must be in keeping with the unique contemporary relationship, grounded in history and policy, between the Crown and Canada's aboriginal peoples. The extent of legislative or regulatory impact on an existing aboriginal right may be scrutinized so as to ensure recognition and affirmation.

The constitutional recognition afforded by the provision therefore gives a measure of control over government conduct and a strong check on legislative power. While it does not promise immunity from government regulation in a society that, in the twentieth century, is increasingly more complex, interdependent and sophisticated, and where exhaustible resources need protection and management, it does hold the Crown to a substantive promise. The government is required to bear the burden of justifying any legislation that has some negative effect on any aboriginal right protected under s. 35(1).

Tsilhqot'in Nation v. British Columbia
Supreme Court of Canada
[2014] 2 S.C.R. 256

In this case the Supreme Court faced the challenge of determining the conditions under which Aboriginal title to land is
established, for the purpose of locating constitutional limits to
provincial and federal actions. The Court developed a test for
claims to Aboriginal title based on the culture and practices of
an Aboriginal people. The Court also laid out terms of the "duty
to consult," whereby provincial and federal governments must
consult with Aboriginal peoples on any infringements to the
exclusive use of lands for which Aboriginal title has either already
been established or potentially might be established in the future.

Following the excerpt is a "letter of understanding" between
the Tsilhqot'in Nation and the Government of Canada, outlin-
ing a commitment and vision to reconciling and strengthening
their relationship.

Chief Justice McLachlin (for the majority):

[32] In my view, the concepts of sufficiency, continuity and exclusivity provide
useful lenses through which to view the question of Aboriginal title. This said,
the court must be careful not to lose or distort the Aboriginal perspective by
forcing ancestral practices into the square boxes of common law concepts, thus
frustrating the goal of faithfully translating pre-sovereignty Aboriginal interests
into equivalent modern legal rights. Sufficiency, continuity and exclusivity are
not ends in themselves, but inquiries that shed light on whether Aboriginal
title is established.

Sufficiency of Occupation

[33] The first requirement—and the one that lies at the heart of this appeal—is
that the occupation be *sufficient* to ground Aboriginal title. It is clear from
Delgamuukw that not every passing traverse or use grounds title. What then
constitutes *sufficient* occupation to ground title?

[34] The question of sufficient occupation must be approached from both
the common law perspective and the Aboriginal perspective (*Delgamuukw*, at
para. 147). [...]

[35] The Aboriginal perspective focuses on laws, practices, customs and traditions of the group (*Delgamuukw*, at para. 148). In considering this perspective
for the purpose of Aboriginal title, "one must take into account the group's size,

manner of life, material resources, and technological abilities, and the character of the lands claimed": B. Slattery, "Understanding Aboriginal Rights" (1987), 66 *Can. Bar Rev.* 727, at p. 758, quoted with approval in *Delgamuukw*, at para. 149.

[36] The common law perspective imports the idea of possession and control of the lands. At common law, possession extends beyond sites that are physically occupied, like a house, to surrounding lands that are used and over which effective control is exercised.

[37] Sufficiency of occupation is a context-specific inquiry. "[O]ccupation may be established in a variety of ways, ranging from the construction of dwellings through cultivation and enclosure of fields to regular use of definite tracts of land for hunting, fishing or otherwise exploiting its resources" (*Delgamuukw*, at para. 149). The intensity and frequency of the use may vary with the characteristics of the Aboriginal group asserting title and the character of the land over which title is asserted. Here, for example, the land, while extensive, was harsh and was capable of supporting only 100 to 1,000 people. The fact that the Aboriginal group was only about 400 people must be considered in the context of the carrying capacity of the land in determining whether regular use of definite tracts of land is made out.

[38] To sufficiently occupy the land for purposes of title, the Aboriginal group in question must show that it has historically acted in a way that would communicate to third parties that it held the land for its own purposes. This standard does not demand notorious or visible use akin to proving a claim for adverse possession, but neither can the occupation be purely subjective or internal. There must be evidence of a strong presence on or over the land claimed, manifesting itself in acts of occupation that could reasonably be interpreted as demonstrating that the land in question belonged to, was controlled by, or was under the exclusive stewardship of the claimant group. As just discussed, the kinds of acts necessary to indicate a permanent presence and intention to hold and use the land for the group's purposes are dependent on the manner of life of the people and the nature of the land. Cultivated fields, constructed dwelling houses, invested labour, and a consistent presence on parts of the land may be sufficient, but are not essential to establish occupation. The notion of occupation must also reflect the way of life of the Aboriginal people, including those who were nomadic or semi-nomadic.

[39] In *R. v. Marshall*, 2003 NSCA 105, 218 N.S.R. (2d) 78, at paras. 135–38, Cromwell J.A. (as he then was), in reasoning I adopt, likens the sufficiency of occupation required to establish Aboriginal title to the requirements for general occupancy at common law. A general occupant at common law is a person asserting possession of land over which no one else has a present interest or with respect to which title is uncertain. Cromwell J.A. cites (at para. 136) the following extract from K. McNeil, *Common Law Aboriginal Title* (1989), at pp. 198–200:

What, then, did one have to do to acquire a title by occupancy? . . .
[I]t appears . . . that . . . a casual entry, such as riding over land to hunt or hawk, or travelling across it, did not make an occupant, such acts "being

only transitory and to a particular purpose, which leaves no marks of an appropriation, or of an intention to possess for the separate use of the rider." There must, therefore, have been an actual entry, and some act or acts from which an intention to occupy the land could be inferred. Significantly, the acts and intention had to relate only to the occupation—it was quite unnecessary for a potential occupant to claim, or even wish to acquire, the vacant estate, for the law cast it upon him by virtue of his occupation alone....

Further guidance on what constitutes occupation can be gained from cases involving land to which title is uncertain. Generally, any acts on or in relation to land that indicate an intention to hold or use it for one's own purposes are evidence of occupation. *Apart from the obvious, such as enclosing, cultivating, mining, building upon, maintaining, and warning trespassers off land, any number of other acts, including cutting trees or grass, fishing in tracts of water, and even perambulation, may be relied upon. The weight given to such acts depends partly on the nature of the land, and the purposes for which it can reasonably be used.* [Emphasis added.]

[40] Cromwell J.A. in *Marshall* went on to state that this standard is different from the doctrine of constructive possession. The goal is not to *attribute* possession in the absence of physical acts of occupation, but to define the quality of the physical acts of occupation that demonstrate possession at law (para. 137). He concluded:

I would adopt, in general terms, Professor McNeil's analysis that the appropriate standard of occupation, from the common law perspective, is the middle ground between the minimal occupation which would permit a person to sue a wrong-doer in trespass and the most onerous standard required to ground title by adverse possession as against a true owner.... Where, as here, we are dealing with a large expanse of territory which was not cultivated, acts such as continual, though changing, settlement and wide-ranging use for fishing, hunting and gathering should be given more weight than they would be if dealing with enclosed, cultivated land. Perhaps most significantly,... it is impossible to confine the evidence to the very precise spot on which the cutting was done: Pollock and Wright at p. 32. Instead, the question must be whether the acts of occupation in particular areas show that the whole area was occupied by the claimant. [para. 138]

[41] In summary, what is required is a culturally sensitive approach to sufficiency of occupation based on the dual perspectives of the Aboriginal group in question—its laws, practices, size, technological ability and the character of the land claimed—and the common law notion of possession as a basis for title. It is not possible to list every indicia of occupation that might apply in a particular case. The common law test for possession—which requires an intention to occupy or hold land for the purposes of the occupant—must be

considered alongside the perspective of the Aboriginal group which, depending on its size and manner of living, might conceive of possession of land in a somewhat different manner than did the common law.

[42] There is no suggestion in the jurisprudence or scholarship that Aboriginal title is confined to specific village sites or farms, as the Court of Appeal held. Rather, a culturally sensitive approach suggests that regular use of territories for hunting, fishing, trapping and foraging is "sufficient" use to ground Aboriginal title, provided that such use, on the facts of a particular case, evinces an intention on the part of the Aboriginal group to hold or possess the land in a manner comparable to what would be required to establish title at common law. [...]

[44] The Court in *Marshall; Bernard* confirmed that nomadic and seminomadic groups could establish title to land, provided they establish sufficient physical possession, which is a question of fact. While "[n]ot every nomadic passage or use will ground title to land," the Court confirmed that *Delgamuukw* contemplates that "regular use of definite tracts of land for hunting, fishing or otherwise exploiting its resources" could suffice (para. 66). While the issue was framed in terms of whether the common law test for possession was met, the Court did not resile from the need to consider the perspective of the Aboriginal group in question; sufficient occupation is a "question of fact, depending on all the circumstances, in particular the nature of the land and the manner in which it is commonly used" (*ibid.*).

Continuity of Occupation

[45] Where present occupation is relied on as proof of occupation pre-sovereignty, a second requirement arises—continuity between present and pre-sovereignty occupation.

[46] The concept of continuity does not require Aboriginal groups to provide evidence of an unbroken chain of continuity between their current practices, customs and traditions, and those which existed prior to contact (*Van der Peet*, at para. 65). The same applies to Aboriginal title. Continuity simply means that for evidence of present occupation to establish an inference of pre-sovereignty occupation, the present occupation must be rooted in pre-sovereignty times. This is a question for the trier of fact in each case.

Exclusivity of Occupation

[47] The third requirement is *exclusive* occupation of the land at the time of sovereignty. The Aboriginal group must have had "the *intention and capacity to retain exclusive control*" over the lands (*Delgamuukw*, at para. 156, quoting McNeil, *Common Law Aboriginal Title*, at p. 204 [emphasis added]). Regular use without exclusivity may give rise to usufructory Aboriginal rights; for Aboriginal title, the use must have been exclusive.

[48] Exclusivity should be understood in the sense of intention and capacity to control the land. The fact that other groups or individuals were on the land

does not necessarily negate exclusivity of occupation. Whether a claimant group had the intention and capacity to control the land at the time of sovereignty is a question of fact for the trial judge and depends on various factors such as the characteristics of the claimant group, the nature of other groups in the area, and the characteristics of the land in question. Exclusivity can be established by proof that others were excluded from the land, or by proof that others were only allowed access to the land with the permission of the claimant group. The fact that permission was requested and granted or refused, or that treaties were made with other groups, may show intention and capacity to control the land. Even the lack of challenges to occupancy may support an inference of an established group's intention and capacity to control.

[49] As with sufficiency of occupation, the exclusivity requirement must be approached from both the common law and Aboriginal perspectives, and must take into account the context and characteristics of the Aboriginal society. The Court in *Delgamuukw* explained as follows, at para. 157:

> A consideration of the [A]boriginal perspective may also lead to the conclusion that trespass by other [A]boriginal groups does not undermine, and that presence of those groups by permission may reinforce, the exclusive occupation of the [A]boriginal group asserting title. For example, the [A]boriginal group asserting the claim to [A]boriginal title may have trespass laws which are proof of exclusive occupation, such that the presence of trespassers does not count as evidence against exclusivity. As well, [A]boriginal laws under which permission may be granted to other [A]boriginal groups to use or reside even temporarily on land would reinforce the finding of exclusive occupation. Indeed, if that permission were the subject of treaties between the [A]boriginal nations in question, those treaties would also form part of the [A]boriginal perspective.

Summary

[50] The claimant group bears the onus of establishing Aboriginal title. The task is to identify how pre-sovereignty rights and interests can properly find expression in modern common law terms. In asking whether Aboriginal title is established, the general requirements are: (1) "sufficient occupation" of the land claimed to establish title at the time of assertion of European sovereignty; (2) continuity of occupation where present occupation is relied on; and (3) exclusive historic occupation. In determining what constitutes sufficient occupation, one looks to the Aboriginal culture and practices, and compares them in a culturally sensitive way with what was required at common law to establish title on the basis of occupation. Occupation sufficient to ground Aboriginal title is not confined to specific sites of settlement but extends to tracts of land that were regularly used for hunting, fishing or otherwise exploiting resources

and over which the group exercised effective control at the time of assertion of European sovereignty.

[...]

The Legal Characterization of Aboriginal Title

[69] The starting point in characterizing the legal nature of Aboriginal title is Dickson J.'s concurring judgement in *Guerin*, discussed earlier. At the time of assertion of European sovereignty, the Crown acquired radical or underlying title to all the land in the province. This Crown title, however, was burdened by the pre-existing legal rights of Aboriginal people who occupied and used the land prior to European arrival. The doctrine of *terra nullius* (that no one owned the land prior to European assertion of sovereignty) never applied in Canada, as confirmed by the *Royal Proclamation* of 1763. The Aboriginal interest in land that burdens the Crown's underlying title is an independent legal interest, which gives rise to a fiduciary duty on the part of the Crown.

[70] The content of the Crown's underlying title is what is left when Aboriginal title is subtracted from it: s. 109 of the *Constitution Act, 1867*; *Delgamuukw*. As we have seen, *Delgamuukw* establishes that Aboriginal title gives "the right to exclusive use and occupation of the land ... for a variety of purposes," not confined to traditional or "distinctive" uses (para. 117). In other words, Aboriginal title is a beneficial interest in the land: *Guerin*, at p. 382. In simple terms, the title holders have the right to the benefits associated with the land—to use it, enjoy it and profit from its economic development. As such, the Crown does not retain a beneficial interest in Aboriginal title land.

[71] What remains, then, of the Crown's radical or underlying title to lands held under Aboriginal title? The authorities suggest two related elements—a fiduciary duty owed by the Crown to Aboriginal people when dealing with Aboriginal lands, and the right to encroach on Aboriginal title if the government can justify this in the broader public interest under s. 35 of the *Constitution Act, 1982*. The Court in *Delgamuukw* referred to this as a process of reconciling Aboriginal interests with the broader public interests under s. 35 of the *Constitution Act, 1982*.

[72] The characteristics of Aboriginal title flow from the special relationship between the Crown and the Aboriginal group in question. It is this relationship that makes Aboriginal title *sui generis* or unique. Aboriginal title is what it is—the unique product of the historic relationship between the Crown and the Aboriginal group in question. Analogies to other forms of property ownership—for example, fee simple—may help us to understand aspects of Aboriginal title. But they cannot dictate precisely what it is or is not. As La Forest J. put it in *Delgamuukw*, at para. 190, Aboriginal title "is not equated with fee simple ownership; nor can it be described with reference to traditional property law concepts."

The Incidents of Aboriginal Title

[73] Aboriginal title confers ownership rights similar to those associated with fee simple, including: the right to decide how the land will be used; the right of enjoyment and occupancy of the land; the right to possess the land; the right to the economic benefits of the land; and the right to pro-actively use and manage the land.

[74] Aboriginal title, however, comes with an important restriction—it is collective title held not only for the present generation but for all succeeding generations. This means it cannot be alienated except to the Crown or encumbered in ways that would prevent future generations of the group from using and enjoying it. Nor can the land be developed or misused in a way that would substantially deprive future generations of the benefit of the land. Some changes—even permanent changes—to the land may be possible. Whether a particular use is irreconcilable with the ability of succeeding generations to benefit from the land will be a matter to be determined when the issue arises.

[75] The rights and restrictions on Aboriginal title flow from the legal interest Aboriginal title confers, which in turn flows from the fact of Aboriginal occupancy at the time of European sovereignty which attached as a burden on the underlying title asserted by the Crown at sovereignty. Aboriginal title post-sovereignty reflects the fact of Aboriginal occupancy pre-sovereignty, with all the pre-sovereignty incidents of use and enjoyment that were part of the collective title enjoyed by the ancestors of the claimant group—most notably the right to control how the land is used. However, these uses are not confined to the uses and customs of pre-sovereignty times; like other landowners, Aboriginal title holders of modern times can use their land in modern ways, if that is their choice.

[76] The right to control the land conferred by Aboriginal title means that governments and others seeking to use the land must obtain the consent of the Aboriginal title holders. If the Aboriginal group does not consent to the use, the government's only recourse is to establish that the proposed incursion on the land is justified under s. 35 of the *Constitution Act, 1982.*

Justification of Infringement

[77] To justify overriding the Aboriginal title-holding group's wishes on the basis of the broader public good, the government must show: (1) that it discharged its procedural duty to consult and accommodate; (2) that its actions were backed by a compelling and substantial objective; and (3) that the governmental action is consistent with the Crown's fiduciary obligation to the group: *Sparrow.*

[78] The duty to consult is a procedural duty that arises from the honour of the Crown prior to confirmation of title. Where the Crown has real or constructive knowledge of the potential or actual existence of Aboriginal title, and contemplates conduct that might adversely affect it, the Crown is obliged to

consult with the group asserting Aboriginal title and, if appropriate, accommodate the Aboriginal right. The duty to consult must be discharged prior to
carrying out the action that could adversely affect the right.

[79] The degree of consultation and accommodation required lies on a spectrum as discussed in *Haida*. In general, the level of consultation and accommodation required is proportionate to the strength of the claim and to the
seriousness of the adverse impact the contemplated governmental action would
have on the claimed right. "A dubious or peripheral claim may attract a mere
duty of notice, while a stronger claim may attract more stringent duties" (para.
37). The required level of consultation and accommodation is greatest where
title has been established. Where consultation or accommodation is found to
be inadequate, the government decision can be suspended or quashed.

[80] Where Aboriginal title is unproven, the Crown owes a procedural duty
imposed by the honour of the Crown to consult and, if appropriate, accommodate the unproven Aboriginal interest. By contrast, where title has been
established, the Crown must not only comply with its procedural duties, but
must also ensure that the proposed government action is substantively consistent with the requirements of s. 35 of the *Constitution Act, 1982*. This requires
both a compelling and substantial governmental objective and that the government action is consistent with the fiduciary duty owed by the Crown to the
Aboriginal group.

[81] I agree with the Court of Appeal that the compelling and substantial
objective of the government must be considered from the Aboriginal perspective as well as from the perspective of the broader public. As stated in *Gladstone*,
at para. 72:

> ... the objectives which can be said to be compelling and substantial will
> be those directed at either the recognition of the prior occupation of
> North America by [A]boriginal peoples or—and at the level of justifica-
> tion it is this purpose which may well be most relevant—*at the reconcili-*
> *ation of [A]boriginal prior occupation with the assertion of the sovereignty*
> *of the Crown.* [Emphasis added.]

[82] As *Delgamuukw* explains, the process of reconciling Aboriginal interests with the broader interests of society as a whole is the *raison d'être* of the
principle of justification. Aboriginals and non-Aboriginals are "all here to stay"
and must of necessity move forward in a process of reconciliation (para. 186).
To constitute a compelling and substantial objective, the broader public goal
asserted by the government must further the goal of reconciliation, having
regard to both the Aboriginal interest and the broader public objective.

[83] What interests are potentially capable of justifying an incursion on
Aboriginal title? In *Delgamuukw*, this Court, *per* Lamer C.J., offered this:

> In the wake of *Gladstone*, the range of legislative objectives that can jus-
> tify the infringement of [A]boriginal title is fairly broad. Most of these
> objectives can be traced to the reconciliation of the prior occupation

of North America by [A]boriginal peoples with the assertion of Crown sovereignty, which entails the recognition that "distinctive [A]boriginal societies exist within, and are a part of, a broader social, political and economic community" (at para. 73). *In my opinion, the development of agriculture, forestry, mining, and hydroelectric power, the general economic development of the interior of British Columbia, protection of the environment or endangered species, the building of infrastructure and the settlement of foreign populations to support those aims, are the kinds of objectives that are consistent with this purpose and, in principle, can justify the infringement of [A]boriginal title.* Whether a particular measure or government act can be explained by reference to one of those objectives, however, is ultimately a question of fact that will have to be examined on a case-by-case basis. [Emphasis added; emphasis in original deleted; para. 165.]

[84] If a compelling and substantial public purpose is established, the government must go on to show that the proposed incursion on the Aboriginal right is consistent with the Crown's fiduciary duty towards Aboriginal people.

[85] The Crown's fiduciary duty in the context of justification merits further discussion. The Crown's underlying title in the land is held for the benefit of the Aboriginal group and constrained by the Crown's fiduciary or trust obligation to the group. This impacts the justification process in two ways.

[86] First, the Crown's fiduciary duty means that the government must act in a way that respects the fact that Aboriginal title is a group interest that inheres in present and future generations. The beneficial interest in the land held by the Aboriginal group vests communally in the title-holding group. This means that incursions on Aboriginal title cannot be justified if they would substantially deprive future generations of the benefit of the land.

[87] Second, the Crown's fiduciary duty infuses an obligation of proportionality into the justification process. Implicit in the Crown's fiduciary duty to the Aboriginal group is the requirement that the incursion is necessary to achieve the government's goal (rational connection); that the government go no further than necessary to achieve it (minimal impairment); and that the benefits that may be expected to flow from that goal are not outweighed by adverse effects on the Aboriginal interest (proportionality of impact). The requirement of proportionality is inherent in the *Delgamuukw* process of reconciliation and was echoed in *Haida*'s insistence that the Crown's duty to consult and accommodate at the claims stage "is proportionate to a preliminary assessment of the strength of the case supporting the existence of the right or title, and to the seriousness of the potentially adverse effect upon the right or title claimed" (para. 39).

[88] In summary, Aboriginal title confers on the group that holds it the exclusive right to decide how the land is used and the right to benefit from those uses, subject to one carve-out—that the uses must be consistent with the group nature of the interest and the enjoyment of the land by future generations. Government incursions not consented to by the title-holding group must be undertaken in accordance with the Crown's procedural duty to con-

sult and must also be justified on the basis of a compelling and substantial public interest, and must be consistent with the Crown's fiduciary duty to the Aboriginal group.

[...]

[142] The guarantee of Aboriginal rights in s. 35 of the *Constitution Act, 1982*, like the *Canadian Charter of Rights and Freedoms*, operates as a limit on federal and provincial legislative powers. The *Charter* forms Part I of the *Constitution Act, 1982*, and the guarantee of Aboriginal rights forms Part II. Parts I and II are sister provisions, both operating to limit governmental powers, whether federal or provincial. Part II Aboriginal rights, like Part I *Charter* rights, are held *against* government—they operate to *prohibit* certain types of regulation which governments could otherwise impose. [...]

Letter of Understanding between the Tsilhqot'in Nation and Canada

Dated for reference January 27, 2017
Between:
The Tsilhqot'in Nation as represented by:
Xeni Gwet'in First Nations Government,
Yunesit'in Government,
Tl'etinqox Government,
ʔEsdilagh First Nation,
Tsi Deldel First Nation,
Toosey Indian Band (Tl'esqox), and
The Tsilhqot'in National Government ("TNG")
(the "Tsilhqot'in Nation")
And:
Her Majesty The Queen in Right of Canada as represented by
the Minister of Indigenous and Northern Affairs Canada ("the
Minister")
("Canada")
(Collectively, the "Parties")

Shared Vision

1. By entering this Letter of Understanding ("Letter"), Canada and the Tsilhqot'in Nation commit to renewing and strengthening their nation-to-nation relationship, and negotiating in good faith to achieve a lasting reconciliation for the Tsilhqot'in people.

2. On June 26, 2014, the Supreme Court of Canada rendered its unanimous judgement in *Tsilhqot'in Nation*, recognizing Aboriginal title for the first time in Canadian history, in the homeland of the Tsilhqot'in people.

3. The *Tsilhqot'in Nation* judgement offers a profound opportunity for Canada, the Tsilhqot'in Nation, and all First Nations to restore Indigenous Peoples to their rightful place as true partners in the economic, political and social fabric of Canada.

4. On May 10, 2016, Canada fully endorsed the *United Nations Declaration on the Rights of Indigenous Peoples* without qualification and committed to implement the *Declaration* in partnership with Indigenous Peoples.

5. The Tsilhqot'in Nation has governed itself since time immemorial, in accordance with its own inherent laws, jurisdiction, governance and responsibilities. For generations, the Tsilhqot'in people have vigorously protected their culture, their homeland, and their right to self-determination as Indigenous Peoples within Canada.

6. The Parties wish to embrace this historic opportunity and explore new ways to achieve a just and enduring reconciliation for the Tsilhqot'in

people and to lead the way forward with new and innovative approaches to reconciliation between Canada and Indigenous Peoples, based on recognition of rights, respect, co-operation and true partnership.

Acknowledgment and Reconciliation

1. The Parties agree to renew and strengthen their nation-to-nation relationship. In this spirit, the Minister accepts the invitation of the Tsilhqot'in Nation to meet with the Tsilhqot'in leadership, elders, youth and communities in Xeni Gwet'in, on Tsilhqot'in Aboriginal title lands, in Summer 2017 or such other time as agreed by the Parties. The Minister will also relay Tsilhqot'in Nation's invitation to the Prime Minister and the Minister of Justice.

2. Recognizing that reconciliation begins with truth telling and healing, the Minister agrees to seek authority for Canada:
   1. to take steps to redress, through a statement issued on a date and location to be agreed upon by the Parties, the wrongful trial and hanging in 1864/65 of the Tsilhqot'in Chiefs, who died defending their lands, their people and their way of life;
   2. to the fullest extent of its authority, to exonerate the Tsilhqot'in Chiefs of any wrongdoing; and
   3. to make deliberative attempts to understand the history of the Chilcotin War of 1864/65 and its aftermath (in particular the Tsilhqot'in perspective) and how these events have shaped the relationship between the Tsilhqot'in and the Crown to date, in an effort to move beyond this history and create a truly reciprocal and respectful relationship.

Reconciliation Framework Agreement

3. The Parties will make best efforts to negotiate a Reconciliation Framework Agreement (Framework Agreement) by January 2019. The Framework Agreement will set out a shared vision, principles, priorities and structures to negotiate a comprehensive and lasting reconciliation between the Tsilhqot'in Nation and Canada.

Priority Issues

4. The Parties commit to working to transform the lives of Tsilhqot'in citizens and communities, in the following priority areas:
   1. closing the profound gaps in education, health and mental health care, housing, infrastructure, access to clean water and the overall health and well-being of the Tsilhqot'in citizens and communities;
   2. addressing criminal justice, community safety and policing issues;
   3. supporting children and families of the Tsilhqot'in people;
   4. jointly reviewing fisheries management in Tsilhqot'in territory;

5. establishing new fiscal relationships based on stable, predictable and flexible funding;

6. exploring and seeking to resolve issues related to Lot 7741 (Chilcotin Military Block);

7. fostering economic opportunities for the Tsilhqot'in;

8. recognizing and implementing Tsilhqot'in governance and law;

9. recognizing and reconciling Tsilhqot'in Aboriginal title and rights;

10. implementation of the *United Nations Declaration on the Rights of Indigenous Peoples*, including the right of free, prior informed consent;

11. negotiating the Framework Agreement, as described above; and

12. other priorities as identified by the Parties.

5. The Parties are committed to making progress in the above areas while the Framework Agreement is negotiated and implemented.

6. In negotiating the Framework Agreement, and making progress in the priority areas, the Parties will draw on the Truth and Reconciliation Commission's recommendations, as set out in its Final Report, for guidance and as a framework for action in achieving reconciliation.

Process

7. The Tsilhqot'in Chiefs and the Minister (the "Leadership") may engage when required to resolve issues as they arise and to ensure the efficient progress of negotiations. The Minister will engage other federal departments as required.

8. The Lead Negotiator for the Tsilhqot'in Nation and the Senior Assistant Deputy Minister, Treaties and Aboriginal Government (the Steering Committee), will meet on a quarterly basis, at a minimum, and are responsible for overseeing the negotiation process.

9. The Parties will establish a technical working group comprised of designates of the Tsilhqot'in Nation, and officials from Indigenous and Northern Affairs Canada, Justice Canada, and other departments, as required (the "Working Group"). The Working Group will hold regular meetings, no less than monthly, and implement direction from the Leadership. The Working Group will also deal with any urgent short-term issues that arise between meetings.

10. Each Party will ensure that its representatives at the Working Group have direct and timely access to their Leadership and to those individuals that are best positioned to provide any required mandate, decision or direction.

11. The Parties will use a flexible and solutions-based approach to develop opportunities and arrangements as required to achieve progress on the priority issues, even if they differ from, or do not fit easily, into existing regimes, laws, programs, policies or structures.

Funding and Resources

12. The Parties agree that the commitment of funding and resourcing by Canada is essential to the success of this Letter and the Framework Agreement. The Parties will determine bridge funding to support the shared priorities and processes identified in this Letter, until the Framework Agreement is concluded and longer-term funding commitments are in place.

Other

13. This Letter does not create, amend, define, affirm, recognize, abrogate or derogate from any Aboriginal rights or title of the Tsilhqot'in Nation which are recognized and affirmed by section 35 (1) of the *Constitution Act, 1982.*

14. This Letter and Framework Agreement which may flow from it are not intended to constitute a treaty or land claims agreement within the meaning of Sections 25 and 35 of the *Constitution Act, 1982.*

15. This Letter does not create, recognize, affirm, deny or amend any legally enforceable rights.

16. This Letter does not preclude the Tsilhqot'in from accessing any funding, program or initiative that Canada might normally make available to other First Nations.

17. This Letter, the negotiations conducted pursuant to this Letter, and all related documents, are without prejudice to the positions of the Parties in any proceedings before a court or other forum and shall not be construed as admissions of fact or liability.

Ktunaxa Nation v. British Columbia (Forests, Lands and Natural Resource Operations)
Supreme Court of Canada
[2017] S.C.C. 54

When the Supreme Court of Canada hears an appeal on a matter involving First Nations, the Court is often required to add incrementally to the growing body of law setting out the relation between First Nations and Canada. At the same time, the Supreme Court may be required to rule on associated matters in which members of First Nations are involved, yet their status as First Nations members plays no special role in the question of law at hand. In this case, the Supreme Court faced both a general question of constitutional law regarding freedom of religion, and a question regarding the duty to consult and accommodate a First Nation. The Ktunaxa First Nation objected to British Columbia's approval of a project to build a year-round ski resort on sacred grounds of the Ktunaxa First Nation. The Ktunaxa challenged the adequacy of the consultation and accommodation, and further claimed that their freedom of religion is unacceptably infringed by building in territory inextricably bound up in the nature and practice of their religious belief. This excerpt focuses on the issue of freedom of religion. In the Court's reasoning you will see the challenge of reasoning about a fundamental freedom when the practice of that freedom may require more than the absence of government interference, and when that freedom is part of the complex and evolving relation between First Nations and the Canadian legal system.

Seven of the Court's nine judges determined that the Ktunaxa's freedom of religion was not infringed, since their religious beliefs were not affected by government interference. The remaining two judges agreed with the majority decision but disagreed with a particular dimension of the majority's analysis. In their minority opinion the two judges asserted that the Ktunaxa's freedom of religion was indeed infringed, and that this infringement ought to be acknowledged as such even while the infringement is justified in this instance.

Chief Justice McLachlin and Justice Rowe (for the majority):

Introduction

[1] The issue in this case is whether the British Columbia Minister of Forests, Lands and Natural Resource Operations ("Minister") erred in approving a ski resort development, despite claims by the Ktunaxa that the development would breach their constitutional right to freedom of religion and to protection of Aboriginal interests under s. 35 of the Constitution Act, 1982.

[2] The appellants represent the Ktunaxa people. The Ktunaxa's traditional territories are said to consist of land that straddles the international boundary between Canada and the United States, comprised of northeastern Washington, northern Idaho, northwestern Montana, southwestern Alberta and southeastern British Columbia.

[3] This case concerns a proposed development in an area the Ktunaxa call Qat'muk. This area is located in a Canadian valley in the northwestern part of the larger Ktunaxa territory, the Jumbo Valley, about 55 kilometres west of the town of Invermere, B.C. [...]

Facts

[11] The Jumbo Valley and Qat'muk are located in the traditional territory of the Ktunaxa. The Ktunaxa believe that Grizzly Bear Spirit inhabits Qat'muk. It is undisputed that Grizzly Bear Spirit is central to Ktunaxa religious beliefs and practices.

[12] The Jumbo Valley has long been used for heli-skiing, which involves flying skiers to the top of runs by helicopter, whence they ski to the valley floor. In the 1980s, Glacier Resorts became interested in building a permanent ski resort on a site near the north end of the valley and sought government approval of the project. [...]

The Scope of Freedom of Religion

[61] The first step where a claim is made that a law or governmental act violates freedom of religion is to determine whether the claim falls within the scope of s. 2 (a). If not, there is no need to consider whether the decision represents a proportionate balance between freedom of religion and other considerations: *Amselem*, at para. 181.

[62] The seminal case on the scope of the Charter guarantee of freedom of religion is this Court's decision in *Big M Drug Mart*. The majority of the Court, per Justice Dickson (as he then was), defined s. 2 (a) as protecting "the right to entertain such religious beliefs as a person chooses, the right to declare religious beliefs openly and without fear of hindrance or reprisal, and the right to manifest religious belief by worship and practice or by teaching and dissemination" (p. 336).

[63] So defined, s. 2 (a) has two aspects—the freedom to hold religious beliefs and the freedom to manifest those beliefs. [...]

Application to This Case

[68] To establish an infringement of the right to freedom of religion, the claim-ant must demonstrate (1) that he or she sincerely believes in a practice or belief that has a nexus with religion, and (2) that the impugned state conduct inter-feres, in a manner that is nontrivial or not insubstantial, with his or her ability to act in accordance with that practice or belief: see *Multani*, at para. 34.

[69] In this case, it is undisputed that the Ktunaxa sincerely believe in the existence and importance of Grizzly Bear Spirit. They also believe that per-manent development in Qat'muk will drive this spirit from that place. The chambers judge indicated that Mr. Luke came to this belief in 2004 but whether this belief is ancient or recent plays no part in our s. 2 (a) analysis. The Charter protects all sincere religious beliefs and practices, old or new.

[70] The second part of the test, however, is not met in this case. This stage of the analysis requires an objective analysis of the interference caused by the impugned state action: *S.L. v. Commission scolaire des Chênes*, 2012 SCC 7, [2012] 1 S.C.R. 235, at para. 24. The Ktunaxa must show that the Minister's decision to approve the development interferes either with their freedom to believe in Grizzly Bear Spirit or their freedom to manifest that belief. But the Minister's decision does neither of those things. This case is not concerned with either the freedom to hold a religious belief or to manifest that belief. The claim is rather that s. 2 (a) of the Charter protects the presence of Grizzly Bear Spirit in Qat'muk. This is a novel claim and invites this Court to extend s. 2 (a) beyond the scope recognized in our law.

[71] We would decline this invitation. The state's duty under s. 2 (a) is not to protect the object of beliefs, such as Grizzly Bear Spirit. Rather, the state's duty is to protect everyone's freedom to hold such beliefs and to manifest them in worship and practice or by teaching and dissemination. In short, the Charter protects the freedom to worship, but does not protect the spiritual focal point of worship. We have been directed to no authority that supports the proposition that s. 2 (a) protects the latter, rather than individuals' liberty to hold a belief and to manifest that belief. Section 2 (a) protects the freedom to pursue prac-tices, like the wearing of a kirpan in *Multani* or refusing to be photographed in *Alberta v. Hutterian Brethren of Wilson Colony*, 2009 SCC 37, [2009] 2 S.C.R. 567. And s. 2 (a) protects the right to freely hold the religious beliefs that motivate such practices. In this case, however, the appellants are not seeking protection for the freedom to believe in Grizzly Bear Spirit or to pursue practices related to it. Rather, they seek to protect Grizzly Bear Spirit itself and the subjective spiritual meaning they derive from it. That claim is beyond the scope of s. 2 (a).

[72] The extension of s. 2 (a) proposed by the Ktunaxa would put deeply held personal beliefs under judicial scrutiny. Adjudicating how exactly a spirit is to be protected would require the state and its courts to assess the content and merits of religious beliefs. In *Amselem*, this Court chose to protect any sin-cerely held belief rather than examining the specific merits of religious beliefs:

In my view, the State is in no position to be, nor should it become, the arbiter of religious dogma. Accordingly, courts should avoid judicially interpreting and thus determining, either explicitly or implicitly, the content of a subjective understanding of religious requirement, "obligation," precept, "commandment," custom or ritual. Secular judicial determinations of theological or religious disputes, or of contentious matters of religious doctrine, unjustifiably entangle the court in the affairs of religion. (para. 50, per Iacobucci J.)

The Court in *Amselem* concluded that such an inquiry into profoundly personal beliefs would be inconsistent with the principles underlying freedom of religion (para. 49). [...]

Justice Moldaver (concurring):

[117] I agree with the Chief Justice and Rowe J. that the Minister reasonably concluded that the duty to consult and accommodate the Ktunaxa under s. 35 was met. Respectfully, however, I disagree with my colleagues' s. 2 (a) analysis. [...]

The Scope of Section 2(a)

[121] All Charter rights—including freedom of religion under s. 2 (a)—must be interpreted in a broad and purposive manner (*Figueroa v. Canada [Attorney General]*, 2003 SCC 37, [2003] 1 S.C.R. 912, at para. 20; *Reference re Prov. Electoral Boundaries [Sask.]*, [1991] 2 S.C.R. 158, at p. 179, per McLachlin J., as she then was). As this Court stated in *R. v. Big M Drug Mart Ltd.*, [1985] 1 S.C.R. 295, at p. 344, the interpretation of freedom of religion must be a "*generous* rather than a legalistic one, aimed at fulfilling the purpose of the guarantee and securing for individuals the full benefit of the Charter's protection" (emphasis added). The interpretation of s. 2 (a) must therefore be guided by its purpose, which is to "ensure that society does not interfere with profoundly personal beliefs that govern one's perception of oneself, humankind, nature, and, in some cases, a higher or different order of being" (*R. v. Edwards Books and Art Ltd.*, [1986] 2 S.C.R. 713, at p. 759).

[122] In light of this purpose, this Court has articulated a two-part test for determining whether s. 2 (a) has been infringed. The claimant must show: (1) that he or she sincerely believes in a belief or practice that has a nexus with religion, and (2) that the impugned conduct interferes with the claimant's ability to act in accordance with that belief or practice "in a manner that is more than trivial or insubstantial" (*Syndicat Northcrest v. Amselem*, 2004 SCC 47, [2004] 2 S.C.R. 551, at para. 65; *Multani v. Commission scolaire Marguerite-Bourgeoys*, 2006 SCC 6, [2006] 1 SC.R. 256, at para. 34; *Alberta v. Hutterian Brethren of Wilson Colony*, 2009 SCC 37, [2009] 2 S.C.R. 567, at para. 32).

[123] The first part of the test is not at issue in this case. None of the parties dispute that the Ktunaxa sincerely believe that Grizzly Bear Spirit lives in Qat'muk, and that any permanent development would drive Grizzly Bear

Spirit out, desecrate the land and sever the Ktunaxa's spiritual connection to it. The central issue raised by this appeal concerns the second part of the test. The Chief Justice and Rowe J. maintain that the Minister's decision does not interfere with the Ktunaxa's ability to act in accordance with their religious beliefs or practices. With respect, I disagree. As I will explain, in my view, the Minister's decision interferes with the Ktunaxa's ability to act in accordance with their religious beliefs and practices in a manner that is more than trivial or insubstantial, and the Ktunaxa's claim therefore falls within the scope of s. 2 (a).

The Ability to Act in Accordance with a Religious Belief or Practice

[124] As indicated, the s. 2 (a) inquiry focuses on whether state action has interfered with the ability of a person to act in accordance with his or her religious beliefs or practices. This Court has recognized that religious beliefs are "deeply held personal convictions...integrally linked to one's self-definition and spiritual fulfilment," while religious practices are those that "allow individuals to foster a connection with the divine" (*Amselem*, at para. 39). In my view, where a person's religious belief no longer provides spiritual fulfillment, or where the person's religious practice no longer allows him or her to foster a connection with the divine, that person cannot act in accordance with his or her religious beliefs or practices, as they have lost all religious significance. Though an individual could still publicly profess a specific belief, or act out a given ritual, it would hold no religious significance for him or her.

[125] The same holds true of a person's ability to pass on beliefs and practices to future generations. This Court has recognized that the ability of a religious community's members to pass on their beliefs to their children is an essential aspect of religious freedom protected under s. 2 (a) (*Loyola*, at paras. 64 and 67). Where state action has rendered a certain belief or practice devoid of spiritual significance, this interferes with one's ability to pass on that tradition to future generations, as there would be no reason to continue a tradition that lacks spiritual significance.

[126] Therefore, where the spiritual significance of beliefs or practices has been taken away by state action, this interferes with an individual's ability to act in accordance with his or her religious beliefs or practices—whether by professing a belief, engaging in a ritual, or passing traditions on to future generations.

[127] This kind of state interference is a reality where individuals find spiritual fulfillment through their connection to the physical world. The connection to the physical world, specifically to land, is a central feature of Indigenous religions. Indeed, as M.L. Ross explains, "First Nations spirituality and religion are *rooted in the land*" (*First Nations Sacred Sites in Canada's Courts* (2005), at p. 3 [emphasis added]). In many Indigenous religions, land is not only the site of spiritual practices in the sense that a church, mosque or holy site might be; land may itself be sacred, in the sense that it is where the divine manifests itself. Unlike in Judeo-Christian faiths for example, where the divine is considered to be supernatural, the spiritual realm in the Indigenous context is inextri-

cably linked to the physical world. For Indigenous religions, state action that impacts land can therefore sever the connection to the divine, rendering beliefs and practices devoid of their spiritual significance. Where state action has this effect on an Indigenous religion, it interferes with a believer's ability to act in accordance with his or her religious beliefs and practices.

[128] Taking this feature of Indigenous religions into account is therefore critical in assessing whether there has been a s. 2 (a) infringement. The principle of state neutrality requires that the state not favour or hinder one religion over the other (see *S.L. v. Commission scolaire des Chênes*, 2012 SCC 7, [2012] 1 S.C.R. 235, at para. 32; *Mouvement laïque québécois v. Saguenay [City]*, 2015 SCC 16, [2015] 2 S.C.R. 3, at para. 72). To ensure that all religions are afforded the same level of protection under s. 2 (a), courts must be alive to the unique characteristics of each religion, and the distinct ways in which state action may interfere with that religion's beliefs or practices.

The Chief Justice and Rowe J.'s Position on the Scope of Section 2 (a)

[129] The Chief Justice and Rowe J. take a different approach. They maintain that the Charter protects the "freedom to worship," but not what they call the "spiritual focal point of worship" (para. 71). If I understand my colleagues' approach correctly, s. 2 (a) of the Charter protects only the freedom to hold beliefs and manifest them through worship and practice (para. 71). In their view, even where the effect of state action is to render beliefs and practices devoid of all spiritual significance, claimants still have the freedom to hold beliefs and manifest those beliefs through practices, and there is therefore no interference with their ability to act in accordance with their beliefs. Thus, under my colleagues' approach, as long as a Sikh student can carry a kirpan into a school (*Multani*), Orthodox Jews can erect a personal succah (*Amselem*), or the Ktunaxa have the ability to conduct ceremonies and rituals, there is no infringement of s. 2 (a), even where the effect of state action is to reduce these acts to empty gestures.

[130] I cannot accept such a restrictive reading of s. 2 (a). As I have indicated, where a belief or practice is rendered devoid of spiritual significance, there is obviously an interference with the ability to act in accordance with that religious belief or practice. The scope of s. 2 (a) is therefore not limited to the freedom to hold a belief and manifest that belief through religious practices. Rather, as this Court noted in *Amselem*, "[i]t is the religious or spiritual essence of an action" that attracts protection under s. 2 (a) (para. 47). In my view, the approach adopted by my colleagues does not engage with this crucial point. It does not take into account that if a belief or practice becomes devoid of spiritual significance, it is highly unlikely that a person would continue to hold those beliefs or engage in those practices. Indeed, that person would have no reason to do so. With respect, my colleagues' approach amounts to protecting empty gestures and hollow rituals, rather than guarding against state conduct that interferes with "profoundly personal beliefs," the true purpose of s. 2 (a)'s protection (*Edwards Books*, at p. 759).

[131] This approach also risks excluding Indigenous religious freedom claims involving land from the scope of s. 2 (a) protection. As indicated, there is an inextricable link between spirituality and land in Indigenous religious traditions. In this context, state action that impacts land can sever the spiritual connection to the divine, rendering Indigenous beliefs and practices devoid of their spiritual significance. My colleagues have not taken this unique and central feature of Indigenous religion into account. Their approach therefore risks foreclosing the protections of s. 2 (a) of the Charter to substantial elements of Indigenous religious traditions.

[Eds. note: while Justice Moldaver held that there was an infringement of s. 2 (a) of the Charter, he concluded that it was nonetheless justifiable.]

RELATED CASES

Calder v. B.C. (A.G.) [1973] S.C.R. 313
(In this historic case the Supreme Court of Canada held that Aboriginal title to land in Canada derived from ancestral occupation and possession, and not from the *Royal Proclamation of 1763* or any other legislative enactment or executive order.)

Guerin v. The Queen [1984] 2 S.C.R. 335
(This case established that Aboriginal rights are only alienable to the Crown and that the Crown is under a fiduciary obligation towards Aboriginal peoples.)

R. v. Van der Peet [1996] 2 S.C.R. 507
(In this case the Supreme Court of Canada set out a general test for identifying Aboriginal rights.)

Delgamuukw v. B.C. [1997] 3 S.C.R. 1010
(In this key case the Supreme Court of Canada describes the scope of protection for Aboriginal title under section 35(1) of the *Constitution Act, 1982.*)

Haida Nation v. British Columbia (Minister of Forests) [2004] 3 S.C.R. 511
(This case establishes a recognized duty to consult with Aboriginal peoples on the part of the Crown where any government action may have an impact on Aboriginal land claims.)

PART VIII

International Cases

It may seem surprising that at textbook focused on Canadian issues includes examination of international cases. The reason for this additional focus is simple: as the processes of globalization result in increased interaction between states and their citizens, the role of law in guiding these interactions and resolving disputes has also increased in importance. Several questions arise in this context of increased inter-action: what are the sources of international law, and who is bound in what ways by that law? And how should we understand the relation between state law and international law? Are there inherent limits to the claims of either?

The Part begins with attention to the nature of international law and its principal actors. The *Lotus* case was decided by the Perma-nent Court of International Justice, the judicial arm of the League of Nations in the period between World War I (1914–18) and World War II (1939–45). In this decision the Court gave voice to a principle still used today—the *Lotus* principle that states are sovereign within their own borders and are bound only by international laws to which they agree. This principle has often been interpreted as having more weight in international law than it actually does. States have long recognized their interdependence and the value of limits to state sovereignty for the sake of global security. A considerable portion of international law involves agreements between states to permit mutually advantageous interactions to occur in ways which decrease the liberty of each state. Many such agreements are instances of "transboundary law" agreed between pairs and groups of states, offering other states examples of laws enabling peaceful achievement of shared goals and resolution of disputes. This layer of transboundary law stands apart from state law, and when taken together with the rise of various global institutions such as the International Criminal Court and the European Court of Human Rights, may be establishing the foundation of global law reaching far more deeply into citizens' lives than the state-to-state agreements of historic international law. The *Trail Smelter Arbitration* case excerpted here shows the growth of transboundary law as a means to resolving disputes where each side seeks a viable way of continuing to live alongside the other. The possibility of global law is explored in various ways in the International Court of Justice Advisory Opinion on the *Legality of the Threat or Use of Nuclear Weapons*, excerpted here. The Court searches the body of international law to determine whether nuclear weapons are prohibited or permitted under international law, and as it does so, has an opportunity to assess and state the fundamental interests and rights of states under international law. The right to self-defence for the sake of survival is often conceived as arising in the contexts of threats from forces outside the state. Yet sometimes the question as to the limits of state action to preserve itself arise in quite different contexts, familiar from history, where one part of a state wishes to separate from the other to create two separate states. The International Court of Justice was asked recently to offer an advisory opinion regarding the way Kosovo declared independence and separated from Serbia. In *Accordance with International Law of the Unilateral Declaration of Independence in Respect of Kosovo*, excerpted here, the Court reflects on the way new states may arise in a world already filled with the claims of state law, transboundary law, and global law.

Trail Smelter Arbitration (United States v. Canada)
United Nations, Reports of International Arbitral Awards
[1941] Volume III, 1905

This case concerns an instance of transboundary air pollution caused by activities in Canada with serious negative environmental, economic, and social effects occurring in the United States. A special Tribunal was created "to reach a solution just to all parties concerned." The Tribunal established the principle that states are responsible for actions occurring on their territory causing injury in another state's territory, justified by the Tribunal's advancing to the international level a principle familiar from state law: the principle that the "polluter pays." The case is important in the development of both transboundary law and environmental law, widely regarded as a key clarification of states' obligations in transboundary law. It is equally important as a demonstration of the capacity of specialized tribunals to resolve disputes between states.

This Tribunal is constituted under, and its powers are derived from and limited by, the Convention between the United States of America and the Dominion of Canada signed at Ottawa, April, 15, 1935, duly ratified by the two parties, and ratifications exchanged at Ottawa, August 3, 1935 (hereinafter termed "the Convention"). [...]

The controversy is between two Governments involving damage occurring, or having occurred, in the territory of one of them (the United States of America) and alleged to be due to an agency situated in the territory of the other (the Dominion of Canada). In this controversy, the Tribunal did not sit and is not sitting to pass upon claims presented by individuals or on behalf of one or more individuals by their Government, although individuals may come within the meaning of "parties concerned," in Article IV and of "interested parties," in Article VIII of the Convention and although the damage suffered by individuals did, in part, "afford a convenient scale for the calculation of the reparation due to the State" (see Judgment No. 13, Permanent Court of International Justice, Series A, No. 17, pp. 27, 28). (*Cf.* what was said by the Tribunal in the decision reported on April 16, 1938, as regards the problems arising out of abandonment of properties, Part Two, Clause (1).)

As between the two countries involved, each has an equal interest that if a nuisance is proved, the indemnity to damaged parties for proven damage shall be just and adequate and each has also an equal interest that unproven or unwarranted claims shall not be allowed. For, while the United States' interests may now be claimed to be injured by the operations of a Canadian corporation, it is equally possible that at some time in the future Canadian interests might be claimed to be injured by an American corporation. As has well been said: "It would not be to the advantage of the two countries concerned that industrial effort should be prevented by exaggerating the interests of the agricultural community. Equally, it would not be to the advantage of the two countries that the agricultural community should be oppressed to advance the interest of industry."

Considerations like the above are reflected in the provisions of the Convention in Article IV, that "the desire of the high contracting parties" is "to reach a solution just to all parties concerned." And the phraseology of the questions submitted to the Tribunal clearly evinces a desire and an intention that, to some extent, in making its answers to the questions, the Tribunal should endeavor to adjust the conflicting interests by some "just solution" which would allow the continuance of the operation of the Trail Smelter but under such restrictions and limitations as would, as far as foreseeable, prevent damage in the United States, and as would enable indemnity to be obtained, if in spite of such restrictions and limitations, damage should occur in the future in the United States.

In arriving at its decision, the Tribunal has had always to bear in mind the further fact that in the preamble to the Convention, it is stated that it is concluded with the recognition of "the desirability and necessity of effecting a permanent settlement."

The duty imposed upon the Tribunal by the Convention was to "finally decide" the following questions:

(1) Whether damage caused by the Trail Smelter in the State of Washington has occurred since the first day of January, 1932, and, if so, what indemnity should be paid therefor?

(2) In the event of the answer to the first part of the preceding question being in the affirmative, whether the Trail Smelter should be required to refrain from causing damage in the State of Washington in the future and, if so, to what extent?

(3) In the light of the answer to the preceding question, what measures or régime, if any, should be adopted or maintained by the Trail Smelter?

(4) What indemnity or compensation, if any, should be paid on account of any decision or decisions rendered by the Tribunal pursuant to the next two preceding questions?

[...]

After long consideration of the voluminous typewritten and printed record and of the transcript of evidence presented at the hearings, the Tribunal formally notified the Agents of two the Governments that, in its opinion, unless the time limit should be extended, the Tribunal would be forced to give a permanent decision on April 2, 1938, on the basis of data which it considered inadequate and unsatisfactory. Acting on the recommendation of the Tribunal and under the provisions of Article XI authorizing such extension, the two Governments by agreement extended the time for the report of final decision of the Tribunal to three months from October 1, 1940.

On April 16, 1938, the Tribunal reported its "final decision" on Question No. 1, as well as its temporary decisions on Questions No. 2 and No. 3, and provided for a temporary régime thereunder. The decision reported on April 16, 1938, will be referred to hereinafter as the "previous decision."

Concerning Question No. 1, in the statement presented by the Agent for the Government of the United States, claims for damages of $1,849,156.16 with interest of 5,250,855.01—total $2,100,011.17—were presented, divided into seven categories, in respect of (a) cleared land and improvements; (b) of uncleared land and improvements; (c) live stock; (d) property in the town of Northport; (e) wrong done the United States in violation of sovereignty, measured by cost of investigation from January 1, 1932, to June 30, 1936; (f) interest on $350,000 accepted in satisfaction of damage to January 1, 1932, but not paid on that date; (g) business enterprises. The area claimed to be damaged contained "more than 140,000 acres," including the town of Northport.

The Tribunal disallowed the claims of the United States with reference to items (c), (d), (e), (f) and (g) but allowed them, in part, with respect to the remaining items (a) and (b).

In conclusion (end of Part Two of the previous decision), the Tribunal answered Question No. 1 as follows:

Damage caused by the Trail Smelter in the State of Washington has occurred since the first day of January, 1932, and up to October 1, 1937, and the indemnity to be paid therefor is seventy-eight thousand dollars ($78,000), and is to be complete and final indemnity and compensation for all damage which occurred between such dates. Interest at the rate of six per centum per year will be allowed on the above sum of seventy-eight thousand dollars ($78,000) from the date of the filing of this report and decision until date of payment. This decision is not subject to alteration or modification by the Tribunal hereafter. The fact of existence of damage, if any, occurring after October 1, 1937, and the indemnity to be paid therefor, if any, the Tribunal will determine in its final decision.

Answering Questions No. 2 and No. 3, the Tribunal decided that, until a final decision should be made, the Trail Smelter should be subject to a temporary régime (described more in detail in Part Four of the present decision) and a trial period was established to a date not later than October 1, 1940, in order to enable the Tribunal to establish a permanent régime based on a "more adequate and intensive study," since the Tribunal felt that the information that had been placed before it did not enable it to determine at that time with sufficient certainty upon a permanent régime. [...]

The period within which the Tribunal shall report its final decisions was extended by agreement of the two Governments until March 12, 1941. [...]

The first question under Article III of the Convention is: "(1) Whether damage caused by the Trail Smelter in the State of Washington has occurred since the first day of January, 1932, and, if so, what indemnity should be paid therefor."

This question has been answered by the Tribunal in its previous decision, as to the period from January 1, 1932 to October 1, 1937, as set forth above. [...]

The second question under Article III of the Convention is as follows:

In the event of the answer to the first part of the preceding question being in the affirmative, whether the Trail Smelter should be required to refrain from causing damage in the State of Washington in the future and, if so, to what extent? [...]

Particularly in reaching its conclusions as regards this question as well as the next, the Tribunal has given consideration to the desire of the high contracting parties "to reach a solution just to all parties concerned."

As Professor Eagleton puts in (*Responsibility of States in International Law*, 1928, p. 80):

"A State owes at all times a duty to protect other States against injurious acts by individuals from within its jurisdiction." A great number of such general pronouncements by leading authorities concerning the duty of a State to respect other States and their territory have been presented to the Tribunal. These and many others have been carefully examined. International decisions, in various matters, from the Alabama case onward, and also earlier ones, are based on the same general principle, and, indeed, this principle, as such, has not been questioned by Canada. But the real difficulty often arises rather when it comes to determine what, *pro subjecta materie*, is deemed to constitute an injurious act.

A case concerning, as the present one does, territorial relations, decided by the Federal Court of Switzerland between the Cantons of Soleure and Argovia, may serve to illustrate the relativity of the rule. Soleure brought a suit against her sister State to enjoin use of a shooting establishment which endangered her territory. The court, in granting the injunction, said: "This right (sovereignty) excludes.... not only the usurpation and exercise of sovereign rights (of another State).... but also an actual encroachment which might prejudice the natural use of the territory and the free movement of its inhabitants." As a result of the decision, Argovia made plans for the improvement of the existing installations. These, however, were considered as insufficient protection by Soleure. The Canton of Argovia then moved the Federal Court to decree that the shooting be again permitted after completion of the projected improvements. This motion was granted. "The demand of the Government of Soleure," said the court, "that all endangerment be absolutely abolished apparently goes too far." The court found that all risk whatever had not been eliminated, as the region was flat and absolutely safe shooting ranges were only found in mountain valleys; that there was a federal duty for the communes to provide facilities for military target practice and that "no more precautions may be demanded for shooting ranges near the boundaries of two Cantons than are required for shooting ranges in the interior of a Canton."

No case of air pollution dealt with by an international tribunal has been brought to the attention of the Tribunal nor does the Tribunal know of any such case. The nearest analogy is that of water pollution. But, here also, no decision of an international tribunal has been cited or has been found.

There are, however, as regards both air pollution and water pollution, certain decisions of the Supreme Court of the United States which may legitimately be taken as a guide in this field of international law, for it is reasonable to follow by analogy, in international cases, precedents established by that court in dealing with controversies between States of the Union or with other controversies concerning the quasi-sovereign rights of such States, where no contrary rule prevails in international law and no reason for rejecting such precedents can be adduced from the limitations of sovereignty inherent in the Constitution of the United States.

In the suit of the State of Missouri v. the State of Illinois (200 U.S. 496, 521) concerning the pollution, within the boundaries of Illinois, of the Illinois River, an affluent of the Mississippi flowing into the latter where it forms the boundary between that State and Missouri, an injunction was refused. "Before this court ought to intervene," said the court, "the case should be of serious magnitude, clearly and fully proved, and the principle to be applied should be one which the court is prepared deliberately to maintain against all considerations on the other side. (See Kansas v. Colorado, 185 U.S. 125.)" The court found that the practice complained of was general along the shores of the Mississippi River at that time, that it was followed by Missouri itself and that thus a standard was set up by the defendant which the claimant was entitled to invoke.

As the claims of public health became more exacting and methods for removing impurities from the water were perfected, complaints ceased. It is significant that Missouri sided with Illinois when the other riparians of the Great Lakes' system sought to enjoin it to desist from diverting the waters of that system into that of the Illinois and Mississippi for the very purpose of disposing of the Chicago sewage.

In the more recent suit of the State of New York against the State of New Jersey (256 U.S. 296, 309), concerning the pollution of New York Bay, the injunction was also refused for lack of proof, some experts believing that the plans which were in dispute would result in the presence of "offensive odors and unsightly deposits," other equally reliable experts testifying that they were confidently of the opinion that the waters would be sufficiently purified. The court, referring to Missouri v. Illinois, said: "...the burden upon the State of New York of sustaining the allegations of its bill is much greater than that imposed upon a complainant in an ordinary suit between private parties. Before this court can be moved to exercise its extraordinary power under the Constitution to control the conduct of one State at the suit of another, the threatened invasion of rights must be of serious magnitude and it must be established by clear and convincing evidence."

What the Supreme Court says there of its power under the Constitution equally applies to the extraordinary power granted this Tribunal under the Convention. What is true between States of the Union is, at least, equally true concerning the relations between the United States and the Dominion of Canada.

In another recent case concerning water pollution (283 U.S. 473), the complainant was successful. The City of New York was enjoined, at the request of the State of New Jersey, to desist, within a reasonable time limit, from the practice of disposing of sewage by dumping it into the sea, a practice which was injurious to the coastal waters of New Jersey in the vicinity of her bathing resorts.

In the matter of air pollution itself, the leading decisions are those of the Supreme Court in the State of Georgia *v.* Tennessee Copper Company and Ducktown Sulphur, Copper and Iron Company, Limited. Although dealing with a suit against private companies, the decisions were on questions cognate to those here at issue. Georgia stated that it had in vain sought relief from the State of Tennessee, on whose territory the smelters were located, and the court defined the nature of the suit by saying: "This is a suit by a State for an injury to it in its capacity of quasi-sovereign. In that capacity, the State has an interest independent of and behind the titles of its citizens, in all the earth and air within its domain."

On the question whether an injunction should be granted or not, the court said (206 U.S. 230):

> It (the State) has the last word as to whether its mountains shall be stripped of their forests and its inhabitants shall breathe pure air.... It is not lightly to be presumed to give up quasi-sovereign rights for pay and.... if that be its choice, it may insist that an infraction of them shall be stopped. This court has not quite the same freedom to balance the harm that will be done by an injunction against that of which the plaintiff complains, that it would have in deciding between two subjects of a single political power. Without excluding the considerations that equity always takes into account.... it is a fair and reasonable demand on the part of a sovereign that the air over its territory should not be polluted on a great scale by sulphurous acid gas, that the forests on its mountains, be they better or worse, and whatever domestic destruction they may have suffered, should not be further destroyed or threatened by the act of persons beyond its control, that the crops and orchards on its hills should not be endangered from the same source.... Whether Georgia, by insisting upon this claim, is doing more harm than good to her own citizens, is for her to determine. The possible disaster to those outside

the State must be accepted as a consequence of her standing upon her extreme rights.

Later on, however, when the court actually framed an injunction, in the case of the Ducktown Company (237 U.S. 474, 477) (an agreement on the basis of an annual compensation was reached with the most important of the two smelters, the Tennessee Copper Company), they did not go beyond a decree "adequate to diminish materially the present probability of damage to its (Georgia's) citizens."

Great progress in the control of fumes has been made by science in the last few years and this progress should be taken into account.

[...] The Tribunal, therefore, finds that the above decisions, taken as a whole, constitute an adequate basis for its conclusions, namely, that, under the principles of international law, as well as of the law of the United States, no State has the right to use or permit the use of its territory in such a manner as to cause injury by fumes in or to the territory of another or the properties or persons therein, when the case is of serious consequence and the injury is established by clear and convincing evidence.

The decisions of the Supreme Court of the United States which are the basis of these conclusions are decisions in equity and a solution inspired by them, together with the régime hereinafter prescribed, will, in the opinion of the Tribunal, be "just to all parties concerned," as long, at least, as the present conditions in the Columbia River Valley continue to prevail.

Considering the circumstances of the case, the Tribunal holds that the Dominion of Canada is responsible in international law for the conduct of the Trail Smelter. Apart from the undertakings in the Convention, it is, therefore, the duty of the Government of the Dominion of Canada to see to it that this conduct should be in conformity with the obligation of the Dominion under international law as herein determined.

The Tribunal, therefore, answers Question No. 2 as follows: (2) So long as the present conditions in the Columbia River Valley prevail, the Trail Smelter shall be required to refrain from causing any damage through fumes in the State of Washington; the damage herein referred to and its extent being such as would be recoverable under the decisions of the courts of the United States in suits between private individuals. The indemnity for such damage should be fixed in such manner as the Governments, acting under Article XI of the Convention, should agree upon.

SS Lotus (France v. Turkey)
Permanent Court of International Justice
[1927] (Ser. A) No. 10 (Sept 7)

The *Lotus* case is famous for its having expressed the "Lotus principle," which holds that the only international law is that law to which states have agreed. The circumstances in which the principle is articulated are of much less interest than the principle itself. The facts of the case are concerned with a collision at sea between a French vessel and a Turkish vessel, and Turkey's subsequent claim to jurisdiction to investigate and find fault. The issue taken by France and Turkey to the Permanent Court of International Justice was not whether the French officers or the Turkish officers were at fault, but whether under international law Turkey could claim jurisdiction over such a matter. In seeking to distinguish binding international law from various other possible sources of guidance, such as historic practice or general requirements of justice, the Court identified as a principle of international law the idea that all international law is a product of the choices of states. This "Lotus principle" is in tension with recognition of customary international law as a primary source of international law, especially when history and present practice show that new states are largely presumed to be bound by customary law even without any formal acts of acceptance of that law. Since assertion of the existence of the principle, the growth of various areas of international law have given at least the appearance of an international legal system whose binding force is an undeniable fact. Yet at the same time, the Lotus principle is still invoked from time to time by states asserting autonomous status as the fundamental actors in international law, and state sovereignty as a fundamental norm of international affairs.

––––––––––––

The Court:

Fundamental Principles of International Law

[44] International law governs relations between independent States. The rules of law binding upon States therefore emanate from their own free will as expressed in conventions or by usages generally accepted as expressing principles of law and established in order to regulate the relations between these

co-existing independent communities or with a view to the achievement of
common aims. Restrictions upon the independence of States cannot therefore
be presumed.

[45] Now the first and foremost restriction imposed by international law
upon a State is that—failing the existence of a permissive rule to the contrary—
it may not exercise its power in any form in the territory of another State. In
this sense jurisdiction is certainly territorial; it cannot be exercised by a State
outside its territory except by virtue of a permissive rule derived from international custom or from a convention.

[46] It does not, however, follow that international law prohibits a State
from exercising jurisdiction in its own territory, in respect of any case which
relates to acts which have taken place abroad, and in which it cannot rely on
some permissive rule of international law. Such a view would only be tenable if
international law contained a general prohibition to States to extend the application of their laws and the jurisdiction of their courts to persons, property and
acts outside their territory, and if, as an exception to this general prohibition,
it allowed States to do so in certain specific cases. But this is certainly not the
case under international law as it stands at present. Far from laying down a
general prohibition to the effect that States may not extend the application of
their laws and the jurisdiction of their courts to persons, property and acts
outside their territory, it leaves them in this respect a wide measure of discretion, which is only limited in certain cases by prohibitive rules; as regards other
cases, every State remains free to adopt the principles which it regards as best
and most suitable.

[47] This discretion left to States by international law explains the great
variety of rules which they have been able to adopt without objections or
complaints on the part of other States; it is in order to remedy the difficulties
resulting from such variety that efforts have been made for many years past,
both in Europe and America, to prepare conventions the effect of which would
be precisely to limit the discretion at present left to States in this respect by
international law, thus making good the existing lacunæ in respect of jurisdiction or removing the conflicting jurisdictions arising from the diversity
of the principles adopted by the various States. In these circumstances all
that can be required of a State is that it should not overstep the limits which
international law places upon its jurisdiction; within these limits, its title to
exercise jurisdiction rests in its sovereignty.

[48] It follows from the foregoing that the contention of the French Government to the effect that Turkey must in each case be able to cite a rule of international law authorizing her to exercise jurisdiction, is opposed to the generally
accepted international law to which Article 13 of the Convention of Lausanne
refers. Having regard to the terms of Article 15 and to the construction which
the Court has just placed upon it, this contention would apply in regard to civil
as well as to criminal cases, and would be applicable on conditions of absolute
reciprocity as between Turkey and the other contracting Parties; in practice,

it would therefore in many cases result in paralysing the action of the courts, owing to the impossibility of citing a universally accepted rule on which to support the exercise of their jurisdiction.

Legality of the Threat or Use of Nuclear Weapons, Advisory Opinion
International Court of Justice
[1996] General List No. 95 (8 July)

In this excerpt, the International Court of Justice considers a matter referred to it by the General Assembly of the United Nations in a process very similar to that seen in reference cases in Canada. The Court is asked to determine whether under international law the threat or use of nuclear weapons is permitted. In portions of the case not included here, the Court deliberates on the question of whether it has jurisdiction to answer the question, and having answered that it does, it proceeds to identify elements of international law bearing on the question. The Court finds that international humanitarian law addressing human rights is certainly relevant, as is the law of conflict, yet neither provide a clear basis for an answer to the question. The Court finds that there is an obligation to support non-proliferation of nuclear weapons, but stops short of any more forceful conclusion. There is insufficient legal basis for a finding of a permission or prohibition of the use of nuclear weapons, the Court concludes, and the right of states to self-defence means there is a weighty legal consideration in favour of permitting use of nuclear weapons in some manner proportionate to a threat to the state's continued existence, even if that requirement seems difficult to achieve in practice. Here we see that even while there are limits to the force of the Lotus principle and characterization of international law as the product of absolutely sovereign states, where questions arise as to limitations of states by international law, the presumption that states are the main subjects and agents of international law remains central to deliberations regarding the requirements of international law.

On the legality of the threat or use of nuclear weapons, THE COURT...*gives the following Advisory Opinion*:

[1] The question upon which the advisory opinion of the Court has been requested is set forth in resolution 49/75 K adopted by the General Assembly of the United Nations (hereinafter called the "General Assembly") on 15 December 1994.... Resolution 49/75 K [...]:

[The General Assembly] Decides, pursuant to Article 96, paragraph 1, of the Charter of the United Nations, to request the International Court of Justice urgently to render its advisory opinion on the following question: "Is the threat or use of nuclear weapons in any circumstance permitted under international law?"

[...]

[90] Although the applicability of the principles and rules of humanitarian law and of the principle of neutrality to nuclear weapons is hardly disputed, the conclusions to be drawn from this applicability are, on the other hand, controversial.

[91] According to one point of view, the fact that recourse to nuclear weapons is subject to and regulated by the law of armed conflict does not necessarily mean that such recourse is as such prohibited. As one State put it to the Court:

> Assuming that a State's use of nuclear weapons meets the requirements of self defence, it must then be considered whether it conforms to the fundamental principles of the law of armed conflict regulating the conduct of hostilities (United Kingdom, Written Statement, p. 40, para. 3.44);
>
> The legality of the use of nuclear weapons must therefore be assessed in the light of the applicable principles of international law regarding the use of force and the conduct of hostilities, as is the case with other methods and means of warfare (United Kingdom, Written Statement, p. 75, para. 4.2(3)); and
>
> The reality...is that nuclear weapons might be used in a wide variety of circumstances with very different results in terms of likely civilian casualties. In some cases, such as the use of a low yield nuclear weapon against warships on the High Seas or troops in sparsely populated areas, it is possible to envisage a nuclear attack which caused comparatively few civilian casualties. It is by no means the case that every use of nuclear weapons against a military objective would inevitably cause very great collateral civilian casualties. (United Kingdom, Written Statement, p. 53, para. 3.70; see also United States of America, Oral Statement, CR 95/34, pp. 89–90.)

[92] Another view holds that recourse to nuclear weapons could never be compatible with the principles and rules of humanitarian law and is therefore prohibited. In the event of their use, nuclear weapons would in all circumstances be unable to draw any distinction between the civilian population and combatants, or between civilian objects and military objectives, and their effects, largely uncontrollable, could not be restricted, either in time or in space, to lawful military targets. Such weapons would kill and destroy in a necessarily indiscriminate manner, on account of the blast, heat and radiation occasioned by the nuclear explosion and the effects induced; and the number of casualties which would ensue would be enormous. The use of nuclear weapons would

therefore be prohibited in any circumstance, notwithstanding the absence of any explicit conventional prohibition. That view lay at the basis of the assertions by certain States before the Court that nuclear weapons are by their nature illegal under customary international law, by virtue of the fundamental principle of humanity.

[93] A similar view has been expressed with respect to the effects of the principle of neutrality. Like the principles and rules of humanitarian law, that principle has therefore been considered by some to rule out the use of a weapon the effects of which simply cannot be contained within the territories of the contending States.

[94] The Court would observe that none of the States advocating the legality of the use of nuclear weapons under certain circumstances, including the "clean" use of smaller, low yield, tactical nuclear weapons, has indicated what, supposing such limited use were feasible, would be the precise circumstances justifying such use; nor whether such limited use would not tend to escalate into the all-out use of high yield nuclear weapons. This being so, the Court does not consider that it has a sufficient basis for a determination on the validity of this view.

[95] Nor can the Court make a determination on the validity of the view that the recourse to nuclear weapons would be illegal in any circumstance owing to their inherent and total incompatibility with the law applicable in armed conflict. Certainly, as the Court has already indicated, the principles and rules of law applicable in armed conflict, at the heart of which is the overriding consideration of humanity, make the conduct of armed hostilities subject to a number of strict requirements. Thus, methods and means of warfare, which would preclude any distinction between civilian and military targets, or which would result in unnecessary suffering to combatants, are prohibited. In view of the unique characteristics of nuclear weapons, to which the Court has referred above, the use of such weapons in fact seems scarcely reconcilable with respect for such requirements. Nevertheless, the Court considers that it does not have sufficient elements to enable it to conclude with certainty that the use of nuclear weapons would necessarily be at variance with the principles and rules of law applicable in armed conflict in any circumstance.

[96] Furthermore, the Court cannot lose sight of the fundamental right of every State to survival, and thus its right to resort to self-defence, in accordance with Article 51 of the Charter, when its survival is at stake.

Nor can it ignore the practice referred to as "policy of deterrence," to which an appreciable section of the international community adhered for many years. The Court also notes the reservations which certain nuclear-weapon States have appended to the undertakings they have given, notably under the Protocols to the Treaties of Tlatelolco and Rarotonga, and also under the declarations made by them in connection with the extension of the Treaty on the Non-Proliferation of Nuclear Weapons, not to resort to such weapons.

[97] Accordingly, in view of the present state of international law viewed as a whole, as examined above by the Court, and of the elements of fact at its disposal,

the Court is led to observe that it cannot reach a definitive conclusion as to the legality or illegality of the use of nuclear weapons by a State in an extreme circumstance of self-defence, in which its very survival would be at stake.

[...]

[105] For these reasons, THE COURT... [r]eplies in the following manner to the question put by the General Assembly... By seven votes to seven [...]:

> It follows from the above-mentioned requirements that the threat or use of nuclear weapons would generally be contrary to the rules of international law applicable in armed conflict, and in particular the principles and rules of humanitarian law;
>
> However, in view of the current state of international law, and of the elements of fact at its disposal, the Court cannot conclude definitively whether the threat or use of nuclear weapons would be lawful or unlawful in an extreme circumstance of self-defence, in which the very survival of a State would be at stake. [...]

Accordance with International Law of the Unilateral Declaration of
Independence in Respect of Kosovo, Advisory Opinion
International Court of Justice
[2010] I.C.J. Reports, p. 403

In 1999 the Security Council of the United Nations intervened in
Serbia and created by Resolution 1244 an interim administration
in the province of Kosovo, known as the United Nations Interim
Administration Mission in Kosovo (UNMIK). Under UNMIK,
a Constitutional Framework for Provisional Self-Government
was created to regulate the role of the United Nations in Kosovo
and to facilitate consultation between Kosovo and Serbia regarding the status of Kosovo. In 2008, representatives of the Kosovo
people unilaterally declared independence from Serbia. In 2010,
the General Assembly of the United Nations requested an advisory opinion from the International Court of Justice on the following question: "Is the unilateral declaration of independence
by the Provisional Institutions of Self-Government of Kosovo in
accordance with international law?"

While international law has historically been restricted to the
relations between sovereign states, beginning in the mid-twen-
tieth century its scope expanded to include individual human
rights and the rights of peoples. Among the issues raised in this
advisory opinion are the grounds for self-determination of peoples within sovereign states, and how such self-determination,
under international law, may compete with and so limit the territorial integrity of states.

The Court (by 10 votes to 4) concluded that the unilateral
declaration of independence by the Kosovo people did not violate
either general international law or the special international law
created by Security Council Resolution 1244 or the Constitutional Framework created by UNMIK.

The Court:

General International Law

[79] During the eighteenth, nineteenth and early twentieth centuries, there
were numerous instances of declarations of independence, often strenuously
opposed by the State from which independence was being declared. Sometimes
a declaration resulted in the creation of a new State, at others it did not. In no

case, however, does the practice of States as a whole suggest that the act of promulgating the declaration was regarded as contrary to international law. On the contrary, State practice during this period points clearly to the conclusion that international law contained no prohibition of declarations of independence. During the second half of the twentieth century, the international law of self-determination developed in such a way as to create a right to independence for the peoples of non-self-governing territories and peoples subject to alien subjugation, domination and exploitation. [...] A great many new States have come into existence as a result of the exercise of this right. There were, however, also instances of declarations of independence outside this context. The practice of States in these latter cases does not point to the emergence in international law of a new rule prohibiting the making of a declaration of independence in such cases.

[80] Several participants in the proceedings before the Court have contended that a prohibition of unilateral declarations of independence is implicit in the principle of territorial integrity.

The Court recalls that the principle of territorial integrity is an important part of the international legal order and is enshrined in the Charter of the United Nations, in particular in Article 2, paragraph 4, which provides that:

> All Members shall refrain in their international relations from the threat or use of force against the territorial integrity or political independence of any State, or in any other manner inconsistent with the Purposes of the United Nations.

In General Assembly resolution 2625 (XXV), entitled "Declaration on Principles of International Law concerning Friendly Relations and Co-operation among States in Accordance with the Charter of the United Nations," which reflects customary international law (*Military and Paramilitary Activities in and against Nicaragua (Nicaragua v. United States of America), Merits, Judgment, I.C.J. Reports 1986*, pp. 101–03, paras. 191–93), the General Assembly reiterated "[t]he principle that States shall refrain in their international relations from the threat or use of force against the territorial integrity or political independence of any State." This resolution then enumerated various obligations incumbent upon States to refrain from violating the territorial integrity of other sovereign States. In the same vein, the Final Act of the Helsinki Conference on Security and Co-operation in Europe of 1 August 1975 (the Helsinki Conference) stipulated that "[t]he participating States will respect the territorial integrity of each of the participating States" (Art. IV). Thus, the scope of the principle of territorial integrity is confined to the sphere of relations between States.

[81] Several participants have invoked resolutions of the Security Council condemning particular declarations of independence: see, *inter alia*, Security Council resolutions 216 (1965) and 217 (1965), concerning Southern Rhodesia; Security Council resolution 541 (1983), concerning northern Cyprus; and Security Council resolution 787 (1992), concerning the Republika Srpska.

The Court notes, however, that in all of those instances the Security Council was making a determination as regards the concrete situation existing at the time that those declarations of independence were made; the illegality attached to the declarations of independence thus stemmed not from the unilateral character of these declarations as such, but from the fact that they were, or would have been, connected with the unlawful use of force or other egregious violations of norms of general international law, in particular those of a peremptory character (*jus cogens*). In the context of Kosovo, the Security Council has never taken this position. The exceptional character of the resolutions enumerated above appears to the Court to confirm that no general prohibition against unilateral declarations of independence may be inferred from the practice of the Security Council. [...]

Interpretation of Security Council Resolution 1244 (1999)

[...]

[97] First, resolution 1244 (1999) establishes an international civil and security presence in Kosovo with full civil and political authority and sole responsibility for the governance of Kosovo. As described above (see paragraph 60), on 12 June 1999, the Secretary-General presented to the Security Council his preliminary operational concept for the overall organization of the civil presence under UNMIK. On 25 July 1999, the Special Representative of the Secretary-General promulgated UNMIK regulation 1999/1, deemed to have entered into force as of 10 June 1999, the date of adoption of Security Council resolution 1244 (1999). Under this regulation, "[a]ll legislative and executive authority with respect to Kosovo, including the administration of the judiciary," was vested in UNMIK and exercised by the Special Representative. Viewed together, resolution 1244 (1999) and UNMIK regulation 1999/1 therefore had the effect of superseding the legal order in force at that time in the territory of Kosovo and setting up an international territorial administration. For this reason, the establishment of civil and security presences in Kosovo deployed on the basis of resolution 1244 (1999) must be understood as an exceptional measure relating to civil, political and security aspects and aimed at addressing the crisis existing in that territory in 1999.

[98] Secondly, the solution embodied in resolution 1244 (1999), namely, the implementation of an interim international territorial administration, was designed for humanitarian purposes: to provide a means for the stabilization of Kosovo and for the re-establishment of a basic public order in an area beset by crisis. This becomes apparent in the text of resolution 1244 (1999) itself which, in its second preambular paragraph, recalls Security Council resolution 1239, adopted on 14 May 1999, in which the Security Council had expressed "grave concern at the humanitarian crisis in and around Kosovo." The priorities which are identified in paragraph 11 of resolution 1244 (1999) were elaborated further in the so-called "four pillars" relating to the governance of Kosovo described

in the Report of the Secretary-General of 12 June 1999 (paragraph 60 above). By placing an emphasis on these "four pillars," namely, interim civil administration, humanitarian affairs, institution building and reconstruction, and by assigning responsibility for these core components to different international organizations and agencies, resolution 1244 (1999) was clearly intended to bring about stabilization and reconstruction. The interim administration in Kosovo was designed to suspend temporarily Serbia's exercise of its authority flowing from its continuing sovereignty over the territory of Kosovo. The purpose of the legal régime established under resolution 1244 (1999) was to establish, organize and oversee the development of local institutions of self-government in Kosovo under the aegis of the interim international presence.

[99] Thirdly, resolution 1244 (1999) clearly establishes an interim régime; it cannot be understood as putting in place a permanent institutional framework in the territory of Kosovo. This resolution mandated UNMIK merely to facilitate the desired negotiated solution for Kosovo's future status, without prejudging the outcome of the negotiating process.

[100] The Court thus concludes that the object and purpose of resolution 1244 (1999) was to establish a temporary, exceptional legal régime which, save to the extent that it expressly preserved it, superseded the Serbian legal order and which aimed at the stabilization of Kosovo, and that it was designed to do so on an interim basis.

The Question Whether the Declaration of Independence Is in Accordance with Security Council Resolution 1244 (1999) and the Measures Adopted Thereunder

[101] The Court will now turn to the question whether Security Council resolution 1244 (1999), or the measures adopted thereunder, introduces a specific prohibition on issuing a declaration of independence, applicable to those who adopted the declaration of independence of 17 February 2008. In order to answer this question, it is first necessary, as explained in paragraph 52 above, for the Court to determine precisely who issued that declaration.

The Identity of the Authors of the Declaration of Independence

[102] The Court needs to determine whether the declaration of independence of 17 February 2008 was an act of the "Assembly of Kosovo," one of the Provisional Institutions of Self-Government, established under Chapter 9 of the Constitutional Framework, or whether those who adopted the declaration were acting in a different capacity.

[103] The Court notes that different views have been expressed regarding this question. On the one hand, it has been suggested in the proceedings before the Court that the meeting in which the declaration was adopted was a session of the Assembly of Kosovo, operating as a Provisional Institution of Self-Government within the limits of the Constitutional Framework. Other

participants have observed that both the language of the document and the circumstances under which it was adopted clearly indicate that the declaration of 17 February 2008 was not the work of the Provisional Institutions of Self-Government and did not take effect within the legal framework created for the government of Kosovo during the interim phase.

[104] The Court notes that, when opening the meeting of 17 February 2008 at which the declaration of independence was adopted, the President of the Assembly and the Prime Minister of Kosovo made reference to the Assembly of Kosovo and the Constitutional Framework. The Court considers, however, that the declaration of independence must be seen in its larger context, taking into account the events preceding its adoption, notably relating to the so-called "final status process" (see paragraphs 64 to 73). Security Council resolution 1244 (1999) was mostly concerned with setting up an interim framework of self-government for Kosovo (see paragraph 58 above). Although, at the time of the adoption of the resolution, it was expected that the final status of Kosovo would flow from, and be developed within, the framework set up by the reso-lution, the specific contours, let alone the outcome, of the final status process were left open by Security Council resolution 1244 (1999). Accordingly, its paragraph 11, especially in its subparagraphs *(d)*, *(e)* and *(f)*, deals with final status issues only in so far as it is made part of UNMIK's responsibilities to "[f]acilitat[e] a political process designed to determine Kosovo's future sta-tus, taking into account the Rambouillet accords" and "[i]n a final stage, [to oversee] the transfer of authority from Kosovo's provisional institutions to institutions established under a political settlement."

[105] The declaration of independence reflects the awareness of its authors that the final status negotiations had failed and that a critical moment for the future of Kosovo had been reached. The Preamble of the declaration refers to the "years of internationally-sponsored negotiations between Belgrade and Pristina over the question of our future political status" and expressly puts the declaration in the context of the failure of the final status negotiations, inasmuch as it states that "no mutually-acceptable status outcome was pos-sible" (tenth and eleventh preambular paragraphs). Proceeding from there, the authors of the declaration of independence emphasize their determination to "resolve" the status of Kosovo and to give the people of Kosovo "clarity about their future" (thirteenth preambular paragraph). This language indicates that the authors of the declaration did not seek to act within the standard framework of interim self-administration of Kosovo, but aimed at establishing Kosovo "as an independent and sovereign state" (para. 1). The declaration of independence, therefore, was not intended by those who adopted it to take effect within the legal order created for the interim phase, nor was it capable of doing so. On the contrary, the Court considers that the authors of that declaration did not act, or intend to act, in the capacity of an institution created by and empowered to act within that legal order but, rather, set out to adopt a measure the significance and effects of which would lie outside that order.

[106] This conclusion is reinforced by the fact that the authors of the declaration undertook to fulfil the international obligations of Kosovo, notably those created for Kosovo by UNMIK (declaration of independence, para. 9), and expressly and solemnly declared Kosovo to be bound vis-à-vis third States by the commitments made in the declaration (*ibid.*, para. 12). By contrast, under the régime of the Constitutional Framework, all matters relating to the management of the external relations of Kosovo were the exclusive prerogative of the Special Representative of the Secretary-General:

"*(m)* concluding agreements with states and international organizations in all matters within the scope of UNSCR 1244 (1999);

(n) overseeing the fulfilment of commitments in international agreements entered into on behalf of UNMIK;

(o) external relations, including with states and international organisations…" (Chap. 8.1 of the Constitutional Framework, "Powers and Responsibilities Reserved to the SRSG"),

with the Special Representative of the Secretary-General only consulting and cooperating with the Provisional Institutions of Self-Government in these matters.

[107] Certain features of the text of the declaration and the circumstances of its adoption also point to the same conclusion. Nowhere in the original Albanian text of the declaration (which is the sole authentic text) is any reference made to the declaration being the work of the Assembly of Kosovo. The words "Assembly of Kosovo" appear at the head of the declaration only in the English and French translations contained in the dossier submitted on behalf of the Secretary-General. The language used in the declaration differs from that employed in acts of the Assembly of Kosovo in that the first paragraph commences with the phrase "We, the democratically-elected leaders of our people …," whereas acts of the Assembly of Kosovo employ the third person singular.

Moreover, the procedure employed in relation to the declaration differed from that employed by the Assembly of Kosovo for the adoption of legislation. In particular, the declaration was signed by all those present when it was adopted, including the President of Kosovo, who (as noted in paragraph 76 above) was not a member of the Assembly of Kosovo. In fact, the self-reference of the persons adopting the declaration of independence as "the democratically-elected leaders of our people" immediately precedes the actual declaration of independence within the text ("hereby declare Kosovo to be an independent and sovereign state"; para. 1). It is also noticeable that the declaration was not forwarded to the Special Representative of the Secretary-General for publication in the Official Gazette.

[108] The reaction of the Special Representative of the Secretary-General to the declaration of independence is also of some significance. The Constitutional Framework gave the Special Representative power to oversee and, in certain circumstances, annul the acts of the Provisional Institutions of Self-Govern-

ment. On previous occasions, in particular in the period between 2002 and 2005, when the Assembly of Kosovo took initiatives to promote the independence of Kosovo, the Special Representative had qualified a number of acts as being incompatible with the Constitutional Framework on the grounds that they were deemed to be "beyond the scope of [the Assembly's] competencies" (United Nations dossier No. 189, 7 February 2003) and therefore outside the powers of the Assembly of Kosovo.

The silence of the Special Representative of the Secretary-General in the face of the declaration of independence of 17 February 2008 suggests that he did not consider that the declaration was an act of the Provisional Institutions of Self-Government designed to take effect within the legal order for the supervision of which he was responsible. As the practice shows, he would have been under a duty to take action with regard to acts of the Assembly of Kosovo which he considered to be *ultra vires*.

The Court accepts that the Report of the Secretary-General on the United Nations Interim Administration Mission in Kosovo, submitted to the Security Council on 28 March 2008, stated that "the Assembly of Kosovo held a session during which it adopted a 'declaration of independence,' declaring Kosovo an independent and sovereign State" (United Nations doc. S/2008/211, para. 3). This was the normal periodic report on UNMIK activities, the purpose of which was to inform the Security Council about developments in Kosovo; it was not intended as a legal analysis of the declaration or the capacity in which those who adopted it had acted.

[109] The Court thus arrives at the conclusion that, taking all factors together, the authors of the declaration of independence of 17 February 2008 did not act as one of the Provisional Institutions of Self-Government within the Constitutional Framework, but rather as persons who acted together in their capacity as representatives of the people of Kosovo outside the framework of the interim administration.

RELATED CASES

Barcelona Traction, Light and Power Company, Ltd., I.C.J. Reports 1970, p. 3
(This case clarifies the role of international courts, who may bring a matter before them, and the interests states can and cannot seek to represent before the court. Belgium asked for compensation from Spain, whose actions harmed the interests of Belgian shareholders in a Canadian-headquartered firm. The Court found that since the firm affected by Spain's action was Canadian, Belgium had no basis for this action, since Belgium had no right to give diplomatic protection to a non-Belgian firm. This case is highly relevant to the question of when a state can offer diplomatic protection to citizens or firms of another—a situation, the Court notes, marked by exploitation as much as protection when it has occurred.)

Delimitation of the Maritime Boundary in the Gulf of Maine Area, I.C.J. Reports 1984, p. 286
(Canada and the United States brought a maritime boundary dispute to the International Court of Justice, which for the first time sat as a body of just five judges rather than the usual fifteen. The Court's holding awarded both Canada and the US jurisdiction over part of the contested territory, in a dispute motivated by interests in access to lucrative fisheries.)

The Prosecutor v. Thomas Lubanga Dyilo, ICC-01/04-01/06, 14 March 2012
(Ten years after its formation, the International Criminal Court handed down its first decision on March 14, 2012. Thomas Lubanga Dyilo, a Congolese militia leader, was convicted of enlisting and conscripting child soldiers—a war crime. This case demonstrates the rise of international criminal law in conjunction with state criminal law.)

Van Gend den Loos (Case 26/62) [1963] ECR 13
(In this case the European Court of Justice identified the European legal order as a new legal order over and above the law of its member states, applicable not just to those states but directly to the affairs of their citizens.)

CANADIAN CHARTER OF RIGHTS AND FREEDOMS

Constitution Act, 1982

Part I

Preamble

Whereas Canada is founded upon principles that recognize the supremacy of God and the rule of law;

Guarantee of Rights and Freedoms

1. The *Canadian Charter of Rights and Freedoms* guarantees the rights and freedoms set out in it subject only to such reasonable limits prescribed by law as can be demonstrably justified in a free and democratic society.

Fundamental Freedoms

2. Everyone has the following fundamental freedoms:
   a) freedom of conscience and religion;
   b) freedom of thought, belief, opinion and expression, including freedom of the press and other media of communication;
   c) freedom of peaceful assembly; and
   d) freedom of association.

Democratic Rights

3. Every citizen of Canada has the right to vote in an election of members of the House of Commons or of a legislative assembly and to be qualified for membership therein.

4. (1) No House of Commons and no legislative assembly shall continue for longer than five years from the date fixed for the return of the writs at a general election of its members.

   (2) In time of real or apprehended war, invasion or insurrection, a House of Commons may be continued by Parliament and a legislative assembly may be continued by the legislature beyond five years if such

continuation is not opposed by the votes of more than one-third of the members of the House of Commons or the legislative assembly, as the case may be.

5. There shall be a sitting of Parliament and of each legislature at least once every twelve months.

Mobility Rights

6. (1) Every citizen of Canada has the right to enter, remain in and leave Canada.
(2) Every citizen of Canada and every person who has the status of a permanent resident of Canada has the right

   a)   to move to and take up residence in any province; and
   b)   to pursue the gaining of a livelihood in any province.

   (3) The rights specified in subsection (2) are subject to

   a)   any laws or practices of general application in force in a province other than those that discriminate among persons primarily on the basis of province of present or previous residence; and
   b)   any laws providing for reasonable residency requirements as a qualification for the receipt of publicly provided social services.

   (4) Subsections (2) and (3) do not preclude any law, program or activity that has as its object the amelioration in a province of conditions of individuals in that province who are socially or economically disadvantaged if the rate of employment in that province is below the rate of employment in Canada.

Legal Rights

7. Everyone has the right to life, liberty and security of the person and the right not to be deprived thereof except in accordance with the principles of fundamental justice.

8. Everyone has the right to be secure against unreasonable search or seizure.

9. Everyone has the right not to be arbitrarily detained or imprisoned.

10. Everyone has the right on arrest or detention

    a)   to be informed promptly of the reasons therefor;
    b)   to retain and instruct counsel without delay and to be informed of that right; and
    c)   to have the validity of the detention determined by way of habeas corpus and to be released if the detention is not lawful.

11. Any person charged with an offence has the right

    a) to be informed without unreasonable delay of the specific offence;

    b) to be tried within a reasonable time;

    c) not to be compelled to be a witness in proceedings against that person in respect of the offence;

    d) to be presumed innocent until proven guilty according to law in a fair and public hearing by an independent and impartial tribunal;

    e) not to be denied reasonable bail without just cause;

    f) except in the case of an offence under military law tried before a military tribunal, to the benefit of trial by jury where the maximum punishment for the offence is imprisonment for five years or a more severe punishment;

    g) not to be found guilty on account of any act of omission unless, at the time of the act or omission, it constituted an offence under Canadian or international law or was criminal according to general principles of law recognized by the community of nations;

    h) if finally acquitted of the offence, not to be tried for it again and, if finally found guilty and punished for the offence, not to be tried or punished for it again; and

    i) if found guilty of the offence and if the punishment for the offence has been varied between the time of the commission and the time of the sentencing, to the benefit of the lesser punishment.

12. Everyone has the right not to be subjected to any cruel and unusual treatment or punishment.

13. A witness who testifies in any proceedings has the right not to have any incriminating evidence so given used to incriminate that witness in any other proceedings, except in a prosecution for perjury or for the giving of contradictory evidence.

14. A party or witness in any proceedings who does not understand or speak the language in which the proceedings are conducted or who is deaf has the right to the assistance of an interpreter.

Equality Rights

15. (1) Every individual is equal before and under the law and has the right to the equal protection and equal benefit of the law without discrimination and, in particular, without discrimination based on race, national or ethnic origin, colour, religion, sex, age or mental or physical disability. (2) Subsection (1) does not preclude any law, program or activity that has as its object the amelioration of conditions of disadvantaged individuals or groups including those that are disadvantaged because of race, national or ethnic origin, colour, religion, sex, age or mental or physical disability.

Official Languages of Canada

16. (1) English and French are the official languages of Canada and have equality of status and equal rights and privileges as to their use in all institutions of the Parliament and government of Canada.

(2) English and French are the official languages of New Brunswick and have equality of status and equal rights and privileges as to their use in all institutions of the Parliament and government of New Brunswick.

(3) Nothing in this Charter limits the authority of Parliament or a legislature to advance the equality of status or use of English and French.

17. (1) Everyone has the right to use English or French in any debates and other proceedings of Parliament.

(2) Everyone has the right to use English or French in any debates and other proceedings of the legislature of New Brunswick.

18. (1) The statutes, records and journals of Parliament shall be printed and published in English and French and both language versions are equally authoritative.

(2) The statutes, records and journals of the legislature of New Brunswick shall be printed and published in English and French and both language versions are equally authoritative.

19. (1) Either English or French may be used by any person in, or in any pleading in or process issuing from, any court established by Parliament.

(2) Either English or French may be used by any person in, or in any pleading in or process issuing from, any court in New Brunswick.

20. (1) Any member of the public in Canada has the right to communicate with, and to receive available services from, any head or central office of an institution of Parliament or government of Canada in English or French, and has the same right with respect to any other office of any such institution where

a) there is a significant demand for communications with and services from that office in such language; or

b) due to the nature of the office, it is reasonable that communications with and services from that office be available in both English and French.

(2) Any member of the public in New Brunswick has the right to communicate with, and to receive available services from, any office of an institution of the legislature or government of New Brunswick in English or French.

21. Nothing in sections 16 to 20 abrogates or derogates from any right, privilege or obligation with respect to the English and French languages, or either of them, that exists or is continued by virtue of any other provision of the Constitution of Canada.

22. Nothing in sections 16 to 20 abrogates or derogates from any legal or customary right or privilege acquired or enjoyed either before or after the coming into force of this Charter with respect to any language that is not English or French.

Minority Language Educational Rights

23. (1) Citizens of Canada

    a) whose first language learned and still understood is that of the English or French linguistic minority population of the province in which they reside, or
    b) who have received their primary school instruction in Canada in English or French and reside in a province where the language in which they received that instruction is the language of the English or French linguistic minority population of the province, have the right to have their children receive primary and secondary school education in that language in that province.

    (2) Citizens of Canada of whom any child has received or is receiving primary or secondary school instruction in English or French in Canada, have the right to have all their children receive primary and secondary school instruction in the same language.

    (3) The right of citizens of Canada under subsection (1) and (2) to have their children receive primary and secondary school instruction in the language of the English or French linguistic minority population of a province

    a) applies wherever in the province the number of children of citizens who have such a right is sufficient to warrant the provision to them out of public funds of minority language instruction; and
    b) includes, where the number of those children so warrants, the right to have them receive that instruction in minority language educational facilities provided out of public funds.

Enforcement

24. (1) Anyone whose rights or freedoms, as guaranteed by this Charter, have been infringed or denied may apply to a court of competent jurisdiction to obtain such remedy as the court considers appropriate and just in the circumstances.

(2) Where, in proceedings under the subsection (1), a court concludes that evidence was obtained in a manner that infringed or denied any rights or freedoms guaranteed by this Charter, the evidence shall be excluded if it is established that, having regard to all the circumstances, the admission of it in the proceedings would bring the administration of justice into disrepute.

General

25. The guarantee in this Charter of certain rights and freedoms shall not be construed so as to abrogate or derogate from any aboriginal treaty or other rights or freedoms that pertain to the aboriginal peoples of Canada including

   a) any rights or freedoms that have been recognized by the Royal Proclamation of October 7, 1763; and

   b) any rights or freedoms that now exist by way of land claims agreements or may be so acquired.

26. The guarantee in this Charter of certain rights and freedoms shall not be construed as denying the existence of any other rights or freedoms that exist in Canada.

27. This Charter shall be interpreted in a manner consistent with the preservation and enhancement of the multicultural heritage of Canadians.

28. Notwithstanding anything in this Charter, the rights and freedoms referred to in it are guaranteed equally to male and female persons.

29. Nothing in this Charter abrogates or derogates from any rights or privileges guaranteed by or under the Constitution of Canada in respect of denominational, separate or dissentient schools.

30. A reference in this Charter to a province or to the legislative assembly or legislature of a province shall be deemed to include a reference to the Yukon Territory and the Northwest Territories, or to the appropriate legislative authority thereof, as the case may be.

31. Nothing in this Charter extends the legislative powers of any body or authority.

Application of Charter

32. (1) This Charter applies

   a) to the Parliament and government of Canada in respect of all matters within the authority of Parliament including all matters relating to the Yukon Territory and Northwest Territories; and
   b) to the legislature and governments of each province in respect of all matters within the authority of the legislature of each province.

   (2) Notwithstanding subsection (1), section 15 shall not have effect until three years after this section comes into force.

33. (1) Parliament or the legislature of a province may expressly declare in an Act of Parliament or of the legislature, as the case may be, that the Act or a provision thereof shall operate notwithstanding a provision included in section 20 or sections 7 to 15 of this Charter.

   (2) An Act or a provision of an Act in respect of which a declaration made under this section is in effect shall have such operation as it would have but for the provision of this Charter referred to in the declaration.

   (3) A declaration made under subsection (1) shall cease to have effect five years after it comes into force or on such earlier date as may be specified in the declaration.

   (4) Parliament or the legislature of a province may re-enact a declaration made under subsection (1).

   (5) Subsection (3) applies in respect of a re-enactment made under subsection (4).

* * *

Part VII

52. (1) The Constitution of Canada is the supreme law of Canada, and any law that is inconsistent with the provisions of the Constitution is, to the extent of the inconsistency, of no force or effect.

   (2) The Constitution of Canada includes

   a) the *Canada Act 1982*, including this Act;
   b) the Acts and orders referred to in the schedules; and
   c) any amendment to any Act or order referred to in paragraph (a) or (b).

   (3) Amendments to the Constitution of Canada shall be made only in accordance with the authority contained in the Constitution of Canada.

Glossary

This glossary contains legal, Latin, and philosophical terms which occur frequently in legal writing and in philosophical writing about law. This is not a comprehensive glossary: a complete account of philosophical and legal terms would run to several volumes. This glossary is meant to be an introductory reference and guide to help the reader bridge the gap between philosophy and law, and to bridge also some of the gaps between American, British, and Canadian usage. We have tried to offer an accurate yet concise definition of each term. Where strict accuracy might require a long explanation of different practices, we have offered a more general definition which explains a main or common sense of the term. If more precise definition of a term is required, it is best to look to a dictionary of law or philosophy which applies to the specific context in which you have found the term used.

We have relied extensively on the following excellent resources:

Bryan A. Garner, ed. *Black's Law Dictionary*, 10th ed. St. Paul, MN: Thomson West, 2014.
Elizabeth Martin and Jonathan Law, eds. *A Dictionary of Law*, 6th ed. Oxford: Oxford UP, 2006.
J.A. Yogis. *Canadian Law Dictionary*, 5th ed. Hauppauge, NY: Barron's Educational Series, 2003.

See also the glossary provided on the Supreme Court of Canada website: http://www.scc-csc.ca/unrep-nonrep/glossary-lexique-eng.aspx.

Accused: in its most general sense, a person charged but not yet convicted of criminal wrongdoing.
Acquit: in contract law, to be released from an obligation; in criminal law, to be not proven guilty and saved from further prosecution for the same crime. Note that acquittal in the criminal courts does not eliminate the possibility of a civil suit treating the same set of events.

Act: 1. intentional conduct. 2. a legislative body's written statement of a legal rule or rules, usually referred to as statute law.

Action: a legal proceeding one party has brought against another in order to have a matter of dispute resolved by a court.

Actus reus: (Latin) the conduct element of criminal wrongdoing. A criminal act is composed of legally prohibited conduct and criminal intention (*mens rea*). Some crimes involve an intentional omission or failure to act.

Adjudication: a judgement which resolves a legal dispute. A theory of adjudication accounts for what courts do (or ought to do) in order to reach a decision which resolves a legal dispute.

Affirm: an appellate court's confirmation of a lower court's decision.

Amicus curiae: (Latin) friend of the court. A representative of the public interest or some other interest relevant to the disposition of a legal action, yet otherwise unrepresented by the parties to the action. The *amicus curiae* typically presents information to the court in the form of a brief.

Appeal: review by a higher court of the decision of a lower court. Appeals may be granted in order for a higher court to evaluate a party's claim that there is a need to remedy such errors of law as misapplication of law to facts, incorrect directions to a jury, or use of legally unacceptable evidence.

Appellant: the party who appeals a decision. An appeal is typically, though not necessarily, made by the party who is dissatisfied with the decision of the lower court.

Appellate court: *see* Court of Appeal

Arraignment: a legal procedure in which the charge against an accused is read out in court and the accused is asked to enter a plea (usually guilty or not guilty).

Arrest: the legally authorized deprivation of a person's liberty in order to bring a charge against that person.

Attorney: generally, a person legally empowered to act as an agent for another; in the USA, a term used to refer to a lawyer legally authorized to practise law.

Attorney General: in Canada and England, the chief legal officer for the Crown, politically responsible for public prosecution and a source of legal advice to government. Attorneys General are elected members of Parliament or the legislative assembly of the jurisdiction for which each is responsible. In the USA, the US Attorney General is the appointed, non-elected chief legal officer of the federal government who also heads the Department of Justice, and advises the government on legal matters. A similar function is performed by the Attorneys General of individual states (elected or appointed, according to individual states' laws).

Bar: 1. the physical or imaginary division in a courtroom between public observers and the judges, lawyers, and persons formally involved in the case at trial. Bar associations comprise members of the legal profession, distinguished from Benchers, the judges who render decisions. 2. prevent. Once a case has been decided by a judge, the fact of that decision bars the parties from bringing the same matter to trial again.

Barrister: in England, a lawyer who argues cases in court. A solicitor is a lawyer who prepares cases and works outside the court in co-operation with barristers. In Canada this distinction is not made, and all lawyers may retain the designation "barrister and solicitor."

Bench: generally, the court and judges. The physical seat used by judges, or the body of judges as opposed to the lawyers who argue cases and are members of the bar.

Bencher: in England, a judge or senior lawyer who is a member of the group which governs the activities of one of the Inns of Court (legal associations in London which govern the activities of barristers and perform an educational function). In Canada, a member of a provincial law society which governs activities of that law society.

Bill: most generally, a document proposing a law, and brought before a legislative body for consideration and approval.

Bill of Rights: a legislative statement of basic rights and freedoms. In England, refers to the Bill of Rights of 1689. In the USA, the first ten amendments of the United States Constitution. In Canada, the Bill of Rights of 1960 has been largely superseded by the *Charter of Rights and Freedoms* which entrenches and protects in a stronger manner the basic rights and freedoms of Canadians.

Breach: to break by action or inaction the requirements of a legal rule.

Breach of contract: failure without legal excuse by a contracting party to comply with certain provisions of a legally acceptable contract.

Brief: in the USA and Canada, a document prepared by a lawyer prior to arguing a case in court. The brief contains the facts of the case, relevant sources of law, and argument showing how the relevant legal rules apply to the facts. In England, a document prepared by a solicitor directing a barrister to argue a case in court.

Burden of proof: (Latin: *onus probandi*) generally, the duty of a party to a trial to prove the party's claims about the way a case at trial ought to be resolved. In criminal trials, it is assumed that the accused is innocent until proven guilty, and the prosecution bears the burden of proving the accused guilty beyond reasonable doubt, with certain exceptions.

By-law: local legislation by authorities who are subordinate to some higher authority. Also rules of an association or corporation.

Canon: general term for a rule, especially in the codes of conduct of professional societies.

Canon law: Roman Catholic church law, used also by the Church of England (Anglican Church), governing activities of the church and some activities of church members who are not also members of the clergy.

Case: a legal controversy to be resolved by a court, and more generally the argument offered by each party to the dispute.

Cause: the reason for some effect, or the reason for bringing a dispute to a court for resolution. Many other legal uses.

Certiorari: (Latin) to be informed. A way of causing a higher court to investigate the decision of a lower court, with the effect of cancelling the practical effects of the lower court's decision. The higher court issues a writ to the lower court, causing the lower court to give to the higher court the records of its reasoning and decision in some matter.

Challenge: 1. to question the legal justification of some state of affairs. 2. the legal right to object to and have a potential juror or jurors removed from a jury. In Canada and the USA, each side to a dispute is allowed a set number of peremptory challenges with which a juror may be disqualified for no stated reason. Peremptory challenges were abolished in the UK by the Criminal Justice Act 1988.

Charge: in criminal law, to formally accuse a person of having committed a specific crime.

Charter: in its most general sense, a foundational document setting out the basic standards according to which a specific wide range of conduct is to be governed. In Canada, an informal way of referring to the *Canadian Charter of Rights and Freedoms.*

Civil action: legal proceeding to resolve a non-criminal dispute over a private or civil right.

Civil law: 1. law concerned with interactions between private individuals and legal persons such as corporations. Concerns rights and remedies in the context of property, family law, contracts, and torts. Distinguished from criminal law, which governs conduct which wrongs society in general. 2. Roman law which formed the basis for civil law in Louisiana, and several states in western Europe. In a form influenced by the Code Napoléon of France, civil law also forms the basis of private law in Quebec.

Civil rights: 1. personal rights protected by law. 2. in American jurisprudence, functionally synonymous with civil liberties. 3. in Canadian jurisprudence, civil rights pertain largely to interpersonal relations, and civil liberties pertain largely to relations between private persons and social institutions.

Code: generally, a systematic assembly of a particular area of law in a particular jurisdiction, e.g., the Criminal Code of Canada.

Comity: a principle according to which courts of one state or jurisdiction will give effect to laws and judicial decisions of another state or jurisdiction, not as a matter of obligation but out of deference and mutual respect.

Common law: generally, the English precedent-based system of law, inherited by Commonwealth nations and the USA. More specifically, that part of the law developed by the courts in their decisions which extend the customs and principles already in place in the practices of the people. More recently, as unwritten customs have been displaced by court decisions, that part of the law developed by the courts.

Competent: generally, having authority and meeting minimum standards of rationality to take some action.

Concurrent sentences: two or more terms of imprisonment, served in whole or in part simultaneously.

Concurring opinion: a separate opinion delivered by one or more judges which agrees with the decision of the majority of the court but offering different reasons for that decision.

Conflict of laws: the branch of jurisprudence concerned with principled resolution of conflicts which arise when the laws of more than one jurisdiction apply to some matter. Private international law treats the ways in which a court in one jurisdiction chooses to interpret the force of laws of some other jurisdiction.

Congress: the federal legislative body of the USA, comprising the House of Representatives and the Senate.

Consideration: in contract law, the valuable thing given over as payment for some present or promised action. Valid contracts generally require consideration.

Consecutive sentences: when one sentence of confinement is to follow another in point of time, the second is deemed to be consecutive.

Constitutional: consistent with, authorized by, or not conflicting with any provision of the constitution or fundamental law of the state.

Construction: interpretation of an unclear part of some legal standard, typically according to accepted construction rules.

Contra: (Latin) against.

Contra bonos mores: (Latin) against good morals.

Contract: a legally binding agreement which gives the contracting parties specific rights or obligations which may be enforced by the courts should either party fail to comply with the conditions of the contract. Valid contracts are characterized by (1) an offer and (2) acceptance by (3) competent parties who exchange (4) consideration and aim at some (5) legal purpose.

Conveyance: a documented transfer of land between persons.

Conviction: the finding in a criminal trial that, according to the standard set by law, the accused is guilty as charged. Conviction typically also refers to the sentence which results from the finding of guilt.

Corporation: an artificial person treated by the law as a single person even though it may in fact be composed of an individual (corporation sole) or many individuals (corporation aggregate). Corporations may hold legal rights and duties.

Corpus delicti: (Latin) body of a crime. The object or the harm resulting from the *actus reus* of a crime.

Counsel: 1. generally, advice given from one to another. 2. in the USA, a general term for an attorney. In the UK, a term for a barrister or barristers. In Canada, a general term for lawyers.

Court Martial: a military court in which members of armed forces are tried for offences against service law. In the US, military courts are responsible for trial and punishment of offences against the Uniform Code of Military Justice committed by those properly subject to that code. The service law of the UK consists of a series of acts and further regulations governing each service. The service law of Canada is specified in the *National Defence Act 1985*.

Court of Appeal: a higher court which reviews a lower court's application of law to a case. Also referred to as "appellate courts" to mark the fact that courts which perform appeal functions need not be explicitly called "Courts of Appeal." Appellate courts evaluate a party's claim that a lower court's resolution of a legal proceeding was in error, for reasons including errors in the conduct of the trial, errors of application of law to facts, and errors in admission of evidence.

Court of King's Bench/Queen's Bench: in the UK, the highest court of common law, forming one division (Queen's Bench Division) of the High Court's three divisions. The other divisions are Chancery and Family. In Canada, this term refers to the trial division of a province's superior or supreme court.

Crime: legally prohibited wrong against society in general.

Crown: in the UK, the office formally held by the reigning monarch as the supreme legal power. In practice, the activities of the Crown are in control of the elected government and the civil service. Barring exceptional circumstances, the monarch does not exercise legal powers except on the advice of elected ministers. In Canada, the Crown generally refers to the elected government and all subordinate officials.

Crown Attorney: in Canada, a lawyer appointed by an Attorney General to prosecute accused criminals on behalf of the Crown. Also called Crown Prosecutor. In the UK, a prosecutor works under a regional Chief Crown Prosecutor.

Culpable: blameworthy. Culpability requires intention, recklessness, or negligence, except in instances of strict liability.

Cumulative sentence: any sentence which is to take effect after the expiration of a prior sentence.

Custom: a long-held practice, standard, or usage in some place which through common acceptance is treated as law.

Damages: compensation awarded a person who has suffered a legal wrong. There are many types of damages.

Decision: used in several senses, often to refer to the formal judgment by a court which resolves a dispute brought before it.

De facto: (Latin) in fact. Often used to contrast actual practice with formal legal requirements.

Defamation: public utterance of claims which tend to harm a person's reputation according to the standards of right-thinking persons. In the USA and Canada, spoken defamation is called *slander*, and published or graphic defamation is called *libel*. In England, defamation of short duration is called *slander*, and more permanent defamation is called *libel*.

Defence: in a criminal trial, the legally acceptable reasons presented to the court in an attempt to have the accused found not guilty. In a civil trial, the legally acceptable reasons presented to the court in an attempt to reduce or eliminate the plaintiff's claim against the defendant. Also used to refer to the pleading given the court by a defendant in response to a plaintiff's claim.

Defendant: in a criminal trial, the person accused of commission of a crime. In a civil trial, the person sued by the plaintiff.

De jure: (Latin) by right, as required by law. Often contrasted with *de facto*, "matter of fact" practice.

De novo: (Latin) fresh, new. A trial *de novo* is held as if the matter had not previously been tried.

Denunciation: the pronouncement or condemnation of an act or person as morally wrong or evil; a common principle or objective or punishment.

Deposition: pre-trial testimony made under oath by a witness in response to spoken or written questions, as part of the process of discovery in which each side gathers evidence for its case. In Canada and the US, depositions are typically taken in the office of the lawyer of one of the parties. In criminal trials in the UK, depositions are taken before the magistrates' court; and in civil trials an examiner of the court (an official) may take depositions.

Deterrence: (specific and general) the action of discouraging conduct through instilling fear of the consequences; a common principle or objective of punishment.

Dicta/dictum: (Latin) words/word. Remarks offered by a judge in the course of resolving a dispute, but not directly connected to the reasons upon which the judge relies in reaching a judgement. *Dicta* usually do not set a binding precedent.

Diligence: many types. Generally, the standard of carefulness reasonably expected of a person in a given situation.

Discharge: generally, a release from some obligation.

Discovery: in the context of trials, the pre-trial process by which opposing parties gather information from one another in order to prepare the arguments to be heard before the court.

Discretion: generally, the power of an official to exercise official powers in accordance with the official's best judgement.

Dismiss: to end a legal dispute prior to or during a trial.

Disposition: final settlement of a matter.

Dissent: in a judicial decision, the fact of disagreement by a judge or judges who are in the minority. A dissenting opinion consists of reasons for disagreement with the majority of the court.

Docket: generally, a record of a court's activities, including a list of disputes to be heard, and the resolution of the dispute.

Double jeopardy: the legal doctrine that an accused person cannot be tried more than once for the same charge on the same evidence.

Due process: US and Canadian doctrine of fairness in both procedural operation of law and its substantive effects.

Duress: coercive or other threat used to compel action against the actor's will.

Duty: an obligation to act or withhold from a particular course of conduct.

Eminent domain: American legal doctrine later adopted in Canada, recognizing a governmental right to take private property for public purposes.

Entrenchment: in constitutional law, a special and elevated kind of recognition of rights, liberties, and freedoms which protects these from change by normal legislative means.

Equity: generally, recourse to considerations of justice or fairness, rather than the strict letter of the law.

Erga omnes: (Latin) against all.

Ergo: (Latin) therefore.

Estoppel: generally, the legal principle that bars or stops party A from denying or alleging that the truth of some matter is different from what A previously represented it to be, and was (usually) taken by B as the truth, so A cannot gain advantage over B through a new, different representation of the truth of some matter. A is bound by A's initial representation of the truth of the matter. Roughly and intuitively stated, you may not change your story now to take advantage of someone else's having relied on your prior story. There are several types of estoppel, whose interpretation must be determined with reference to the specific jurisdiction.

Et al.: (Latin) and others.

Ethics: 1. the branch of philosophy concerned with the nature of the good life and right conduct. 2. in the legal context, often used to refer to standards of professional conduct which apply to members of the legal profession. *See also* moral philosophy.

Evidence: legally acceptable matter such as testimony, documents, substantial objects used to prove or disprove the existence of some claimed fact.

Exculpatory: legally admissible evidence or other facts which tend to relieve a defendant from legal liability. *See* inculpatory.

Excuse: a legally acceptable reason for relief from legal liability. *See* exculpatory.

Ex parte: (Latin) on behalf of one side only.

Ex post facto: (Latin) after the fact.

Extradition: the process in which a person is returned to a state in which he or she is to stand trial for a criminal offence. Extradition treaties between states provide for the giving over of fugitives from other states' criminal law.

Felony: in the USA, especially serious crimes, contrasted with less serious misdemeanours. In Canada and England this term has largely fallen out of use, and carries on in England only in pre-1967 criminal statutes. Especially serious crimes are now called indictable offences, and less serious crimes are now called summary offences.

Fraud: intentional misrepresentation of the truth of some matter for the purpose of gain.

Gratis: (Latin) free.

Guilty: a plea before the court or a finding by a court that an accused has committed the crime charged.

Habeas Corpus: (Latin) you have the body. A *writ* used in the procedure of judicial determination of the legality of detention of a person. If the detention is illegal, the accused is released.

Hearing: a proceeding held to resolve issues of fact and of law. Can refer to proceedings of courts, or quasi-judicial institutions.

House of Commons: in the UK and Canada, the lower house of Parliament, composed of elected Members of Parliament who serve terms of up to five years.

House of Lords: formerly the highest appellate court in the UK. In 2009 its judicial authority was transferred to the newly created Supreme Court of the UK, in accordance with the *Constitutional Reform Act 2005.*

House of Representatives: one-half of the United States Congress, composed of elected members who serve terms of two years.

Ibid.: abbreviation for (Latin) *ibidem*: in the same place.

I.e.: abbreviation for (Latin) *id est*: that is.

Ignorantia legis non excusat: (Latin) ignorance of the law is no excuse.

In camera: (Latin) in private. Proceedings of courts are typically public, yet some matters warrant being considered without public observation.

Inculpatory: legally admissible evidence or other facts which tend to incriminate or contribute weight to the case aimed at proving a defendant's legal liability. *See* exculpatory.

Indictable offence: In Canada and the UK, a criminal offence involving a matter more serious (e.g., murder) than matters involved in a summary offence (e.g., assault). Typically heard by courts higher than those which deal with less serious summary offences, and typically involving the option of a trial by judge and jury. Distinction no longer clearly evident in Canada. *See also* summary offence, felony.

Indictment: a written charge of a serious criminal offence which must be proved before a court.

Infra/Supra: (Latin) below/above. *Infra* indicates a following provision of reference information; *supra* indicates previously provided reference information.

Injunction: a judicial direction to a specific party to refrain from or to carry out certain conduct.

Inter alia: (Latin) among others.

Invalidation: the nullification, typically by appellate level courts, of legislation, rendering that legislation or some particular legislative provision of no force or effect. *See also* striking down.

Ipso facto: (Latin) by the fact.

Judgement: a decision by a court of competent jurisdiction regarding a dispute brought before it.

Judicial review: a practice established for courts to assess the legality or constitutionality of government actions, laws, or policies.

Jurisdiction: 1. the area of law to which a specific court's authority extends. 2. generally, a particular legal system.

Jurist: a person knowledgeable in law.

Jury: a number of persons selected to decide the facts of a case at trial, and to render a verdict. Grand juries traditionally composed of twenty-three persons are still used in the USA to determine whether facts and charges brought by a prosecutor are sufficient for the matter to go to trial. In England and Canada, grand juries are no longer used. Trial juries are typically composed of six or twelve persons.

Jus: (Latin) law or right.

Jus belli: (Latin) law of war.

Jus cogens: (Latin) known law. Refers to the doctrine of public international law which declares invalid any new agreement which conflicts with the overriding, peremptory norms of the widely accepted body of fundamental international legal norms.

Jus gentium: (Latin) law of nations. Refers to international law generally.

Leading case: a particularly important decision which has resolved a dispute in a way which is later relied upon as a strong guide for similar cases.

Leading question: a question which suggests to the witness the answer desired by the questioner, typically a "yes" or "no" answer. Usually allowed only in cross-examination or examination of a witness hostile to the questioner.

Legislation: generally, written law enacted by an authoritative body.

Legislative history: the background and events, including committee reports, hearings, and floor debates, leading up to enactment of a law. Such history is important to courts when they are required to determine the legislative intent of a particular statute.

Liability: term broadly used to include obligation, duty, responsibility, in civil and criminal contexts.

Libel: generally, defamation of longer duration, typically printed, written, or graphic as opposed to verbally issued defamation. May include cartoons, sketches, sculpture, films, or audio recordings.

Litigants: the persons engaged in a civil dispute brought before a court.

Litigation: generally, the activity of bringing a civil dispute before a court for resolution.

Locus poenitentiae: (Latin) place for repentance. An opportunity for a change of mind prior to completion of some act.

Logic: the branch of philosophy concerned with the characteristics of good and bad arguments.

Malum in se: (Latin) evil or wrong in itself. Evil according to the standard of civilized society even in the absence of specific limiting legislation.

Malum prohibitum: (Latin) evil or wrong because it is prohibited.

Martial law: government of civilians by military authorities in a time of emergency.

Material: important, necessary, substantially relevant.

Mens rea: (Latin) guilty mind. The mental element of the type of crime which requires for its commission both *mens rea* and the actual criminal conduct, called *actus reus*. The *mens rea* requirement for particular crimes is specified by legislation or precedent as intention, recklessness, or negligence. Strict liability criminal offences have no *mens rea* requirement. *See* strict liability.

Mercantile law: the body of law regarding commercial transactions.

Misdemeanor: in the USA, a crime less serious than a felony. Distinction eliminated from English and Canadian law.

Mistrial: a failure of a trial for a fundamental reason.

Moral philosophy: the branch of philosophy which examines the nature of the good life and right conduct. *See also* ethics.

Natural justice: generally, principles of procedural fairness which prohibit bias on the part of the judge, and require that both sides to a dispute be heard.

Necessity defence: a defence against a criminal charge on the ground that no alternative legally permissible course of action was available to the defendant.

Negligence: conduct which is assessed careless when measured against the standard of what a reasonable person could be expected to do or not do. Aspect of *mens rea.*

Non-performance: the failure of a contracting party to adhere to the terms of a contract.

Non sequitur: (Latin) it does not follow. A conclusion which does not follow from the premises or reasons given.

Normative jurisprudence: the branch of philosophy of law concerned mainly with evaluation and justification of law and legal practices.

Nota bene: (Latin) note well. Abbreviated N.B.

Not guilty: a plea made by the accused to deny charges, and a verdict which indicates that the case against the accused was not proven beyond reasonable doubt.

Nulla poena sine lege: (Latin) no punishment without law. The principle that no punishment shall be given unless the punishment is set by law.

Offence: generally, a crime.

Opinion: a judge's or court's reasons for a decision regarding a dispute.

Overrule: the overturning of a decision in a particular case by the same court or a higher court of the same jurisdiction.

Pacta sunt servanda: (Latin) agreements must be served. General legal principle that what is agreed must be carried out.

Parens patriae **jurisdiction:** (Latin) literally, "parent of the country," refers traditionally to the role of the state as sovereign and guardian of persons under legal disability, such as juveniles or the insane.

Parliamentary sovereignty: legal doctrine that Parliament is supreme and can make or eliminate any law.

Party: persons with a direct interest in a legal proceeding.

Per curiam: (Latin) by the court.

Performance: the carrying out of an obligation, e.g., the terms of a contract.

Perjury: knowingly giving false testimony while under oath to give true testimony.

Person: an individual human or a group of persons such as a corporation or a union.

Plaintiff: a person bringing civil suit or action against another before a court.

Plea bargaining: a practice of negotiating a reduction in charges or sentence in exchange for the accused pleading guilty to agreed charges.

Pleadings: written statements of fact given by each party to the opponent reporting facts used in support of each party's case, used to make plain the issues to be resolved at trial.

Positive law: law actually put into place by an authority for government of a law-governed society.

Positive morality: the actual current moral beliefs of a particular society.

Precedent: legal doctrine by which previously decided cases are authoritative sources for settlement of later similar cases. *See also stare decisis.*

Preponderance of evidence: more probable than not. The standard of proof used in civil law, contrasted with the higher standard of reasonable doubt used in criminal law.

Prima facie: (Latin) on its face. On initial appearance or examination.

Private international law: *see* conflict of laws.

Pro bono: (Latin) for the good. Often used to refer to legal work undertaken by lawyers on an unpaid, voluntary basis.

Proceeding: generally, the form and manner of operations before a court, and the steps in the course of judicial resolution of a dispute.

Prosecutorial discretion: the power of a prosecutor to rely on his or her best judgement as to whether criminal charges ought to be laid.

Question of fact: a dispute over facts, decided by a jury.

Question of law: a dispute over a matter of law, decided by a judge.

Ratio decidendi: (Latin) reason for decision. The *ratio* of a case binds lower courts by the doctrine of precedent.

Reading down: where a court gives an over-inclusive statute a sufficiently narrow interpretation to bring it into line with the demands of the constitution.

Reading in: where a court adds something to a statute to make it conform to the constitution.

Reasonable doubt: the standard of proof used in criminal trial. A person guilty of a crime must be guilty beyond reasonable doubt, according to the standard of the reasonable person.

Rechtsstaat: (German) a state under the rule of law. This complex term expresses the ideal of a state whose nature and existence is intrinsically tied to a commitment to the principles of the rule of law.

Reckless: heedless, rash conduct which is indifferent to the existence of recognized danger. More serious than negligence. Aspect of *mens rea.*

Remedy: a means to enforce a right or to redress violation of a right.

Repeal: a legislative act which eliminates a previous law.

Retribution: in criminal law, it is punishment based strictly on the belief that every crime demands payment in the form of punishment, as a matter of desert.

Reversal: the overturning of the decision of a lower court by a higher court.

Senate: in the USA, one-half of the United States Congress (the other half being the House of Representatives). Senators are elected to six-year terms. In Canada, the upper house of Parliament, composed of appointed members who serve until age seventy-five.

Sentence: the punishment given a defendant upon conviction of criminal wrongdoing.

Slander: spoken defamation. *See also* defamation.

Sovereign immunity: legal doctrine which prevents a suit against the government without the consent of the government.

Stare decisis: (Latin) stand by decided matters. The doctrine that courts follow precedent, and lower courts treat decisions of higher courts of the same jurisdiction as binding, and decisions of higher courts in other jurisdictions as only persuasive.

Statute: a written legislative act by an authoritative body.

Strict liability: a type of offence in which responsibility is assigned without a finding of fault. Strict liability offences are typically matters where the value of efficient regulation and nominal penalties outweigh the danger of omitting an assessment of fault.

Striking down: a court decision to invalidate or nullify legislation or some particular legislative provision. *See also* invalidation.

Summary offence: In Canada and the UK, a criminal offence involving a matter less serious (e.g., assault) than matters involved in an indictable offence (e.g., murder). Typically heard by a single judge in a lower court for speedy resolution of the charge. *See also* indictable offence, felony.

Supra: (Latin) above. Often used in legal writing to indicate that a full reference to some source of information has already been given, and may be found in an earlier part of the work. E.g., *supra* n. 17 means that a fuller reference may be found in note 17 which occurs in the preceding text.

Testimony: a witness's statement of evidence, given under oath.

Tort: a civil wrong remedied by an award of damages.

Tortfeasor: a person who commits a tort, called a "tortious" act.

Ultra vires: (Latin) outside of or beyond the powers. An action beyond the authorized power of the actor.

Unconstitutional: refers to a law which is inconsistent with provisions of a constitution.

Viz.: abbreviation for (Latin) *videlicet*: namely.

Volenti non fit injuria: (Latin) no injury or wrong is done to a consenting person. Defence in tort law which claims that plaintiff consented to damage or risk of damage suffered.

Writ: generally, a written court order giving authority and direction to carry out some act.

From the Publisher

A name never says it all, but the word "Broadview" expresses a good deal of the philosophy behind our company. We are open to a broad range of academic approaches and political viewpoints. We pay attention to the broad impact book publishing and book printing has in the wider world; for some years now we have used 100% recycled paper for most titles. Our publishing program is internationally oriented and broad-ranging. Our individual titles often appeal to a broad readership too; many are of interest as much to general readers as to academics and students.

Founded in 1985, Broadview remains a fully independent company owned by its shareholders—not an imprint or subsidiary of a larger multinational.

For the most accurate information on our books (including information on pricing, editions, and formats) please visit our website at www.broadviewpress.com. Our print books and ebooks are also available for sale on our site.

broadview press
www.broadviewpress.com